P9-CSH-365

*Abraham*
*to the Middle-East Crisis*

# Abraham
# to the
# Middle-East
# Crisis

*by*

G. FREDERICK OWEN

*Member of*
The Palestine Oriental Society and Associate Member of the
American Schools of Oriental Research
(*Jerusalem and Baghdad*)

•

WITH ILLUSTRATIONS

•

*Wm. B. Eerdmans Publishing Company*
*Grand Rapids, Michigan*

ABRAHAM TO THE MIDDLE-EAST CRISIS

*by* G. FREDERICK OWEN

---



*Fourth edition, revised*

*First printing, October,* 1957

LIBRARY OF CONGRESS CATALOG NUMBER
57-13039

Printed in the United States of America

To the memory of

OLIVE NANCY OWEN

*faithful mother, devout Christian, and efficient teacher; who, during the early morning years of life, instilled in the author's heart and mind a deep and abiding interest in Palestine.*

## ACKNOWLEDGMENTS

It is a pleasure to express appreciation for the warm interest, helpful criticism, and sympathetic advice given by friends, fellow research workers, and able scholars.

Dr. J. L. Kelso, Professor of Biblical Literature and Semitics at Pittsburgh-Xenia Theological Seminary has read the first sixteen chapters and given many helpful suggestions; Dr. O. E. Brown, Professor of Church History and Dean Emeritus of Vanderbilt University School of Religion, has read the manuscript, acted in an advisory capacity, and encouraged publication; Dr. Eugene D. Owen, research worker in the field of Ancient History at Washington, D. C., has read the manuscript and been exceedingly helpful with his scholarly advice; Dr. Nelson Glueck, former Director of the American School of Oriental Research in Jerusalem, Palestine, and present President of the Hebrew Union College, Cincinnati, Ohio, has placed valuable material at the disposal of the writer and shown warm interest in the publication of the manuscript. Mr. Thomas A. Sturm, U. S. Government historian, has read the final chapter on the Middle-East Crisis.

Dr. W. F. Albright of Johns Hopkins University, Dr. O. R. Sellers of the Presbyterian Theological Seminary of Chicago, Mr. Eric Matsen of the American Colony of Jerusalem, Mr. C. Raad of Jerusalem, and the University of Pennsylvania Museum and the Israel Information Office have kindly furnished illustrative materials.

To the writers and publishers whose names appear in the bibliography, thankful acknowledgment is given, and assurance expressed that there has been a conscientious and continuous effort made to give due credit where the writer has quoted from or been influenced by the work of others.

G. F. O.

# INTRODUCTION

Palestine has played an important role in the great movements which have shaped character and directed the destinies of mankind. It has given liberally in the fields of law and architecture, and has bequeathed the best in morals, in religion, and in literature. As the world's most resplendent stage, it has given color, vividness, and vitality to the most thrilling, sublime, and worthwhile dramas of all time — the Old and the New Testaments. With good reason the land looms large in the minds of men, broadens their vision, deepens their determination, and sweeps their emotions to the loftiest heights.

Palestine is so strategically located, and has had such a mission in the earth, that its story easily becomes a composite picture of the human family at peace, at worship, and at cross purposes. Borne on by the urge of conquest, prompted by mighty moral motives, or tantalized by prospects of revenge, world-renowned characters, great nomadic hordes, and vast armies have come and gone, and marched again or slept with the dead on this unique land-bridge which connects the old-world continents.

Those who have read Palestinian history and perceived only the clashing of interests, looked only upon the conflict, and heard only the clangor of arms, need a spirit of readiness to evaluate the purposes which lay in the background, and the forces which forged to the front years and even centuries after the marchers were still in death and the din of battle had died away on distant shores.

In the present volume the aim of the writer is to picture the tides of humanity, point out the ebb and flow of ideas, and so interweave sacred and secular history as to form a thread of consecutive thought that, in the light of modern archaeological research, will constitute a readable account of the principal events which have transpired in or near Palestine during the past four thousand years — from Abraham to the Middle-East Crisis.

G. Frederick Owen

## CONTENTS

## ILLUSTRATIONS

*Abraham*
*to the Middle-East Crisis*

## Chapter I

# WESTWARD HO!

The white city of Ur lay shimmering under the dazzling rays of an oriental sun that shown from a cloudless sky. The land was languourous with tropical inertia. Sharp commands from half-groggy taskmasters rang out on the dust-laden air, while ant-like armies of strong-armed brown and black slaves passed to and from heavily laden ships roped to the quay at the canal-head which connected the city with the nearby Euphrates river.

Busy clerks took the tally, while scribes carefully recorded with three-pointed styluses each item on tablets of soft moist clay with which slaves hurried up to the nearby temple archives where the tablets were registered and filed for future reference. White-tunicked priests, bearded and grave, attended the count to verify the correctness of the tithe laid aside as sacred in the service of the gods of the land.[1]

From the height of the towering ziggurat smoke was wafted heavenward and the savory odor from the properly prepared sacrifices settled back over the prosperous pagan city, and was a welcome and most acceptable incense — to all except Abram, the son of Terah. The refined sensibilities of his innermost soul vibrated to the message of monotheism. His spiritual ear had caught that directing message from on high:

> Get thee out of thy country, and from thy kindred, and from thy father's house, unto a land that I will shew thee; and I will make of thee a great nation, and I will bless thee, and make thy name great; and thou shalt be a blessing; and I will bless them that bless thee, and curse him that curseth thee; and in thee shall all the families of the earth be blessed.[2]

The sun had not glided down half the semicircle when the civic and religious leaders of the city learned that their prominent and prosperous fellow citizen, Abram, of the generation of Terah, was sacrificing his immovable property at attractive prices and gathering his cattle and camels, purchasing stout sackcloth-of-hair tents, and making ready to leave Ur with its flourishing arts and sciences, and to trek westward where he might avoid the heavily laden paganistic atmosphere of the Euphrates valley and find a more sparsely settled land where he might prepare a constituency for the propagation of the gospel of *one* supreme Being, Creator and Preserver of men and all things material.

Movable belongings were carefully made into bales or packed in boxes, and securely strapped on diminutive donkeys and groaning camels. It was early in the morning when the tinkle of the bells of Abram's camels announced to early risers the departure of the caravan for the western land, commonly known as Canaan.

A small, white-haired, shriveled old man, perched high on the hump of a camel, Terah, rode as the honored member of the caravan. Of medium height and of noble proportions, the figure of the feminine member of the party was remarkable for its symmetry and modest grace; Sarai, the wife of Abram, rode seated high on the back of the whitest and most graceful camel forming the line.

Trusted servants, long in the employ of the family, worked under the oversight of a lithe, aggressive, yet sympathetic young man, Lot, who had been bereft of his father only a short time when his uncle Abram permitted him to enter his employ. The final decision to trust his future with his highly respected uncle had come as a result of his appreciation for the wholesome, untrammeled life of Abram.[3]

With the gleam before him, Abram readily left the easier civilization for the newer western country, which to him was the divinely appointed land. The caravan moved northwestward along the well-beaten path, now over fertility and again over extensive fields of shifting sand, but always with the urge within and the goal ahead.

So did he travel in cheerful godliness
On life's common way,
And yet his heart the lowliest duties
On himself did lay.

The immediate goal was Haran, "the city of Nahor," — the abode of Terah's father and Abram's grandfather.

Pleasant and prosperous days among kinsmen at Haran were saddened by the passing of Terah. No sooner were the days of mourning ended than Abram and Lot gathered all, and going westward followed the curve of the "Fertile Crescent" until they reached Damascus, the "Pearl of the East." Here, amid gurgling fountains, fruitful vines, and laden orchards, Abram tarried for a time, while getting his bearings and learning more about the nearby land to which he journeyed. Eliezer — a man of the western mind — was employed as a "smoother of the way" among the Canaanites, and as steward of Abram's ever-increasing caravan.

From the vast fertile stretches of the Damascus plain the camels, with their inimitable swinging motion, moved along the foothills of Jebel esh Sheikh — Mount Hermon, — passed the beautiful sea of Chinnereth and entered Canaan, where in the very heart of the land Abram, in sacred devotion, erected an altar at Shechem, and while worshipping, heard these striking words:

"UNTO THY SEED WILL I GIVE THIS LAND"[4]

Years swiftly passed; years in which Abram and Sarai shared the common toils of life. He, with the help of Eliezer, had the care of those who tended the flocks, the camels, and the cattle; and she with queenly grace, quietly directed the daily routine of labor and relaxation common to the inner circle of those great encampments of black bat-like, sackcloth-of-hair tents which, city-like, occupied some hillside adjacent to profitable pasture lands.

The promise of a son had been given, yet time with its hardening and aging process had slowly wrought upon body and womb of the mistress of the clan. Visions of lonely tomorrows appeared wherein she should go down to the grave without having presented a son to him who by promise was to be the father of uncounted millions. Faith died. Then one day in the privacy of her tenthouse, Sarai urged that Abram accept Hagar, her Egyptian maid, so that by proxy she might yet be honored as the mother of that Semitic seed destined to bless the ends of the earth.

Ishmael, the fruit of this frenzied frame-up, had attained the age of fourteen when, contrary to all natural expectations, Sarah gave birth to a boy baby whom she named Isaac — laughter. For this child of remarkable origin the parents bore mutual love and respect, and at weaning time made merry with a gay feast, but the occasion ended in sorrow and bitterness.

Ishmael, half Hebrew and half Egyptian, in light jest and mockery, made sport of the lad of laughter whom the others were praising. Seeing the unwarranted provocation, Sarah asserted her authority, and brought on a sharp domestic brawl, the effects of which forty centuries have not sufficed to wipe out. "Cast out this bondwoman and her son, for the son of this bondwoman shall not be heir with my son, even with Isaac."[5] The thought of such a course gripped Abraham's heart with grief, yet he yielded when he heard Jehovah say, "In Isaac shall thy seed be called. And also of the son of the bondwoman will I make a nation, because he is thy seed."[6]

Burning thirst, gnawing hunger, and provoking hardship pursued Ishmael and his mother far into the Sinai desert where they sought sustenance amid barren wastes. Under a bush the lad lay in the throes of desperation; Hagar sadly turned away lest her eyes should look upon the death struggle of her only offspring; divine help came, hope revived and more prosperous days ensued. Ishmael grew and learned well the art of making his way with bow and arrow amidst the wild life which roamed the rocky wastes, tracked the fields of sand, and visited the oases of Sinai. His mother took him a wife out of the land of Egypt, by whom he begat twelve princely sons, who gave rise to as many tribes. In time they became a well-known people who dwelt "from Havilah unto Shur."[7]

The black-horse-rider visited Abraham's tent encampment and bore away Sarah, whose earthly remains the great patriarch buried in the cave of Machpelah, which, at the gate of the city, he purchased from Ephron, the Hittite. Now old and well stricken in years, and being blessed of God "in all things," Abraham took an oath of Eliezer, the Damascene steward, that he would go again to Mesopotamia and seek a wife for Isaac among Abraham's kindred of whom the news had come that God had prospered them with many children.[8]

One half the arc of the Fertile Crescent[9] Eliezer's caravan trekked before it came to the well of Padan-Aram where Rebekah, Isaac's first cousin, came to water the flocks. In the home that night the agreement was reached. On the following day, with the blessing "be thou the mother of thousands of millions," she left with the caravan which moved steadily along the old trail and brought them to Hebron. Here the maiden lighted from her camel to be greeted by Isaac, who, at eventide, strolled in the field for meditation. In the tent, so recently made vacant by Sarah's death, they plighted to each their all, and comfort came to him on whom the patriarchal mantle should fall.

Aged Abraham again embarked on the sea of matrimony. Keturah, his new wife, bore him six sons, yet Abraham "gave all that he had unto Isaac."[10]

Unto Isaac and Rebekah were born twins — Esau and Jacob. Even before their birth it was revealed that they represented *two nations and two manner of people.*[11] At their birth "the first came out red, all over like a hairy garment; and they called his name *Esau.* And after that came his brother out, and his hand took hold of Esau's heel, and his name was called *Jacob.*"[12] Each of the brothers was destined to be father of a famous nation whose people were to be after the similitude of their respective founders both in name and in attitude toward life. The children of Esau were to be called *Edomites;* while Jacob's descendants came to be known as *Israelites.*

The boys grew to manhood and Esau became a cunning hunter, a man who roamed far afield, while Jacob was only a plain man, living in tents and raising cattle.[13] Jacob was a producer; Esau sought that which had grown of itself. The producer, in keeping with his name and nature, was a supplanter — a schemer. Even at birth he had "grasped" his brother's heel, and he continued this policy as he grew older. He was ever watchful of his opportunities.

One day Esau wandered farther afield than usual, and was faint from hunger by the time he reached home. Jacob took advantage of his famished condition by feeding him in return for a promise that he (Jacob) should have the birthright which was due the first-born.

Esau took unto himself two wives, both daughters of Hittite families. These daughters were "a grief of mind" unto Isaac and Rebekah. Rebekah insisted that Jacob's matrimonial career should be charted on a different sea — he was to wed a wife of his mother's kinsmen. In the meantime the mother and son unscrupulously set about to enhance Jacob's fortune at the expense of Esau, who waited for the inheritance even though he had already given private oath that the birthright should be Jacob's.

By a gigantic piece of fraud the elderly father was induced to will the family fortune to Jacob by pronouncing the birthright blessing upon him. Esau returned from his hunt, heard what had happened and became sorely displeased. This piece of perfected trickery contributed to the ever-widening breach between the fathers of two peoples later to be known as Jews and Arabs.

At that time only Jacob's absence could in any way relieve the tension. Fearful lest his scheming should cost him his head, his frightened feet took him to Beth-el before the day was done. With a stone for a pillow he sought rest, but the activities of the day put him to sleep with a troubled brain and thoughts of his father's God. He dreamed of a ladder suspended between heaven and earth and up and down its golden rounds were angels ascending and descending on errands for God.

With the dawn of day he declared the place to be Beth-el — "the house of God, and the gate of heaven." Pledging God one tenth of his income[14] he went on his journey northeastward until he came to Padan-Aram (Haran) where he worked for Laban — his mother's brother —

and in course of time married Laban's daughters — Leah and Rachel. By diligent toil and careful scheming great flocks and herds were accumulated after which Jacob fled from his uncle and returned to Canaan."[15]

Arriving at the border he halted and sent messengers to inform his brother Esau of the increase which had come to him while he had sojourned in the far country, and asked that he might find grace in his sight. On hearing the news, Esau gathered four hundred armed men and hastened to the border to meet the younger brother. The schemer was face to face with the feud of former years. The situation grew tense.

In the late afternoon, Jacob the schemer selected the choicest of his sheep, cattle and camels, as a present to Esau. Twilight stole in, mellowing the distance over Gilead's hills and vales; night came and the hours dragged heavily.

At midnight torchlights gleamed on the oleanders lining the brink of the Jabbok, and glistened on the waters that sang their way to the Jordan. Sheep, goats, donkeys, cattle, and camels plunged in and struggled for the further side; uncertainty and fear tightened the atmosphere, while cries from women and children arose to add to the confusion. Finally all had crossed, and passed on — save Jacob the heel-grasper.

Having relinquished his hold upon earthly things and separated himself from everyone, even those whom he held dearest, he was left alone for the night, to reason with himself and to wrestle with God. The vicissitudes of a strange, checkered career gripped him. Schemes and dreams, broken vows and wayward ways passed before him like a panorama. He had been altogether too supercilious, worldly, and avaricious. His present danger had brought his feeling of unworthiness to the fore. Realizing that his destiny hung on the decision of those hours, he became desperate.

The wrestlings of that night — with his inner self and his Maker — can never be forgotten as long as the sons of Jacob shall live. Grey dawn broke on a changed life and "crippled Israel" crossed the river and met an estranged brother who forgave and embraced him.[16]

After a brief visit, accompanied by the customary hospitalities of dining, Esau returned to the south country, while Jacob passed into the central portion of Palestine and took up his abode in the city of Shechem, where Abraham had once sojourned. Here the younger brother purchased land, digged a well, and met with considerable prosperity. He then moved to Beth-el and erected an altar where God had appeared unto him when he fled from the face of Esau. During his hours of devotion and worship he heard the voice of Jehovah saying:

> Thy name shall be called no more Jacob, but Israel; . . . I am God Almighty; be fruitful and multiply; a nation and a company of nations shall be of thee, and kings shall come out of thy loins; and the land which I gave Abraham and Isaac, to thee I will give it, and to thy seed after thee will I give the land.[17]

Journeying from Beth-el the caravan passed Salem and was nearing Bethlehem when Israel's beloved Rachel sickened and died. Bereft of the nearest and dearest that should ever enter his earthly life, Jacob set up a suitable memorial stone and passed on "beyond the tower of Edar," where he pastured his flocks and herds for a time, then joined his aged father who soon passed to the bourne from whence no traveler returns.

From Edom came a caravan that halted at the great encampment of the late Sheikh Isaac. Bent low with grief, the two brothers — Jacob and Esau — met at the cave of Machpelah where, with great respect and reverence, they buried their father in the common tomb of the patriarchs.

## Chapter II

# THE RISE OF THE ARABS

When the days of mourning were ended Jacob was in possession of their father's estate — the birthright blessing had held good. We do not know the extent of Esau's irritation over the outcome; the records merely suggest that when the last wail of the mourners had died away on the Judean hills the elder brother took the last vestige of his belongings and "went from the face of his brother" and dwelt in Mount Seir, south of the Dead Sea.[1]

The country to which Esau moved is a most interesting section of a range of mountains which stretches almost the entire distance of 112 miles from the Dead Sea southward to the Gulf of Akabah. Through the center of this range is a rift extending from the Dead Sea to the Gulf. Geologists think it must have been the channel through which the Jordan river ran to the Gulf. It is now called *Wady el-Arabah,* and during the early Mohammedan period it was used as a highway of commerce[2] connecting Syria with the harbors at the head of the Gulf. The spices of southern Arabia and the gold of Africa were shipped to Elath and Ezion-Geber, and from thence were carried by camel caravans over this and the important Transjordan highland route to the nations of the north.

Near the center of this mountain range are Jebel Harun (Mount Hor of Biblical fame), and that enchanting city of Petra (Sela of the Bible) which, because of the nature of its topography, is one of the best natural fortifications to be found in the Near East.

There are many reasons why Esau should have chosen this section of the country as a future dwelling place for himself and his descendants. It was rocky and wild and in part woody.[3] It abounded in wild life of almost every kind, thus affording an outlet for the hunter spirit of Esau and his people. To the Egyptians, this country, along with the desert that stretched westward, was known as "The Red Land"; "Edom" is merely the Hebrew or Canaanitish translation of the Egyptian title.[4] The name was descriptive of the red cliffs of Seir as well as of the first born of Isaac. When Raymond Hull looked upon this country he exclaimed:

> Never before have I seen colors of such depth and variety of pattern. The walls of rock remind one of patterns on highly painted wall, Eastern carpets, or other fanciful fabrics of the loom. The deepest reds, purples, and shades of yellow are here arranged in alternate bands, shading off into each other, and sometimes curved and twisted into gorgeous fantasies.[5]

Esau's very nature, as disclosed in his name, and the nature of the country must have produced a harmony of singular satisfaction. There is little doubt but that he first located this congenial country on one of his hunting expeditions. He seems to have been impressed with it from the first; and the Horites, who dwelt there before his coming, appear to have greatly appreciated him. He was in Mount Seir when Jacob's messengers sought him out to inform him of his younger brother's return from Padan-Aram.[6] He married into the family of one of the Horite chiefs, and he and his descendants, partly by conquest and partly by absorption, planted themselves securely in the country which was henceforth to be called Edom.[7]

Esau had married four wives: two daughters of the Hittites, one of the Horites, and one of the Ishmaelites (Ishmael's daughter).[8] By these wives were born unto him many sons who were known as princes, or "dukes." These intermarried with the people among whom they lived, founded many tribes, and soon became a mighty people — the highlanders of this section of the country.

To the northeast of Edom and just east of the Dead Sea lived the well-known Ammonites and Moabites — descendants of the daughters of Lot.[9] As kinsmen, there was close affinity between them and the Edomites.

The larger part of northern Arabia, however, was inhabited by the Ishmaelites and their allies. They dwelt "from Havilah unto Shur"[10] — from the border of Egypt stretching away toward the border of Mesopotamia. Many of the foremost of the Ishmaelites lived in walled cities. These people, for the most part, were merchants and travelers.

The southern portion of Edom was known as Teman; and just to the east of Teman dwelt the Kadmonites, or "children of the East." Both Tema and Kedemah were sons of Ishmael.[11] An Egyptian papyrus of the twelfth dynasty mentions the Kadmonites as having received a political fugitive from Egypt, who married one of their princesses and became one of their chiefs. Their wisdom was celebrated, as was that of their kinsmen of Teman, and later King Solomon was praised with the statement that his "wisdom excelled all the wisdom of the children of the east."[12]

Not far from the Kadmonites was the land of Uz, famous as the home of Job. In the book of Lamentations we read: "Rejoice and be glad, O daughter of Edom, that dwellest in the land of Uz."[13] And this leads us to believe that Uz was not only inhabited by some of the Edomites, but must have been a province of Edom, at least these people were closely related.

Nebaioth (Nebajoth) was the eldest son of Ishmael, and father of the Nabatheans who, at a later date, partially displaced the Edomites and dwelt in and around the cliff city of Petra. Known as the "Nabathean Arabs," they enjoyed unusual prosperity just preceding the Christian era. Hareth III (Aretas), one of their foremost kings, was a well-known figure during the rise of Herod the Great.

Others of Ishmael's descendants — such as Kedar — herded their flocks and were known for their archery.[41] Some of us can almost fancy we see an Arab village or encampment being attacked when we read the words of the prophet:

> Arise ye, go up to Kedar, and spoil the men of the east. Their tents and their flocks shall they take away; they shall take to themselves their curtains, and all their vessels, and their camels; and they shall cry unto them, Fear is on every side.[15]

The Midianites were half-brothers to the Ishmaelites. It will be remembered that Abraham married Keturah, after the death of Sarah, and by her six sons were born unto him. These did not inherit with Isaac, but were sent away with gifts only, much the same as Ishmael had been. They settled near the Ishmaelites and soon came to occupy the lower section of the Sinai Peninsula and the country stretching along the eastern coast of Akabah toward Mecca.

The Midianites mingled, intermarried and merged their interests with the Ishmaelites until others came to use their names interchangeably, as was the case in the narrative concerning the sale of Joseph:

> Then there passed by *Midianites*, merchantmen; and they drew and lifted up Joseph out of the pit and sold Joseph to the *Ishmaelites* for twenty pieces of silver; and they brought Joseph into Egypt.[16]

Moses, on fleeing from Egypt, found a refuge in Midian, and it was one of their number — the daughter of "the priest of Midian" — who became his wife. The father-in-law visited Moses at Mount Sinai and there gave him a very profitable lesson in political organization.[17] A Midianite was guide to the Children of Israel during their wanderings in the wilderness.[18]

The Midianites became known as Nomads of the desert wastes who had no permanent dwellings, but moved their tents according to seasons and conditions. They roamed through an extensive territory ranging from south and east of the Gulf of Akabah to the northern portions of Transjordania. The Biblical references are in perfect keeping with the habits of these peoples, and their places of sojourn.

The Amalekites are generally supposed to have descended from Amalek, the grandson of Esau, yet a people by that name is mentioned as being in existence during Abraham's day, when Chederlaomer devastated the country.[19] It is possible that Essau's grandson, Amalek, and his descendants were merged with the older stock of Amalekites, and he became their ruler as Esau had with the Horites of Edom. At any rate they dwelt near the Edomites, and were the most war-like people of their day.

The peoples throughout this region so merged their interests, married and intermarried, that the Ishmaelites, Edomites, Midianites, Horites, Amalekites Ammonites, Moabites, and other cognate tribes became known as the "Westerners," or "Arabs" — those who lived in or adjacent to the Wady el Arabah. However, to the people of Palcstine they were often "the Children of the East." Today we know them as the "Maadites," or Northern Arabs. To their extreme south — far down toward the southernmost portion of the Arabian peninsula—lived another people known as the "Himyarites," or "Yemenites," as we now know them. They claim to have sprung from Joktan, or, as the Arabs call him, "Kahtan," the son of Eber and grandson of Shem.[20]

These Yemenites seem to have enjoyed an advanced civilization, ana to have engaged in a "far-reaching commercial activity" long before much human history was written in many other countries of the world. Saba (the same as *Sheba*), whose queen paid a visit to King Solomon, was one of their two important kingdoms, the other being Main, which was, in later times, more closely connected with the Midianites.[21]

Southern Arabia (Yemen) was a very fertile and productive country in those days when the rainfall was more plentiful. Its inhabitants produced perfumes and spices and sold them to the world. Their boats plied the waters between India and the Red Sea ports. Many were their cargoes which were unloaded at Elath and Ezion-Geber, at the head of the Red Sea. Here the Ishmaelites, or "Maadites," took charge of the cargoes and transported them to the north by means of their camel caravans. It is difficult for us to conceive of the vast extent of this caravan commerce, which, however, did not reach its full development until the establishment of Roman power in the East.

Two great caravan routes left the Himyarite cities, one skirting the Persian Gulf and the Euphrates to Chaldea and Assyria, and thence by Tadmor, or Palmyra, to Damascus: the other following the coast of the Red Sea, until it passed Akabah, where it branched into two lines, one passing up Wady el Arabah then turning westward to Gaza, Phoenicia, and Egypt, the other going north on the Transjordan highlands to Petra and from thence to Damascus.

The caravans which pursued these routes were in size like small armies. They had their regular times of starting, of passing their several stages, and of intersecting other routes. Large towns grew up at their stations; while great centers of the caravan trade, like Damascus, Palmyra, and Petra, rose to rank among the famous cities of the world.

The early kings of Israel seem to have been intimately concerned in this overland commerce. Solomon built Palmyra and Tadmor, and fortified Petra; and his successors, as late as Jehoshaphat, had a naval station at Ezion-Geber (Akabah).[22] After a time, however, the increase in shipping left the great caravan trade to fall into decay; and long before the time of Mohammed it had been reduced to comparative insignificance.

This decline in their great business was very disastrous to the Arabs, and threw their whole economic life into confusion. "Old settlements were broken up, great cities were abandoned; and whole tribes reduced from opulence to poverty."[23] Forsaking their ancient seats, with their hand against every man, and every man's hand against them, they went out to provide for themselves as best they could.

During this period of confusion, the Arabian nation, as it is known to modern history, seems to have been formed. The Yemenites, or Himyarites, had lost their ancient language — how long before does not appear; and "the two races, although still retaining their traditional jealousy and hostility, had become everywhere and to a foreign eye indistinguishably fused into one people. The nation thus formed was disstinctively and thoroughly Semitic in character and language, and in both physical and mental characteristics was entitled to a high rank among the families of mankind. It has remained essentially unchanged to the present day."[24]

## Chapter III

# ISRAEL AND EGYPT

A few years after Esau's departure from his father's funeral at Hebron the curtain again rose on Jacob and his descendants in Palestine. The scene was somewhat strange. A boy of seventeen summers left the vale of Hebron and journeyed northward along the high road until he had passed his mother's grave, Salem's sanctuary, Jacob's well, and come to Dothan where he met his shepherd brothers, and became the victim of a plot by which he was sold to Ishmaelite merchantmen, carried to Egypt and there sold as a slave to one of the chief officers of that wealthy nation.[1]

An attempt at seduction; a diabolical plot; base ingratitude; the prison with all its attendant horrors. Yet his unimpeachable manliness, his faithfulness in doing the right, and his loyalty to the God of his fathers brought the young man into the palace — he became governor of the land of the Pharaohs.[2]

A great drought parched the Levant, and extended into the usually well-watered valley of the Nile. Egypt's surplus supply of grain was in demand and was sold to the people of the surrounding nations. Ten guilty brothers appeared before the governor of Egypt; they desired corn. They were tested, one kept as surety, the others returned to Palestine, finally to be driven back to Egypt by the famine. Further testing and humiliation of the ten men; then, at the opportune moment, as if by magic, the scene reached its climax — the governor revealed that he was brother to the ten guilty men. Memories were revived, confessions were made, peace was restored, the tide of feeling ran high; a caravan was seen on the march — going toward Palestine.

An old man stood shading his eyes from the glare of the evening sun, when there swung into the Vale of Hebron a strange company — camels, donkeys, wagons, grain and gold, — with Jacob's ten sons leading the procession. The old man fainted — overcome with joy at the news that his beloved son, Joseph, whom he thought long since slain by wild beasts, was then governor of all Egypt.[3] Great was the commotion in that home, and in Hebron when the entire household and the inhabitants of the city understood that Skeikh Jacob was moving into the valley of the Nile where he would have plenty and be near his prosperous son.

Goshen,[4] a fertile section in northeastern Egypt, was assigned to the newcomers, where away from the Canaanites and segregated from the Egyptians, they would have opportunity to develop into a people, strong enough to maintain their identity and propagate the truth of monotheism — that God is one. The place hummed with activity as the Hebrews pitched their tents, erected more permanent dwelling places, shepherded their flocks, and lived the round of daily life.

The old father, who had become a favorite with Pharaoh, approached the end of his earthly pilgrimage, delivered his final words to the future leaders of Israel, and like a clock, worn out with beating time, the weary wheels of his life at length stood still — the one time "schemer," long since changed into a "prince with God," yielded up the ghost[5] and was "gathered unto his people" within the never-ending promised land.

The "black horse and his rider" later invaded the Nile valley and called for the governor who gave his parting words concerning Israel's return to Palestine, then breathed his last earthly breath and departed for that heavenly land — a place far more pleasant than even the hills and vales about his childhood home at Hebron.

Generations passed, and the Hebrews multiplied and prospered in Goshen until, after a rule of two centuries, their protectors — the Shepherd Kings, called the Hyksos, — grew weak and were driven from the throne and thrust out of the land by Amosis I, the leader of an active Berber family, who established the powerful eighteenth dynasty at Thebes.[6]

Amosis, the new Pharaoh, cared not for Joseph nor his kinsmen, for they were shepherds, and every shepherd was "an abomination" unto the native Egyptians. Seeing the Hebrews outnumbered his own people, and fearing lest they usurp the throne, the new Pharaoh reduced them to slavery. This measure failing to curb their growth, the royal decree went forth that all male children among the Hebrews should be killed at birth.[7]

A Hebrew mother of the priestly tribe of Levi hid her darling baby away in the dense papyrus growth along the backwaters of the Nile river. Pharaoh's daughter went to bathe, and found him. Her sympathy led her to adopt the child; thus making him a member of the royal household and a student of all the learning of the land.

Having drawn him from the bulrushes she named him "Moses."[8] What a name! And how significant of his life's work! At maturity he made his decision — he would consider the treasures of Egypt as naught when compared with the privilege of being counted among the ever-increasing number of righteous slaves — better a slave with an objective than the anointed of the land with no goal ahead.

Borne on by an inner urge, Moses began his life's work, but the sadness of tragic failure attended his first futile attempt to deliver his brethren from bondage. His frightened feet carried him across the wilderness of Sinai, past the mountain called Horeb, into the country of the Midianites. A pretty little scene had its setting at a Midianitish well — in chivalrous style Moses pushed back the thoughtless shepherds and watered the flocks attended by seven young women.[9] This gallant act brought him into the household of "the priest of Midian."

As a faithful son-in-law he cared for the sheep — protected them, watered them, sought proper pastures and led them where they might graze. One day the graduate student finished the work for his higher degree, had a burning bush commencement exercise at Mount Horeb, where he received his commission to return to Egypt and lead the Hebrews to the "Promised Land."

Forty years of schooling in God's university subdued impulsiveness and banished uncertainty from the man Moses. With the composure befitting a monarch he, accompanied by his brother Aaron, appeared before Pharaoh and began to effect the deliverance of Israel. Pharaoh was indignant that anyone should suggest that his great army of Hebrew slaves be manumitted for the mere purpose of worshipping their God in a distant land which they said had been promised them.

Ten plagues, save one, came, yet Pharaoh was unwilling to let Israed go. Then came the tragedy of the tenth plague — the destroying angel passed through the land and bore away the firstborn of every Egyptian home. Egypt's eastern doors swung wide and Moses marched out with more than a million Hebrew slaves from whom the shackles had just fallen.

With the "mountain of God" as their immediate goal, they marched in an easterly direction; then turned southward. Everything went well until there came a turn in the tide of affairs; when by what seemed an inexplicable circumstance they found themselves shut in by the wilderness, between Migdol and the Red Sea, and pursued by Pharaoh and his army. Moses bade the people stand still and see the salvation of God.

A strange awe settled over the Israelites as they beheld the waters pushed back and heard their leader urging them on. As soon as they reached the distant shore, they looked back and beheld the waters as they returned and engulfed their enemies who had pursued them with the expectation of bringing them again into slavery.

For the first time the children of Israel felt their entire freedom. They joined in heart and voice to praise God. Triumphantly they sang:

> I will sing unto the Lord
> For he hath triumphed gloriously;
> The horse and his rider
> Hath he thrown into the sea.[10]

The tides of joy rose until Miriam, the sister of Moses and Aaron, took up a timbrel and led the women as they marched on with the refrain:

> Sing ye to the Lord,
> For he hath triumphed gloriously;
> The horse and his rider
> Hath he thrown into the sea.[11]

The march continued until they were past the bitter spring of Marah and had reached the palm grove of Elim. At Rephidim the Amalekites took up arms and Israel was engaged in battle for the first time with the peoples of Western Arabia — their distant kinsmen.

## CHAPTER IV

# WILDERNESS WANDERINGS

WITHIN JUST FORTY-SEVEN DAYS after the passover in Egypt Moses and the people arrived at Mount Horeb (Sinai) close by the territory of Midian, where the people encamped in the broad plain (since known as "the Plain of the Tribes"), and Moses ascended the mountain to receive the foundation stone of Hebrew national unity and the Magna Carta of Hebrew religious liberty.

On the third day there were thunders and lightnings, and a thick cloud upon the mountain. A trumpet sounded long, and waxed louder and louder, and Jehovah spoke in thundering tones:

> I am the Lord thy God. . . . thou shalt have no other gods before me.
> Thou shalt not make unto thee any graven image, nor any likeness of any thing . . .
> Thou shalt not take the name of the Lord thy God in vain . . .
> Remember the sabbath day, to keep it holy . . .
> Honour thy father and thy mother . . .
> Thou shalt not kill.
> Thou shalt not commit adultery.
> Thou shalt not steal.
> Thou shalt not bear false witness . . .
> Thou shalt not covet.[1]

The book of the covenant was given and Israel became party of the second part of a religious, civil, and social covenant which has since been a potent factor in the cultures of all the earth. In their awe the people accepted with readiness the prerogatives and duties of the divine election constituting them a holy nation.[2]

But alas! When Moses stayed long on the mount the majority of the people removed portions of their recently acquired golden ornaments and made a molten calf — the likeness of the sacred bull, which the Egyptians had so commonly worshipped — and erected an altar before the image. Night closed in and Sinai, like an aged sentinel, towered mutely above a stage set for sacrilege, carnal pleasure and paganism.

At early dawn the following day, the people came with their offerings to the idol, sat down to feast, and rose up to play. The spirit of revelry arose until the more brazen souls removed their clothing and threw themselves into the whirl of a heathenish dance. On coming down from the Mount, Moses beheld the orgy of apostasy and was so taken back by their affront to Jehovah that he dashed the stony tablets[3] against the gray granite sides of Sinai, and broke them to pieces.[4]

An awful plague broke out and many of the idolaters were swept into eternity. Yet God, through Moses, salvaged the most of the people. These, in turn, clothed themselves in modesty, "stripped themselves of ornaments," and "sought the Lord" in sincerity. Moses again ascended Mount Sinai and "was there with the Lord forty days and forty nights . . . and he wrote upon the tables the words of the covenant, the ten commandments" and returned from the mount "with the two tables of testimony."

When he had worshipped before the Lord, Moses read the words of the covenant and asked all those "of a willing heart" to bring of their gold, and silver, and brass, and blue, and purple, and scarlet, and fine linen, and goats' hair, and rams' skins dyed red, and badgers' skins, and acacia wood, and oil, and spices and various precious stones. With these they erected a most unusual portable tabernacle, and made ready to resume their journey.

Marching northward, they encountered barren wastes, towering mountains, and refreshing oases. The air was often filled with complaint, the seeds of disloyalty germinated in the hearts of many, and mutiny was a constant danger to be feared and forestalled. Yet history knows of no other army, without a base of supplies, whose material needs were so adequately met.[5]

In the second summer after leaving Egypt, Israel arrived at Kadesh-Barnea, the extreme southern point on the frontier of Canaan. Here the rock was smitten; Miriam, the sister of Moses and Aaron, died and was buried; spies were sent out and returned saying there were giants in the land and that Israel was unable to take it; but two of the spies, Joshua and Caleb, declared that Israel was "well able to go up and take the land at once.[6] For accepting the majority report the Hebrews were forced to wander in the wilderness until the bones of the men of that generation had bleached in the mountains, valleys and shifting sands of the Sinai peninsula.

When the next generation was grown they passed around to the south of the Dead Sea; and in coming to the rocky region of the land of Edom the people discovered that the Edomites had their country protected by *four* lines of strong fortresses and watch-towers — a line of forts guarding their country on all four sides.[7]

Moses sent messengers to Edom's king asking permission to pass through their country with their pledge that they would "go by the king's highway" and "not pass through the fields, or through the vineyards, neither drink of the water of the wells." But the Edomites refused to give Israel passage through their country. Therefore they turned southward and encamped at the foot of Mount Hor, where Aaron died and was buried on the mountain, after which Israel moved eastward and northward skirting Edom and finally encamped on the desert fringes of eastern Moab.[8]

Following Israel's triumphs over Og, king of Bashan, and Sihon, king of the Amorites; the Midianites and the Moabites grew uneasy. Balak, king of Moab, attempted to hire the prophet Balaan to curse the newcomers, but alas for the Midianites and Moabites: while the savory odors ascended from the sacrifices on the rock-hewn altars on Moab's mountain heights, the venerable old prophet broke forth in that exceedingly significant language:

> How shall I curse, whom God hath not cursed? or how shall I defy, whom the Lord hath not defied? From the top of the rocks I see him, and from the hills I behold him: lo, the people shall dwell alone, and shall not be reckoned among the nations. Who can count the dust of Jacob, and the number of the fourth part of Israel? Let me die the death of the righteous, and let my last end be like his! . . . There shall come a Star out of Jacob, and a Sceptre shall rise out of Israel . . . and Israel shall do valiantly.[9]

Balaam saw the chains of Balak's hot anger loosed and heard him mutter: "Lo, the Lord hath kept thee back from honor." The elderly prophet turned aside to a Midianite encampment, leaving Israel in peace and Moab in consternation.

While encamped near the Jordan river, among the beautiful acacias in the plains of Moab, Moses heard God calling time on him. With a brave heart the mighty leader assembled the people, appointed his successor, urged the people to be loyal, bade them farewell, passed the top of Mount Nebo, viewed the promised land, died and was buried in a valley in the land of Moab.

> This was the bravest warrior
>   That ever buckled sword;
> This was the most gifted poet
>   That ever breathed a word;
> And never earth's philosopher
>   Traced with his golden pen,
> On deathless page, truths half so sage
>   As he wrote down for men.

Thirty days of sincere mourning came to an end and the children of Israel accepted the leadership of Moses' successor — Joshua. He received his charge from God, gave marching orders, and in a brief time more than a million Israelites crossed the Jordan river, encamped at Gilgal, ate of the old corn of the land, underwent circumcision, and at the appointed time began the conquest of Palestine.[10]

Strange was the method of attack on Jericho, the "city of palm trees." Forming a line with the priests in the front rank bearing the ark, the Israelites marched about the city thirteen times, after which the priests blew their trumpets, the people shouted, and the walls "fell down flat." The soldiery of Israel charged the place, put the inhabitants to the sword, took their vessels of gold, silver, brass, and iron, then "burned the city" so thoroughly that recent excavators found reddened masses of bricks, cracked stones, charred timbers, and beds of ashes several inches thick.[11]

Covetous, disobedient Achan, the son of Carmi, was stoned and burned in the valley of Achor for his theft of a gorgeous Babylonish garment, two hundred shekels of silver, and a wedge of gold. Israel then took Ai by ambushment, burned the city,[12] and passed on northward to Shechem, where, with the mountains of Ebal and Gerizim rising on either hand, in obedience to Moses' command,[13] Joshua assembled all Israel."[14]

On Gerizim — the "Mount of Blessing" — stood the tribes of Simeon, Levi, Judah, Issachar, Joseph, and Benjamin. On Ebal — the "Mount of Cursing" — stood the tribes of Reuben, Gad, Asher, Zebulun, Dan, and Naphtali. In the midst of the valley separating the two mountains stood the ark of the covenant.

With the elders, officers, and judges arranged about the sacred symbol, and the vast multitudes covering the mountain sides and filling the plain below, the loud-voiced Levites turned their faces Gerizimward and uttered the blessings that would certainly visit the lives of those who lived righteously; then turning their faces Ebalward, they uttered the evil that was destined to descend upon those who transgressed the law. A tremendous *Amen!* arose from the mighty congregation, tenfold louder as it reverberated from Ebal to Gerizim and from Gerizim to Ebal. The scene was impressive and the effect upon the vast assembly was extremely wholesome.

The kings of Canaan formed a league and fought Israel with the ferocity and desperation of those who fight for their homes; but they were overcome and perished in the narrow defiles of the Beth-Horon pass. The elements and even the sun and moon are said to have favored the hosts led by the intrepid Joshua.[15]

Victory followed victory in their gradual conquest, until thirty-one kings were conquered, and the children of Israel came into possession of a great portion of the highlands from Bethel northward. At Shiloh they set up the tabernacle, established their central sanctuary, and divided the land by lot. But ere long many among them became enamored of the false gods of the land.

Being fully cognizant of the drift, Joshua gathered all the tribes at Shechem,[16] and bringing the leaders nearest him, spoke to them in a very heart-to-heart fashion, stressing the reality of Jehovah and the unreality of the false gods about them. Then placing the issue squarely before them, he declared that he and his house would "serve the Lord"; but required an answer as to whom they would serve.

With a sincere purpose the people took their stand with Joshua, to serve the Lord *only*. A stone was lifted, and their pledge engraved upon it as a memorial. Joshua soon died and was buried at Timnath-Serah, south-west of Shechem. The people, in keeping with their parting promise, put away their strange gods and settled upon their estates on both sides of the Jordan.

### Chapter V

## IN THOSE DAYS THERE WERE JUDGES

For a time the children of Israel sought diligently to clear the land of idolators and serve Jehovah with singleness of heart, then becoming too content to reach so tranquil a goal, they put to tribute those who worshipped idols and little imagined the outer and inner conflicts destined to beset them as a penalty for their failure to stamp out pagan practices and firmly establish the worship of Jehovah.

Within their own homes "another generation" arose that failed to experience true regeneration of soul, dropped their highest ideals, slipped into the ways of the people about them, and drifted downward in ease and withering tolerance. Decades passed, but they only drifted farther down the defiles of ruin until an oppressor arose from without and a judge or prophet arose from within.[1]

Having intermarried with the people round about, and turned to the groves for Baal worship, they possessed no further claim on Divine aid, therefore fell an easy prey to the armed forces of the Arameans who oppressed them for eight years until they repented and cried unto the Lord for deliverance. The spirit of the Lord came upon Othniel, Caleb's nephew, who led the people to victory and gave the land rest for forty years.[2]

A coalition under Eglon, King of Moab, brought Israel into servitude for eighteen years when for the second time they did evil in the sight of the Lord. Then from the Israelitish host arose Ehud, a left-handed Benjamite, who wrought himself a two-edged dagger of a cubit length; girded it under his garment and walked briskly along the pass of Michmash to Jericho bearing a present from the children of Israel to the alien ruler. Under pretense of having a message from God for Eglon, the two retired to the king's quiet, cool summer parlor, when with his unerring left hand, the Israelite stealthily thrust the dagger into the stomach of the portly king who had confided in him so sincerely. After locking the doors of the parlor, Ehud passed out across the side porch, made his way into the mountains of Benjamin and Ephraim where he gathered the forces, took the fords of the Jordan, slew the prosperous Moabite leaders and brought to an end their oppression.

Following this unusual victory, Shamgar, the son of Anath, walked westward and attacked the Philistines single-handed, slaying six hundred of them with an ox goad. Thus Israel was delivered from both the Moabites and Philistines.[3]

With the death of Ehud the children of Israel fell into gross sin; then Sisera, the captain of King Jabin's Canaanitish forces, came against them with nine hundred chariots of iron and such a formidable host that the people of Israel forsook the daily round of life and sought refuge in concealment lest they be found and destroyed by the enemy.

The highways of Israel that echoed
The tramp of the traveler's tread,
Deserted and silent ran on,
As though through the realms of the dead;
The straggler that journeyed alone,
In his fear of the foeman's wrath,
In the dark shades of evening stole
Through the wild hills' wildest path.
The villages ceased to assemble,
So greatly increased were their woes,
They shrank from the prospect of battle,
And cowered from the sight of their foes.[4]

Men strong in qualities of leadership, and firm enough in their beliefs to withstand the tendencies of the age, were wanting. It remained for deliverance to come through Deborah, a woman courageous enough to refuse the lines of least resistance, and passing over the opinions of the people, steadfastly declared her unbounded faith in God as the determining factor in deciding questions of right and wrong. People who had been thrown into spiritual darkness by yielding to the currents of thought and worldly ways about them had seen the demoralizing effects upon their own lives and had made paths to Deborah's dwelling under the palm tree "between Ramah and Beth-el."[5] All who knew her were convinced that she was on such intimate terms with God that she could point the way of deliverance in this day of dire need.

Instead of making the occasion an opportunity to magnify her own importance, she modestly and wisely sought the assistance of Barak,[6] the best and most courageous of her acquaintances. Together they rallied Israel in a glen well up on the side of Mount Tabor, where Barak "watched till the lengthening line of his enemy's chariots drew out from the western angle at Tel el-Kassis and stretched opposite to him with Ta'anach and Megiddo behind them, then gave them battle in a fierce highland charge."[7] The huge Canaanitish army broke rank and retreated in wild disorder across the Great Plain.

From the north a terrific storm in all its fury suddenly burst upon the Canaanite army which fled back the way it had come, so that it madly crowded the narrowing plain while horses and men became mixed in wild confusion as they jostled and trod down one another in their attempt to escape through the pass of the Kishon at Tel el-Kassis and Tel Harosheth. At the height of the confusion the swollen waters of the ancient river Kishon surged in swirling torrents through the pass and swept the proud Canaanites to their ruin.

Trusting to his frightened feet to carry him away from danger, Sisera had in the meantime broken away from the main army and made his escape by a solo flight eastward. Jaded and exhausted, he sought refuge in the tent of Jael, the wife of Heber. After eating he fell asleep from sheer exhaustion, when Jael took one of the pins of the tent and, lifting a hammer, drove the nail through the temples of the famous general.[8] The grandest battle song in the world was composed and sung to commemorate this great deliverance.[9]

The children of Israel again fell into evil ways and so weakened themselves that they were unable to ward off the Midianite nomads who crossed the Jordan river and pushed up the valley of Jezreel. Seeing their opportunity they overran Palestine for seven years. The tinkling bells of their browsing camels sounded from many a hillside and Israel dared to do nothing about it.

In dens, caves and strongholds Israel lived, and was permitted to go abroad only to sow their fields. At harvest time the Amalekites brought their cattle and their tents, joining the Midianites and the two infested the land until "the increase of the earth" was destroyed. Israel's distress was great, so great that she "cried unto the Lord" who sent a prophet to deliver them and help them recapture their freedom and their moral and spiritual ideals.[10]

In secrecy Gideon threshed wheat by the winepress intending to hide it from the Midianites when a heavenly messenger assured him that the Lord was with him and as a man of valor he would deliver Israel. He pled his poverty, yet arose to throw down the altar of Baal and cut down the grove.[11] With the blast of a trumpet he gathered Israel on the northern slope of Gilboa above the well of Harod, which had long been "a favorite resort for herdsmen, and camping place for caravans and military bands."[12] Here, where a copious spring sends forth a large stream of crystal clear water from the foot of Mount Gilboa, the "deep bed and soft banks of the stream constitute a formidable ditch in front of the position on Gilboa, and render it possible for defenders of the latter to hold the spring at their feet in face of an enemy on the plain."[13]

The invaders' headquarters were northward from Gilboa over against the hill of Moreh. The Midianites, Amalekites, and other Arab bands were encamped along the entire length of the Jezreel valley "like grass-hoppers for multitude; and their camels were without number."[14] Twice did this cautious yet courageous man "put out the fleece" to ascertain God's will, and twice did he winnow his army; then exploring the ground two miles in breadth between his men and the Arab tents, he overheard two soldiers talking of the recognition of the power of Gideon which had taken possession of the Midianites.[15] This decided the issue in his mind.

Returning to his camp he divided his three hundred courageous men into three companies, and giving to every man a trumpet, a pitcher and a torch to be placed within the pitcher, he ordered his men to certain designated positions about the enemy encampment. When every man "stood in his place round about the camp" Gideon gave the signal and every man broke his pitcher, blew his trumpet and shouted, "the sword of the Lord, and of Gideon."[16]

The move was so sudden and the effect so instantaneous that the host of Midianites and Amalekites thought themselves hopelessly surrounded by a vast army. Concern for their tents, cattle and camels brought on a sudden rush, attended by confusion and panic in which many died at the hands of their fellows. The mighty host broke away from the field of battle and fled down the valley of Jezreel. Hot pursuit on the part of Gideon and the various recruits from nearby tribes sent the flying Arabs across the Jordan river past Succoth, beyond Penuel, to Karkor where they met final defeat.[17]

When Gideon returned in triumph to his native city, Ophrah, his own tribe of Manasseh and adjoining tribes made him ruler of the whole countryside. Thus, Israel was delivered from the nomadic hordes and the glory of God was not lost in the glamour of hero-worship.[18]

The country was in quietness for forty years, but Gideon was no sooner dead than Israel drifted back to the misty flats of Baal worship and its attendant degradation. In their confusion there arose one Abimelech, who by political trickery, got himself made petty "king," which caused Jotham to stand upon Mount Gerizim and utter "the parable of the bramble brier king" — one of the greatest and most effective pieces of irony ever spoken:

> The trees went forth on a time to anoint a king over them; and they said unto the olive tree, Reign thou over us. But the olive tree said unto them, Should I leave my fatness, wherewith by me they honour God and man, and go to be promoted over the trees? And the trees said to the fig tree, Come thou, and reign over us. But the fig tree said unto them, Should I forsake my sweetness, and my good fruit, and go to be promoted over the trees? Then said the trees unto the vine, Come thou, and reign over us. And the vine said unto them, Should I leave my wine, which cheereth God and man, and go to be promoted over the trees? Then said all the trees unto the bramble, Come thou, and reign over us. And the bramble said unto the trees. If in truth ye anoint me king over you, then come and put your trust in my shadow; and if not, let fire come out of the bramble, and devour the cedars of Lebanon.[19]

The evil principles adopted by Abimelech brought on cruel civil war in which many cities were destroyed and many people lost their lives. For the next forty-five years Tola and Jair judged Israel. But these were no sooner gone than Israel forsook the Lord and served the strange gods of the land until the anger of the Lord was hot against them and He sold them into the hands of the Ammonites.

Tribute and oppression were their portion until the Hebrews east of the Jordan gathered at Mizpah of Gilead and promised Jephthah, the brave chief of a robber band, that he should be judge of the land if he would lead them in a victorious campaign against their enemies, the Moabites.

Accepting the responsibility of so great an undertaking, the new leader turned to God in unselfish earnestness. "When I return in peace from the children of Ammon, whatsoever cometh forth from the doors of my house to meet me, I will offer it up for a burnt offering."[20] Twenty cities fell in rapid succession and the children of Ammon were subdued before Israel. Laden with honors, the victorious general was returning to his home when his bronzed cheek paled and his voice faltered as he beheld his only daughter with her maidens and their timbrels coming to celebrate his victory. When informed of the vow the maidens returned their musical instruments, discarded their pretty garments, donned drab-colored mantles and retired to the mountains, where for two months they bewailed her virginity, only to return for the consummation of the vow.

> Though the virgins of Salem lament,
> Be the judge and the hero unbent.[21]

After six years Jephthah died and Israel again ventured into idolatry, and for many years was tormented and harrassed by the Philistines. Then, in a home at Zorah, on "the hillside facing south against the sunshine"[22] where sea breezes often blew, a boy was born over whose head no razor was to pass and who should consume no strong drink. Angels talked with the mother before his birth, declaring that he was to be a "Nazarite."

Here, "in as fair a nursery for boyhood"[23] as was to be found in the land, Samson "grew, and the Lord blessed him, and began to move him at times in the camp of Dan."[24]

On coming to manhood he might have had the hand of one of the choicest maidens among the Danites, or he could have ascended the Judean hills and won the affections of one of the noble young women among the Judeans. But, alas! he overlooked the "modest sweetness of the daughters of his own people,"[25] neither sought he the gentle graces of any Jewish maiden, but became enamored of the seductive charms of the women down across the Philistine border. Uncurbed passions caused this brawny man to cross and recross the valley of Sorek while consorting with those women whose wild, fierce natures were eventually to defeat him in his God-ordained purpose.[26]

At Timnath, where he wedded the object of his first love, he perplexed the Philistines at the wedding feast by putting forth a riddle, then wrought havoc in their midst when they plowed with his heifer.[27] Samson burned the fields of the Philistines, carried away the gates of Gaza, achieved a victory with the jawbone of an ass and dealt such destruction that the Philistines dared not make aggressive war on Israel. For twenty years the Philistines were confused and weakened by this strange, strong man from across the valley of Sorek.

In Israel Samson was rated as a judge and a deliverer, and what a record he made when he trusted in God, but what inglorious defeat was his portion when he became actuated by personal motives rather than by love of country or of God! What a descent he made "from the pure home and the mother who talked with angels, to the heathen cities, with their harlots and their prisons."[28]

When Samson met Delilah, he fell under her spell. She drew him into her house where she wove about him a web "much as a spider weaves his silken tendrils around a helpless fly."[29] Delilah bargained with the lords of the Philistines, and wheedling Samson with soft enchantments, drew the strong man to the brink of the precipice. A few times he amused himself by deceiving Delilah with plausible inventions, but finally "she wrung from Samson the divine secret which ought never to have left his lips."[30] With the passing of his strength he went out to shake himself, only to find that his presumption had betrayed him and the Lord had departed from him.

The Philistines "took him, and put out his eyes, and brought him down to Gaza, and bound him with fetters of brass; and he did grind in the prison house."[31] What a pathetic sight! Israel's judge grinding at a tread mill in a Philistine prison; and what a pathetic story, the story of this man and his uncurbed strength which like one of Canaan's native brooks, "at first tumbled and sported with laughter, then like them, also ran to the flats and the mud, and, being darkened and befouled, was used by men to turn their mills."[32]

One day in this center of Philistine government before a large assemblage of lords and ladies the once invincible Samson, now a blinded man serving as a beast of burden, was led in to make sport for the spectators; while thus engaged, the pent up sorrows of his outraged soul poured in piteous agonizing anguish of spirit into the ears of the God of his strength, brought the power of God upon him; and the blind prince, with the Philistine host, lay crushed beneath the ruins of the temple. In this final act he destroyed more enemies than he had killed during his lifetime.

The story of this strange life across which fitful winds of fate had wafted, bringing defeat and death was now history; and the tribe of Dan of which he was such an illustrious leader, wearied by the turmoil of so many invasions, moved northeastward to the foot of Mount Hermon, to Laish, which they called Dan.

## CHAPTER VI

# THE RISE OF THE HEBREW MONARCHY

DURING THE LATTER PART of the twelfth century B. C. there was little unity in Israel and less true worship. For almost three centuries she had oscillated between victory and defeat, between success and failure, between the worship of Jehovah and that of the false gods about her. Her high priest was weak and his sons wayward. Sacred devotion had long since departed and selfish license held sway. The people were on a long drift from God.

One night at the well-known city of Shiloh, a lad lay sleeping in the temple court, when amid the quietness of the night, he heard Israel's doom pronounced.[1] Before long the time came when Israel was smitten, the ark of the covenant was taken, and the Philistines ruthlessly overran the country. In the eyes of the people the lad, Samuel, was the personification of faithfulness to God, a light in the prevailing spiritual darkness, and the one to whom they instinctively turned in the hour of dire need. Through his devout example and wise leadership the tide in the affairs of Israel took a decided turn for the better. The Philistines were made to fear the God of Israel, the ark was returned, and temporary peace prevailed between the two peoples.

Samuel was both good and great, and through him righteousness was exalted, a love for Jehovah inspired, and the people were welded together in their purposes and plans so that once again they faced the greater issues of life with courage and determination. To the people Samuel was a prophet, a deliverer, and a judge. He traveled in circuit and held court, and his presence as their leader brought peace and satisfaction throughout the realm.[2]

After a time, however, the Philistines renewed their aggression and the Israelites took fright and pled for a king so that Israel might have a militarist to lead her out to battle like the nations round about her. The lot fell upon Saul, a young man who stood head and shoulders above those about him, and who was distinguished for personal dignity and manly beauty.[3]

In his morning years God gave him "another heart" and by a clean, humble and positive life he pleased God, endeared himself to the nation and was recognized as a great and useful leader. But Saul's scepter was lifted in troublous days when as a warrior king he was obliged to brandish the sword and reign with the military camp as his court. When on a mission to "utterly destroy" the wicked and war-like Amalekites the king harkened to carnal counsel and carried out only a part of the divine plan. As a reward for his disobedience Saul incurred God's displeasure, lost Samuel's support, and imbibed an "evil spirit." After this he often fell a victim to inaction, jealousy and discouragement.

By the highways and through the wadies of the Shephelah the Philistines persistently penetrated the southwestern domains of Israel's first king, until with his army Saul marched westward to contest their further progress. He pitched camp in a commanding position just north of the valley of Elah, and the Philistines pitched theirs in an equally strong position just south of the valley, at Shocoh. There was long hesitation of the armies to face each other in battle.[4] Saul, who had come to love the camp more than the battlefield, had no plans for the offensive but clung close to his policy of "watchful waiting" while his soldiers shuddered at the sound of every unusual noise.

Over the hills and down through *Wady es Sunt* came David, the son of Jesse, wearing the usual shepherd's *abayah,* carrying his scrip in which was an ephah of parched corn and ten cheeses. In his girdle was a simple sling like that carried by many a shepherd.[5]

Passing well down the Judean mountains, he paused for a long moment in the cool peaceful upland which rose a few hundred feet above the low lying hills of the "Shephelah," then started, but suddenly stopped to stare — as one who saw strange sights. Before him on the lower hills of the Shephelah, two armies were enrange of Azekah. The beautiful valley of Elah with its smoother camped, the one on Mount Zechariah, and the other along the contour lay between the two hostile and elevated camps. Only the advance guards occupied either side of the level terrain.

Coming from the peaceful haunts of those shepherd runs the lad gazed into all that war arena, and began to breathe the air of conflict. For a moment strange thoughts gripped his consciousness, stirred his emotions and did exquisite things to his soul. Then recalling the green-carpeted hills of peace about Bethlehem, his father and his home, he flung soldier ambitions with their danger-fraught paths back into the secret recesses of his heart, and descending to the Shephelah, went directly to the front ranks of Israel's army. The cause for which Israel strove and the atmosphere in which he moved reawakened the lad's emotions. He shouted for the battle.

Looking across the beautiful valley — two miles wide and about five long — he beheld a giant who wore a helmet of brass and a coat of mail as he strode forth toward Israel's ranks, with a roaring challenge. When the shepherd lad perceived the tenseness of the atmosphere and saw the faces of strong men go pale with fear he asked what the affair was all about and was told that it was Goliath from the city of Gath, who for some days had been hurling a challenge twice a day to Israel to send a man to fight with him to decide the issue whether Israel was to serve the Philistines or the Philistines were to serve Israel.

The lad felt a strange stirring in his breast when he understood that the challenge was a defiance of the armies of the living God and the cause of righteousness. He startled the bystanders and his brothers with his positive and fearless declaration, "I will accept the challenge." Eliab, his eldest brother, reminded the lad of his humble shepherd duties, and jealousy assailed him with the belittling charge that the "pride" and "naughtiness," of his heart had caused him to come over only to *"see* the battle," but met with the ready reply, *"Is there not a cause?"* Knowing that his words rang true, one carried the news to the King, who immediately sent for David.

When he stood before King Saul, the shepherd lad was conscious that his royal master was making comparisons between him and the giant, and missing the mark by thinking only in terms of the physical. "Thy servant kept his father's sheep," said the lad, "and there came a lion, and a bear, and took a lamb out of the flock; and I went out after him . . . and slew both the lion and the bear; and this uncircumcised Philistine shall be as one of them, seeing he hath defied the armies of the living God. . . Moreover, the Lord that delivered me out of the paw of the lion, and out of the paw of the bear, he will deliver me out of the hand of this Philistine."[6]

Willing to make a contribution to the warfare, King Saul armed David with his own armor, put a helmet of brass upon his head, clad him in a coat of mail, and gave to him his sword. But the armor did not fit, nor did it harmonize with the plan that God had in mind for David; therefore, all the king's contribution was laid aside, and the shepherd lad went from the king and his court with no other armor and battle equipment than the simple sling he had frequently used while tending his father's flock on the Judean hills.

Passing along the battle line he was cheered by many a soldier who wondered at his lack of armor, yet admired his courage and indomitable spirit. Passing the foremost soldier, the lad went out upon the battlefield alone, so far as human resources were concerned, to entrust to God his future and the issues of the battle. From the bed of the brook he chose five smooth stones and placed them securely in a shepherd's scrip — a small leather bag which every shepherd carries — and went on to meet the giant.

Goliath, the huge, brass-encased man of war, strode forth to meet his opponent but on seeing the strippling appear with no armor bearer, and not even the semblance of armor, he disdained the youth as unworthy of combat with a warrior so renowned as himself. Then, as if urged to battle by the necessity of the occasion, the giant harangued the lad for coming out to meet him after such a fashion and declared his purpose to give the lad's flesh to the fowls of the air.

David then recounted the cause of the conflict and dictated the terms of battle:

> Thou comest to me with a sword, and with a spear, and with a shield; but I come to thee in the name of the Lord of Hosts, the God of the armies of Israel, whom thou hast defied.
>
> This day will the Lord deliver thee into mine hand; and I will smite thee, and take thine head from thee; and I will give the carcasses of the host of the Philistines this day unto the fowls of the air, and to the wild beasts of the earth; that all the earth may know that there is a God in Israel.
>
> And all this assembly shall know that the Lord saveth not with the sword and spear; for the battle is the Lord's and he will give you into our hands.[7]

In the conflict which ensued every man on either mountainside stood breathless for a moment while the shepherd lad thrust his hand into his scrip and taking out one of the smooth stones, he placed it in his sling, whirled it over his head, took aim and let the stone drive through the air to its mark — the massive forehead. Goliath fell; David ran up, unsheathed the giant's ponderous sword, cut off his head and started for the King's camp. Israel shouted and the Philistines fled and the louder Israel shouted the faster the enemy fled.

As he stood before the king and recounted his exploits, David was overheard by Prince Jonathan who fell desperately in love with the shepherd lad — he liked the kind of mettle that was in the noble youth. King Saul kept David and let him go home no more. When they passed a crowd soon after this, the women shouted: "Saul hath slain his thousands and David his ten thousands," and from that time forth an "evil spirit" increased Saul's jealousy and often threw him into mad fits.

At times David swept the strings of his beautiful harp and consoled the king by the sweet strains that floated through the rooms of the royal palace; at other times the young giant-killer was hunted on the Judean hills as the old king would hunt for a partridge.

A few times, when his full-orbed self came to the fore, the king entertained regrets of his badly balanced moral life. "I have played the fool, and have erred exceedingly," he once said, half reproachfully and half repentant, when standing in the white light of undeserved mercy.[8]

The climax came at that Mount Gilboa encampment, at *Ain Harod,* when Saul and his army were soon to do battle with the superior forces of the Philistines, who encamped with their horses and chariots just below Shunem (the present village of *Solam*) and spread themselves over the valley of Jezreel, including their old fortress of Beth-Shean.[9]

Night stole down from the east, shrouding Gilboa in purple, softening its sharp outlines, and making them seem gentle and easy. But none of the soft gentle influences of nature affected Saul. An ugly, nervous tension had taken possession of the Hebrew military encampment; especially was the atmosphere tense for the king who had now reigned forty years. The sighing night winds which arose on Gilboa spoke to him of impending evil.

In the still watches of the night while darkness hung about Gilboa like a dark velvet curtain, reality gripped him, and his thoughts turned back over the years he had served Israel — stern, eventful years in which he had hardly ceased to wield the sword. Prior to those were better years that did not mock him; years in which he took time to serve God. When innocency, simplicity, and humility bore the fruit of righteousness. But those years were gone and he could no longer get help through prayer — God had departed from him and answered him no more.

Across the valley of Jezreel and along the mountain pathways, stealthily moved the ill-fated king, going to consult the wily, old witch at Endor. Disheartened, gloomy, and dejected, he returned to his camp; where, the poet says, he pronounced his own doom:

> My kingdom from me rent, my children slain,
> My army lost, myself from hope cast out —
> The seer hath spoken well. All is achieved,
> David, thou art avenged.[10]

During the night the Philistines marched southward, circled Gilboa, and with the morning light made the onset from the southwest, thus availing themselves of Gilboa's easy ascent and charging Israel's left rear flank. The battle went sore against Saul. Tragedy stalked across Gilboa's heights when Israel's first king was wounded by the Philistine archers; and to cheat the uncircumcised of a measure of their victory, he fell upon his own sword and took his life.[11] The army of Israel was destroyed or scattered upon the mountains like sheep without a shepherd. In hot haste the Philistines removed the bodies of Saul and his sons from the lofty battle field and hung them upon the walls of Bethshan, in the lower reaches of the valley of Jezreel.

When the news of the disaster reached David, the tenderness of his nature rose superior to every feeling of revenge or ambitious rivalry. From this fertile brain, backed by a soul stirred to the depths, there came the most pathetic, and yet the most beautiful lament ever recorded in the annals of history:

> The beauty of Israel is slain upon the high places;
> How are the mighty fallen!
> Tell it not in Gath, publish it not in the streets of Askalon,
> Lest the daughters of the Philistines rejoice,
> Lest the daughters of the uncircumcised triumph.
> Ye mountains of Gilboa, let there be no dew,
>
> Neither let there be rain, upon you, nor fields of offerings;
> For there the shield of the mighty is vilely cast away,
> The shield of Saul, as though he had not been anointed with oil.
> How are the mighty fallen in the midst of the battle!
>
> O Jonathan, thou wast slain in thine high places. „
> Anguish is mine for thee, O my brother Jonathan,
> Dearest wert thou to me. Thy love to me was wonderful,
> Passing the love of women.
> How are the mighty fallen, and the weapons of war perished![12]

David was crowned in Hebron, then passing by all other recognized Israelitish centers, he stormed Jerusalem and made it his capital city. Before his day Jerusalem was a small, but well-fortified sanctuary city of the Jebusites; but with thought of the future he began at once to make it a worthy capital for all Israel. He enlarged it by making the fortress of Zion on the neighboring hill, taking in the valley which separated the two, and surrounding the whole with a good substantial wall. Then "with dramatic pageantry" he brought into Jerusalem, the Ark of the Covenant which had long been in the hands of the Philistines. "With this act of consecration began the romantic history of Jerusalem, as the religious and civil center of the State, and physical symbol of Hebrew unity."[13]

Everything favored national prosperity for Israel. There was no great power in Western Asia inclined to prevent her becoming a powerful monarchy; the battle of Kadish on the Orontes (1272 B. C.) had been fought. The Hittites had been humbled; and Egypt, under the last kings of the twenty-first dynasty, had lost her prestige and had all but collapsed. The Philistines were driven to a narrow portion of their old dominion, and the king of Tyre sought friendly alliance with David.[14]

With a steady hand David set out to force back and defeat Israel's enemies who had constantly crowded, horned and harrassed the Hebrews; Moab and Ammon were conquered; then the Edomites, alarmed at the ever-increasing power of Israel, rose against David, but were routed by Abishai, who penerated to Petra and became master of the country.

The Arameans and Amalekites were in turn conquered. Commercial highways were thrown open and in came merchandise, culture, and wealth from Phoenicia, Damascus, Assyria, Arabia, Egypt and more distant lands. To his people David was king, judge and general, but to the nations round about, he was the leading power in all the Near Eastern world — the mightiest monarch of the day.[15]

Years sped by and David the king and Nathan the prophet planned how they would build the house of the Lord — a mighty temple to be dedicated to the worship of God Almighty. Then came a fair night when sleep fled from King David, and in his wakefulness he arose and walked the garden roof of his great palace. Across the narrow street, in a nearby apartment, beautiful Bath-sheba bathed with her window blinds undrawn.[16] Her physical and intellectual beauty, coupled with her carelessness, presented an appeal which only the strongest and bravest of men could resist; and just at that juncture David was neither strong physically nor well fortified spiritually.

For more than thirty years he had borne an unsullied name, and had been "a model of reproachless chivalry" but just previous to this he had been adjudged unable personally to bear the fatigues of the field of conflict and had been left behind. The delicacies of the palace had "softened and ungirt his spirit" while state duties coupled with responsibilities for war had drained his great soul of much of its divine power which he had formerly possessed. In his spiritually depleted state the great hero "fell by a glance," then set about the task of covering his tragic tracks.

Uriah, Bath-sheba's warrior husband, fought in David's army in quelling an uprising at ancient Rabbath-Ammon. Eastward the messenger hurried across the Jordan valley rift and brought Uriah to the King's palace at Jerusalem. But faithful Uriah slept beside the King's palace gate and went not down to his house. This complicated matters, but David and the devil arranged for Uriah to be sent to the battle front where he fell, faithful to Israel and faithful to the King who had proven him false.[17]

Then came a day when the prophet Nathan appeared before the King and gave forth a tale of two men in one city; "the one rich and the other poor. The rich man had exceeding many flocks and herds but the poor man had nothing, save one little ewe lamb which he had bought and nourished up . . . it did eat of his own meat, and drink of his own cup, and lay in his bosom, and was unto him as a daughter. And there came a traveler unto the rich man, and he spared to take of his own flock and of his own herd, to dress for the wayfaring man that was come unto him; but took the poor man's lamb, dressed it for the man that was come to him."

When the story had ended, David's spirit of gallantry arose and he pronounced death for the one guilty of such gross injustice. "And," said the King, "he shall restore the lamb fourfold, because he did this thing, and because he had no pity." Then with simple directness Nathan pointed an index finger at the King and said, "Thou art the man, thou hast killed Uriah the Hittite with the sword, and hast taken his wife to be thy wife." David proved his manhood by owning his guilt and going on his face to fast and pray and repent. God forgave and he took again the high white line of a clean, honorable, spirit-filled life.[18]

David's self denial and devotion to the interest of the nation became widely known, yet his children were rapidly growing to maturity and would try his metal from many other angles. The beauty of his wives and the physical completeness of David combined to make their children the most attractive and the most intelligent of their day. "In all Israel there was none to be so much praised as Absalom for his beauty: from the sole of his foot even to the crown of his head there was no blemish in him." And his sister Tamar excelled all the daughters of Israel in beauty and grace.

Engrossed with state affairs, King David left his lovely children to provide their own entertainment and go the way of their immature choices. Tamar was attacked and humbled by Amnon, her half brother. Handsome Absalom resented the horrid affront and heightened the tragedy by slaying Amnon at the sheep-shearing in Baal-hazor (Tel-Asur). To avoid the consequences Absalom fled to Geshur, northeast of the sea of Galilee, where for three years he dwelt with King Talmai, his grandfather on his mother's side.[19] Then his father permitted him to return to Jerusalem where he was given access to the royal exchequer and left in idleness.

Absalom's ambitions were in the direction of law — he longed to be the appointed judge who should sit at the royal gate of the Holy City and judge the cases of those who came with controversies. When David ignored his son's ambition, Absalom prepared him chariots and horses and fifty men to run before him. With these he gained the attention of the people, and by rising early and standing beside "the way of the gate" he conversed with those who were in trouble, kissed them and deplored the fact that he was not deputed to favor their cause. Thus did the fast young man "steal the hearts of the men of Israel."[20]

Four years of this political trickery ripened into a plot to take the throne from his overburdened father. Under the guise of worship Absalom went to Hebron accompanied by two hundred men out of Jerusalem, while his spies went throughout all the tribes of *Israel* to urge them to pledge allegiance to the handsome young man who promised a more liberal rule.

At the psychological moment the trumpet of revolt was sounded in Hebron and a messenger hurried into Jerusalem saying that the hearts of the men of *Israel* were after Absalom. David gathered his household and those who were loyal to him, and with a bodyguard of six hundred men he passed over the brook Kidron and went up barefoot and with covered head by the ascent of the Mount of Olives, weeping as he went on eastward to the fords of the Jordan river. Marching into the land of Gilead, David established his base of supplies at Mahanaim, numbered the people that were with him and set captains of thousands and captains of hundreds over them, and divided his army into three divisions.

In hot pursuit Absalom followed across the Jordan where the battle was joined in the woods of Ephraim. Upon a fine mule the handsome young rebel rode as he reeled with intoxication at the prospect of a throne. But his hilarity did not last long, for when the battle was joined twenty thousand of Absalom's men were slain and confusion among those that remained soon turned into a riot. Absalom clamped the spurs to the royal mule and was attempting to make his escape when he ran directly into a band of David's soldiers. Swerving to one side the reckless Prince was hurrying on through the wood when his unfortunate *head* was caught in the forked boughs of a great oak. The royal mule ran on, leaving the rider suspended between heaven and earth, while Joab and his soldiers surrounded him and riddled him with darts and javelins.

Joab blew the trumpet, and the people ceased the battle. They took Absalom's body and cast it into a great pit in the forest, and raised over it a very great heap of stones. The beauty of Israel was slain.

Overcome with grief at the tragedy of a son's ruined life, King David walked to and fro on the ramparts of Mahanaim's citadel tower and wept bitterly while he gave voice to that classic parental wail: "O my son Absalom, my son, my son Absalom! would I had died for thee, O Absalom, my son, my son!" Only "Absalom's Pillar" which he had raised up during his life time, stands "in the King's vale" near Jerusalem to keep alive memories of Israel's beautiful, reckless son. Strange shaft is this that pierces the blue! Yet stranger still was the life of that fast young Prince who reckoned without Jehovah and came to such a tragic end.[21]

On David's return to Jerusalem, one Sheba, a son of wickedness, took advantage of a minor difference between Judah and Israel, and blew the trumpet of revolt; but David and Joab quelled the revolt. David satisfied the people throughout Israel, quieted the Philistines for all time to come, then in the midst of peace and plenty wrote many psalms of praise to Jehovah. The elderly king gathered vast stores of stone, iron, brass, and cedar for the erection of the temple of God, gave his parting charge, and closed the most successful royal career recorded in the annals of history.

Had it not been for his temporary moral breakdown David might have achieved far more, but as it was he turned over to his successor the most powerful kingdom of Western Asia — the fruit of the labors of Samuel, Saul, and David, of Abner and Joab. It was bounded by Lebanon and the Euphrates on the north, the Euphrates and the desert on the east, Egypt on the south, and the Mediterranean on the west. Palestine was then exceedingly fertile, and sustained a large population. Its hills were crested with fortresses, and covered with cedars and oaks. The land was favorable to both tillage and pasture, abounding in grapes, figs, olives, dates, and every species of grain.[22]

Solomon was the divinely appointed son of David who succeeded him. In answer to prayer he was given such wisdom as no other before nor since. During the early part of his reign he subjected himself to discipline and divine direction, and endeavored, in an intelligent way, to give life a spiritual yet practical basis. His proverbs were not only profound lessons of moral wisdom, but were also a guide to his people. He ruled by combining moral and military strength. He formed alliances with most of the surrounding nations, subsidized and protected the caravan routes, built a fleet of ships to engage in trade with distant countries, and brought peace and plenty to his subjects until every man sat under his own vine and fig tree in perfect security.

The royal stables contained forty thousand horses and fourteen hundred chariots.[23] The palace glistened with plates of gold, and the parks and gardens were watered from immense reservoirs, but of all King Solomon's accomplishments none in any way rivaled the erection of the Sacred Temple on Mount Moriah — an enterprise which David had longed to accomplish. By the aid of one hundred and sixty thousand men the stones were quarried, the timbers hewn, and the magnificent structure completed. This far-famed king left as his monument a temple with foundations timeless in their security, furnishings surpassingly rich, and its architecture the pride and glory of its time and the admiration and envy of generations to come.

## Chapter VII

# THE RENT GARMENT

Wisdom, loyalty, faithfulness and efficiency characterized the attitudes and acts of David's brilliant son for the first few years of his reign. Then, as if he had attained the mastery of man and God, he turned from following the Lord, and selfishly seizing the reins of wrong, drove to the misty flats of licentiousness, pride and paganism.

Maddened with the love of show, Solomon swung into a feverish career of wastefulness, impropriety, and oppression. Not satisfied with the necessary buildings and legitimate progress of his past years, he over-burdened his people with taxation, enslaved some, and ruthlessly instigated the murder of others.

All Solomon's drinking vessels were of gold, and those of his house were of pure gold. The shields of his mighty men were made of beaten gold, and his great throne was made of ivory and overlaid with the finest gold. Silver in Jerusalem became as common as stones.[1]

Solomon literally built himself a *paradise of pleasure.* One of his chief resorts was Etham[2] where, when the mornings were beautiful, he often went in stately progress, "dressed in snow white raiment, riding in his chariot of state which was made of the finest cedar, decked with gold and silver and purple, and carpeted with the costliest tapestry worked by the daughters of Jerusalem; and attended by a bodyguard of sixty valiant men of the tallest and handsomest of the young men of Israel, arrayed in Tyrian purple, with their long black hair, freshly sprinkled with gold dust every day, glittering in the sun."[3]

The verdict of history, that "wine and women" are the causes of many a wrecked career, is not far amiss in the story of Solomon's pathetic decline. His love for *many* women caused him to marry and pamper numerous foreign, heathen wives, who not only robbed him of his excellency of character, humility of spirit, and efficiency in state affairs, but dominated him and turned his heart to seek "after other gods." Just across the "king's vale" on a hill overlooking the village of Siloam, strange edifices arose before the eyes of the awe-stricken Hebrews. Solomon was building temples for the strange gods he and his strange wives were serving.

> And the Lord was angry with Solomon because his heart was turned from the Lord God of Israel, which had appeared unto him twice. And had commanded him concerning this thing, that he should not go after other gods; but he kept not that which the Lord commanded.[4]

Solomon, like many another absolute monarch, drove too fast and traveled too far. Israel's religion became mixed with idolatry, the state burdened with debt, and the people dissatisfied. Revolt within and a breaking away of vassal states without followed in the wake of a rule so romantic and irrational. The monarch became debauched and effeminate; an egotist and cynic, so satiated with the sensual and material affairs of life that he became skeptical of all good — to him, all became "vanity and vexation of spirit."

In building Millo and repairing the breaches of Jerusalem, a young man named Jeroboam, the son of an Ephrathite widow, proved himself so industrious as to come under the eyes of King Solomon, who promoted him to become the "keeper of the house of Joseph" — overseer of all the relays of labor furnished by the tribes of Ephraim and Manasseh. His might and valor increased until one day when he went for a stroll in the fields outside Jerusalem, suddenly Ahijah, a well-known prophet from the city of Shiloh, hurried up to him, removed his own garment, rent it into *twelve* pieces and presented *ten* of the twelve to Jeroboam, with the words:

> Thus saith the Lord, the God of Israel, Behold, I will rend the kingdom out of the hand of Solomon, and will give ten tribes to thee . . . Howbeit . . . I will make him prince all the days of his life for David my servant's sake, whom I chose, because he kept my commandments and my statutes; but I will take the kingdom out of his son's hand and will give it unto thee, even ten tribes. . . .
>
> And it shall be, if thou wilt hearken unto all that I command thee, and wilt walk in my ways and do that is right in my sight, to keep my statutes and my commandments, as David my servant did; that I will be with thee, and build thee a sure house, as I built for David, and will give Israel unto thee.[5]

The news of this garment-rending episode no sooner reached the palace than the jealous old king set about to take the life of the industrious young man. However, he was foiled in his sinister design, for Jeroboam secretly fled into Egypt where he received the hospitality and protection of Shishak, King of Egypt, until the year 931 B.C., when the sable curtains were drawn and Israel's most spectacular king passed to that bourne from whence no traveler ever returns.[6]

Rehoboam, Solomon's son and successor, ascended the throne at Jerusalem without opposition, but the ten tribes of the north took little interest in the coronation. Their messengers urged their camels over the Sinai desert as they pushed on toward the Egyptian court to inform Jeroboam that Solomon was dead and his presence was desired at Shechem.[7]

In harmony with a well-established custom of the day, Rehoboam journeyed to Shechem where Israel gathered to ratify his succession, but the crowning was delayed, for Jeroboam arrived and entered into conference with Israel's representative men; then he and they appeared before the new king and promised the allegiance of the ten tribes if the oppressive yoke of high taxes and forced labor were made lighter. Granted three days in which to consider the matter, Rehoboam consulted with the older men who served his father, and they advised *moderation* but after consultation with his fastidious, younger associates, he returned the answer:

> My father made your yoke heavy, and I will add to your yoke; my father also chastised you with whips, but I will chastise you with scorpions.[8]

The arrogant answer no sooner reached the ears of the men of Israel than on every hand the shout was heard:

> To your tents, O Israel!

The King sent his treasurer for an interview, but the sight of him who handled the tribute only further irritated the grieved tribes. They stoned him to death. King Rehoboam took fright, fled to his royal chariot and hastily covered the forty miles between Shechem and Jerusalem. His young, fastidious associates, with their short-sighted views, were insufficient to keep up the king's courage. They, like many a younger set, were bringing a cause to ruin and their leader to sorrow.

The incensed tribes encamped about Shechem would no longer follow one who hearkened to the voice of an immature group and refused to heed their plea for a return of a more moderate pace in state affairs. The name *Jeroboam* was heralded from tent to tent until with passionate enthusiasm Israel called an assembly of all the people, and before this vast congregation they summoned the *widow's* son and crowned him King over the ten tribes of Israel. Thus the Hebrew nation was rent in twain. *The ten pieces of the rent garment,* according to the prophecy of Ahijah, *passed into the hands of Jeroboam.*

## Chapter VIII

# ISRAEL KISSING CALVES

Jeroboam's first move was to rebuild and fortify Shechem[1] as the capital for his new kingdom, then to fortify Penuel,[2] his principal outpost; after which he paused for a mental review of his realm. The new king had not long sat thus in his reverie until with a start he hurried to his feet with the words:

> If this people go up to do sacrifice in the house of the Lord at Jerusalem, then shall the heart of this people turn again . . . unto Rehoboam king of Judah, and they shall kill me, and go again to Rehoboam, King of Judah.[3]

The idea that man would ultimately go the way of his emotions — especially his religious emotions — was old in the realm of thought. Yet the occasion challenged the best there was in the man of valor. He resolved to provide a religion the practice of which would *not* take the people from his dominion. He determined furthermore to make it *both easy* and *convenient* for them. Doubtless he considered the words of Ahijah regarding his walking in the ways of the Lord and keeping his statutes, but knowing so well his own state of spiritual bankruptcy, and being unwilling to restock, he easily restorted to human devices.

His stay in Egypt had provided him with ready knowledge of their worship of the live bull, and all Israel was acquainted with the old Canaanitish practice of worshipping the image of the calf or bull as a symbol of strength, endurance, and productivity. The moral and spiritual standards were not lofty; yet it was fascinating, and could be made popular. Moreover, it would be *different* from Jehovah's way, and this fact would aid him in gaining his political ends, even though it be at the cost of moral and spiritual values.

> Whereupon the King took counsel, and made two calves of gold, and said unto them, It is too much for you to go up to Jerusalem; behold thy gods, O Israel.[4]

One of these golden calves was lifted to its pedestal and an altar placed before it in *Beth-el,* and the other in *Dan.* Both cities were dignified with the rank of official, national, religious shrines — and both of them strongly fortified as military centers. The former was fairly convenient for those of the south, and the latter for those in the north. Priests were ordained and feast days appointed. The people donned their finest apparel, decked themselves in their ornaments[5] and filed into the newly appointed place of worship, and heard the priests say,

> Let the men that sacrifice kiss the calves.[6]

The new way made few demands except in ritual, and none for noble character, but permitted large freedom, gave rise to riotous self-indulgences and encouraged immoral innovations.[7] Spiritual men protested, but seeing that nothing could be done to remedy the matter, the Lord's faithful priests and the Levites forsook their possessions and *all* the people in Israel who *set their hearts to follow the Lord God* joined them and they went to Jerusalem to join themselves to Rehoboam who, in the meantime, had been cured of catering to the notions of the younger set. Thus the Kingdom of Judah was greatly strengthened morally as well as politically. With few spiritual people in her midst, Israel was left to speed on down the costly way of compromise and outbroken sins.

The kingdom of Israel existed for only a little over *two* centuries, and was almost continually troubled from within and frequently beset by enemies from without. From Jeroboam to Ahab — a period of sixty-six years — there were six kings, three of whom were assassinated. During Asa's reign of forty-one years (in Judah) eight kings sat on the throne of Israel. There was a succession of idolatrous, violent and bloodthirsty usurpers, whom the army raised to the throne, then assisted in disposing of the survivors of the preceding king's family. None of these kings, except Omri and Jeroboam II, seems to have been marked by signal ability.

Omri built the city of Samaria[8] on a high hill and so strongly fortified it that it remained the capital until the fall of the kingdom. He also made an alliance with Phoenicia, the foremost commercial center of that day, and one of the wealthiest countries of antiquity. He subdued the Moabites,[9] indelibly stamped his name on the country which he ruled and left to his son a kingdom laden with vast possibilities.

Ahab, his son and successor, was young, handsome and friendly. He loved amusements, luxuries, beautiful things; as a prince he never learned to curb his desires. Religiously he showed little active interest in the worship of God, yet openly payed his respects to the golden calves at Beth-el and Dan. In his love affairs he passed the bounds of

Israel and won the affections of a fashionable princess of Phoenicia, who was pleasure-loving and fond of the ostentatious. Nature had generously endowed Jezebel with that type of beauty that troubles and fascinates the world, yet leaves no lasting good.

This Jezebel stepped into the Palestinian arena to play her part within the tragic drama; to make such a contribution to the decline of Israel as no other woman could or would even dare do. Under her supervision the new ivory palace at Samaria shone in the finery of the day. Its atmosphere spoke of a different era. Coming from Phoenicia she brought with her "a whole cycle of ideas in government and worship which were repugnant to the sturdy, conservative mind of the Israelite."[10]

To gratify her religious inclinations, Ahab erected an unusually fine temple which was dedicated to Baal. Within its precincts, beside the altar, he set up a memorial pillar of this immoral cult, and nearby the capital on an eminence he planted a grove where the worship of Baal could be carried out on an extensive scale.[11] After this unusually fine introduction, Jezebel encouraged Phoenician Baal worship throughout Israel. Soon it was merged with the Beth-el-Dan calf cult, and established on such a large scale that it became the dominant type of worship throughout the northern kingdom.

The air became rank with a spirit of apostasy. In sheer disregard for their early leader's command[12] Hiel of Beth-el rebuilt Jericho, after the order of heathenish building practices. He "laid the foundation thereof in Abiram his first born, and set up the gates thereof in his youngest son Segud,"[13] as Joshua had predicted.

The people in general, and the rich and influential in particular, attempted to move forward with a swaggering arrogance as though there were no Jehovah who had led their fathers from Egypt into Canaan and who had warned them of the evil consequences of forgetting Him and traveling the evil and danger-fraught way. In this attempt to forget they were not very successful, for there came one Elijah, a plain but powerful prophet who rebuked Ahab and Jezebel and the people at every turn of the road. Following a prolonged drought the king and his people thronged the mountain side of Carmel and witnessed a fair and impartial test which struck Jezebel's Baal worship a staggering blow.

For a time there loomed on the horizon great possibilities of Israel's following God in righteousness and true holiness. Convinced that Jehovah was the living God, Ahab encouraged Jehovah's prophets, built cities and steadily rose to power until he held within his grasp the opportunity of turning Israel into the very paths ordained for her by Jehovah, but he faced the final turning point of his life when thirty-two kings joined forces under the general leadership of Benhadad of Damascus, and the entire coalition came against Israel.

In this crisis there were indications that Ahab would break away entirely from the religious falsity which had so long divided his kingdom and become a co-worker with Jehovah. He did gather all Israel, along with levies of soldiers from Judah, and met the invaders in victorious conflict, but when Benhadad was delivered into his hands, Ahab showed unseasonable leniency, and thus compromised for gain and carried out only a part of God's will. This act proved the turning point of his life.[14] After this he was not only weak and vacillating, but was in many respects only a puppet in the hands of his wicked wife, who led him and Israel farther down the defiles of ruin.[15]

According to the constitution governing Ahab, he was limited in his rights over the persons and property of his subjects. Yet when he was refused possession of Naboth's vineyard near Jezreel, he fell sick with covetous disappointment. Reared in an atmosphere of "irresponsible despotism" Jezebel took the matter in hand and brought about the death of Naboth and handed to Ahab a title to the coveted vineyard.

As Ahab walked about his new possession with childish glee and gloated over it as over a new toy which had been stolen for him, he lifted his eyes and looked upon the sternly righteous face of the prophet Elijah. Staring at him for a time, the king broke the silence with the pointed question, "Hast thou found me, oh, mine enemy?" To which he received the quiet reply, "I have found thee; because thou hast sold thyself to work evil in the sight of the Lord. . . . In the place where the dogs licked the blood of Naboth shall dogs lick thy blood, even thine. . . . And the dogs shall eat Jezebel by the wall of Jezreel.[16]

Three years after this Ahab strove to wrest Ramoth-Gilead from the forces of Benhadad, when, in the midst of the battle, a certain man "drew a bow at a venture, and smote the king of Israel . . . and the king was stayed up in his chariot against the Syrians" and watched the ebb of battle until he died at even. His blood was spilt in the midst of the chariot, and there went a proclamation throughout the host, saying, "Every man to his city, and every man to his own country." The body of the disobedient king was brought to Samaria and his chariot was washed at the pool of Samaria and the dogs licked his blood which had poured over his armor and stained his chariot.

Ahaziah, the crippled son of Ahab, succeeded to the throne of Israel, but let the kingdom drift from bad to worse. His brother, Jehoram, followed him as king. He began with what seemed to be a sweeping religious reformation, but lacking genuine religious convictions he soon compromised and was dominated by Queen-mother Jezebel. King Mesha of Moab found the Jehoram-Jezebel combination too weak to offer effectual resistance when he arose to gain complete independence from Israel.[17]

Fourteen years after the death of Ahab, when the idolatrous dynasty of Omri had filled their cup of wickedness to overflowing, Elisha anointed Jehu king over Israel and commissioned him to inaugurate a new regime. Disdaining delay, this, the world's most famous charioteer, assumed the royal title, then leaped into his chariot and drove furiously up the Valley of Jezreel. He met Jehoram in the vineyard of Naboth, just below the city of Jezreel, and surprised him when he "drew a bow with his full strength" and shot Jehoram through the heart. He also pursued and mortally wounded Ahaziah, King of Judah, who was at that time visiting his kinsmen.

When Jehu was returning to Jezreel, Jezebel heard of it and painted her face, attired her head, and sat in the window waiting for him, as if her "flapperish" appearance would detract him from his mission. As Jehu's chariot clattered through the street she taunted him and laughed in his face, but Jehu met her taunt with the command, "Who is on my side, throw her down." Under the chariot wheels she met her death and was eaten by the dogs "by the wall of Jezreel."[18]

Under the preaching of Elijah and the teaching of Elisha there had arisen a general protest against Phoenician influence in Church and State. Therefore, Jehu was enabled to complete the work of executing the seed royal and the leaders in the Baal cult. His action, however, was resented by Phoenicia and even by some within his own land. To secure his throne he did not rely on Jehovah as the prophets had expected him to do, but appealed to Assyria for help, accepting the suzerainty of Shalmaneser II, to whom Jehu paid tribute.[18] Israel was saved but as a consequence she fell under the influence and power of the Assyrians and speedily underwent a "far-reaching economic and social change."[20] The middle and lower classes became impoverished, mortgaged and lost their holdings to the powerful wealthy class who had little to do with the land, but lived luxuriously in the great cities.[21]

Near the middle of the eighth century B. C. Israel, under Jeroboam II, conquered the small tribes bordering her territory, established friendly relations with the surrounding nations and began commercial activities with them. Wealth poured into the country, fortunes were quickly made, the arts flourished, and cities began to grow in number and size. There was ushered in a period of magnificent ease such as had never been enjoyed by the northern kingdom. The wealthier classes imported new comforts and enjoyed undreamed-of luxuries.[22] But the poor profited little from the new commercial relations for they had no capital to invest. Beneath the glamour of the wealthy class were terrible social evils, — their comfortable prosperity had passed into excess and debauchery. Associated with the poverty of the lower classes was discontent. Both the rich and the poor seemed inclined to forget Jehovah.

Almost a century had passed since Elijah, "in his flowing hair" had denounced Ahab and Jezebel. Then began to appear on the Palestinian stage a succession of faithful, inspired prophets who were animated by a desire to instill into the soul a deep sense of the Divine, "ennoble the heart by moral aspirations and inspire men to lofty ideas." Two of these — Amos and Hosea — directed their prophecies toward Israel (the Northern Kingdom). They looked past the glamour of wealth and apparent prosperity and pointed to a dark cloud that was rising on the distant horizon. They cried against the corruption of the day, shamed the people for their shams and warned them of their impending doom if they turned not from the path of wrong.

The first of these "lofty figures" was *Amos,* the inspired herdsman of Tekoa.[23] His prophetic voice began to be heard at Beth-el about 755 B. C. when the northern kingdom under Jeroboam II was enjoying this period of unprecedented prosperity and felt herself to be almost as strong as when Judah and Israel flourished together under King David.

Previous to his prophecy Amos had probably gone to market his annual crop of wool in these prosperous centers of Palestine, and while there he saw the rich growing richer and the poor becoming poorer. In the market places he saw the people "multiply their transgressions" by injustice and immorality, and in the sanctuaries he saw them bring a sacrifice "every morning," and either kiss the golden calf, or bow before Baal; but manifest no signs of repentance or true worship toward Jehovah.

He saw that the well-to-do lived in elegant houses built of cedar and ceiled with ivory.[24] They had summer and winter homes which were gorgeously furnished. The beds in which they lolled were inlaid with beautifully carved ivory. They dressed in expensive silks, drank fine wines and ate delicate foods. On the other hand, Amos was well acquainted with the meagre fare of the poor. Their domestic lives were spent in the black sack-cloth-of-hair tents, and rude stone houses. Very familiar, indeed, was he with the *abayeh* or shepherd's cloak which the poor man wore by day and wrapped in at night; but which the rich sometimes took as the poor man's pledge and refused to return at sundown,[25] thus leaving the poor man to shiver or shift as best he could.

> Ill fares the land, to hastening ills a prey.
> Where wealth accumulates and men decay.[26]

The herdsman, accustomed to the clear atmosphere of the desert and the open pastures where he questioned every suspicious sight or sound, certainly looked upon these strange doings with no degree of tolerance. On returning home, he must have reviewed God's laws as given by Moses, thought deeply, meditated and prayed, until one day he heard God saying unto him, "Go prophesy unto my people Israel." Nathan had dealt with David, Gad with Solomon, and Elijah with Ahab and Jezebel, but Amos rose up from among the shepherds and went with his message to the people as a whole.

Appearing at Beth-el on the occasion of one of their festivals, the inspired herdsman thus faced Israel at one of their religious headquarters, and the calf-cult upon one of its high days. As Luther at the Diet of Worms, as Savonarola at the Duomo in Florence, as Paul on Mars' Hill, as Peter at Pentecost, or as Elijah on Mount Carmel; so Amos faced idolatrous Israel at Beth-el. Thousands of gaudily dressed worshippers probably alighted from their chariots, presented their offerings, listlessly attended the white-robed priests as they went through the routine of offering the sacrifices, bowed before and kissed the golden calf, then moved to and fro about the temple as they exchanged the latest gossip.

The simple man from the sheep runs stepped to the front, gained a commanding position from which he could be heard distinctly, and with an ease and inspiration befitting the occasion, he opened his impressive message with these striking words:

> The Lord will roar from Zion, and utter his voice from Jerusalem; and the habitations of the shepherds shall mourn, and the top of Carmel shall wither.[27]

The speaker readily gained audience with the people. They could not keep from both looking and listening; for the prophet was so plain in appearance, so other-worldly in his bearing, and yet so dramatic in style that he commanded the respect of the most careless. Nor was he wanting in his method of approach, for he tactfully won the sympathy of his hearers by calling their attention to the enormities of guilt in their neighbors. Beginning with the more distant and alien peoples of Damascus, Tyre, and Gaza (the Syrians, Phoenicians, and Philistines), he then "turned his prophetic guns" on the nearer and kindred peoples of Edom, Ammon, and Moab; the borders of whose possessions lay almost within sight of those who heard this message.

The Israelites probably said, "Yes, those enemies of ours have been wicked and are deserving of divine wrath. That is right, go on, O thou Seer, and pronounce their just dues." Then his hearers must have been greatly, yet agreeably surprised to hear this southerner expose the evils of his own people (Judah), and announce the heavy price they were to pay for their unfaithfulness to God.

Then as one who had labored long to come into his desired haven, Amos came to the point of delivering the words meant for Israel. For this purpose God had sent him, and this his soul was bent on doing. All his previous preaching had been true, as well as divinely inspired, yet it was little more than the introduction to the principal message, the inspired herdsman began to say:

> Thus saith the Lord; For three transgressions of Israel, and for four, I will not turn away the punishment thereof; because they sold the righteous for silver, and the poor for a pair of shoes; that pant after the dust of the earth on the head of the poor, and turn aside the way of the meek . . . They lay themselves down upon clothes laid to pledge . . . and they drink the wine of the condemned in the house of their god. Yet destroyed I the Amorite before them, whose height was like the height of the cedars . . . Also I brought you up from the land of Egypt, and led you forty years through the wilderness, to possess the land of the Amorite. I raised up your sons for prophets, and your young men for Nazarites. . . . But ye gave the Nazarites wine to drink; and commanded the prophets saying, Prophesy not. Behold, I am pressed under you, as a cart is pressed that is full of sheaves. . . . You only have I known of all the families of the earth; therefore I will punish you for all your iniquities. Can two walk together except they be agreed? . . . An adversary there shall be even round about the land; and he shall bring down thy strength from thee, and thy palaces shall be spoiled. . . . In the day that I shall visit the transgressions of Israel upon him, I will also visit the altars of Bethel; and the horns of the altar shall be cut off, and fall to the ground. And I will smite the winter house with the summer house; and the houses of ivory shall perish and great houses shall have an end. . . . I have overthrown some of you, as God overthrew Sodom and Gomorrah and ye were as a firebrand plucked out of the burning; yet have ye not returned unto me,

saith the Lord. . . . As a shepherd taketh out of the mouth of the lion two legs, or a piece of an ear; so shall the children of Israel be taken out that dwell in Samaria. . . . Therefore thus will I do unto thee, O Israel; and because I will do this unto thee, prepare to meet thy God. . . .

The virgin of Israel is fallen;
She shall no more rise;
She is forsaken upon her land;
There is none to raise her up. . . .

Seek ye me, and ye shall live; but seek not Beth-el, nor enter into Gilgal, and pass not to Beer-sheba; for Gilgal shall surely go into captivity, and Beth-el shall come to naught. Seek the Lord, and ye shall live.[28]

In condemning the oppression of the poor, the perversion of justice and the taking of bribes he told them only that which all Israel should have known from the law. In speaking of clothes taken in pledge he merely echoed the command, "If thou at all take thy neighbor's raiment to pledge, thou shalt deliver it unto him by that the sun goeth down."[29] And when he denounced those who made "the ephah small, and the shekel great" and who dealt falsely "with balances of deceit," his words only agreed with the well-known law, "Ye shall do no unrighteousness in judgment, in meteyard, in weight, or in measure. Just balances, just weights, a just ephah, and a just hin, shall ye have."[30]

Amos condemned their shams and cried against their substitutes. He urged the people to leave off their idolatrous sacrifices, and even their feasts and so-called solemn assemblies, and to "let judgment run down as waters, and righteousness as a mighty stream." He reproached those who were "at ease in Zion," those who were guilty of luxurious indulgence, and those who were so commercially minded as to say, "When will the new moon be gone, that we may sell corn? And the sabbath, that we may set forth wheat?"[31] He declared the Lord "stood upon a wall with a plumbline in his hand," and that uncompromising justice required that they go into captivity "*beyond* Damascus."

Then the high priest of Beth-el endeavored to stop the preaching. He first sent a message to King Jeroboam, saying that Amos had conspired against the king, then he drew near the prophet and said:

O thou seer, go, flee away into the land of Judah, and there eat bread, and prophesy there: But prophesy not again any more at Beth-el; for it is the king's chapel, and it is the king's court.[32]

But Amos' reply was:

I was no prophet, neither was I a prophet's son; but I was an herdsman, and a gatherer of sycamore fruit; and the Lord took me as I followed the flock, and the Lord said unto me, Go, prophesy unto my people Israel.[33]

Only a few seasons had passed after the shepherd-prophet's voice had died away on the Samaritan hills when Jeroboam II died, and the empire began to crumble away. Within seven months two of his successors had been assassinated; and Menahem, the usurper, who followed in 749 B.C. attempted to rule with an iron hand, but his reign was marked by continuous strife within and his foes from without were preparing to crush him.

Tiglath-Pilesar III (known in Babylon as Pul) at the head of his Assyrian host, fell upon the cities of Transjordan in 734 and took their inhabitants captive. He then devastated the possessions of Zebulun and Naphtali. King Menahem hastened to meet the oncoming army and offered to pay tribute and swear allegiance to Tiglath-Pilesar if only he would spare his life and secure him on his throne. The monarch charged him one thousand talents[34] which Menahem raised by levying a tax for fifty shekels of silver on sixty thousand of his wealthy men. This was the beginning of the end.

The days of luxury and prosperity passed, as Amos had said they would, and for a few years crime and confusion ran rife, chaos was on every hand, and anarchy reigned supreme. Then in the midst of this confused, struggling mass of erring humanity was heard the voice of Hosea, who, from a life-long residence in their midst, knew well the people, their sins and sorrows. He had begun to prophesy before the death of Jeroboam II but now his words were weighted with the experience of the years.

At God's command Hosea had wedded a maid of his country who had proven as unstable morally as was Israel spiritually. Through the years of suffering caused by their waywardness, infidelity, and immorality, the prophet had come to understand God's attitude toward the people upon whom He had lavished His loving kindness, and constant care.

The first child born unto the pair had been named *Jezreel* which intimated that Jehovah would *"break the bow of Israel in the valley of Jezreel."*[35] The second child had been called *Loruhama,* which indicated that Israel had *not* obtained mercy — that she had not qualified by repentance and turning to God; therefore God would be obliged to "utterly take them away." The third child was a son who was given the name of *Loammi,* voicing the lament of God over Israel's persistent course of drifting which had carried her so far from righteousness that He could *no* longer be her God or call her his people.

Once while the children were at play, the prophet heard one of them call the other *Ammi* and in return was called *Ruhamah.* The children had merely dropped the *lo* (no), which, when combined in the new form, meant: *My* people who *have* obtained mercy. He not only corrected the children but urged them to go and "plead" with their mother, and to urge upon her the fact that they could not rightfully be called by such names because of her disobedience and infidelity.

After pleading and warning to no avail, Hosea decided to "hedge up" her way "with thorns," and build a wall across her path that she might be prevented from going after others; he would then allure with kind words and choice gifts[36] and offer to betroth her unto him forever in righteousness. But alas! notwithstanding all his efforts she continued to play the harlot and as often as he reclaimed her she slipped back like a "backsliding heifer." Israel had been just this to Jehovah, therefore, he decided to leave her to her fate and turned his back with the words:

> Ephraim is joined to idols; let him alone.[37]

but being grieved with such a course, lamented:

> O Ephraim, what shall I do unto thee? O Judah, what shall I do unto thee? For your goodness is as a morning cloud, and as the early dew it goeth away![38]

Then the observation:

> Ephraim, he hath mixed himself among the people; Ephraim is a cake not turned. Strangers have devoured his strength, and he knoweth it not; yea, grey hairs are here and there upon him, yet he knoweth it not. And the pride of Israel testifieth to his face; and they do not return to the Lord their God, nor seek him for all this. Ephraim also is like a silly dove without heart; they call to Egypt, they go to Assyria.[39]

In the midst of the message of doom, the prophet paused and reviewed the beautiful relationship of the past:

> When Israel was a child, then I loved him, and called my son out of Egypt. . . . I taught Ephraim also to go, taking them by their arms; but they knew not that I healed them. I drew them with cords of a man, with bands of love; and I was to them as they that take off the yoke on their jaws, and I laid meat unto them.[40]

Then in pitying yet helpless compassion he said:

> O Israel, thou hast destroyed thyself.[41]

Lastly came the appeal and promise which Hosea left with Israel as his parting message ere she began her exit from the stage on which she had so poorly played her part:

> O Israel, return unto the Lord thy God; for thou hast fallen by thine iniquity, Take with you words, and turn to the Lord; say unto Him, Take away all iniquity, and receive us graciously; so will we render the calves of our lips.
>
> I will heal their backsliding, I will love them freely; for mine anger is turned away from him. I will be as the dew unto Israel; he shall grow as the lily, and cast forth his roots as Lebanon. . . . They that dwell under his shadow shall return; they shall revive as the corn, and grow as the vine. . . . Ephraim shall say, What have I to do any more with idols?[42]

Throughout Hosea's prophecy ran that note of hope, and that tenderness was ever present with the sway of his emotions. Israel had sinned. She had betrayed the trust of Jehovah, merited the worst, and was rapidly approaching the end, yet Jehovah loved her and it pained Him to see her headed for her ruin.

> How shall I give thee up, Ephraim?
> How shall I deliver thee, Israel?
> How shall I make thee as Admah?
> How shall I set thee as Zeboim?
> Mine heart is turned within me,
> My repentings are kindled together.[43]

God would forgive her, and save the land — if only she would repent. But weak and wayward Israel did not repent, therefore, her doom came at last.

Hoshea, the son of Elah, murdered King Pekah, and after some hesitancy ascended the throne at Samaria and reigned for nine years. He seems to have been somewhat better than his predecessors, yet while a tributary to Assyria he held secret communications with Egypt, Tyre, Philistia and Judah.[44] Having formed an alliance with these powers he refused to pay his annual tribute to Assyria. Shalmaneser V, King of Assyria, immediately gathered his armies, crossed the Euphrates and Lebanon, and fell upon Sidon and Acre, then came into the plain of Esdraelon where the cities of Israel surrendered or the inhabitants fled to the capital.

Hoshea prepared for a long siege with the hope of receiving help from Egypt, but for this he looked in vain. The siege of Samaria continued for two years — 724 to 722 B.C. — under Shalmaneser V; then Sargon II, his successor, continued it for another year. At last Samaria's heights were stormed, King Hoshea was led away to spend the rest of his life in an Assyrian prison, and the people were deported to Assyria where they were sent to various sections of the country to be absorbed by the people among whom they dwelt,[45] or finally to journey to other lands.

Sargon's own account of the incident is given on an Assyrian cylinder:

> At the beginning of my reign, in my first year . . . Samaria I besieged, I captured. 27,290 people from its midst I carried captive. 50 chariots I took there as an addition to my royal force . . . I returned and made more than formerly to dwell. People from lands which my hands had captured I settled in the midst. My officers over them as governors I appointed. Tribute and taxes I imposed upon them after the Assyrian manner.[46]

Little is known concerning the destiny of these captives, other than that they were settled in northern Mesopotamia and Media, and soon faded out of history's picture. They have frequently been designated as the *"Lost Tribes of Israel."* Their downfall was attributed by the prophets Amos and Hosea to infidelity to God which took the form of idol worship — *"kissing calves,"* as it was called in irony.

## CHAPTER IX

# THE RISE OF THE SAMARITANS

WHEN THE NORTHERN KINGDOM of Israel fell with its capital, the city was not completely destroyed nor all the inhabitants of the land removed.[1] The wealthiest and most powerful were deported to avoid conspiracy, while the humblest of the Israelites — the peasants, the slaves, and the small tradesmen — were left to care for the country. To assist them in farming the land and populating the cities, Sargon imported Mesopotamian settlers, or captives, from the cities of Babylon, Cutha, Ava, and Sepharvaim in the middle section of the Tigris-Euphrates valley, and from Hamath, the Syrian stronghold, located at the entrance to the Lebanon area.[2]

The Israelite stock, already enfeebled by foreign admixtures from Phoenicia and surrounding countries, absorbed the Mesopotamian settlers and produced a racial amalgamation which came to be known as the Samaritans,[3] who were all ruled by an Assyrian governor. The residue of the Israelites had at best only a mixture of the Mosaic law, the tenets of Baalism and those of calf worship. All these, when practiced in a state so small, produced an unusual medley of strange cults, none of which were very strictly followed.

The foreign elements brought with them their various gods and goddesses. The process of amalgamation tended toward deterioration of morals; therefore wickedness throve as the weeds of the field and irreligion soon came to characterize the colonists. Since the inhabitants were few and wicked, the wild beasts of the Jordan valley and nearby mountains spread over the country and attacked the people, and slew so many of them that the Assyrian rulers became concerned, and not only increased the number of colonists, but sent them priests of the Lord to instruct them in the true worship of Jehovah, to preach to them, and to guide them in better ways.[4]

The captive Jewish priest sent to teach them "how they should fear the Lord" was faithful to the task assigned him, yet he had no little task in changing the religion of a group of people so composite. The result appears to have been that the Samaritans adopted the Pentateuch in respect to the leading features of the Jewish faith, and made use of the Jewish ritual, but combined the worship of Jehovah with that of the graven images. Many years after this, numbers of their high places and altars were destroyed during the reforms of Josiah.[5]

On the return of the Jews to Jerusalem, after the Babylonian captivity, the Samaritans offered their assistance to Zerubbabel in the work of rebuilding the Temple, but on account of their foreign extraction and religious innovations the proffered aid was stoutly refused and the Samaritans excluded from all participations in the Jewish work or worship.

The Samaritans naturally resented the affront and attempted to hinder the rebuilding of Jerusalem.[6] The quarrels which arose increased as time went on until a bitter and lasting feud developed between the two peoples. Through the generations which followed there were frequent outbursts of active hostility. The Samaritans were ready to claim kinship with the Jews when the latter were prosperous.[7] But at other times they repudiated the relationship and acknowledged their Assyrian origin.[8]

A rival temple was built upon Mount Gerizim and an entire set of traditions grew up to substantiate the claim that their temple on Mount Gerizim was "the place where men ought to worship."[9] The Samaritans observed the Passover, read from the law and taught that the true site of the temple was on Mount Gerizim, rather than at Jerusalem.

Many Samaritans served in Alexander's army in Egypt, after which some settled there, and by the order of Ptolemy I others from Palestine joined them.[10] These contended with Alexandrian Jews that the site of the temple was on Mount Gerizim rather than on Mount Moriah at Jerusalem.[11]

In 332 B.C. Alexander the Great destroyed the city of Samaria, and the Samaritan temple on Mount Gerizim was destroyed by John Hyrcanus, the Maccabean in 129 B.C.[12] However, the Samaritans continued to gather on Mount Gerizim for sacrifice each year, and in later years seem to have restored their temple.

In the days of Jesus Christ the Samaritans were a despised race, and so depreciated by the Jews as to be designated "Samaritan dogs." To avoid contamination by contact with the Samaritans, many of the Jews who lived in Galilee made a practice of crossing the Jordan and coming up to Jerusalem by the Jericho road.[13] Nevertheless, Christ, the personification of love, showed them favor and offered salvation to those who believed.

The most remarkable sermon ever preached to a single individual was the one that Christ preached to the Samaritan woman at Jacob's well. On one occasion ten lepers approached Christ for cleansing. As they went on their way, in obedience to His command, they were cleansed but only one of them was sufficiently grateful to return and thank the Master: and this one who returned *"was a Samaritan."*[14] The Samaritans were immortalized in history by Christ's parable of "The Good Samaritan."[15] Yet despite all Christ's kindness and the gospel which was later preached to them by the apostles they did not become Christians in very large numbers; but more than once came into conflict with the Roman emperors and the Christians.

During the time of Pilate there arose a deceiver who told the Samaritans that he had discovered the sacred vessels of the Temple, and that they should gather on Mount Gerizim where he would reveal the vessels to them. They came to Tirathoba where they were joined by others, then started their march to Mount Gerizim. Hearing of the march Pilate, fearing an insurrection, sent out "a great band of horsemen and footmen" and not only intercepted their march, but killed their leader and many of the people. The injustice was so great that the Samaritan senate sent messengers to Rome to make complaint, which caused the authorities at Rome to recall Pilate and place Vitellius, a more kindly and considerate governor, over Palestine.[16]

Later there was a threatened uprising among the Samaritans when Vespasian sent Cerealis in command of the fifth legion with six hundred horsemen and three thousand footmen, who surrounded the vast concourse of Samaritans gathered on Mount Gerizim. In the hot oriental summer sun, many perished for lack of water, others deserted to become slaves of the Romans, and eleven thousand six hundred were slain.[17]

After this the Samaritans gradually dwindled in numbers and strength until today only about one hundred and six survive. Since they are unwilling to intermarry with others their number is gradually diminishing. Recently the Jews offered to permit some of their maidens to intermarry with the young men of the Samaritan group. The Samaritans finally accepted the generous offer, but the experiment proved unsuccessful for the eccentric and exclusive manners of the Samaritans proved intolerable for the two Jewish maidens who so kindly offered themselves as a step toward rebuilding the Samaritan group.

They believe as firmly as in the days of Christ that in the mountain of Gerizim men ought to worship, and there only will they offer their sacrifices. They have a priest, who, they claim, is a lineal descendant of Aaron, and they assert that the priesthood has continued in an unbroken succession among them. Their scriptures are the five books of Moses. Of these they claim very ancient copies which they prize very highly.

Like the Jews they keep the sabbath, on which they hold three services — morning, noon, and afternoon — in their ancient synagogue at Nablus. When they pray they bow themselves toward the summit of Mount Gerizim. They practice circumcision and keep the Jewish feasts, (except the Feast of Dedication).[18] They believe in the existence of angels, in a resurrection, as well as future rewards and punishment. They expect the Messiah to come as a prophet only.

The anniversary of the Passover is their great annual festival. For this occasion, all that are able — men, women, and children — leave their homes a fortnight before the Passover, and encamp in tents on a level space a few hundred yards below the actual summit of Gerizim, the "Mount of Blessing." The women are left in the tents while the men assemble in sacred costume, with fifteen of the elders attired in long white robes together with six youths dressed in white, all of whom, on this solemn occasion, stand with bare feet.

The six young men, each with a sheep, arrange themselves in a circle around a certain cluster of stones; the priest stands upon an eminence and recites in a loud chant the history of the Exodus while he watches the setting sun. When the sun touches the horizon the chant becomes louder and the six youths burst into a wild murmur of their own and draw forth their long bright knives. The moment the sun disappears below the horizon the word is given; the sheep are thrown on their backs, and the flashing knives drawn across their throats. Blood flows freely from the quivering victims, then after a few convulsive but silent struggles, the innocent sheep are quiet in death — insufficient sacrifices for the sins of the most ancient religious sect on the face of the earth.

Then, as if in congratulation at the completion of the ceremony, they kiss each other, in oriental fashion, on both sides of the head. Boiling water is poured over the slaughtered sheep, and while their fleeces are being plucked, bitter herbs wrapped in strips of unleavened bread are handed round, followed by the recital of a short prayer.[19]

Long poles are brought, on which the sheep are thrust into a deep, circular pit in the earth, with a bed of coals at the bottom. The pit is sealed, night comes on and the whole community sleeps for five hours, after which a voice announces that the feast is ready. Then the covering is removed from the pit and the six sheep are laid out, between the two lines of Samaritans, who stand in readiness with shoes on their feet, staves in their hands, and ropes around their waists. Sitting on their haunches they thrust their fingers into the roasted sheep and feast until late in the night. On the following day they return to their homes which form a small colony in the suburbs of Nablus at the foot of Mount Gerizim.

## Chapter x

# THE LION'S WHELP LED CAPTIVE

Israel had been in captivity one hundred and thirty years ere Judah suffered the same fate, but during this period she was often humbled and her strength enfeebled until her moral and military powers were subjected to exceeding great strain.

The rebellion at Shechem had come near costing Rehoboam his life, and had lost him the ten tribes, yet he learned a never-to-be-forgotten lesson — the advice of the young and inexperienced was not only inadequate but extremely expensive. Goaded to the exercise of his better senses, he set himself to the task of strengthening and building up the small portion left him. Fifteen strategically located cities of Judah were fortified,[1] strong walls erected about the principal cities of Benjamin, and all the people encouraged to journey to the temple at Jerusalem for wholehearted worship of Jehovah who had been the strength of all the sons of Jacob. This encouraging outlook resulted in an increase of population which strengthened his kingdom, for the Israelites residing in Judah swore allegiance to him, and the priests, Levites and laymen who refused to associate themselves with the calf cult in Israel found their home in Rehoboam's realm.[2]

For three years the king and his people "walked humbly" with Jehovah, then feeling themselves "established" they "forsook the law of the Lord" and followed their own ways,[3] for which they were to pay very dearly.

Solomon had been dead but five years when Shishak I, King of Egypt — who was probably influenced, if not incited, by Jeroboam who had previously found his palace a safe retreat — invaded the territory of Judah with an immense army including *sixty* thousand cavalry and twelve hundred chariots. Many places suffered severely and Jerusalem itself escaped capture only by yielding up much of the vast wealth stored in her temple, great treasure from the royal palace, and the famous golden shields which David had taken from the Syrians, and those made by Solomon for his bodyguard.[4]

Humiliated Judah turned again to the Lord; and His temple, standing in the midst of their capital, became the object of veneration for all who worshipped Jehovah in sincerity and in truth. But Judah was not to be spared the fatal consequences of the pernicious practices of Baal worship which was prevalent in the neighboring kingdoms, including Israel. These innovations were introduced by a woman, as they had been in Israel.

The inroads were made during the prosperous reign of Jehoshaphat (of Judah) when he allied himself with Israel and sealed the alliance by marrying his son, Jehoram, to Athaliah, the daughter of weak, vacillating Ahab and wicked, conniving Jezebel. Athaliah inherited a large measure of her mother's bigotry, and cruelty, as well as her idolatry. Under her influence the worship of Baal and Astarte was disseminated throughout a large portion of the kingdom of Judah.

After the magnificent funeral of king Jehoshaphat in Jerusalem, his son Jehoram ascended the throne, but lacking moral sinew he did Judah more harm than good. Edom revolted and took possession of Elath, Judah's seaport on the Red Sea. The Arabians and Philistines invaded Judah and slew all the king's sons but one, and the king himself died of a painful and loathsome disease, so little honored that he was not buried in the sepulchre of the kings of Judah.[5] Ahaziah, his son, succeeded him as king, but Athaliah really held the reins and drove the state toward paganism, as her mother had done before her in Israel.

While Ahaziah was visiting at Jezreel, Jehu arrived and made quick work of slaying Israel's king, Jehoram, Jezebel, and the rest of the family of Ahab. Ahaziah escaped but received a wound of which he died at Megiddo, and his body was taken back to Jerusalem. Wicked, worldly Athaliah then openly seized the scepter and ordered the slaughter of her own children and grandchildren rather than suffer David's line to continue on the throne.[6]

However, Joash, her infant grandson, was rescued by Jehoshabeath (the wife of the high priest, Jehoiada), and was secretly brought up in the temple. Six years passed during which Athaliah led Judah into many a hurtful practice, chief of which were worldliness and idolatry; then was enacted one of the most dramatic scenes in all Biblical history. Jehoiada, the high priest, led the conspiracy against the Baal-worshipping queen. The royal guards were enlisted in the cause, and the Levites in the temple were furnished with arms. On a sabbath day the seven-year-old lad was brought from the inner temple to the platform outside where the high priest placed a copy of the Law before him and a diadem upon his head. Then after the child was anointed with the holy oil, all the people clapped their hands, blew the trumpets and shouted "God save the King!"[7]

Athaliah, realizing something unusual had happened, hastened to the temple, and seeing the crowned and anointed child-king standing beside the high priest, rent her clothing and cried, "Treason, treason!" but her voice was drowned by the trumpets and cries of the multitude. Incapable of resistance she was led away from the temple precincts and was slain with the sword at the entering in of the gate near the king's house.

> And all the people of the land went into the house of Baal, and brake it down; his altars and his images brake they in pieces thoroughly, and slew Mattan, the priest of Baal before the altars . . . And all the people of the land rejoiced, and the city was quiet.[8]

During the reign of the child-king large contributions were made for the repair of the Temple, reformations were inaugurated, and Judah made progress. But when Jehoiada, the good priest, had died, the higher social set "made obeisance" to the king, and thereby influenced him to permit them to leave "the house of the Lord God of their fathers," and serve the idols of Baal and Ashtaroth in the groves.

Zechariah, the son of Jehoiada, became priest and prophet and denounced the prevailing apostacy.[9] Urged on by the desire to follow their own worldly way, the king and the people brushed aside memories of past services rendered them by Jehoiada, conspired together and on a sabbath day murdered Zechariah, the good high priest, thus becoming guilty of one of the worst crimes ever committed in either Judah or Israel. Thus the misguided king, in the latter part of his life, belied the promise of his earlier years.

Not long after Zechariah's martyrdom, the Syrians, under Hazael of Damascus, marched across Palestine, totally discomfited the Hebrew army, destroyed the worldly princes of the people, and took their spoils. The frightened king stripped the temple of much of its remaining treasure which he gave to the Syrian general, who then marched away, leaving him suffering from a loathsome disease. To avenge the disgrace of the nation the people broke into the king's quarters and murdered him in bed.[10] Thus defeat and death swiftly followed the ingratitude and apostacy of Joash. Nor was he accounted worthy of a place in the sepulchres of the great kings of Judah.

Amaziah, the son of Joash, succeeded his father as king of Judah. Successful campaigns against the Edomites "turned his head," and he challenged Jehoash of Israel to a trial of their military strength, "the result of which was that Amaziah was defeated and taken prisoner, the temple and palace rifled, and breaches made in the walls of Jerusalem. The people of Judah, indignant, rose up against their king and slew him."[11]

During the eighth century B.C. Judah — under Uzziah and Jotham — reconquered the nearby nations, extended the kingdom, and opened up new trade routes; and as a result the kingdom enjoyed prosperity, as her sister state, Israel, did at the same period. In this "golden age of merchants, usurers, and money-mongers" there appeared extraordinary greed for riches among the men and fickle desire for fashion and ostentation among the women. Class distinctions became rife, foreign fashions were introduced, and the people became so informal in their worship and so enamoured of the things of this life that Isaiah — the statesman prophet — received the Divine call to denounce in no uncertain terms the frivolity, laxity, luxury, and vice so prevalent about him.

The worldliness of women caused them to neglect their higher calling of usefulness, modesty and motherhood; and adorning themselves with jewels, painting their eyes with kohl, and decking themselves with the finery of the day, they haughtily walked with "stretched forth necks and wanton eyes, walking and mincing" as they went and making a tinkling with their feet.[12] Isaiah denounced their frivolity and pointed out their inevitable ruin and destruction but most of them no more heeded the warning than the masses of modern times heed the present day warning of the inevitable dangers ahead. Calamity was not long in overtaking "the vain Judean show.'"

Rezin of Damascus and Pekah of Israel united their forces in battle against Judah. Judah's slain were one hundred and twenty thousand men; and two hundred thousand men, women, and children were led into captivity. The frightened king, despite the pleading of Isaiah, threw himself at the feet of the Assyrian king, who granted the desired aid, but claimed the treasure of the temple in return, reduced Judah to a vassal state and burdened her with a heavy tribute.

Under the influence of Isaiah, Hezekiah came to the throne, cleansed the temple and restored the solemn rites, reinstated the Levites, demolished the false gods, removed the groves, threw down the high places, and destroyed the brazen serpent which was being superstitiously worshipped in the temple.[13]

With a renewal of religious and commercial life, Judah was so strengthened that she appeared to be able to break Assyria's humiliating yoke. "Patriots" arose and urged that the tribute be withheld, but others felt certain that nothing could be gained by revolting against the powerful Assyrian monarch. Ultimately the "patriots" triumphed, and Hezekiah joined in a league with Egypt, Moab, Edom, and the Philistine cities; and when Azuri, king of Ashdod, withheld his tribute, all who were in the league boldly followed his example.

Sargon the Assyrian King, "quickly accepted the challenge, hurried his armies westward, captured some of the Philistine cities and deported their people, bringing settlers from other parts of the empire to build up the ruins. The example was effective, for the other conspirators at once ran to cover and kept their peace for a number of years."[14] Then in 705 B. C. Sargon, the most powerful of all Assyrian rulers, fell in battle and Sennacherib took over the kingdom.

When the Mediterranean countries again revolted, Sennacherib amassed a huge army and marched on Tyre and Sidon, then on the Philistine cities. After Edom and Moab capitulated Sennacherib and his mighty host appeared before Jerusalem and laid siege to it, shutting up King Hezekiah "like a bird in a cage." Consternation reigned in Jerusalem that evening, for the besiegers boldly sent up their written demands. Hezekiah took the missive and went to the sacred precincts where he spread it before the Lord and pled for succor.

Ere long the king stood high on the wall and by his side as counsellor stood Isaiah, the venerable statesman-prophet, who half a century before had "seen the Lord sitting upon a throne high and lifted up," and since that time had foreseen and foretold many events. Now this messenger of the Lord held the position of chief counsellor to the king. His words of assurance were satisfying indeed:

> This is the word that the Lord hath spoken concerning Sennacherib: The virgin, the daughter of Zion hath despised thee and laughed thee to scorn; the daughter of Jerusalem hath shaken her head at thee . . . By thy messengers thou hast reproached the Lord, and hast said, with the multitudes of my chariots I am come up to the height of the mountains, to the side of Lebanon, and will cut down the tall cedar trees thereof, and the choice fir trees thereof . . . and the forest of his Carmel . . . Therefore, thus saith the Lord concerning the king of Assyria. He shall not come into this city, nor shoot an arrow there, nor come before it with shield, nor cast a bank against it. By the way that he came, by the same shall he return, and shall not come into this city, saith the Lord.[15]

That night God intervened in behalf of his people. An event occured which will ever puzzle the "skeptical" mind which finds it difficult to believe in miracles.[16] Lord Byron has summed up the event in the following lines:

The Assyrian came down like a wolf on the fold,
And his cohorts were gleaming in purple and gold;
And the sheen of their spears was like stars on the sea,
When the blue wave rolls nightly on deep Galilee.

Like the leaves of the forest when summer is green,
That host with their banners at sunset were seen;
Like the leaves of the forest when autumn hath blown,
That host on the morrow lay withered and strown.

For the Angel of Death spread his wings as the blast
And breathed in the face of the foe as he passed;
And the eyes of the sleepers waxed deadly and chill,
And their hearts beat once, heaved, and forever grew still.

And there lay the steed with his nostrils all wide,
But through it there roll'd not a breath of his pride;
And the foam of his gasping lay white on the turf,
And cold as the spray on the rock-beating surf.

And there lay the rider distorted and pale,
With the dew on his brow and the rust on his mail,
And the tents were all silent, the banners alone,
The lances uplifted, the trumpet unblown.

The widows of Ashur are loud in their wail,
And the idols are broken in the temple of Baal;
And the might of the Gentile, unsmote by the sword,
Hath melted like snow in the glance of the Lord.

Judah made little of her deliverance, for soon Hezekiah passed on, and Manasseh, his easy-going son, began his administration, in which he sat idly by while "witchcraft, divination, and wizardry became common." Even child sacrifice was again permitted in the valley of Hinnom.[17]

Urged on by the liberals, Manesseh mercilessly persecuted those who advocated reform, and "devoured the prophets like a destroying lion." Even aged Isaiah, after a long and useful career in state and church affairs, so tradition says, was sawn asunder near the pool of Siloam.[18] Fifty-five years did this wicked king reign, then in the last days repented and was forgiven ere he went to reap the reward of his checkered career.

The dawning of better days brought to the foreground Zephaniah and Jeremiah, who began their prophecies after Josiah, the new king, ascended the throne. Zephaniah was "a brilliant, forceful orator" who went forth "seeking sinners with the lantern of the Lord." Jeremiah, conscious of a divine destiny, wept as he pointed out the wicked principles and practices which had undermined the very foundations of the state. The combined efforts of these two faithful prophets, the high priest and other righteous men and women brought about marvelous results in the life of the young king.[19]

Josiah set out to destroy the evils which had grown up during the long and wicked reign of Manasseh. He repaired the temple, found the book of the law, had it read to all the people, and required strict obedience to its precepts. Full time service from the singers and ministers was expected, tithe was required of the people, judges were appointed, justice meted out, and far reaching reforms inaugurated. Modesty and proper attitudes were enjoined, shrines destroyed and idol worship entirely abolished.[20] All was summed up in those striking words:

> Hear, O Israel, The Lord our God is one Lord; and thou shalt love the Lord thy God with all thy heart, and with all thy soul and with all thy might.[21]

The vessels and all that had to do with Baal worship were burned in the Kedron valley, the "chariots of the Sun" were consigned to the flames and the valley of Hinnom entirely renovated.

The king entered into a solemn covenant with all the people to obey the law. Common interests and clear consciences made the people exceedingly happy. Peace and prosperity reigned as they had not for many a generation. But all too soon this period of peace and tranquillity was brought to an abrupt end, and that by a strange and pathetic incident which bereft Judah of her good king and counsellor.

Pharaoh-Necho II, king of Egypt, invaded Palestine on his way to measure swords with the newly established king of Babylon who had defeated and destroyed the old Assyrian kingdom and held first place in the Euphrates Valley, as Assyria had done before him.

Josiah, a vassal of the king of Babylon, felt that he should go out to arrest the advancing army. The king of Egypt assured him that his advance was not against the kingdom of Judah and that there was no reason whatsoever for battle; nevertheless, Josiah led out his army and took his stand at the pass of Megiddo to oppose the passage of the Egyptians. In the battle of Megiddo which followed, Judah was defeated and Josiah received a mortal wound. His body was returned to Jerusalem, where his death was lamented as few others had been.[22] Pharaoh-Necho marched on northward to Carchemish, where, in that decisive battle, fought in the year 605 B. C., he was utterly defeated and the rule of the Near East was decided in favor of Babylon.

After Josiah was gone the people lapsed into their old ways of wrong doing, the days of prosperity passed, and evil began to collect its sad toll.

Then the prophet Jeremiah's voice was heard once more. Shocked by the wholesale sinning of the people, he exclaimed:

> Run ye to and fro through the streets of Jerusalem, and see . . . if ye can find a man . . . that executeth judgment, that seeketh the truth.[23]

Then after the reflection he said:

> Surely these are the poor and foolish, they do not know Jehovah's way, nor the law of their God; I will go unto the great men and will speak unto them, for they have known the way of the Lord, and the judgment of their God.[24]

But alas! The prophet found that the leading men had not only "broken the yoke" but were strong in their backslidings. The heart of the faithful messenger was broken, as has ever been the case when godly men see their leaders fail to carry out the original purpose of a sacred cause to which they have devoted their lives. In tears he pled with the people to "amend" their ways that Jehovah might permit them to remain in the land. Choosing to continue their wicked ways, some mocked at Jeremiah's warnings, others probably laughed at his tears and told him that he was causing undue excitement.

Jeremiah became "the most unpopular man in Jerusalem. The priests derided him, the patriots denounced him, the mobs reviled him. He was publicly struck by a temple priest and placed in the stocks to be taunted by the passing crowds."[25] When the king renounced the authority of Babylon and prepared for war, Jeremiah announced that Jerusalem should be conquered and the people carried away into captivity unto the third generation. The king became furious and accused him of mortal crime. But he was rescued by a friend and placed in concealment.

When he was released, he wrote out the sermons which he had preached and sent them to the king. Jehudi read them "in the ears of the king, and in the ears of all the princes that stood beside the king," whereupon the king cut them with his pen knife and threw them into the fire.[26] Jeremiah rewrote and elaborated upon them, declaring that "Judah would fall; it was unworthy to continue. Jehovah would have to refashion His work, for Judah had failed Him. The potter was often obliged to do his work over when clay proved to be not good."[27]

Not long after Jeremiah's words had been spoken, Nebuchadnezzar came with a large army and King Jehoiachin surrendered the city and Nebuchadnezzar deported the king, the queen-mother, the soldiers and some ten thousand leading men with their wives and children to

Babylon, where Jehoiachin had ample time to reflect on Jeremiah's prophecy while he languished in prison for thirty-seven years.

Jerusalem was left in the hands of Zedekiah, who was soon influenced by the patriots to believe that they could yet throw off Babylonian control. Jeremiah, still undaunted, walked through the streets of Jerusalem with a yoke on his shoulders to illustrate what must happen to Judah in the near future. The yoke was torn from his shoulders, and he was spat upon by his opponents, yet he persisted in proclaiming the doom of Judah.[28]

Impatient at the Hebrew spirit of defiance, Nebuchadnezzar led his army around the fertile crescent and over the Palestinian bridge, until he came to the very gates of Jerusalem which he "invested and slowly starved into submission. The sufferings of the besieged, prolonged for more than a year and a half, were dreadful." The people perished so rapidly that it was impossible for the survivors to properly bury them. "Corpses decayed in streets and in cellars, pestilence engendered by the poison stench of the city and by the lack of sanitary measures, added further horrors to the siege.[29]

When the leaders reduced some of the Hebrew debtors to serfdom, the prophet Jeremiah pronounced the death of Zedekiah and his adherents, and the ruin of the temple, the city, and the land. This so enraged the nobles that they caused him to be arrested for sedition and after scourging him, threw him into prison. Becoming uneasy, the king secretly brought forth Jeremiah who fearlessly told him he should be delivered into the hands of the king of Babylon.[30]

Zedekiah was greatly impressed with the frankness of the man of God, and having great respect for him, ordered him to be kept in the outer court of the prison and supplied with food during the terrible famine. The princes, however, clamored for his blood, and the king, through his own weakness of character, surrendered the prophet into their hands. They took him and cast him into a deep dungeon heavy with mire, that his voice might no longer be heard, and that he might die by the most agonizing slow torture.

An Ethiopian palace servant went to the king and informed him of the pitiable plight of the prophet. Unwilling to become a party to the death of such a good man, the king ordered Jeremiah to be lifted out of the dungeon and brought to the temple court. There, during a private interview, the king promised him protection if he would inform him as to the outcome of the siege. Jeremiah plainly told the king of the evil that would befall him and the city if he and the princes persisted in their course of resisting the besiegers. Had the king been a strong character he might have allied himself with Jeremiah and saved the city from destruction, but his miserable cowardly nature shrank from the very prospects of opposition from his carnal counsellors. His mild reply was: "Let no man know of these words." In the outer court of the prison, Jeremiah remained in safety until the day the Chaldeans broke through the walls of the city and ended the Jewish resistance.[331]

Evening came on and the Babylonian princes took their seats at the 'middle gate.' That night the king of Judah and his chief men fled by the way of the king's garden and attempted to escape, but were overtaken in the plains of Jericho and carried into the presence of Nebuchadnezzar, who was then encamped at Riblah in the land of Hamath.

Nebuchadnezzar gave sentence and the firm executioner began his work. The sons of Zedekiah, and certain of the Judean noblemen, were put to death before the eyes of the captured king, then with such gruesome scenes last upon his vision, the eyes of the once proud king of Judah were put out and in chains he was taken to Babylon.[32]

Nebuzaradan, the captain of the guard, took possession of the gold, silver, and brass vessels of the temple, burned the temple and all the principal buildings of Jerusalem, and sent many of their goodly stones rolling to the bottom of the valley of the Kedron. He took the chief priest, the second priest, the three doorkeepers, the chief officers and the chief scribes, and all the people save "the poor of the land" which were left to be "vine dressers and husbandmen." With his captives the captain of the guard started marching northward to present the captives to Nebuchadnezzar at Riblah.[33]

Along the highway the venerable old prophet, with his captive fellow-countrymen, went until the sad and disheartened procession reached Ramah, a few miles north of Jerusalem, when the captain of the guard stopped the procession and said to the prophet:

> I loose thee this day from the chains which were upon thy hand. If it seem good unto thee to come with me unto Babylon, come; and I will look well unto thee; but if it seem ill unto thee to come with me into Babylon, forbear; behold, all the land is before thee; whither it seemeth good and convenient for thee to go, thither go.[34]

Long had the old prophet's heart yearned over the people and his fatherland. He had warned the people against the course which led to their present plight; they had more often depreciated than appreciated his efforts and tears. To go as a privileged character into the country where they would be captives did not appeal to him. With graciousness befitting the magnanimous soul that he was, the venerable old preacher with frosted locks, turned back with the thought of completing life's cycle in his beloved land in company with the small remnant of Hebrews under the command of Gediah, an officer whom the Babylonian monarch had left in charge of affairs in Palestine.

So fell Judah and Jerusalem in the year 587-6 B. C. and four hundred and seventy years after the dedication of the temple by Solomon. Secure in her mountain fortresses, with Jehovah her "first line of defense," Judah might have continued, but for her departure from God and her faith in force which led her to lean on "bruised reeds which offered no effective assistance."[35]

After returning to the city and viewing the scene of devastation and woe, the faithful prophet went outside the walls, within the old grotto, under a gray hill, now known as "Gordon's Calvary," and there penned his pathetic lament:

How doth the city sit solitary
That was full of people!
How is she become as a widow! ,
That was great among the nations!
And a princess among the provinces,
How is she become tributary!

Is it nothing to you, all ye that pass by?
Behold, and see if there be any sorrow like unto my sorrow,
Wherewith the Lord hath afflicted me
In the day of his fierce anger.

All that pass by clasp their hands at thee;
They hiss and wag their head
At the daughter of Jerusalem,
Saying, is this the city that men call
The perfection of beauty, the joy of the whole earth?[36]

Only three months had passed when, on a day, one Ishmael, of the seed royal, who acted under Ammonitish influence, treacherously slew Gedaliah, the governor, while they ate bread together at Mizpah. Johanan attempted to avenge his death, but Ishmael took refuge with the Ammonites and Johanan and the rest of the Hebrews, apprehensive lest they should be called to account for the death of Gedaliah, fled to Egypt and carried Jeremiah with them. There the prophet often cried out against the silly, degrading form of worship adopted by the Judeans, but for this he was rewarded with a martyr's death; his words went unheeded, until the people took time to reflect.

## Chapter XI

# BESIDE THE WATERS OF BABYLON

When the great throng of Judean captives was carried away from their beloved land by Nebuchadnezzar's army, the people made their long mournful march around the entire circle of the Fertile Crescent, and came finally to the central portion of Babylon itself. Here in the heart of this great plain, famed for its beauty and fertility, the tower had been presumptuously begun which resulted in the confusion of tongues; near here also was the city of Ur, from which some fourteen hundred years before their father Abraham had set out on his quest for Canaan.

Those fourteen centuries had been filled with a variety of experiences that ran almost the entire gamut of life. Abraham's descendants had been pioneers in sparsely settled Canaan; they had been favored freemen, and then bondmen in the most fertile region of the far-famed valley of the Nile; they had been wanderers in the wilderness wastes of the Sinai Peninsula; they had led in the conquest of Canaan; gone through the uncertain period of the judges; risen to the most magnificent monarchy of their day; finally to separate into two nations. They had repeatedly fallen into the pernicious practices of paganism, and for their many deflections from the worship of Jehovah they were now in the process of being punished.

They had traveled far, suffered much; and satiated with their own ways were again brought near the very spot where Abraham, their father, had heard the words "Get thee out of thy country to a land that I will show thee." *That Land of Promise* had been their home, but now they were captives and would serve their captors in the land from whence their famous and faithful ancestor had set out.

Babylon was then a mighty metropolis, situated on the left bank of the great Euphrates river which formed a mighty channel of commerce for imports as well as exports. The city's outer wall was fifty miles in length, pierced by one hundred gates of bronze. The wall was so thick that four chariots could drive on it abreast. The streets were at right angles to one another, as in our modern cities, and a splendid canal, parallel to the nearby Euphrates, furnished an abundant water supply. Its mighty temples adorned with jewels and precious metals, its far-famed hanging gardens, and its many palaces brilliant with colored bricks and tiles, were unusual sights to many of the Hebrews.

In this cultural center, located at the crossroads of world commerce and communication,[1] the Jews might have been happy but for the memory of their glorious past and thoughts of a world mission of divine appointment which their leaders had ever beheld. As it was, the *early* stage of their captivity was one of the most grievous and humiliating experiences ever undergone by any people. It seemed to contradict the promises of a glorious future for Israel that had been foretold from the time of Abraham. It completely broke and humbled the hearts of many of the Hebrews. Their faith was kept alive only by the consciousness that their captivity was temporary and provisional; that when their sinfulness had been expiated, and when their beloved land had enjoyed her sabbaths their afflictions would come to an end.

The people were separated from their beloved yet desolate country by a thousand miles of desert; the city and temple of the most high God was a rubbish heap. Yet their loyalty to their city upon the Judean hills was the most passionate and enduring patriotism that this world had seen.

Others might have settled in a land so wonderfully favored and put away thoughts of Padestine; but it could not be so with those who were faithful among the Hebrews. Few passages in the languages of literature are more pathetic than the following:

By the rivers of Babylon,
There we sat down, yea, we wept,
When we remembered Zion.
Upon the willows in the midst thereof
We hanged our harps.[2]

Oh Salem! its sound should be free;
And the hour when thy glories were ended
But left me that token of thee;
And ne'er shall its soft tones be blended
With the voice of the spoiler by me![3]

Sadly they gazed on the river which rolled on in freedom before them. The Babylonians urged them to sing away their sorrow, but filled with anguish and stirred by genuine but elated devotion to their native land, they uttered that plaintive cry:

How shall we sing the Lord's song
In a strange land?
If I forget thee, O Jerusalem

Let my right hand forget her cunning.
If I do not remember thee,
Let my tongue cleave to the roof of my mouth —
If I prefer not Jerusalem
Above my chief joy.[4]

Within the hearts of the Hebrews there was little sense of any injustice being meted out to them, for they were conscious that they were suffering for their sins. Then, too, Nebuchadnezzar adopted a liberal policy of dealing with them, which was followed by his son.[5] The Hebrews were assigned quarters in the cities and positions in the market places. Some were settled in colonies north of Babylon, and some in similar colonies south of the great city. They were treated very kindly, and not at all like slaves.

Later the *Rosh Galutha,* or Prince of the Captivity, was created and given his seat, where he played an important part in the life of the Hebrews of Babylon. He was fourth in rank from the king himself, and his power over all the Hebrews was almost equal to that of a sovereign over his people. He appointed judges, inflicted corporal punishment, imposed fines, and had the power to cast in prison.[6]

The Hebrews had their own laws, maintained their own schools and academies; they were merchants and agriculturists, cultivating and exporting their own grain, wines, dates, sesame, figs and vegetables.[7] They controlled their own flocks, fattened their own animals, led their own caravans. Situated at the "cross-roads of world trade and communication," they became practiced in commercial affairs, and developed a most remarkable business genius that has since attracted unusual attention from the commercial world.

Many of their young men were given the best education to be had in Babylonia. Some of these were greatly appreciated and became exceedingly prominent in state affairs; among whom was Daniel. As a young man of sixteen, Daniel had been taken to Babylon in Nebuchanezzar's first invasion of Palestine, nineteen years before the destruction of the temple. He never swerved in his devotion and loyalty to Jehovah, yet he rose to the highest position in the state, and served during a period of sixty-nine years, exercising a very great influence during the three kingdoms of Babylon, Media, and Persia. Notwithstanding his service to the state he was primarily a servant of Jehovah. At various times he uttered prophecies, particularly regarding the future of Gentile nations, prophecies which are among the most remarkable in the whole Bible.

The exiles of the northern kingdom had for the most part apparently abandoned all semblance of loyalty to God and to their ancestral religion.

They had put aside thoughts of returning to Palestine, and were rapidly losing their identity. But not so with many of the people of Judah. They possessed and now appreciated the prophesies of Isaiah and Jeremiah, and in their very midst God had raised up Ezekiel.

This young priest belonging to the aristocracy of Jerusalem,[8] was carried captive eleven years before the destruction of the temple of Jerusalem and began his active ministry six years before the last group of Jewish captives arrived in Babylon. Ezekiel endorsed all that Jeremiah had said, and endeavored to convince the people that they could never hope to return to Jerusalem until they returned to the Lord.[9] In an admirable way he compared Israel's bondage in Egypt to their captivity in Babylon and pointed out the fact that Satan had long been man's adversary, but that man was to overcome him by strict obedience to God. His warnings, rebukes, and directions were invaluable in helping the Hebrews regain their religious consciousness.

Deprived of their central sanctuary at Jerusalem, and thus cut off from the place of sacrifice and ritual, it was impossible for them to practice their religion as they had done on the Palestinian hills. In their attempt to solve the problem and bury their grief, they devised a place of meeting which came to be known as the *"synagogue"* — the house of study and prayer. This place of meeting became the "unifying bond, and center of their social and religious activities."

In Babylon the exiled Hebrews saw their sad mistake and turned to God. They were cured of their idolatry. They were purified as by fire. So thorough was the process that few times since have the sons of Jacob been known to revert to idolatry.

## Chapter XII

# THE REMNANT THAT REBUILT JERUSALEM

In 550 B. C. Cyrus, an amiable and generous prince of the Oriental world, became king of the Medes and Persians and by a series of rapid conquests took possession of the country from the Caspian Sea to the Persian Gulf; then, as a fitting climax to his campaigns, he turned and captured the supposedly impregnable Babylon in 539 B. C.; and the Empire of Babylon perished forever from the earth. Cyrus, being kindly disposed toward the Jews, freed them to return to their beloved Palestine. Undoubtedly this was brought about by Daniel, who for sixty years had been the most influential person of the Empire and of that age.

The decree sent out by Cyrus is rather striking:

> Thus saith Cyrus, king of Persia, The Lord God of Heaven hath given me all the kingdoms of the earth; and he hath charged me to build him an house at Jerusalem, which is in Judah. Who is there among you of all his people? His God be with him, and let him go up to Jerusalem, which is in Judah, and build the house of the Lord God of Israel, (he is the God) which is in Jerusalem. And whosoever remaineth in any place where he sojourneth, let the men of his place help him with silver, and with gold, and with goods, and with beasts, beside the freewill offering for the house of God that is in Jerusalem.[1]

As a proof of his sincerity and generosity the king returned the sacred vessels of gold and silver which Nebuchadnezzar had taken from the temple at Jerusalem and which Belshazzar had desecrated by drinking wine from them on the occasion of his impious feast.[2] This magnanimity resulted in a wave of Jewish rejoicing which is summed up in the following psalm:

> When the Lord turned again the captivity of Zion,
> We were like them that dream.
> Then was our mouth filled with laughter,
> And our tongue with singing;
> Then said they among the heathen,
> The Lord hath done great things for them.
> The Lord hath done great things for us;
> Whereof we are glad.[3]

Cyrus evidently supposed that large numbers of his subjects would gladly take advantage of the opportunity to return to their beloved fatherland. But notwithstanding his gracious permission and encouragement only a few more than forty-two thousand presented themselves to recognize the land of their fathers.[4]

Many who had acquired position and wealth rejoiced because of the new freedom and favor shown them, yet "stayed behind," says Josephus,[5] "being unwilling to leave their possession." They were content in the belief that Jehovah could be worshipped in spirit and in truth, by prayer, reading the sacred record, and observance of a part of the law, without sacrifices and the mercy-seat which were associated with the solemn temple. They were willing to give of their means toward the cause of reclaiming their fatherland, but left the actual work to those who were more pious, more patriotic, and more enthusiastic. Babylon had come to be their home, and they cared not to go elsewhere.

Zerubbabel, a lineal descendant of David, was appointed as prince or governor of Judah; to lead and govern those who should return. Joshua, a descendant of Zadok, of the house of Aaron, was appointed their high priest. Led by their newly appointed prince and pontiff, the willing and enthusiastic remnant set out across the desert with a police escort to protect them.

They were accompanied by Mithredath, the treasurer, who had charge of the numerous precious vessels of the temple, and who bore a letter to the governor of Syria stating the purpose of the coming of the Jews and asking that he assist them with choice lumber from the Lebanon mountains and whole-hearted service in the rebuilding of the temple, "on the same place where it was before."[6]

Upon the completion of their toilsome journey, coming at last to Jerusalem, they gazed with mingled joy and grief upon a scene of gray desolation — ruined walls, scattered blocks, and shattered stones. Only a ruinous heap where once stood their beloved temple. After they secured food and shelter, their first thought was to restore the worship of Jehovah on the sacred precincts of Mount Moriah. All classes set to work at once to clear away the rubbish which surrounded and covered the great sacrificial stone that marked the place where the temple had once stood upon the sacred hill.

Discovering the former foundations of the altar of burnt offering, they hastened the erection of the altar, then all the returned exiles gathered as one man to the sacred mount to be present at the festivals of the season, when for the first time, after half a century, priests and Levites once more performed their office upon the soil of Palestine. Daily, at morning and evening, sacrificial blood flowed freely on Mount Moriah.[7]

After this they began to gather materials and make contributions for the rebuilding of the temple. When the work was begun, the task of overseeing the workmen was entrusted to the priests and Levites, as in the days of Solomon. Masons and builders were employed, as formerly, from Tyre and Sidon. Cedar trees from Lebanon were floated by sea to Joppa, and thence transported thirty-eight miles over rough roads to Jerusalem,[8] while stones were taken from nearby quarries. While they laid the foundations of the sacred edifice all the people chanted the refrain:

Praise the Lord, for He is good!
For His mercy endureth forever!

Difficulties soon arose when the Samaritans came to Zerubbabel and Joshua requesting permission to assist in rebuilding the temple, with the statement that they too, were worshippers of Jehovah.[9] Their offered assistance was refused on the ground that the Samaritans were mixed both in blood and religion. The Jewish leaders were sincere in their refusal. Their determination was to re-establish the worship of Jehovah free from the taints of false religions and directed by those of pure Hebrew blood.

Resenting the rebuff, and fearing the future political power of the Jews, the Samaritans took advantage of the unsettled state of the Persian empire by using intrigue and bribery to frustrate the purpose and plans of the Jews "all the days of Cyrus, king of Persia."[10] When Cyrus had fallen in battle, his son, Cambyses, began to direct the affairs of the Empire. Taking advantage of the change of rulers, the officials of Samaria wrote a letter in which they represented the Jews in such an unfavorable light that Cambyses wrote a letter demanding that the building of the city and the temple be suspended "until another commandment should be given from him.[11] Armed with such an effective epistle the Samaritan leaders, accompanied by many of the people, quickly mounted their horses, rode to Jerusalem, and by force and power caused the work to cease.[12]

Building operations were at a standstill for about nine years, throughout the reign of Cambyses and until the second year of Darius. Then, when peace and order were restored throughout the western provinces of the Empire, Zerubbabel and Joshua took heart and stirred up the people to recommence the building of the temple; but in the meantime the people had become absorbed in affairs pertaining to their homes, their fields, and their wasted vineyards.

*Endor, where King Saul met the witch.*

*Entrance to the Cave of Adullam. The large rooms within can accommodate a thousand men.*

Below left: *Absalom's Pillar in the King's Vale at Jerusalem.*

Below right: *Ahab and Jezebel often passed up these steps as they entered their palace at Samaria.*

*Coins which were minted and used by the Maccabeans. Numbers 236, 237, and 238 are those of John Hyrcanus, 252 of Alexander Jannaeus.*

*Tombs of the Maccabean leaders at Modin.*

*Bethlehem.*

Their enthusiasm for the rebuilding of the temple and the city walls had fallen to such a low ebb that it took months of preaching, admonitions, and predictions by the ministers of their day to arouse them to renewed interest. Haggai urged them to leave off their sinful sloth and despondency, then in passionate and pathetic outbursts of prophetic truth, foretold the future glories of the then uncompleted Temple, while Zechariah recounted his visions, and counselled his countrymen to lift up their eyes from the sad present to the glories of the future. Stirred by this ministry they again arose to the task of constructing the sacred edifice.

When Tatnai, the Persian governor of the western province, heard of the fresh activity among the Jews, influenced by the Samaritans among whom he dwelt, he came to Jerusalem with the pointed question, "Who hath commanded you to build this house and to make up this wall?" Taking the names of those who sponsored the building operations, the governor sent a letter to Darius the king, stating what was taking place and asking his mind regarding the matter.

Zerubbabel, the governor of the Jews, went to Darius in person,[13] and as friend to friend conferred with him in regard to the matter. This resulted in a decree from Darius to the effect that the governor of the Western portion of the Empire should not only "let the governor of the Jews and the elders of the Jews build this house of God in His place," but that financial assistance be given them that they be not hindered.[14]

Assisted by the governor and encouraged by the continued prophecies of Haggai and Zechariah, the people carried forward the work and in four years completed the temple and in the year 516 B.C. joyfully dedicated it.

After priests, Levites, and temple servants were arranged in order, the "remnant" kept the sacred feasts, killed the passover and endeavored to enjoy emotional tides similar to those which surged within the Hebrew breasts during the days of the first temple. The building, ever afterwards known as Zerubbabel's temple, was "humble, plain, undecorated," but important in Jewish history.

Since the Jews were again in favor with the king and his satraps, and had restored their temple, the priesthood soon satisfied itself with the keeping of feasts, the offering of sacrifices and the mumbling of words connected with these ceremonies. Once form caught their fancy, reality in religion quickly vanished. Their concern to honor the Persian satrap was greater than that to honor God.[15]

With fervor did the prophet Malachi plead with the people not to lose faith in God because of the pious hypocrisies they saw about them but to comply with God's will and law, and His blessings would again be poured out without measure upon them. But, despite all entreaties, a spirit of tolerance and compromise crept into their consciences and led them to intermarry with the Samaritans and with their idolatrous neighbors. Various forms of unrighteousness became common, Jewish exclusiveness gave way and they seemed little more than just *another* colony.

Some years later, in Shushan (Susa), the earnest, sincere religious and professional life of Ezra, a "ready scribe of the Law of Moses," gained favor with the king, and at his request he was granted a permit to return to Palestine and a commission to take others with him.

With much gold and silver and a second installment of vessels for the temple, the new recruits — numbering about six thousand — arrived in Palestine only to find that those who had first come had so intermingled with neighboring peoples that they had all but forfeited the right to be called Jews. When Ezra saw that the chief of the princes and rulers had led in this trespass he rent his garment and his mantle and plucked off the hair of his head and sat down in astonishment.[16] After prayer and conference with those who were concerned about the spiritual welfare of the group, Ezra became the leading spirit in bringing about reform.

In the years that followed the Jews sank to low spiritual levels and suffered many reverses. Just what the catastrophe or destruction was which all but withdrew them is not quite clear. In First Esdras 4:45-50 we are informed that the Edomites burned the temple and occupied a part of Judah. The land was laid waste by marching armies, droughts parched the fields, the herds lowed piteously in their withered pastures; and the hostility of surrounding nations was shown by continual invasions and plunderings.[17]

Many Jews were taken captive and sold in the Grecian markets, those who were left were reduced to such dire need that the daily sacrifices had to be suspended. The Persian officials were no longer able to subsidize the little kingdom; therefore, the Jews were reduced to dire straits and no one seemed ready or able to help. Some of them deserted the enterprise and returned to Babylon.

In the year 446 B.C., Hanani, a Jew, who had returned from Palestine, was visiting at the palace of Shushan and met Nehemiah, the king's cupbearer, who asked him concerning the welfare of their countrymen who had returned to Palestine under Zerubbabel. Hanani and his brethren informed Nehemiah that the remnant of the captivity there was in great affliction and reproach; and that the wall of Jerusalem was broken down and the gates burned with fire.[18]

The news so saddened Nehemiah that he mourned and fasted and prayed, until King Artaxerxes inquired the cause of his sadness. The answer given by Nehemiah was, "Why should not my countenance be sad, when the city, the place of my fathers' sepulchres, lieth waste, and the gates thereof are consumed with fire?"[19] When the king asked him to make a request in the matter, Nehemiah asked that he be sent to Palestine for the purpose of rebuilding the city.

In granting the request the king sent a letter to Asaph, the keeper of the king's forest, asking him to supply the timber needed for rebuilding the gates and walls and house for Nehemiah. When he arrived in Palestine, accompanied by captains of the army and horsemen, Nehemiah was received with joy by his countrymen, but Sanballat and Tobiah of Samaria were grieved that there was come a man to "seek the welfare of the children of Israel.[20]

On the third night after his arrival, without having explained the object of his mission, Nehemiah set forth with only two or three attendants on his famous "night ride," which he describes in the following language:

> I went out by night by the Valley Gate, even toward the Dragon's Well, and to the Dung Gate, and viewed the walls of Jerusalem, which were broken down, and the gates thereof were consumed with fire. Then I went on to the Fountain Gate and to the King's Pool, but there was no place for the beast that was under me to pass. Then went I up in the night by the brook, and viewed the wall, and I turned back and entered by the Valley Gate, and so returned. And the rulers knew not whither I went or what I did; neither had I as yet told it to the Jews, nor to the priests, nor to the nobles, nor to the rulers nor to the rest that did the work. Then said I unto them: Ye see the distress that we are in, how Jerusalem lieth waste, and the gates thereof are burned with fire; come, and let us build up the wall of Jerusalem, that we be no more a reproach. And I told them of the hand of my God which was good upon me; as also of the king's words that he had spoken unto me. And they said, Let us rise up and build. So they strengthened their hands for this good work.[21]

After he had carefully thought out plans and specifications for the work, Nehemiah assigned the many sections of the wall to various groups. Every portion of the wall was in the plan, and no man was exempted from either financial or physical service.[22] Everywhere about the wall tasks were begun with zest, and Nehemiah pushed the work with haste lest "sinister influence should poison the mind of the Persian king and destroy his plans."[23] The sound of the trumpet served as a signal while Nehemiah and the people worked night and day, none of them putting off their clothing except when it needed washing.

Nehemiah's fears were fully justified, for no sooner had Sanballat, governor of Samaria, heard of the building operations than he became indignant and made light of the project. To his soldiers he said, "What do these feeble Jews? Will they fortify themselves? Will they sacrifice? Will they make an end in a day? Will they revive the stones out of the heaps of the rubbish which are burned?"[24]

Tobiah, the governor of Ammon and an ally of Sanballat, being of Jewesh origin,[25] should at least have been sympathetic toward the Jerusalem project, but instead he quickly responded in derision, "Even that which they build, if a fox go up, he shall break down their stone wall."[26]

Mockery having failed to stay the activities of the workmen, Sanballat led the formation of a coalition of the Samaritans, Ammonites, Arabians, and Ashdodites. He at first planned to stop the work by an unexpected onslaught. When the news of this anticipated attack came to the ears of the Jews, they armed themselves for defense against the coalition.

The surrounding groups dared not attack under these circumstances; therefore they devised a plan whereby they hoped to induce Nehemiah to attend a conference that they proposed to hold in the plain of Ono, supposedly in the village of Lydda.[27] In reply to their invitation Nehemiah wrote: "I am doing a great work, so that I cannot come down: why should the work cease, whilst I leave it, and come down to you?"[28] Four successive efforts along this line came to nought, while the Jews vigorously pushed the work of fortifying their beloved city.

As soon as the wall was well under way Nehemiah called an assembly of the chief men in Jerusalem and pointed out the fact that the poor in the surrounding country had, in their recent days of poverty and distress, mortgaged their small homes and holdings to the rich in order to pay their taxes to the government or to support their families; and that as these debts came due, the holders of the mortgaged property had shown no mercy. Some poor men had mortgaged the services of their children and many other complaints of cruel usage had reached the ears of Nehemiah. Addressing the leaders he said, "Ye exact usury, every one of his brother . . . we, after our ability, have redeemed the Jews, which were sold unto the heathen; and ye even sell your brethren? or shall they be sold unto us?"[29]

Urging the men to walk in the fear of God because of the reproach of the heathen about them, he said: "I pray you let us leave off this usury, restore to the poor even this day their fields, their vineyards, their olive yards, and their houses; also the hundredth part of the money and of the corn, the wine and the oil that ye exact of them." "We will do as thou sayest," was the hearty reply. Nehemiah then called upon the priest to administer to all an oath, and *shaking out his lap* he cried, "So God shake out every man from his house, and from his labor, that performeth not this promise, even thus be he shaken out, and emptied."[30] Setting a worthy example, Nehemiah declined the usual salary of the governor and instead gave liberally of his own means to assist the needy. No sincere soul could do other than appreciate such a governor.

When the walls were completed and the gates set up Nehemiah examined the credentials of those who were ordained to the priesthood, excluded those who were unfit, and made ready for the services of the others. The tithes and dues for the support of their religion were required of all the people. Ezra who yet survived was chief of the priests. He assembled the people in an open space before the west gate and there from a pulpit of wood he read to them from the book of Deuteronomy a synopsis of the law. When Ezra unrolled the book of the law all the people stood up, and during the reading he stopped to explain until all the people understood.[31]

The people felt that the law was the word of God ordering the daily round of their existence both as individuals and as a nation, therefore they wept over their neglect of God's commandments. The reading was continued for a week, until the season came for the feast of the Tabernacles, when the people went into the mountains, cut down palm trees and boughs of other trees and prepared booths in the city in which to dwell during the days of the feast.[32]

When the portions of the law forbidding mixed marriages with the heathen were read and expounded, the people were greatly affected. First the atmosphere was tense, then there was a general acknowledgement of the sins of which many of the people had been guilty. All these promised to put away their foreign wives and to live thenceforward in all things obedient to the law. Furthermore, they promised to keep the sabbath, observe the Holy days, let the land lie fallow during the seventh year, and remit all debts when that year came round. Each man promised to give one third of a shekel each year to the temple treasury and carefully to pay his tithes and give of his first fruits.

Following this, they joyfully dedicated the new wall at Jerusalem. Half of the procession, accompanied by Ezra, marched in one direction and the other half, accompanied by Nehemiah, marched in the opposite direction upon the wall. Each was accompanied by a band of Levites and singers who sang songs and played upon musical instruments as they marched. The two companies met when they had completed the circuit of the walls.[33] Many reforms were put in operation and careful business-like arrangements were made for those who should serve about the temple and order the affairs of the country. When twelve years had passed Nehemiah took his departure to go again to Shushan.

Soon after the restorer of Jerusalem departed the enemies round about began to meddle in the affairs of the Jews. Sanballat's daughter had married the daughter of one of the leading men of Jerusalem, and his son, Johannan, had become the husband of a Jewish lady. Seeing their opportunity, these men entered Jerusalem with the help of certain of their in-laws and friends and began the sad work of compromise which brought confusion. After the death of Ezra the worldlings made swift work of liberalizing the Jewish church.

When twelve more years had passed Nehemiah heard of the state of affairs and returned to Jerusalem to right the irregularities. He found that the singers and Levites had not been paid because the people had drifted from God and failed to pay their tithes. He organized a board composed of a priest, a scribe, a Levite, and a layman to look after the affairs and distribute supplies of the temple.

In one of Nehemiah's sabbath day walks he saw men treading the winepress, while others brought through the gates their beasts burdened with market produce to be sold that day in the markets of Jerusalem. He discovered men of Tyre and Sidon who upon the sabbath sold fish to rich people who did not hesitate to buy them. Nehemiah warned the offenders, closed the gates and ordered them not to be opened again until the sabbath was over.[34]

Nehemiah then gave his attention to the evils of mixed marriages, and pointed out the fact that Solomon was led astray by strange wives. That which had already taken place along this line was destined to bring grief to Israel. Joida, the son of Elishib, the high priest, had married a woman of mixed race, and his son Manasseh wedded Nicaso, the daughter of Sanballat the Horonite. Upon the death of his father, Joida in his turn, became high priest. Nehemiah could not displace him, but he drove his son, Manesseh, from Jerusalem. Manasseh carrying with him a copy of the law took refuge with his father-in-law in Samaria. He was afterwards made high priest of the new temple which Sanballat and the Samaritans set up on Mount Gerizim.[35]

Nehemiah, the able, ardent, kind-hearted, pious, and efficient administrator, continued in Jerusalem and died there on ald man. He has been recorded in history as one of the most interesting and dynamic characters of the Old Testament. The little state continued but since it lay in the pathway of invading armies, it often became a prey to foreign conquerors, and was, therefore, hindered from growing to any great size.

CHAPTER XIII

# THE CLASH BETWEEN JUDAISM AND HELLENISM

WHEN CAMBYSES, the son and successor of Cyrus, had conquered Egypt, he handed on to his successor an empire that was "unparalleled in history for continuous extent." When rebellion broke out among the Hellenic cities on the Aegean Coast of Asia Minor, Darius investigated and found that they were encouraged and helped by their sister cities in the Hellenic motherland which we call Greece.

Desiring to crush the nuisance at its source, Darius sent his fleets across the Aegean Sea in 490 B.C. and fought with the men of Athens and Plataea, but the ferocity of the Greek soldiers in the battle of Marathon drove the men away from their undertaking. Ten years later his son, Xerxes, massed together mighty armies with soldiers from all his provinces — India, Persia, Media, Babylonia — and attacked Greece both by sea and land, only to suffer defeat in the naval battle of Salamis (480 B.C.) and in the following year crushing and final defeat at the battle of Plataea.[1]

Influenced by these signal victories the separate Hellenic city-states, both in Greece and on the Asiatic shores of the Aegean Sea, formed a league of "defense and defiance," encouraged their arts, and prepared for a future far more secure than the past. After a few generations passed, Alexander, the son of Philip II of Macedonia, and a pupil of Aristotle, at the head of his Macedonian and Greek world, marched eastward to conquer the Persian Empire, and startled the world with his military achievements.[2]

Alexander was young and brave and charming.[3] As a great general and ardent advocate of Hellenic[4] culture, he extended his imperial mandate "from the Balkans to the Punjab, and from the Nile and the Persian Gulf to the Black Sea and the Caspian."[5] Wherever he went Greek colonies sprang up, Greek language and arts were introduced, and Greek sports encouraged. Some seventy cities located at strategic points on the great commercial highways, became outstanding centers of Greek life, thought and speech.[6] Then, in his thirty-third year, following a night of debauchery, Alexander died (June 13, 323 B.C.) either in or near

Nebuchadnezzar's palace in Babylon, and his vast empire was divided among his generals who were supposed to rule in the name of Alexander's infant son.

Egypt, together with Palestine, fell to the portion of Ptolemy I, (Soter) son of Lagus, who ruled merely as a governor until 306 B.C. when he took the title of king. Asia Minor fell to Seleucus, one of Alexander's most distinguished cavalry officers, who recaptured Babylon, fought the battle of Ipsus in 301 B.C., and founded his new capital at Antioch on the Orontes.[7]

The Ptolemies in Egypt held Palestine principally for the sake of trade and tribute, and that they might be assured of a timber supply from the Lebanon. They permitted the High Priest and the Sanhedrin[8] considerable freedom in the administration of the internal affairs of their small but important country. Seleucus coveted Palestine, especially the Phoenician seaports, from which he might draw recruits for his army. The frontier between the two great countries shifted from time to time, and small Judea became like a ship in a storm smitten on either side by waves.[9]

From 311 to 198 B.C. Palestine was generally under the control of the Ptolemies of Egypt, but in 198 B.C. all was changed, for Antiochus III, called "the Great," met Scopas, Ptolemy's [10] general, in the battle of Paneas (Banias), at one of the sources of the Jordon river, and gained a decisive victory which established the Seleucid dynasty in Palestine.

Greek influence had already infiltrated into Palestine through such trading centers as Gaza, Joppa, Acre, Amman, and Beisan. Under Ptolemy II Gaza and Joppa became royal cities where government mints turned out Ptolemaic coins which were distributed throughout the country.[11] The name of Acre was changed to "Ptolemais," Amman became "Philadelphia," and Beisan was called "Scythopolis." Yet the Hellenizing of Palestine by methods of force was never a part of the deliberate policy of the Ptolemies themselves. The methods employed by them "took more the form of permeative and fusive attempts,"[12] and were accomplished quietly and peaceably. All was different, however, when the Seleucids took control, for they were not only militant in their attitude toward the Jews, but penetrated Palestine with a purpose to plant and water the seeds of Hellenic culture.

The Greek way of life was opposed by all those in Palestine who were true to all that pertained to Jewish culture and morality. They felt that the Hellenistic program would discount monotheism, encourage paganism, and bring on a reign of unbridled selfishness and shameless sensuality.

The Seleucids were not obliged to work alone, however, in their attempt to Hellenize Palestine; for the liberals, a large and influential worldly-minded group of Jews, had often chafed under the restraint of the law; therefore they viewed with genuine pleasure the coming of a non-spiritual culture wrought on broad lines of personal freedom.

Doubtless others among the more earnest souls had become aware of the fact that Judaism had come to be weighed down by ceremonial laws, and had often felt "the burden and uselessness of empty formalism" void of the stirrings of positive spiritual life. Coming into contact with a new culture fostered by a powerful ruling class, many probably considered worldly Hellenism almost as worthwhile as formal Judaism, and far more profitable; for Antiochus the Great was ready to bestow many favors and privileges on the Jews who showed ability to achieve success in public life and were willing to imitate Greek manners.[13]

Such a set-up, of course, brought the two cultures into conflict — Judaism against Hellenism. And a conflict it was; for Judaism had its origin and basis in the idea of "*one* supreme, transcendant Ruler, ordaining all things in heaven and earth, far removed from all human qualities, yet in close communion with men through the law of righteousness which he revealed to them." On the other hand Hellenism's best in the realm of religion would transform each object and phenomenon of nature — day and night, sleep and death, earth and sun, winds and rivers, vegetation and variableness, love and hate, peace and war — into a separate divine and conscious agent. Incarnated in Aphrodite was the passion of love, in Ares the lust of war, in Athena the acme of wisdom, and in Apollo the perfection of the arts.[14]

The Jew at his best stressed monotheism, reliance upon that one omnipotent God, and conformity to a divinely sanctioned moral law. He was serious, restrained and willing to admit limitations. To seek God was ultimate wisdom and to follow His precepts the ultimate virtue. Thoroughly ingrained in his mental and emotional makeup was the feeling that in the fullness of time the mountain of the house of God was to be established in Jerusalem where, in their effort to follow after righteousness, all nations would flow into it.

Hellenism offered enrichment for the intellectual, poetical, and artistic life, yet would accept no revelation as ultimate or final. The Greek "strove to penetrate to the core of his conceptions," and to "analyze the very basis of his knowledge." He was blessed with a subtle reason and with a keen desire to use it. If need be he would attempt to open and lay bare the very heart of any reality, even invading what others considered the most sacred realms.

With the Hebrew the uppermost idea was a love for God and a *proper conduct* among men, while with the Greek the uppermost idea was to *see* things as they really were.[15] The Greek respected no law but that of "complete self-expression." At his best he loved beauty in art, language, and literature. But when pursuing his goal along the lower levels he revelled in outdoor life and every aspect of the *physical* realm which contributed to his *material* and *sensual* success.

Modesty had small place in the life of the Greek; in fact, he flouted conventional standards of modesty. The very etymology of one of the chiefest of their buildings — the gymnasium — was derived from *gymnos,* which meant "nude." According to their customs those who took part in their games and contests were to remove all clothing and bend every effort toward making a worthy record — which to them was the acme of life.

All this instinctively shocked the refined moral sensibilities of the Jews who prized modesty as one of the highest virtues. Their law required long skirts for the priests and forbade steps forming the ascent to the temple altar lest their nakedness be revealed while ascending to officiate at the elevated altar.[16] Modesty pervaded every act and movement in the Hebrew physical life. They not only observed it with jealous care but considered public nudity an incentive to vice.

Obviously the two points of view conflicted, and in the individual could not be reconciled: one could not accept a *revealed* law as ultimate, and yet question everything that was right and holy, even the very foundation of life itself. One could not submit to moral law and modesty and yet dissipate or "exploit one's capacities without restraint" in the round of sports and worldly pleasures.

> Thus the sharp contrasts of the Sculptor's plan
> Showed the two primal paths our race has trod;
> Hellas, the nurse of man complete as man,
> Judea, pregnant with the living God.[17]

Had the Greeks brought their best to Palestine, the story might have been different; but as it was, the splendid achievements of their philosophers and artists and the search for truth and beauty had, for the most part, been left behind. Their degraded Hellenism led them to spend much of their time in the gymnasium and amphitheatre, which meant that the trend of their lives was toward *physical* development and satisfaction, which often ended in licentiousness. They virtually gave morality the lie, as so many have done since their day. They were quick to tear down what to the Jew was sacred, yet made no move to put in its place anything but jest and sports.

In 175 B.C. Antiochus IV lifted the scepter at Antioch, and began to try his hand in Palestinian affairs. Being ambitious to strengthen his kingdom against Rome, he first set himself to the task of bringing Egypt under his sway; and second, to that of welding his dominion into a real unity of Hellenistic culture.[18] Himself a "sincere lover of Hellenism" he began to spread the seeds of Hellenic culture with the passion of a madman who would sow broadcast in a field of his own possession. He not only made Antioch a beautiful and brilliant center, but made short work of filling and encircling Palestine with Greek cities and Greek practices. His was a brilliant and ambitious program; so phenomenal as to cause him to regard himself as the god Zeus in human form, therefore he called himself "Antiochus Epiphanes," (Antiochus, the visible god). His "foolish excesses," however, caused popular wit to change his name to Epimanes, "the madman."

Such places as Ashkelon, Azotus, Appolonia, Dora, Gadara, Gamala, Jamnia, Joppa, Marisa, Eaphia, Samaria, Sepphoris and Straton's Tower rapidly adopted Greek architecture, Greek speech, Greek fashions, and Greek sports. With these prospering on every hand and the way to success in public life lying through imitation of Greek manners; the temptation to conformity was exceedingly powerful.[19]

At first only the more hardened, daring, brazen souls had stepped out for Hellenism, but their number had grown until the youth of the land were becoming bewildered and confused. To adopt one view of life was to abandon the other. Yet to be popular was to harmonize with Hellenism; therefore, many eventually gave way to shameless immodesty by exposing their nakedness in Greek places of sport. They united in an effort to get all possible pleasure from their new mode of life.

Many among the masses were confused and bewildered, but traveled in the path where the stronger leaders led, and perhaps wondered where the quarrel lay; but this could not long continue. Soon there arose a strong party known as the Hasidim, later called *Pharisees,* who contended that Israel should live as directed by her sacred law; in contrast to these were the Letzim, or *Sadducees* as they were later called, who held that the pleasures offered by the Greeks could be enjoyed along with the practice of their religion. The two groups gathered in the synagogues and each sought to discredit the other. Thus the battle raged *between the two factions within the pale of Judaism.*[29]

Judah soon was rent by quarrels between the two factions. Even families became divided and what was sacred and right to one group was but jest to the other. Those who loved Hellenism found Judaism "crude and self-repressing." Those who loved Judaism resented the attack on their morals and mode of life, thus came to hate lasciviousness and all that was Hellenistic, including the beautiful. They hated irreverence; therefore decried all that the Greek philosophers taught. They hated vice so ardently that they came to love their fellowmen too little. A growing spirit of aversion and implacable hatred so far divided them that no compromise could be effected and little hope of future unity entertained.[21]

The king joined power with the worldly-minded party and appointed so many of their number to important offices that promising Jews turned to advocate the Hellenizing program as ardently as any had advocated Judaism. Soon there was strong competition for the lucrative positions.[22]

In the book of First Maccabees we read of one Jason, the brother of Onias III, the high priest, who had Hellenized his Jewish name Joshua into Jason.[23] As leader of the Jewish radical party, he ingratiated himself with the new king (Antiochus Epiphanes) by his eagerness to adopt Hellenistic ways. He asked to be made High Priest as a reward for his loyalty and offered the king four hundred and forty talents in return for the appointment. Furthermore, he offered to pay the king one hundred and fifty more for the privilege of erecting a gymnasium in Jerusalem, and the right of conferring Antiochian citizenship, which would include the privilege of participating in the plays and games.[24]

The king granted Jason's request and in a brief time the gymnasium was built just below the citadel, and the exercises were given the "official" stamp. Those who professed the old faith and observed the sacred laws raised their voices in protest, but nothing came of it. Young men from prominent Jewish families purchased Antiochan citizenship, enrolled for the sports and shocked their pious elders by artificially removing the traces of circumcision and entering the games partially or entirely nude.[25]

The custom was a far cry from that of Moses' law which enjoined extreme modesty; nevertheless it was so popularized that many priests who desired the applause of the people and the "freedom" of Hellenism hurried through their duties at the temple and hastened to the gymnasium to participate in games and to win Greek honors. To the "Antiochites" the

Jewish law was not binding, therefore as liberals they threw off restraint, forsook the holy covenant and made bold to do mischief.[26]

Jason's liberalizing program was carried on for three years (174-171 B.C.), when he was supplanted in the high priesthood by one Menelaus, his lieutenant, who went to represent him before the king in certain necessary matters. But in the course of his work he praised the king, made great promises and thus secured the priesthood for himself. It was a scandalous piece of infidelity, but Menelaus simply outdid Jason in politics, and afterwards in rascality; for he shamefully robbed the temple treasury, caused rebellion and bloodshed and became a relentless enemy of those simple, God-fearing puritans who were sternly moral and yet sincere to the core. On being tried and condemned at a court session in Tyre he secretly bribed one of the king's confidents.

> Whereupon Ptolemie, taking the King aside into a certain gallery, as it were to take the air, brought him to be of another mind; insomuch that he discharged Menelaus from the accusations, who notwithstanding was the cause of all the mischief.[27]

The three envoys of the Jews who testified against him were put to death, yet "through the covetousness of them that were in power, Manelaus remained still in authority, increasing his malice, and being a great traitor to the citizens."[28] What an unworthy successor to Aaron! Yet compromise coupled with greed make almost any depth of crime possible.

Antiochus made three expeditions into Egypt in the successive years, 170, 169, 168 B.C.; the first was successful; the second indecisive; the third failed because of Roman intervention. During the first of these a false rumor of Antiochus' death spread in Jerusalem. Immediately Jason, the banished high priest, came from his hiding place across the Jordon and invaded Jerusalem. Menelaus fled to the citadel, but many of his followers were put to death. Hearing of the trouble and considering the proceeding a slight to his majesty, Antiochus hastened from Egypt to Jerusalem. He felt he must not only settle the affair in favor of Menelaus, but must also subdue the Jews who were thoroughly embittered because of the unjust execution of their envoys, and the unJewish practices foisted upon them.

He entered the city and ordered a fresh and more terrible massacre. In company with Menelaus he entered the temple and seized the golden altar of incense, the seven-branched candlestick, the table of shewbread, the golden vessels, and even stripped the gold plating from the front of the temple itself; then with these sacred treasures he marched away to his capital at Antioch.[29]

Two years later Antiochus returned to Egypt for more plunder, but in the midst of his merciless task orders came from the Roman senate demanding that he leave the country. Having been foiled in his plan to bring Egypt under his control, he returned to Palestine and Syria in an exceedingly bad humor. With the thought of directing all his energies toward the goal of attaining his ideal of *unity* in the empire, he deemed it expedient to make the Jews like the remainder of his subjects, therefore wrote to the whole nation that "they should be *one* people and that each should forsake his own laws."[30]

He mistook the temper of the Jews and was destined to meet with stout-hearted opposition in his designs to reduce Palestine to a "monotonous uniformity of culture." His was a direct attack on Judaism itself, and the Jews above all other people of the earth would maintain that which marked them off from other peoples — their cultural and spiritual ideals. The more orthodox Jews not only refused to make any effort to change their culture and forms of religious worship, but outwardly showed resentment toward the imperial order and those who promulgated it. From this time on the country was faced with a more decided conflict of ideals — *Hellenism pitted against Judaism,* — which could result in nothing short of war.

One Apollonius, an officer capable of almost any dark deed, was placed in command of an army of twenty-two thousand soldiers and sent into Palestine with orders to "slay all those that were in their best age and to sell the women and children."[31] Arriving at the gates of Jerusalem, he assured the people that he had come with friendly intentions. On the first sabbath the Jews were somewhat apprehensive, but Apollonius made no move to molest them. On the second sabbath the unsuspecting Jews began to worship when the soldiery fell upon them and carried out a bloody massacre. Thousands who were not murdered were carried away captive to be sold as slaves. Those friendly to the Hellenizing program went unmolested.

The walls of the ancient city were demolished and many of the houses were burned or pulled down. The old city of David, south of the temple, was fortified anew and made into a powerful stronghold, in which a Syrian garrison was placed. The temple was stripped of its ornaments, a swine was sacrified on the altar and its blood sprinkled in the Holy of Holies. A statue of Jupiter was placed on the altar and a decree went forth that sacrifices should be offered to it. Only Gentiles and Hellenized Jews were to reside in the city. Thus Jerusalem, like many another city, was made an habitation of heathen and "became strange to those that were born of her."[32]

The king's edict went forth requiring that "all should be one people, and that every one should forsake his own laws." The rite of circumcision, keeping the sabbaths, and the observance of feasts were prohibited under pain of death. Copies of the Mosaic law were destroyed, and to have such in one's possession was made a capital offense. Officers were sent into all the districts, charged with the duty of seeing that the commands of the king were strictly obeyed. Heathen practices, including idolatry, were instituted throughout the country.[33]

The temple "was filled with riot and revellings by the heathen who dallied with harlots and had to do with women within the sacred precincts, and moreover, brought forth things that were not befitting. The king's birthday was celebrated each month. Instead of the sabbaths and the feasts, the Jews were forced under penalty of death to partake of the sacrifice for the king and to wear wreaths at the feast in honor of Bacchus."[34]

Two women who had circumcised their children were "openly led about the city with their babes hanging from their breasts, and they cast them down headlong from the wall."[35] Eleazar, an aged scribe, was executed because he would not transgress the law by eating swine's flesh. His death served *"for an example of a noble courage,* and a memorial of virtue, not only unto young men, but unto all his nation."[36] In the many towns and villages heathen altars were set up and participation in the sacrifices was made a test of loyalty. Many obeyed the king's edict either from choice or from force; while some refused and were put to death. Many fled and concealed themselves in the caves and ravines of the Judean mountains.

With Jewish ritual made illegal and apparently crushed out, the people shut away from their temple, derided and shamed for their respect for the ancient standards, and their freedom taken from them; poor Judah seemed friendless and helpless. To all human calculations the cause of monotheism seemed hopelessly lost. Yet future events were to prove that the indomitable Jewish spirit had by no means been quenched. Oppression from without was gradually fusing the sons and daughters of Israel into a group with common interests. Each began to pray for deliverance from some source. And that help came in an unexpected manner and from a natural source. The spirit that was to guide them was in their midst. The occasion of a proper crisis was to bring him to the fore.

## Chapter XIV

# THE TRIUMPH OF THE MACCABEES

Out in the village of Modin, twenty miles northwest of Jerusalem, lived an aged priest named Mattathias, who was of the Hasmonean family. His five sons — John, Simon, Judas, Eleazar, and Jonathan — possessed courage and bravery equal to that of their sire. On seeing the desecration of the temple and hearing the blasphemies that were committed in Judah and Jerusalem, the aged father is said to have uttered the sad lament:

> Woe is me that I was born to see this misery of my people, and of the Holy City. It is delivered into the hands of the enemy and her temple is become as a man without glory. Her glorious vessels are carried away into captivity, her infants are slain in the streets, her young men with the sword of the enemy. What nation hath not had a part in her kingdom, and gotten of her spoils. From being a free woman she is become a bondslave. To what end therefore shall we live any longer?[1]

Then Mattathias and his sons rent their clothes, and fasted and mourned very sorely. Soon the aged priest reached the decision that he would not remain quiet, but would cry out against the evils and help the good cause or die courageously for it. The Syrian officer representing the king's cause heard of the pious acts and intentions of the Hasmonean family, and came to the village of Modin. The inhabitants were summoned to abandon the Law and to come forth to sacrifice to the Greek deities. Mattathias, because he was so influential, was offered gifts and urged to set an example of submission, but he refused with the following words:

> If all the nations that are under the King's dominion obey him, and fall away every one from the religion of their fathers and give consent to his commandments: yet will I and my sons and brethren walk in the covenant of our fathers.[2]

Then — as if to break the tension of the dread occasion — there came forth a craven Jew to offer sacrifice to Jupiter. Mattathias rushed upon the apostate Jew and killed him at the altar, then slew the king's officer who stood by to superintend the ceremony. With the challenge: "Whosoever is zealous of the Law, and maintaineth the covenant, let him follow me."[3] The priest with his five sons (later known as "the Maccabees") led the way to a mountain fortress where they raised the standard of revolt. Judah and Judaism were at war with Hellenism and the Syrian Empire![4]

Many of the Jews hastened to join these brave men who led them through the country destroying heathen altars, reviving Jewish rites, and reopening synagogues. Priests, pious scholars, singers, and peaceful rustics became heroes.[5] The army grew in size from day to day and new life was infused into Judaism — it was as if a religious giant had been raised from the dead. Judah, as well as Syria, was surprised, but Mattathias was an old, old man and could not continue as the inspiration of the army. He had, however, no thought of seeing the cause die ere it had accomplished the desired end — ridding Palestine of the irreligious foreign rulers.

After one year the aged and courageous priest died. His deathbed scene was highly dramatic: calling his family and friends about him, he put them under solemn obligation to God and their country. After recounting what God had been to Israel and what Israel's heroes, by their faith in God, had done, he said, "Therefore, my sons, be valiant and show yourselves men in behalf of the law for by it shall ye obtain glory." He then appointed Judas Maccabeas, his third son, to be the leader of the great reformation which he had inaugurated. "As for Judas Maccabeas," said he, "he hath been mighty and strong even from his youth up: let him be your captain, and fight the battle of the people. Take also unto you all those that observe the law. Avenge ye the wrong of your people. Recompense fully the heathen, and take heed to the commandments of the law."[6]

After the old priest's death Judas Maccabeas succeeded to the leadership and proved to be one of the bravest men that ever lived. He combined faith, courage, and piety; and under him the mysterious strength of the Jews was again manifest before a wondering world. *Maccabeus* is said to mean "the *Hammer*" — *the hammer of his foes*.[7] Judas Maccabeas certainly lived up to his name.

With an armed force of about six thousand men he set out to oppose a kingdom that extended from the Egyptian border on the south to Armenia on the north. This was a bold venture — recklessly bold, as most militarists would view it — yet the first Syrian army sent against him under Seron was hemmed in the narrow Judean mountain passes about Beth-horon and so completely defeated and scattered that there were only enough left to tell the story.

Lysias then commissioned Nicanor, in conjunction with Gorgias, to lead a vast army of forty-seven thousand to overwhelm the Jewish forces led by Judas. The large and well-disciplined army inspired such confidence that they were joined by a large group of coast slave dealers provided with cash and fetters, who fully expected to purchase the Jewish captives that would be taken by the great army.

Moving along the coastal plain, Nicanor refused to move very far up the valley of Ajalon which would entangle his army in the hill passes about Beth-horon, but chose rather to encamp on the foothill near Emmaus (later Necopolis, now Amwas) where he would have ample ground on which to make use of his cavalry and phalanx. Here he awaited Judas' expected attack.

The odds seemed against Judas and his small force; yet they read their Bibles, brought in their tithes, and fasted and prayed all day. At evening Judas gathered his men and delivered the following short but impressive and inspiring address:

> With the God of heaven it is all one, to deliver with a great multitude, or a small company; for the victory standeth not in the multitude of an host, but strength cometh from heaven. We fight for our lives and our laws, wherefore the Lord himself will overthrow them before our face; as for you, be not afraid of them.[8]

Gorgias led his forces out of Jerusalem and marched westward to assist Nicanor. But Judas was too much in earnest to be caught napping. By a forced march he took the road ahead of Gorgias, and rested his brave troops in the darkness near Emmaus. At dawn they looked from the hills and saw the strongly fortified and well-patrolled Syrian camp facing the *east.* Swinging his forces to the left, Judas, in light formation, charged the huge Syrian force from the *south,* while Nicanor expected him from the east or north. Panic seized the Syrian host and they "fled to the plain" of Sharon.

The Jews followed in hot pursuit, and after slaying three thousand of the enemy, returned and took possession of the Syrian camp with all its weapons of war, supplies of food, gold, silver, and Syrian silk. They were almost in the act of giving themselves up to the enjoyment of the spoils, when Judas warned them to be ready for the other division commanded by Gorgias. The warning was timely, for the Jews had no sooner gained battle array than Gorgias, with his army, appeared on the Judean heights and stood gazing at his fellow-general in flight. The sight was sufficient; he turned back lest his army be defeated and destroyed by the rapid and resourceful Maccabeans.

Exasperated by the failure of two armies, Lysias himself, during the following autumn, led a vast army of sixty thousand infantry and five thousand cavalrymen into Palestine to hunt down Judas and put a stop to the guerilla warfare which had so effectively outwitted his best generals. Entirely avoiding the Beth-horon pass, Lysias led his army along the Maritime plain by Gaza, eastward over the hilly region and northward on the Hebron road where they encamped "beside the city" of Beth-zur.[9]

The army was so large and the elephants looked so ferocious that terror spread among the Maccabean forces, and many fell away. On seeing this Judas followed the example of Gideon and winnowed his army. To the faint-hearted he called, *"Fall out of line."* With the three thousand who remained he had prayer, then, during the night, threw himself upon the last vast host led by Lysias. Five thousand of the enemy were killed, and the Syrians fled in panic through the whole night, while the victors sang Psalm 136 — their national anthem — enumerating the enduring mercies of their God.[10]

The way now lay open for Judas to enter Jerusalem. On marching his forces into the city he found the temple in ruins and shrubs growing in its courts. Here a pathetic scene occurred; those valiant warriors, who had destroyed three armies, fell on their faces, threw dust on their heads, and wept aloud.[11] They then entered the temple, destroyed its pagan altars and ornaments, cleansed it thoroughly, relighted the perpetual lamp, and with ceremonies befitting the occasion, rededicated it to God amid the rejoicings of the people. This year 165 B.C. — was glorious in the annals of Judea, and indeed of the world.[12]

Encouraged by such signal victories, Judas erected stone forts within the temple area, strongly fortified and garrisoned Beth-zur, then attacked and forced back the Ammonites and Edomites — Arabs, as they were later called — who had crowded in and settled in Judea during the decline of Jewish power. Galilee, Gilead, and Philistia were overcome and the Jews had a brief period of rest from their foes from without. Syria took no concern for its attention was entirely taken up elsewhere.[13]

In 164 B. C. Antiochus Epiphanes died while on an expedition in the Far East. One year later Lysias heard that Judas laid siege to the Syrian garrison in the citadel of Jerusalem. Accompanied by the young king, the general gathered a formidable host of one hundred thousand footmen, twenty thousand horsemen, and thirty-two elephants and marched around to Beth-zur. After capturing this ancient citadel Lysias pushed on northward to Beth-Zacharias where he met Judas in Battle.

The splendid advance of the great army arranged about the elephants as centers deeply impressed the Jews; but having successfully faced so many Syrian armies, they advanced to the attack with unbounded confidence. Six hundred of the king's men were slain; and Eleazar, the brother of Judas, thinking he had discovered the elephant on which the young king was riding, fought his way single-handed to the beast, crept under it, and inflicting a fatal stab, was himself crushed by the animal's fall.[14] But valor availed not. The odds against the Maccabeans were too great. They were obliged to retreat.

Marching on northward, Lysias laid siege to the Holy City. With the enemy already in the citadel and the vast army without the walls, there seemed little hope. The dread cloud that hovered over Judea took on a darker hue due to a scarcity of food supplies, for it was a sabbatic year, in which no grain had been sown. Then in the midst of the siege, Providence seemed to intervene. News came to Lysias that Philip, with the army of Antiochus Epiphanes, was marching to Antioch "to assume the government" in accordance with the dying wishes of the former king.[15]

Seeing that its hands were so full at home, the Seleucid government, as represented by Lysias and Antiochus V. indicated a readiness to come to terms with the Jewish patriots. A treaty was drawn up by which the walls of the temple were to be spared, the Jews were to be granted peace and be at liberty "to make use of, and live according to the laws of their fathers." Since religious liberty was vouchsafed to the Jews the most religious section of the people, the *Hasidim* or *Pharisees* were satisfied that the rebellion should go no further.

When the king set out for Antioch, Lysias influenced him to take with him Menelaus, the high priest. He aimed to remove the man who had originated so much trouble, and thus provide against future disturbances among the Jews. The move, however, was not so successful in accomplishing its intended purpose, due to the fact that Alcimus, the man appointed to his place, was strongly Hellenistic in his leanings, and received no encouragement to officiate while Judas was at the head of affairs in Jerusalem.

The end aimed at by Judas and his followers was no longer the preservation of religious freedom, but to decide the question whether those friendly to the Greeks or those within the national party of the Jews should have the supremacy. However, the opposition was sufficient to bring complications between Judas and the Seleucid authorities of Antioch. Demetrius, the new Syrian monarch, not only reappointed Alcimus high priest, but also sent a Syrian army under the command of Bacchides to reinstate him. Alcimus made "quieting assurances" which immediately won the acknowledgement of many among the strictest section of the Jews. Bacchides returned to Syria, but Judas and his adherents continued their opposition to Alcimus on the grounds that they had no faith in his promises.[16]

Alcimus ordered the execution of sixty men belonging to the party of the Hasidaeans. This aroused renewed opposition and brought on an open war in which the tide turned in favor of Judas and those attached to the faith of their fathers. Alcimus fled into Syria where he laid his case before Demetrius. Presently the Syrian general, Nicanor, appeared in Judea with a great army. He sought through stratagem to take Judas, but having failed in this, he marched on Jerusalem where he "wreaked his vengeance on the innocent priests," then with a threat to burn their temple if they did not deliver up to him Judas and his army, he returned and encamped in the district of Beth-Horon, where on March 13, 161 B.C., Judas and his forces fell upon them in a surprise attack. The Syrians were not only utterly defeated, but Nicanor fell in the tumult and his soldiers were cut down while they attempted to flee the battle-field.[17]

Judas now stood at the head of the Jewish commonwealth, and as such he sent two men of his party as ambassadors to Rome to secure the help of the Romans against the Syrians. These and similar procedures caused Judas to lose the support of the more religious section of the Jewish people. They had come to feel that Judas and his brethren were growing worldly in the process of their "struggling and scheming" in political affairs.[18] The true situation was revealed during the following month when Bacchides, the Syrian general, marched against Judea with an army of twenty-two thousand. So little interest was manifest in the new issues that few of the Jews cared to fight, since their religious liberty had already been gained.

The army dwindled to three thousand, while the Syrian forces so outnumbered the small army commanded by Judas that twenty-two hundred of his soldiers deserted, and the remaining eight hundred advised a retreat until their forces could be augmented; but with the words: "Let not the sun ever see such a thing, that I should show my back to the enemy," Judas fell upon the opposing army's left flank and crushed it, but the right flank then turned and charged him. All day he strove with superhuman valor against overwhelming forces, then toward evening the enemy beset him round about, and "Not being able to fly, Judas stood still, and he and those that were with him fought; when he had slain a great many of those that came against him, he at last was himself wounded, and fell, and gave up the ghost, and died in a way like his former famous actions."[19]

During the rule of Jonathan, who succeeded Judas, the gradual disintegration of the Syrian (Seleucid) monarchy and their weariness of the struggle caused them to change their policy and begin, by political strategy, to win the Jews to their side. In Jonathan they met their political match. In fact, his crafty diplomacy caused him often to anticipate possible benefits, then after paving the way with gifts, to propose to the Seleucid officials his desired plans, and gain their support of his project.[20]

In 152 B.C. Jonathan was installed as high priest by the Seleucid government, and thus became both the temporal and spiritual leader of his people. As governor of Judea, he renewed friendship with Rome, and received many concessions for his people.

Then, after eighteen years he was taken at his own game of craftiness. Trypho desired to be king of Syria. The chief obstacle in his way was Jonathan, who remained loyal to the Syrian king. Trypho came to Beth-shan and Jonathan met him with an army of forty thousand chosen men. Trypho evaded him, then later by flattery and gifts persuaded Jonathan to meet him at Ptolemais (Acre) for an interview. Blinded by ambition or possessed by mad heedlessness born of long immunity, he walked into the trap, was made a prisoner and his bodyguard of one thousand soldiers was massacred. A ransom of one hundred talents of silver was collected from the Jews, but it bought no freedom for Jonathan. Trypho put him to death and Simon buried him in the family sepulchre at Modin.[21]

Soon after Simon's succession to the throne he sent assurance of his support and loyalty to Demetrius II (Nicator) who reciprocated by con-confirming Simon as high priest, renewing all the covenants made with Jonathan and removing the last mark of Jewish dependence — the payment of the tribute.[22]

Having already conquered Joppa and annexed the city definitely as a part of the Jewish state, Simon captured Gazara and thus secured an open road to the port of Joppa. Beth-zur was captured and fortified.[23] Then the Syrian garrison, so long stationed in the Akra citadel of Jerusalem, was expelled and the Jews began to feel fully independent.

During September of that same notable year (141 B.C.) it was resolved in a great assembly "of the priests, and the people, and the princes of the people, and the elders of the land," that Simon should be high priest and military commander and civil governor of the Jews "for ever until there should arise a faithful prophet" to determine otherwise.[24]

Appointing his son John captain of all his hosts, Simon devoted his attention to the management of the civil and religious affairs of the nation. Commercial relations were established with the various Mediterranean countries, Jewish slaves were redeemed, and the Jews, so writes the author of the book of Maccabees,

> tilled the land in peace, and the land gave her increase, and the trees of the plains their fruit. The old men sat in the streets, they talked together of the common good, and the young men put on glorious and fine apparel. Every man sat under his own vine and his fig tree, and there was none to frighten them.[25]

## CHAPTER XV

# THE DECLINE OF THE JEWISH STATE

MATERIAL PROSPERITY continued under John Hyrcanus, who became ruler of the country when Simon, his father, was treacherously assassinated. There was too much prosperity for the moral welfare of the people. Hyrcanus assumed the role of an earthly monarch, coined money bearing his insignia,[1] employed mercenary troops in larger number than Jewish soldiery and proceeded to conquer the smaller kingdoms about him.

Medeba fell after a trying siege of six months, then the army returned from across the Jordan, subjugated the Samaritans, and in 129 B.C. destroyed their rival temple on Mount Gerizim.[2] His sons laid siege to the city of Samaria and razed it to the ground. Gezer, Beth-shan, and other chief cities which commanded the highways of the land, were taken over and a strip of land east of the Jordan river was taken from the Nabatean Arabs. The Edomites (Idumeans) were conquered and given the alternative of exile or the acceptance of Judaism. Desirous of remaining "in the country of their forefathers" they embraced Judaism, underwent circumcision and submitted to the Law.[3]

The kingdom soon became almost as extensive as that of Solomon but was far less stable. The use of such faulty, degenerate methods of carrying on conquests and making converts with the sword was certain to result in a harvest, the fruits of which would be bitter indeed. The Maccabees were but one generation from their heroic efforts to maintain religious freedom for themselves. Capturing other peoples and forcing them to abandon their own religion was certain to fall with dire consequences on the heads of the Hasmoneans.

On John's death in 104 B.C. he was succeeded by his eldest son, Judas Aristobulus, who continued his father's policy. After conquering Galilee he had himself crowned and let it be known that he was "King of the Jews," but like many another monarch, he soon adopted the dreadful practice of destroying or imprisoning the members of his family who could become a threat to the security of his throne.[4]

One brother, Antigonus, was given a place of honor because of the affection which the ruling brother bore toward him. During the king's illness, politics wrought remorse and havoc as is so often the case. Enemies of Antigonus persuaded Aristobulus to believe that his beloved brother was intriguing to supplant him. At first the sick man would not believe the charge, but with suspicions aroused he requested that his brother come to him unarmed. Should he appear in arms, he was to be killed. Antigonus was then informed that Aristobulus wished to see him in the glory of the new armor which he had just purchased, and, suspecting nothing, he went in full armor to the palace, where, in a secret passage way, he was murdered.[5] Stricken with grief over his brother's death, Aristobulus suffered a hemorrhage that brought to an end his rule which had extended over a period of only one year.

In the meantime the Pharisees had increased in number and in strength. These "Puritans" or "Separatists" who had been the leading spirit in the Maccabean wars, were unable to appreciate the worldly conquests, the secularizing policy, the bigotry, and the political intrigue so foreign to the Hasmonean ideal. They had been heart and soul with Judas and Jonathan in their noble struggles to secure their freedom and protect and further their religious interests; but they could not and would not follow their leaders whose chief ambitions were to gain worldly powers and honors. To them there was something more important thon material gain, and more enduring than crowns which would tarnish and pass away. They desired a continuation of that faith and those practices held so sacred by their fathers. To them departure from these principles meant a breakdown of their faith and the introduction of certain malignant forms of paganism against which they had so courageously fought.

The Sadducees, like liberals of any other age, did not seem to be troubled over the trend of affairs in state and church. They were among the aristocracy of the land and held views that were saturated with Hellenism. John Hyrcanus and Judas Aristobulus had favored the Sadducees, thereby re-enacting the age-old drama of a leader taking sides with the wealthy and influential when he has acquired an appetite for power. Since they were in favor with the rulers, the Sadducees had come to look with disdain on the Pharisees who foresaw certain trouble in the approaching storm.

During the reign of Alexander Jannaeus, who succeeded his brother, Aristobulus, the policy of conquest and subjugation was continued. The former country of the Philistines was added to Judea and whole populations were forced to submit to Jewish rites and account themselves Jews. With hired soldiers from Cyprus and Asia Minor, Jannaeus fought to subjugate neighboring countries. Judas had been a warrior of necessity, but Jannaeus was a warrior by choice. Fascinated by conquest, he incurred the ill will of the deeply religious among his subjects who held him in low esteem as a high priest.

During the Feast of Tabernacles early in his reign, he poured the water, the symbol of fruitfulness, not upon the altar but on the ground at his feet. This bold departure from the usual ritual caused the people to pelt him with citrons and charge him with being unworthy of the priesthood. He retaliated by calling in his mercenaries who slew six hundred Pharisees before the temple inclosure was cleared.[6]

Some time after this, while leading an expedition against Obedas, an Arabian sheikh, he was lured into a rough and dangerous region and then attacked. His army was destroyed, and he barely escaped with his life. When he appeared in Jerusalem he found that the conflict between the Pharisees and the Sadducees had reached the point of civil war. Throwing the weight of his influence on the side of the Sadducees, he brought on additional sorrow by his unwise and heartless deeds.

Eight hundred Pharisees who had held a fortress against him were hung upon crosses in the midst of the city and the throats of their wives and children were cut before their dying eyes. Eight thousand others fled into Egyptian exile.[7] Many turned away in disgust, and some longed to be delivered from self-government. After a quarter of a century of misrule, the king grew weary, sad, and disillusioned. Beset by haunting memories, he drank himself to death, and in 78 B.C. his sordid reign came to an end and his widow, Alexandria, succeeded him.

Alexandria, whose Jewish name was Salome, was a very pious woman and strongly attached to the Pharisees. She had always deprecated the harsh treatment meted out to the Pharisees by her husband. On becoming queen she showed the rare judgment and good sense to appoint her eldest son, Hyrcanus, to the high priesthood. Greatly influenced by Simon ben Shetach and other rabbis, she did much to promote peace. Almost everything in Judea was again carried out in accordance with the Mosaic law. Courts of justice were re-established and religious observances resumed, education was promoted by the establishment of schools, and other praiseworthy and peaceful moves inaugurated.[3]

The exiles returned, foreign wars ceased, and the old religion was practiced without hindrance. The Sadducees uttered few complaints for they felt themselves fortunate to escape with a small measure of persecution.

The queen repealed all the ordinances contrary to the traditions of the Pharisees and encouraged the people to follow the strict rules of the

Mosaic law. She was very popular with the people but neglected the army, and in time fell into ill-favor with a majority of the soldiers.

In an hour when the queen was very ill her younger son, Aristobulus, placed himself at the head of the army and demanded recognition. Sick and near the end of her earthly career, Salome offered no resistance. Shortly afterward she died and he at once assumed the title of king. His brother Hyrcanus, then acting as high priest, was also proclaimed king, as Hyrcanus II. The two brothers gathered their armies for battle near Jericho. Having the good will of the soldiers, Aristobulus won out in the brief contest and Hyrcanus' life was spared with the understanding that he was to be deprived of his position as high priest, to enjoy his fortune, and live in seclusion.

During his idleness he had considerable association with Antipater, the son of the governor of Idumea, who often reminded him that his life was unsafe as long as he lived in Judea. Finally he was influenced to leave Palestine and take refuge among the Arabs, where he put himself under the protection of Hareth, in the cliff city of Petra. Antipater, who soon succeeded his father as governor, induced the Arabian king, Aretas, to assist in re-establishing Hyrcanus II in Palestine, on condition that when he should become ruler he would give back to the Arabs the cities which his father Jannaeus, had taken from them.

With an Arab army of fifty thousand, Aretas defeated Aristobulus, and drove him into the temple area. Deserters flocked to the standard of Hyrcanus II, their former high priest, who took up the siege against his brother. After some weeks in the approach of the Passover season the followers of Aristobulus, who were being besieged within the city, begged the besiegers to allow cattle for the sacrificial offering to be brought into the city. "They passed money through an opening in the wall, only to discover that their brethren were taunting them. There were no passover sacrifices that year in the Holy City. War was war, even between Jews."[9]

Not only were the two brothers at war with each other, but neither of them had scruples against asking aid from outside rulers. In the spring of 63 B.C. Pompey came to Damascus and *three* embassies appeared before him, Hyrcanus, Aristobulus, and a committee representing the people of Palestine. Hyrcanus and Aristobulus maligned each other. But the messengers from the people suggested that they preferred not to be under the rule of a king, but under that of their high priest, as their fathers had often been before them.[10]

Pompey promised to give decision after he had made an expedition against the Nabateans. But this expedition was postponed and Pompey marched into Judea, not as a friend, but as a conqueror. Sweeping aside all resistance, he laid siege to the city, and on October 10, in the year 63 B.C., Jerusalem was taken and twelve thousand of the Jews put to the sword.

Pompey and his officers, out of curiosity, entered the Holy of Holies within the temple, and finding everything as the Jews had represented it, ordered the temple thoroughly cleansed and the services continued. Hyrcanus II was confirmed as high priest *without* secular authority, while Aristobulus and his sons were taken captive to Rome, where later they appeared in Pompey's triumphal march. Rome assumed nominal control of Palestine, and the independence of the Jewish people, which had lasted for nearly eighty years, was brought to an end.

## CHAPTER XVI

# THE RISE OF HEROD THE GREAT

FOR MORE THAN a quarter of a century thereafter the country was in a turmoil. Various Jewish leaders raised the standard of revolt, ever to be met with bloodshed and defeat. Then, too, there was strife among the Roman masters, and Palestine changed hands four times in a few years. Crassus, of the second triumvirate, became proconsul and twice plundered the temple at Jerusalem. At his death a new insurrection broke out, which the Roman legions under Cassius suppressed, and thirty thousand Jews were made prisoners and sold into slavery.

In the midst of all these disturbances, Antipater of Idumea made himself valuable and well pleasing to the Romans. They came to prize his advice and to favor him in many ways. In turn he sought to serve Rome and win her applause. His wife, Kypros, was the daughter of King Aretas of Arabia, and their sons were *Phasael,* and *Herod.*

In 48 B.C. Antipater supplied men and money for Caesar's campaign in which Rome conquered Egypt. To show their appreciation, they granted Antipater Roman citizenship with complete exemption from all taxes and promoted him to the position of governor of Judea. This arrangement was quite satisfactory with Hyrcanus, since Antipater had often befriended him in days gone by. When they were both in Jerusalem they spent many hours in each other's company and undertook together the repair of the walls of Jerusalem. This pleasant arrangement continued for four years, then the career of Antipater was brought to an end by a cup of poison given him during a banquet with Hyrcanus. One year before passing from the Palestinian stage his son Phasael had been made military governor of Jerusalem and his son Herod, then a young man of twenty-five years, was made governor of Galilee.[1]

For some years Galilee had been infested with a band of men calling themselves "patriots," but who, in reality, were robbers living from the spoils of the government and its officials. They lived securely in a cluster of well known caves on the high cliffs near the Sea of Galilee. The young governor had iron cages constructed, placed armed men in the cages and let them down over the precipice, where they killed and captured the culprits. Some of these Galilean "Robin Hoods" were popular with the Jewish Nationalists, and enjoyed a measure of sympathy from the people, due to the fact that they preyed largely on government property. Their destruction raised Herod in the esteem of the Romans, yet it greatly angered the Jews, for the Jewish law held that these men, being Jews, could not lawfully be put to death unless the execution had been sanctioned by the Sanhedrin.

Fired with the fiercest indignation, the Sanhedrin demanded that the young governor be summoned to Jerusalem to answer to them for executing men without warrant.[2] He came, but attended by a band of brave soldiers ready to obey his bidding to the last command. To the trembling Sanhedrin he answered as one who speaks to abject subjects, then returned to Galilee without waiting for their verdict. The Jews came to dislike him because he, a descendant of Esau, disregarded their wishes.

Ere long Julius Caesar promoted Herod to the governorship of Coele-Syria, the long and fertile strip of territory which lies between the Lebanons. Then Caesar fell, and Cassius, one of his murderers, came to the Near East as ruler. Herod gained the friendship of Cassius and remained governor, but when the battle was joined at Philippi, Cassius fell and Mark Antony became the mightiest ruler of the Roman world.

Cleopatra, the beautiful but wicked queen of Egypt, went to meet Antony at Tarsus. She sailed down the river Cydnus in a ship whose sails were of purple silk, and its oars of silver. While incense burned on board the ship the queen reclined on a couch spangled with stars of gold, and the rowers kept time to the sound of flutes and cymbals.

Cleopatra's beauty, coupled with her charming personality and the unusual exhibition, so captivated Antony that he followed her back to Egypt, where, charmed by her presence, he spent much time. Thither went Herod with gold seeking the favor of Antony. Not only did he beome Mark Antony's friend, but returned from Egypt as the governor of Judea and the ruler of those who had dared accuse him and seek his life for the execution of the Galilean outlaws.[3]

Herod remained in Jerusalem but a short time for the Near East seethed with discontent and many of the Jews longed for Antigonus, one of their own number, to return as their ruler. The Parthians, a fierce tribe of the Persians living near the Caspian Sea, taking advantage of Antony's absence, swept down through Syria, joined hands with Antigonus and forced their way into Jerusalem. Hyrcanus was captured and his ears shamefully mutilated,[4] thus depriving him of an opportunity to ever again be high priest. He was then sent into exile beyond the

Euphrates. After desperate fighting, Herod barely escaped with his household and fled to Masada[5] where he left his family and himself went on into Arabia, and from thence to Egypt whence he sailed for Rome and laid his case before Antony and Octavius.

Both the Roman leaders felt that Herod was just the man to hold Palestine for Rome; therefore they acclaimed him "King of the Jews," which made him and his children the successors of the royal line of David and his descendants. Doctor Sachar points out the fact that history presents few sights stranger than the spectacle which followed: Herod, half Jew and half Idumean (Edomite), accompanied by Antony and Octavious, proceeding to the Temple of Jupiter on the Capitoline hill, where sacrifices were offered in thankfulness for Herod's having been named king of the Jews.[6]

Returning to Palestine with Roman legions, Herod conquered the surrounding country and in the spring of 37 B. C. laid siege to Jerusalem. He made his headquarters on the acropolis of Samaria, where, on the eve of his final drive he celebrated his marriage with Mariamne, the beautiful Hasmonean princess, for whom he had waited five years.[7] From a political point of view the marriage was a master stroke, for Mariamne was a direct descendant of Mattathias who had raised the standard of revolt. The Jews dearly loved the Maccabean line; therefore, Jewish hatred for Herod was modified by the marriage. But the marriage was more than political, for Herod was desperately in love with Mariamne. Her beauty and purity appealed to him, and he loved her with the passionate ardor of the Oriental.[8]

Leaving his beautiful bride in the palace at Samaria, Herod hastened to his armies now closing in on Jerusalem. Within a few hours they swept into the city where they captured and scourged Antigonus, the last of theMaccabean rulers, and freely took life and destroyed property until Herod raised his voice in protest: "Will the Romans deprive the city of all its inhabitants and possessions and leave me king of the wilderness?"[9]

Queen Mariamne had a brother to whom she was especially devoted. He was but seventeen years old, and with Mariamne represented the royal priestly line of the Maccabees. Desiring to please Mariamne and further ingratiate himself with the Jews, Herod made the young man high priest. But alas! when the people saw him step forth as a reminder of the Maccabean heroes they sent up a chorus of shouts that made the Judean hills echo the joy of a grateful people. The young high priest was so praised and appreciated that Herod's blood boiled with envy. A bit later the young man was invited to Herod's gorgeous winter palace at Jericho, where he was drowned, *accidentally,* as he bathed in the royal reservoir in the gardens of Jericho. The king styled it "a most unfortunate, deplorable accident," but the queen knew better, and her love for Herod cooled.

Alexandria, the queen's mother, denounced the murderer of the high priest to Cleopatra who hated Herod, her near neighbor and constant rival, whom she could not control as was her wont with others. Cleopatra denounced Herod to Mark Antony, and Herod was summoned to Rome to answer before Antony and Octavius for the infamous assassination of the young high priest.[10] He left the government to his uncle Joseph, who had married Herod's sister, Salome. And among all the wicked feminine intriguers Salome will ever hold a prominent place in the world's checkered history. If Herod was given to dark deeds, then Salome was given to darker. "As Mariamne was Herod's good angel, so Salome was the devil's efficient agent to drag her brother to the blackest depths of crime."[11] Of course, Mariamne and Salome had nothing in common and could not agree, yet they were obliged to live in the same palace.

On leaving Jerusalem, Herod had ordered Joseph, his vice-regent, to execute Mariamne *if* he fell by shipwreck or by execution at Rome. So great was his love for the queen that his jealous heart desired that she should not become the wife of another man, in case of his death. Salome questioned her uncle-husband, and finding the secret, told all to Mariamne.

Herod won his case at Rome, and returned to his lovely Mariamne, but alas! she met his warm love with coldness and rigid upbraiding. He had ordered her death in case of his. She denounced him and his murderous intent. In a tempest of jealousy, fury and rage, Herod ordered Joseph's immediate execution. The crisis passed with one murder and left domestic affairs at the palace in a worse plight than before.

The Roman world was the world, in general, and was controlled by two men — Anthony and Octavius (or Augustus as he was later known). Antony held the East; Octavius, the West.

There was not enough room for both. They met at Actium off the classic shores of Greece to fight it out. Cleopatra was with Antony. When the battle began to rage she fled, whereupon Antony left the battle field and followed Cleopatra to Egypt where they both soon came to ruin.

On hearing of Antony's downfall, Herod appointed Soemus as his deputy, moved his family to the city of Samaria, ordered out his royal galleys, and sailed to meet Augustus at the historic island of Rhodes. He bowed before the Roman conqueror, reminded him of his fidelity to Mark Antony, and pled for the privilege of giving Augustus the same allegiance that had proven Antony's staff and stay in Palestine. It was a political appeal that not only succeeded in winning the favor or Octavius, but meant that all that Antony had given Cleopatra at Jericho and on the Philistine plain was returned to Herod, and his empire became almost as vast as that ruled over by David.[12]

He hastened back from Rhodes with youthful enthusiasm to tell Mariamne the great news of his success. Urging his steed along the Palestinian roadway, he arrived at his Samaritan palace where he flung himself on his couch and commanded that Mariamne be brought before him at once. But she came "as cold and proud as a marble statute." She refused to rejoice at his success. She scorned his affectionate caresses, groaned at his ardent demonstration of love, and positively refused all his demands. It was a tragic scene.

Then the secret was revealed — before leaving for Rhodes the king had given Soemus, his faithful servant, the same cruel charge relative to the queen: "*If* I die she is to be executed." She taunted him with this repeated command to take her life in the event of his death, and denounced him for the murders of her kindred — her brother, her uncle, and her aged grandfather.

The king was first troubled, then grew angry. The restless tides of his fury came in and he raved like a maniac, fell ill, and all but lost his reason. Some say he was never mentally normal after this.[13] During this illness his sinister sister, Salome, gained access to him and insisted that the queen had been faithless in his absence. In his jealous rage the king ordered the instant execution of Soemus, and the arrest and trial of Mariamne. At the trial the tension of the scene was heightened by the queen's own mother taking sides with her enemies, yet Mariamne bravely faced all her accusers with scorn, and stood her ground as heroically as had her Maccabean ancestors. The court said she was guilty, but her purity and innocence caused King Herod to stay the hand of the executioner for many days.

Had she returned his love she might have lived, but how could she care for such a bloody, brutal man; and how could she freely roam the halls of his palace where political intrigue and domestic hatred made the place to her little less than a living hell? In a fit of anger he ordered her execution. As Mariamne was being led forth to execution, her mother rushed forward and struck her in the face, charged her with ungratefulness, and said that she was about to suffer only what she deserved. Bystanders uttered astonishment, but Mariamne said not a word. With the calmness and dignity befitting a righteous queen, she met her fate as a relief, and without even casting a reproachful look on those who condemned her.[14]

Soon after the execution of his beautiful and beloved queen, Herod became a victim to mad paroxysms of remorse. His love and ardor returned upon him, and a passionate longing for the touch of her hand tormented him. He roamed through every room in his palace and walked along the marble colonnades, calling piteously, "Mariamne, Mariamne." He fell into fits and writhed like a serpent, crying and demanding that Mariamne come to comfort him.[15] Oh, for Mariamne, the only being he ever loved, or could love!

Oh, Mariamne! now for thee
  The heart for which thou bled'st is bleeding.
Revenge is lost in agony,
  And wild remorse to rage succeeding.
Oh, Mariamne! where art thou?
  Thou canst not hear my bitter pleading.
Ah! couldst thou — thou wouldst pardon now
  Though Heaven were to my prayer unheeding.

And is she dead? — and did they dare
  Obey my frenzy's jealous raving?
My wrath but doom'd my own despair;
  The sword that smote her's o'er me waving —
But thou art cold, my murder'd love!
  And this dark heart is vainly craving
For her who soars alone above,
  And leaves my soul unworthy saving.

She's gone, who shared my diadem;
  She sank, with her my joys entombing;
I swept that flower from Judah's stem,
  Whose leaves for me alone were blooming;
And mine's the guilt, and mine the hell,
  This bosom's desolation dooming;
And I have earn'd those tortures well,
  Which unconsumed are still consuming![16]

He had the servants call her, and listened as they went down the long arcades and through the royal gardens summoning the dead queen into the presence of her royal husband.

Rallying from his "demented grief" King Herod gave his attention to a phenomenal building program that has few parallels. On the seacoast, bordering fertile, flower-embowered Sharon, he built a Roman seaport and named it Caesarea — for Caesar, his royal patron. Ancient Samaria was built with strong walls, graceful gates, elegant buildings, and a magnificent boulevard. To it he gave the name of *Sebaste,* the

Greek for Augustus. At Jericho he built a theatre, circus and hippodrome. Near the hot Springs of Callirrhoe, at Machaerus, he erected a fort with rooms of marvelous beauty, beneath which were dungeons, and inexhaustible cisterns cut in the solid rock.

Sixteen years before the birth of Christ, Herod began his contribution toward beautifying and perpetuating Jerusalem. His decision to convert the temple into a magnificent modern edifice was not at all welcomed by the representative men of the nation. They feared that Herod merely intended to destroy their old temple, and endlessly protract the new, thus robbing them of their sanctuary.

But he pacified them by assuring them that the old temple would stand until the workmen were on hand ready to commence the new structure. A thousand carts for transferring quarry stone and marble appeared on the scene and ten thousand skilled workmen made ready to begin operations.[17] The temple area was greatly enlarged by a huge platform of stonework, which was supported by arches and pillars.[18] Around this area of about one thousand square feet, were beautiful colonnades of marble, roofed with cedar. Here the people found a pleasant promenade and lounging place, and here the rabbis held school.

In 20 B.C., the eighteenth years of Herod's reign, the building was begun, and in one year and a half the inner part of the sanctuary was finished so that services might be resumed. The building of the outer walls, courts and galleries occupied a period of eight years, and the completion of the entire edifice took forty-six years.[19] This temple was a magnificent structure, the pride and joy of the Jewish people.

The dimensions were vaster and the decorations richer and more ornate than were those of Zerubbabel's temple. Nine gates, thickly coated with silver and gold, led the way into the temple. The inner sanctuary was covered on all sides with gold plate, and was dazzling to the eye. The various courts and porticos and palaces with which it was surrounded gave it a very imposing effect. Josephus says that from a distance the whole resembled a snow-covered mountain, and that the light reflected from the gilded porch dazzled the eyes of the spectator like "the sun's own rays."[20] In those days it was a common saying, "If you have not seen Herod's Temple you have seen nothing at all," and undoubtedly it was one of the most beautiful buildings ever constructed.[21]

At Jericho Herod constructed a large reservoir, arranged a royal garden, and built a magnificent winter palace. At the Springs of Callirrhoe, just across the north end of the Dead Sea, he constructed yet another palace where he might indulge in hot mineral baths and find a measure of relief from his bodily ailments and cares of state.

Herod was efficient in state affairs, enjoyed the applause of Rome, and did many things which should have merited the favor of the people he ruled. He craved the love and affection of his subjects, yet received little praise because there was little in common between the king and his people. His marriage with Mariamne might have accomplished much, but its possible wholesome effect was dissipated by his murdering episodes.

Beyond all this was the fact that he was an irreligious Idumean Arab, backed by Roman authority, reigning over Jewish subjects. The combination was not a happy one. Love and respect were almost impossible. With criticism, curses, and opposition from the Jews; and pride, bigotry and deviltry on the king's part, there was created an atmosphere of mistrust, hatred, and rebellion in which it was well nigh impossible for anything to be done satisfactorily.

The latter years of Herod's life were wretched beyond expression. The tale of his domestic tragedies has no parallel in the annals of history. Queen Mariamne left him *five* children, two daughters and three sons. The boys were educated at Rome where they would be near the great Augustus Caesar. One of them died there. The other two were looked upon as "crown princes" who would succeed their father.

When they finished their education and returned from Rome, they were "tall, noble-looking men, conscious of the royal blood in their veins." The hearts of the Jewish people went out to them, but their half-brother plotted against them. By treachery and political intrigue Salome helped to bring them into question. They were first tried at Rome, but acquitted themselves with such manliness, and showed such affection for their father as to cause Caesar himself to warmly commend them.[22]

Jealous intrigue and persistent whispering about the Palestinian royal palace apparently gave their half-brother the advantage. In 7 B.C. King Herod had them tried before a Roman court at Beirut, and later they — Alexander and Aristobulus, the last of the Maccabees — were strangled in the palace of Samaria.

Such scenes as had taken place in that palace! Here their mother, Mariamne, had wedded Herod; here she finally broke with him; here she was tried and assassinated; now her two noble sons were brought hither and strangled. Once again right was on the scaffold and inglorious wrong on the throne. Ah! what tragic scenes have been enacted on that ancient and oft ruined acropolis of Samaria!

The princes[23] were laid in the Alexandrium, in the province of Samaria, two years before the close of the Jewish era. After this, Herod grew melancholy, or as Josephus says, was "depressed by the calamities that had happened to him in connection with his children, so that he had no pleasure in life, even when he was in health."[24]

In the thirty-sixth year of Herod's reign, and while Augustus was yet emperor at Rome, JESUS CHRIST the Saviour of the world was born in Bethlehem, according to the word of the prophets. Herod first heard of Him through the "wise men" who came from the East.[25]

Misled by the opinion prevalent among the Jews that the Messiah was to be a military prince who would rule in regal power, Herod sought advantage by feigning a worshipful interest in the Bethlehem babe. Foiled in his hypocritical plans, he sent the soldiery to Bethlehem and slew the children under two years of age. Thus he hoped he had destroyed one whom he considered a rival of himself and family. But the Christ child was to be known millennia after Herod's hand had laid down the Judean scepter.

That same year Herod lay racked in pain with an incurable cancer. He resorted to the hot Springs of Callirrhoe, near the fortress of Machaerus, where he took hot mineral baths. But no relief came, for death was upon him! On returning to Jericho, he recalled his oldest son from exile that he might succeed him, but just five days before the old king died, he discovered the treachery of his undeserving son and had him executed.

Fearing lest there should be no one to mourn his death, Herod summoned "the most illustrious men out of every village in all Judea" and had them imprisoned at Jericho, where he spent his last weary days in his beautiful winter home. To his sister, Salome, he gave the order that as soon as he was dead, all these men should be put to death, "and then" said he, "all Judea and every family will weep at my death." What actually did happen was that at his death the illustrious Judeans were released, and a wave of rejoicing swept the country from one end to the other.

Four miles southeast of Bethlehem, on one of the high points of the wilderness of Judea, Herod, during latter years, had erected an artificial peak to a lofty height and crowned it with the "Herodium" — one of the most spectacular tombs known to man. At his death the royal hearse left Jericho, passed through Jerusalem to Bethlehem and to the Herodium.

The selfsame shepherds that heard the angels sing and saw the Christ child, also probably saw the royal hearse go by and heard the wail of the *hired* mourners. Many looked on while they buried King Herod the Great on top of Frank Mountain, that to this day towers above the

"Shepherd fields" and the peaceful little city of Bethlehem where the "King of the Jews" was born and the innocents perished at Herod's command. Both Jewish and Christian writers have only evil to speak of Herod. One historian aptly summed up his career when he said that, "he stole along to the throne like a fox, he ruled like a tiger, and he died like a dog."

## Chapter XVII

# IN THE FULLNESS OF TIME

During Herod's life time the Roman world had come to assume vast proportions. It was bounded on the west by the Atlantic ocean, on the north by the Rhine and the Danube, on the east by the Euphrates, and on the south by the Sahara desert. The empire abounded in cities, each having its walls and gates, colonnaded streets, baths, libraries, and temples. When on missions of commerce and communication, the people traveled over a network of substantial roads from Hadrian's wall in Britain to the white city of Damascus and to the plunging cataracts of the Nile.[1]

Imperial discipline made the people exceptionally safe, and the Greek language made it convenient for them to converse freely throughout the far-flung empire. An element of informality and of popular opportunity made promotion possible for even the commoner. From the lower ranks Herod had arisen to rule over Palestine, Perea, and a large portion of Syria.

Not long before his death Herod made his will, dividing the kingdom among his three sons: Archelaus, Herod Antipas, and Herod Philip. The will was ratified by the emperor Augustus in its most important points. Archelaus, who retained the government of Judea, proved himself a cruel tyrant. After he had reigned ten years, the Jews complained, and Augustus banished him to Gaul where he died in disgrace.

Augustus Caesar then sent Publius Quirinus (Luke calls him "Cyrenius," which was the Greek form of his name), the former governor of Syria, to reduce the countries over which Archelaus had reigned to the form of a Roman province.[2] Judea was made subordinate to the president of Syria, with Coponius, a Roman, as its procurator, or Lieutenant governor.

The power of life and death was taken out of the hands of the Jews, and taxes became payable direct to the Roman Emperor. Justice was administered in the name and by the laws of Rome. Still, in that which pertained to their religion, their own laws, the power of the high priest and the Sanhedrin, the Jews were permitted to retain. Jerusalem was thronged with men of all nations; the Greek, the Roman and the Jew predominating.

In "the fifteenth year of the reign of Tiberius Caesar,"[3] Pontius Pilate being at that time governor of Judea, John the Baptist appeared in the sterile wastes between the wilderness of Judea and the Jordan river, heralding the message: "Repent ye: for the kingdom of heaven is at hand. . . . Prepare ye the way of the Lord, make his paths straight." Clothed in a mantle of camel's hair, with a girdle of leather about his loins, living on locusts[4] and wild honey, and preaching conformity to the great traditions of the prophets, he offered a marked contrast to the scribes and Pharisees of his day.[5]

Passing beyond the bounds of creed, nationality, and race, John aimed his message of repentance at the conversion of the children of Israel and all others who would meet conditions as laid down by his rugged gospel. It was the year of release — 779-780 according to Jewish reckoning — and the people being free from the soil, from labor and from debt, were at liberty to attend. From the hills and vales of old Judea, and the busy marts of Jerusalem, farmers, shepherds, merchants, officials, soldiers and people from all walks of life gathered in vast throngs to hear the profound yet practical messages of the plain, transparent wilderness preacher.[6]

The fame of the Baptist reached the high functionaries of the Jewish Church who sent a delegation to inquire if he were the Messiah. Representing himself as "a voice crying in the wilderness," he said: "I indeed baptise you with water unto repentance: but he that cometh after me is mightier than I, whose shoes I am not worthy to bear."[7]

When John announced that the Kingdom of Heaven was at hand, and that the King would soon appear it awakened a sympathetic chord in the hearts of the Hebrews. Like a rainbow the vision of the Messiah had hung over the whole of the Old Testament. It had broken forth in choicest prophecy, quickening hope, sustaining faith, and inspiring endurance. It alone had kept the Jewish people from national despair when blight was on the face of every other hope.

They kept believing that Heaven's pledge of universal love would be fulfilled. The prophecies had suggested a "messenger" who would go before and "prepare the way" and they firmly believed that John was that long-looked-for messenger.

When they heard him preach just reparations, a change of the inner life, and a purpose to please God in righteous living; many submitted to baptism and glorified God for such a message and messenger. To John, baptism was the outward sign of true conversion.[8]

Six months of John's intense evangelism had passed when Jesus of Nazareth reached the age of thirty years, left behind the carpenter shop at Nazareth, made His way along the great rift valley and appeared on the banks of the Jordan, at Bethabara, to be baptized of John.

When John saw Jesus coming unto him, he cried with an earnest, animated voice: "Behold the Lamb of God, which taketh away the sin of the world."[9] John suggested that he was not qualified to administer baptism to so great a personage, but for the sake of "fulfilling all righteousness," Jesus received baptism and thus signified His willingness to "Make common cause" with sinful men.[10]

The Spirit of God descended "like a dove" and rested upon Him in confirmation of His Messiahship, but He did not tarry for the adoration of the people. Withdrawing into the vast solitudes of the sterile wastes of the wilderness of Judea, He spent forty days in fasting and communing with God, where, under the burning heat of an oriental sun, His sensitive body famished with hunger, His mouth and tongue parched with thirst or His shivering form enveloped in the black, chilling folds of a wilderness night, He ran the gamut of temptation — the appeal to the physical appetites; the desire to be praised and worshipped as one under the protection of Heaven; and the desire for worldly power and possession.

There in full command of His own will He rose in the sublime strength of His Holiness to do the "will of Him who had sent Him," and faced His fiendish intruder and declared him a defeated foe as He stood above the world — yet in the world — the spotless "Lamb of God."

Defeated in his designs the devil departed for a reason.

> And to his crew, that sat consulting, brought
> Joyless triumphals of his hoped success,
> Ruin, and desperation, and dismay,
> Who durst so proudly tempt the Son of God.[11]

Having vanquished the prince of the kingdoms of this world, Christ descended from the high wastes of the wilderness, passed along Jordan's brink and tarried over the sabbeth near where John the Baptist was preaching. Andrew and John were so drawn to Him that they followed Him to His sabbath abode where they heard His mighty word, then went for their brothers, James and Simon Peter, saying: "Come see the Messiah."[12]

On the following day Jesus and the four left Bethabara and began their journey back to Galilee. Philip met the group and was invited to join them. His acceptance of Jesus was so wholehearted that he hurried away and found his close friend Nathanael (Bartholomew) seated under a fig tree reading his Bible. Hurrying up to him, Philip said: "We have found Him of whom Moses in the law, and the prophets, did write, Jesus of Nazareth, the son of Joseph." When Nathanael questioned if any good thing could come out of Nazareth, Philip said: "Come and see." Nathanael came and as he saw and heard the Master his doubt disappeared and he said: "Rabbi, thou art the Son of God; thou art King of Israel." So they journeyed on together, Jesus and the first six disciples.[13]

Soon after reaching His home at Nazareth, Jesus and His disciples attended a marriage feast at Cana (four miles east of Nazareth) then went to the beautiful Sea of Galilee where nine cities nestled on its enchanting shores, four thousand boats plied its blue waters, and four great caravan routes "led away in as many diverging directions." Here, where "rose the wide murmur of busy life," Jesus completed the choosing of His disciples that should be with Him, then "launched forth on a ministry which was to change the history of civilization."[14]

Meanwhile the great crowds, to which John continued to preach, seemed ready to do anything he advised. Even Herod Antipas came often to hear him, and did "many things" for the fearless evangelist.[15] Then one day John's preaching became rather personal — he reproved Herod for having divorced his wife, the daughter of King Aretas of Arabia, and having married Herodias, his brother Philip's wife.[16] Herod knew John was a great and good man and that he had told him the truth, therefore received the reproof with fair equanimity, but from that time forth Herodias became "the chief foe of the rigid preacher of repentance."[17]

When John was preaching on the east side of the Jordan, Herod had him arrested under the pretext of fear lest the powerful preacher raise a rebellion, but in reality because Herodias urged his arrest to stop the denunciations of the sinful lives of her and her husband. Herod, undecided as to what disposal to make of the Baptist, placed him in the strong prison at Machaerus.

The final decision was reached through Herodias, John's avowed enemy, when on the occasion of the celebration of Antipas' birthday in the palace of Machaerus, a great banquet was given in his honor. Salome, the daughter of Herodias and granddaughter of Herod the Great and Mariamne, by her dancing so delighted the half-drunken king that he promised to fulfil to her any wish she might express. At the instigation of her mother she asked for the head of John the Baptist. The request surprised and sickened Herod, yet his wicked heart and weak will made it impossible for him to deny the request.

Immediately orders were given and the head of the Baptist was brought on a charger of gold and given to the young dancer who had it carried to the banqueting table upon which it was placed "a supreme offering, before a treacherous and evil woman."[18]

Herodias was revenged. But "vengeance is mine; I will repay, saith the Lord;" and vengeance came swift and terrible, for before another decade passed Herod Antipas and Herodias were banished to Gaul. Salome died an early and violent death.

The wheels of God grind slowly
  But they grind exceedingly small,
Though with patience stands He waiting
  With exactness grinds He all.

Meanwhile, Jesus entered the Galilean synagogues and preached saying: "The time is fulfilled, and the Kingdom of God is at hand; repent ye and believe the gospel."[19]

After a short time He went to Jerusalem to attend the Feast of the Passover where He preached the way of life, wrought many miracles, met Nicodemus, an exceedingly powerful Jewish leader, and expounded unto him the chiefest of all miracles — the spiritual birth.

Soon after the feast Christ began His return journey to Galilee. He disdained the longer route by the way of the Jordan Valley, and with His followers left by the Damascus gate of Jerusalem and took the direct way northward, for "He must needs go through Samaria." For long centuries the Samaritans had been looked down upon as "dogs," and had received little attention or sympathy from the Jews, but it was not to be so with Jesus, for He was the personification of love, and

Love hath a hem of its garment
That reaches the very dust,
  It can touch the stains
  In the streets and the lanes,
And because it can it must.

It dares not rest on the mountain,
It is bound to come to the vale,
  For it cannot find
  Its fullness of mind,
Until it falls on the lives that fail.

On the way He stopped to rest by the side of Jacob's well near Sychar and preached the most remarkable message ever delivered to an individual. The Samaritan woman was converted and hurried to the city and told the people that she had met the Messiah who had told her "all things" that ever she did. Then the people of Sychar welcomed Jesus, and He tarried with them two whole days, during which period many believed on Him as the Saviour.

When He arrived in Galilee His fame spread so rapidly that the buildings became too small to accommodate the throngs that attended His ministry. He was obliged to turn to the fields, the sea-side, and the mountain tops; where His audiences numbered into the thousands.

To Him they came — the blind, the dumb,
The palsied, and the lame,
The leper with his tainted life,
The sick with fevered frame.

On hearing of the death of John He went aside for a brief time, then resumed His ministry to the masses. His many miracles, His mighty deeds, and His weighty words caused His fame to be spread abroad. Herod Antipas heard of Him, and being tormented by an evil conscience, felt convinced that John the Baptist had risen from the dead, and that "mighty works" were being shown forth in Him.[20]

Fearing the "miracle-worker" who preached in Galilee, Herod desired to be rid of Him. In craven, fox-like fear, he craftily influenced certain Pharisees to go to Jesus and tell Him that Herod sought His life, hoping thereby to intimidate Him until He would voluntarily quit the country. Manifesting no signs of fear, Christ said: "Go ye, and tell that fox, Behold, I cast out devils and do cures today and tomorrow, and the third day I shall be perfected.[21] It was as if the Master were saying: "This year, and the next, then the third year I shall carry on this ministry, and complete it in Jerusalem."

Whether Herod would have been bold enough to touch Him we know not, but his brazen daring need not be tested. That year Aretas of Arabia made war on Herod; attacked and destroyed his army. Herod's time and energies were demanded in the south portion of his small, earthly dominion, while in the north portion Jesus proclaimed happy tidings of open gates to the Kingdom of God and of Heaven — the realm of goodness, of sincere humility, of love, of the spirit and the soul — into which men could enter only by complete change of heart — the transformation of the soul by a rebirth in harmony with the spirit realm. "That which is born of the flesh is flesh; that which is born of the spirit is spirit."

Following a night spent in solitary prayer He ascended a mountain and when the masses gathered about Him, He delivered unto them what men have called *"The Sermon on the Mount"* — words weighted with divine glory, with authority, and yet with infinite mercy. No one has dared question the simple yet sublime statements of that message, nor deride the sweet spirit in which it was pronounced. It was not only wise, but divine. Its sentences burned like fire into human hearts, and the message itself has gone down in history as the most positive declaration of the way of righteousness ever spoken to mankind. Like a flood it has swept everything before it.

Christ's radiant personality, His tenderness and humility captivated the masses wherever He went. He preached by day saying, "I must work the works of Him that sent me," and He prayed by night. He opened blinded eyes, unstopped deaf ears, with the touch of His tender hands healed the sick, and with a word raised the dead to renewed life. He wore a seamless garment, trod the land footsore and weary, paid His taxes with money secured from a fish's mouth, and commanded the turbulent sea to be silent.

He was conscious of the possession of divine power, yet was so real that He refrained from employing sensational methods in displaying that power. He could have changed stones into bread, leaped from the pinnacle of the temple unhurt, and subdued the kingdoms of the world by force, but He would do none of these things.

His audiences were composed of the learned scribe, the proud-hearted Pharisee, the place-seeking Sadducee, the fervid Zealot, and the many classes in the lower brackets of society. He moved on the highest intellectual levels, yet by the use of a vivid, picturesque language He cast His teaching into a form so simple as to be understood by a child.

He talked of lilies in their bright array,
He spoke of ravens being fed.
'Have faith,' He said to anxious men, 'You, too,
Shall all be dressed and given bread!'[22]

Christ did not mistake symbols for reality, nor share the narrow prejudices and contemporary fancies of His day, but taught in harmony with all scientific fact; taught as one who knew the things of life and death. Others took a short view of life — looked "only at the near side of near things" — while Jesus "saw both sides of things far and near,"[23] and taught in terms of eternity. For Him the tomb was not a blind alley, but a thoroughfare that closed on the twilight and opened on the dawn.[24]

Confucius confessed to know "little or nothing about God and how the universe came to be. His teachings were confined mainly to human relations." Buddha knew very little of God, but taught of the *fact, cause,* and *remedy* for human suffering. The Greeks taught many gods, "often wicked and always impersonal." Even Socrates, Plato, and Aristotle pathetically groped in the darkness trying to find "the great first cause," the ultimate reality that lay behind the universe that appeared to their senses. Christ taught one personal and righteous God who was not only available to the individual, but who delighted in supplying the needs of His children. Christ constantly spoke of God as "Father." To Him God was "more real than His mother, Mary."[25]

Jesus Christ had about Him a depth that "did not depend upon clothes or pose, or *assumption* of supernatural power,"[26] but lay in the very nature of His divine-human being. There was something about Him "that made the best of men feel they were in deepest need, and yet the worst of men felt drawn to Him." "He was goodness that was approachable," says Dr. E. Stanley Jones; "not meticulous, but merciful, not standing on pedestals to be worshiped, but bending in lowly service over the lost." He was friendly and tender and "in that very tenderness and friendliness there was a regal something that made men's consciences flutter and tremble like an aspen leaf . . . . Never did majesty and meekness so blend and become so beautiful . . . . Never did word and work so blend in harmony as they did in Him."[27]

He was not the product of the natural order — no order existing could have produced such. He was a new order who marched across that decisive century and not only gave to the world a mark by which to reckon time, but a moral and spiritual standard which would be the norm for all time to come.

This unquestionable difference between Christ and others was apparent in all that He said and did, and even more so in all that He was. His person bore the stamp of other-worldliness, and miracles not only formed a great part of His work and ministry, but were so wrought into the warp and woof of all that He did and said that to remove them would wreck the story of His life.[28]

The Stoic emphasized the self and strove to protect that self in tranquility but Christ taught that men should forget the claims of their own selves and be lost in service to God and man that they might be saved eternally. The Stoics believed that the universe moved on in great cycles; and that when the circuit was complete all would begin again and happen once more exactly as it did the last time, but Christ replaced this "monotonous repetition" with the teaching that man could yield himself body and soul to God Almighty, and constrained by His love, could work for others, have constant communion with God and at the close of "life's little day" go to be with Him and live eternally in that many-mansioned country.

The inadequacy of human effort and human philosophy had been evident wherever man had tried them. Christ came teaching that the supreme issue of life was not one of the philosophical nor of the sociological order but one of the spirit which was to be settled down deep in the soul of the individual; that righteousness did not lie in ceremony and ritual or technical purity, but was an affair of the heart, of the nature and the will, as the Hebrew prophets had previously urged.

Christ did not minimize outward conflict — the pressure of environment — but taught that "the greatest of all troubles and the grimmest of all conflicts was the unseen battle that was waged on the field of the divided heart."[29] His teaching did not consist of a system of subterfuges, false inferences and superficialities, but bore the mark of the absolute and infallible — the way of life proceeding from the heart of divinity. He did not base His religion on error and endeavor to make it adjustable to carnal passions and impulses, but led His followers directly to the heights of moral regeneration where human nature is transformed, the sensibilities refined, and love perfected. Others came to lead in war, politics, and philosophy, but the Man of Galilee held true to His confidence in "inner values," and to His ever present thought of a Kingdom — within.

His words were refreshing and inspiring. Men never tired of them, even when they tarried long to hear Him expound the gospel that applied to their everyday lives; "Because I live, ye shall live also." His logic was true, His technique without a fault, and His teaching as unanswerable as the ages.

On a day Jesus told His auditors of a man blest of God in the fertility and increase of his lands. He took them into the man's very thoughts, invoice, and plans, then quickly and with such vividness as the technique of no other teacher has taught — He had the wealthy farmer *face to face with God whom He had forgotten* — "this night shall thy soul be required of thee, then whose shall those things be which thou hast provided?" The people all perceived the immense spiritual and intellectual wealth that lay ready to His hand, and were whole-hearted in rendering the verdict that He "spoke as never man spoke," and taught "as one having authority and not as the scribes."[30]

The Master was "a man of sorrows, and acquainted with grief," yet was known for His delight in the lilies of the field, birds of the air, and little children who were so plentiful in Palestine. He loved home, exalted womanhood and gave the incomparable parable of the good Samaritan as the world's greatest lesson against class distinction. His teachings not only "squared with the world's best intelligence," but tended to "stabilize society without sterilizing it."[31] He often spoke of the Kingdom of God — a Spirit-born organism based on the fundamental ideas of God — in which there was "neither Jew nor Greek . . . . bond nor free," but all one in Jesus Christ, redeemed with His precious blood.[32]

He recognized the inexorable law of justice, yet manifested a sympathetic understanding toward those who strayed from the right. He perceived the prodigal son's blindness, coming ruin and remorse, yet thrilled with joy as He so plainly described his home-coming.

In fulfilling "the law and the prophets" He was so very original that "they of the deepest insight were amazed."[33] Yet comparatively few Jews were ready to receive Him as the Messiah for whom they had waited. The prophets had pictured the coming Messiah as kind, humble, and meek — the personification of love, mercy, justice and truth. They had also pictured Him as coming in power, might, and regal splendor — the conqueror of the universe and the judge of the ages.

These teachers of His day, and later, were able to give the minutest delineations and interpretations of the law in regard to *diet* and the *sabbath,* but perceived not that the prophets had written of two appearances of the Messiah — the first in His *humility,* and the second in His *glory.*

They seized upon the passages referring to His coming in power, and conceived the idea that He was coming as the military conqueror of the world, the judge of the ages, and the restorer of the Jewish state. They were looking for a king to slay their foes and lift the Jewish nation to lofty heights. Convinced in their own minds that He was to reign over a *temporal* realm, they steadfastly refused to give careful consideration to those passages depicting Him as a Saviour and Ruler in the *spiritual* realm.[34]

The law of Moses was the guide for the overwhelming majority of Jewish leaders, yet these God-given laws were so overlaid with tradition and so dimmed with emandations that the substance had long since become so hidden in its own shadow that to them it was little more than a system requiring correct eating, ostentatious fasting and alms giving; the tithing of mint, anise, and cummin; the washing of cups and platters, and the garnishing of the sepulchres of the prophets.

They had placed the ceremonial laws on the same level with moral regulations, and had become so disciplined in these laws that they were unprepared to accept Christ's teaching that *love* was the fundamental law of life and the conquering power of human society. With meticulous care they watched the correctness of every move, "from the eating of a meal to the wearing of a new cloak,"[35] yet overlooked regenerating grace for the individual heart and life, and failed to perceive that *love* toward God and man was necessary before they could fully live here, or hope to live in that eternal country where love is the law of the land. They were sick, sad, and sinful, yet trusted in the outer trappings of their religion, and understood not their Messiah who had come to regulate their spiritual, social, and moral well-being.

> He came unto His own, and His own received Him not. But as many as received Him, to them gave He power to become the sons of God.[36]

Christ recognized none of the rabbinical traditions and emendations of His day but inculcated the one great duty of *love*. He recognized neither Jerusalem nor Mount Gerizim as the exclusive place of worship, but declared that God, as a spiritual Being, was to be addressed with sincere and spiritual worship at *all* times and in *all* places. He accepted men on their highest level, yet never condoned nor excused sin. He proposed a religion and public policy which not only cut straight across the usual religious practices of the day but exposed the hollowness and shallowness of formal religion and public policy of His day.

Christ was peaceful in His bearing, yet exceedingly unswerving in His loyalty to love, mercy, and truth. He lived an immaculately clean life and made no compromise with unrighteousness, but proclaimed His standards boldly. Religious authorities of His day measured themselves by those standards and were embarrassed, because He taught and lived a higher righteousness than that which they taught and exemplified.

Churchmen never relish reproof for leniency in upholding moral standards, nor for dereliction of duty when they permit politics and formality to take the place of fervent piety. Down from the temple at Jerusalem went spies to dog the footsteps of Jesus Christ in Galilee, to report the nature of His teachings, and if possible, to entrap Him into some false word or deed which would give the Sanhedrin a chance of suppressing this strange Galilean if they thought best.

They soon understood that the broad stream of Christ's policy and purpose tended toward encouraging Israel's rulers to abandon their ill-judged hope of nationalistic triumph over Rome and make their mission one of evangelizing the world for true righteousness in God and of the Spirit. This teaching evoked further resentment on the part of many Jews who held tenaciously to the concrete side of religion and to a national exclusiveness.[37] This resentment on their part led to opposition, and opposition to implacable hatred. Nothing less than His death would satisfy them.[38]

Yet the farthest reaches of the human imagination can but fail to grasp the far-reaching results of a wholesale turning of the Jewish people to the person and teachings of the Messiah — the mediator between God and man. With his legal, economic, and ethical background submerged in *love,* the regenerated Jew, amplified and tempered by the gracious love and power of Jesus Christ, would have become the man of the ages, the evangel of all times.

To the frozen regions of the north, the burning sands of India, and wherever man is found, He would have gone with a clear mind, a warm heart and a soul aflame with a passion to gather men and teach them the right; even as He has gone to every part of the globe to gather the shekels of the commercial world. Judging from the unparalleled results following the labors of those few who did accept Him, one could imagine the entire world won for love, righteousness, and justice.

But the masses did not accept; indeed could not, unless they were willing to forsake their decadent formality and seek for the way of life in something more potent than the keeping of certain days and observance of certain laws of dietics — good within themselves, but made rigid and *all* important by the tradition of the elders.

In the autumn of the third year of His ministry Jesus withdrew, with His disciples, to hold a religious retreat at the northern end of the Jordan valley among the foothills of Hermon. During this retreat He schooled His spirit for the end, and talked frankly with His disciples that they might be enlightened, purged, and disciplined for the days to come. Accompanied by Peter, James, and John, He ascended Mt. Hermon where He was transfigured while Moses and Elijah appeared and talked with Him about His decease which He should accomplish at Jerusalem.[39]

On coming down from the mount Christ healed many who had patiently waited his coming. He then spent a brief time in the environs of Capernaum where He taught the people, opened the eyes of the blind, visited with those who invited Him to their tables, and conversed with His disciples.

When the winter was past, and the rain was over and gone, and the flowers were appearing in the gardens, along the wadies, and on the hillsides, He left Galilee and with His disciples went up through Samaria to Jerusalem. There He taught the masses, wrought miracles, and had much to do with the Pharisees, the temple officers, and the Sanhedrin.

He then crossed into Perea (Transjordan) where He was busy teaching the people when there came a message from Bethany saying that Lazarus was dead. Crossing the Jordan He ascended the Judean mountains by the Jericho road and came to Bethany where He not only declared Himself to be "the resurrection and the life" but wept with those who sorrowed, and called His friend Lazarus from the tomb.[40]

The raising of Lazarus led many Jews to believe on Him, and this wholesale turning to Christ stimulated such opposition on the part of His opposers that a council was called in which the high priest frankly told the council that it was better that Jesus die instead of the whole nation. To avoid their plots Christ withdrew with His disciples to a small city called Ephraim (perhaps the present *Ta-iyibeh,* an out-of-the-way mountain village five miles northeast of Bethel) where He conversed often with His disciples that they might be prepared for the final solemn charge.

Then when the time for the Passover season was drawing near He and His disciples joined a Jerusalem-bound Galilean caravan at some point along the Jordan valley road and moved on down the world's greatest rift valley. At Jericho, Zacchaeus, a Jew small of stature, yet a rich and influential tax-gatherer, climbed a sycamore tree where he could watch the procession and see into the eyes of the Man of Galilee. The eyes of the Master and those of the tax-gatherer met, and the Master caught the eager hunger lurking in the worldly man's heart and bade him hasten down from the tree. Zacchaeus squared his life by repentance and restitution, hospitably entertained Jesus and on the following day sent Him on His way.[41]

Throngs followed Jesus as He left out of the city, but blind Bartemaus, a wayside beggar, lifted his voice to call on the Christ. The Master not only heard, but commanded Bartemaus to come. Throwing aside his *abayeh* the beggar ran and threw himself in humility before the Master, and pleaded for restoration of his sight. Christ granted his request and Bartemaus "followed Him in the way." With a supreme purpose and absorbing passion "the Lamb of God" pressed toward the Holy City to die for humanity.

There had been a "simple and virgin beauty" about the first months of His ministry, and a "certain rush and splendor about His crowded second year when He was in the full-tide of His popularity," but in these closing months, when the shadow of the cross fell athwart His pathway, His Passion to fulfill the divine will became more intense and His life rose to a sublime holiness that awed His disciples as they followed Him in the way going up to Jerusalem.[42]

They arrived at Bethany six days before the Passover, and were entertained with great honor in the house of Simon the leper. The next day large numbers of Christ's followers gathered on the Mount of Olives, while two went to the nearby village of Siloam and returned with a colt "whereon yet never man sat." Some of His followers spread their *abayehs* (cloakes or outer coats) on the back of the donkey and others spread theirs in the way making a carpet for the roadway.

As He rode down the Mount of Olives along the winding westward road the people waved palm branches while they shouted, "Hosanna, to the Son of David. Blessed is He that cometh in the name of the Lord; Hosanna in the highest." The valley and mountainside rang with His praises. Some grew nervous and wanted the shouting stopped, but Christ's declaration was that if men did not praise Him, the rocks and the hills would.[43]

Pausing for a moment, Christ beheld the famous city, and discerning its approaching doom, told the bystanders of a day when the enemy should cast a trench about it and compass it round, and keep it in on every side, and lay it even with the ground, not leaving one stone upon another. Then, with the yearning spirit of love, He uttered that pathetic lament:

> O Jerusalem, Jerusalem, thou that killest the prophets, and stoneth them which are sent unto thee, how often would I have gathered thy children together, even as a hen gathereth her chickens under her wings, and ye woul dnot! Behold, your house is left unto you desolate.[44]

After crossing Brook Kedron Christ rode up the circling way to the Eastern Gate where He dismounted and passed through the gate and entered the court of the temple. The place was loud with the bleating of sacrificial sheep, lowing cattle, moaning pigeons, cooing doves, and arguing, boisterous merchants and money changers who sought to fleece the uttermost farthing from the patient pilgrims who changed their money into temple currency and purchased beast and bird for sacrificial purposes. The sight so grieved the Master that He paused long enough to plat a whip of cords; then with the words: "Ye have made my Father's house a den of thieves," He raised the cord-whip above His head and charged the atmosphere rank with secularism; nor did He stop until He had driven out the many traders and money changers who had established their stalls, booths, and money tables within the sacred precincts of the holy temple.

Having been licensed by the high priests, these merchants in hot anger made complaint, and the authorities gloried in the fact that they then had more just grounds for action against the divinely strange Man of Galilee.

Definitely determined to press for the immediate execution of Jesus, the high priests and their associates worked rapidly for they knew they must complete their thankless task before the Passover actually began — there remained but two days. Deciding upon a desperate yet dangerous course, they secretly sent a messenger pleading with Judas — the treasurer of the twelve — to meet them for a private interview. Once in their company Judas yielded to their suave offer, and the bargain was made — the treasurer was to betray the Christ to the high churchmen for thirty pieces of paltry silver.[45] From then on all the opposition bent their energies to the completion of the sordid plan.

On the evening of the thirteenth of Nisan (April 2) just after the sunset flared against gray walls and cast its parting rays on Olivet's brow, the Master met in the familiar room with His twelve. With them He could eat the supper which He knew would be the last. Judas was there, but before the meal was finished the traitor left — actuated by sinister motives and bent on an evil mission.

Once the traitor was away, the Master unlocked His heart and poured forth His secret confidences to the eleven trusted disciples. He talked to them at length of the other "Comforter" — the Holy Spirit, — whom they would receive to comfort them in His absence. Then there fell from His lips the grandest message ever spoken regarding the vine, the branches, their fruit and their relationship. All this natural phenomenon, He said, was like to Him and His followers.[46]

While night hung fantastically about the Holy City, Christ passed from the upper room and led eleven faithful men along the narrow street, passed the guard at the gate, and took the roadway leading by the terraced vineyards and oliveyards on Kedron's western slope.

When He had crossed the steep valley of Jehoshaphat and the Brook Kedron He entered the garden of Gethsemane where He left His apostles and withdrew a little farther into the olive grove where He prayed with agonizing earnestness while His disciples slept. A prevision of His death at the hands of sinners brought a chill upon His heart, and in the midst of His most earnest praying

A vision rose before His eyes,
A cross, the waiting tomb,
The people's rage, the darkened skies,
His unavoided doom.

Yet there was holy calm in His Spirit in suffering the will of God and abiding joy in the anticipation of the redemption He was to attain for man.

With orders from the "expounders of the law and the devotees of ritual," the temple police, accompanied by Judas and an anxious mob, closed in on Jesus at the end of His prayer.[47] Judas gave the kiss of betrayal, the arrest was made, and the crowd jeered while they led Him away a prisoner to the house of Annas; where before the elders and scribes the formidable elderly high priest emeritus questioned Him, then sent Him to his son-in-law Caiaphas, the active high priest, who lived on Mount Ophal. Torches gleamed, night loafers were driven from the way, and wicked men in their litters were borne at a gallop through the narrow streets.

During the cross-examination before Caiaphas, His enemies gave testimony in such a manner as to make it sound as though Christ had spoken publicly of destroying the temple and rebuilding it in three days, and of Jerusalem being trodden down by the Gentiles. They then accused Him of claiming to be the Son of God. When He frankly admitted His divine origin and assured them that He would make His second appearance on earth — as a judge and conqueror — they declared they had no need of further proof, therefore they imprisoned Him until early morning when the entire Sanhedrin could be present to give the condemnation a more nearly legal aspect.[48]

Had it been a charge meriting anything less than death, the Jewish Sanhedrin could have passed and executed the final sentence,[49] but having no power to carry out the sentence of death, they met while the morning was yet young and readily *condemned* Him of blasphemy, then *delivered* Him to Pontius Pilate, the governor, with the instruction that Jesus was disloyal to the government and guilty of blasphemy, therefore should be put to death.[50] The priests themselves refused to cross the threshold of the Praetorium for fear of pollution on the eve of the sabbath.

Judas, on seeing that Christ was condemned, returned the thirty coins to the crief priests saying, "I have sinned in that I have betrayed the innocent blood." The priests refused to accept the coins, whereupon Judas threw the money on the floor, and went hurriedly to the well-known precipice south of Jerusalem and hanged himself.[51]

Pilate heard that Jesus was a Galilean, therefore sent Him to Herod Antipas who was then in the city on a visit. Herod was elated over the turn of the tide that sent Jesus to him; for he had often heard of the marvelous miracles of the Man of Galilee and "of a long season" had hoped to see Him perform one of these wondrous deeds. However, when they were face to face, Herod fell to questioning Him. Christ ignored all the wicked, worldly man's vain curiosity and it so nettled Herod that he, "with his men of war set Him at nought, and mocked Him, and arrayed Him in a gorgeous robe, and sent Him again to Pilate."[52]

Pilate's task was not easy, for many of his soldiers and at least one of his trusted centurions paid Christ homage, and many Jewish leaders secretly worshipped Him.

Pilate was governor of the Romans who held their heads high, while Christ was the Prince of Peace ruling in a sphere where the most obscure slave "could pluck a Roman by the sleeve and call him brother."[53]

Pilate inquired regarding the "Great Galilean's" Kingdom, and heard Him say: "My kingdom is not of this world: if my kingdom were of this world, then would my servants fight, that I should not be delivered to the Jews; but now is my kingdom not from hence." But Pilate's concepts were so shot through with materialism that he failed to perceive the distinction between a *spiritual* and an *earthly* kingdom. Then, as if successful in securing His confession, Pilate said: "Thou art a king, then?" Christ's straight-forward reply was: "Thou sayest that I am a king. To this end was I born, and for this cause came I into the world, that I should bear witness unto the truth. Everyone that is of the truth heareth my voice." Inferring that Jesus spoke of some certain philosophy, Pilate uttered that famous question: "What is truth?"[54]

The trial was only in its initial stages when Pilate's wife, who is said to have once heard Christ talk to a multitude, sent her governor husband an urgent note saying: "Have thou nothing to do with that just man." But the governor could not easily stay the trial for he was urged on by the rabble who clamoured for Christ's blood.

Pilate drew the Man of Galilee into a room "away from the noisy riffraff of the High Priest" and "stared intently into His eyes to catch even a glint of fear that comes to men who are in the shadow of death,"[55] and finding such innocence and manliness as he never knew, the provincial governor came back to the rabble with those trenchant words, "I find no fault in Him." They cried the more exceedingly, demanding vengeance for blasphemy.

Pilate might have disregarded the High Priest — who enjoyed but small honor in his community — and with a word turned the market-place and forum loose to the eloquence of Jesus. Perhaps for a fleeting second he thought to do so, and, for the sake of time, suggested to the crowd that they make choice between Jesus and Barabbas. When this strategy failed Pilate chose Rome rather than "the new kingdom to which Jesus had given the name Heaven."[56] Without, the rabble cried, "Crucify Him! Crucify Him!"; within, Pilate's worldly ambition cried, "Rome! Rome! Rome!" And, for the sake of position and prestige the provincial governor gave orders that He should be crucified. And yet for conscience' sake and for the sake of his wife, the governor "held his fingers forth over a fine silver bowl into which a young servant poured water upon them from a silver ewer."[57]

Christ was before Pilate less than an hour, but that morning hour tested everything that Pilate was or had hoped to be. Judgment was passed on Pilate, "as well as on Jesus in that short span."[58] In vain had he washed his hands in the presence of the multitude with water drawn from the great cistern which he had built in Jerusalem.

Roman soldiers led Jesus away into the hall of the Praetorium where in jest they clothed Him with a purple robe, crowned Him with thorns and placed a reed in His hand for a sceptre, and in mockery saluted Him as King. "Prophesy," said one, and smote Him, but in meekness Christ bore it without a word. They then took from Him the mock reed, removed the purple robe, and clothing Him in His own garments, led Him along the *Via dolorosa* to a lone gray hill outside the gaunt, gray walls; while the Romans, the Jews, the Christians and the world looked on.

At nine o'clock in the morning Roman hammers swung low as servants of the far-flung empire nailed the Great Galilean to a crude wooden cross, then lifted Him for crucifixion between two malefactors — one repentant and the other adamant. Nearby the soldiers parted His garments among them, and cast lots to know who would receive His seamless *abeyeh,* and sitting down they watched Him there. "Earth which has ever slain her noblest sons, slew also her Redeemer!" Above Him, written in Greek, in Latin, and in Hebrew, they placed the inscription

*Jesus of Nazareth, the King of the Jews*

When they had read the inscription the chief priests of the Jews went to Pilate with the suggestion that he change it to read: "He *said,* I am king of the Jews." But Pilate's pointed reply was: "What I have written I have written."[59]

Varied emotions surged through the souls of the moving, restless mass of living beings who milled about the brow of the lone gray hill — ever to be kept at a fair distance by the Roman legion thrown about the Man of Sorrows. Once the tumult of shouting, moaning, and jeering was quieted when the suffering Saviour prayed for the people, saying: "Father, forgive them, for they know not what they do." Henceforth, the cross was to be regarded as love rising to sublime heights — the "fingerpost pointing from time to eternity, directing man's conscience to the Father's heart."[60]

At high-noon, 'mid the glory of an oriental sun, a strange darkness settled over the face of the earth and lingered until three o'clock in the afternoon. Then while the paschal lamb was being prepared His choice spirit left the tenement of clay. Joseph of Arimathaea begged His body and Nicodemus furnished a hundred pounds of myrrh and aloes. With loving hearts and tender care they worked in the spices as they wrapped the body in fine linen and laid it in Joseph's new tomb. On the third day Christ claimed His body, burst asunder the bars of death and left the tomb in triumph. His redemptive work was complete. The guard missed Him, the gardener knew not where He was, and His disciples lovingly sought His body; only to find an angel within the tomb.

Since then, for His devoted followers, Easter has supplanted the Passover; for He was "the Lamb slain" for our sins, but He arose, and ever liveth to make intercession for the saints. Forty days He walked among His followers and then ascended from the Mount of Olives. His influence in shaping the history of mankind has been eloquently summed up in the words of Richter: "With his pierced hand he has lifted empires off their hinges, turned the stream of centuries out of their channels, and still governs the ages."[61]

No religious teacher or philosopher in either Asia or Europe had ever even suggested that he had any element of deity in his physical makeup — nor had any suggested even the possibility of such a thing as a remedy for sin, much less that he could offer himself as a redemption for sin. Yet through all the teachings of the Great Galilean there ran the thought that He was truly God and truly man — divinity wrapped in humanity.

To substantiate His claim, the world is faced with the fact that Christ was "unlike all the rest of us,"[62] and that during His brief lifetime of thirty-three years He inaugurated a movement that has virtually captured the world, lasted for more than nineteen centuries, and continues to loom larger and larger with each succeeding generation. Questions concerning other leaders have been settled, but the question "What think ye of Christ? Whose son is He?" is "invested with perpetual youth."[63]

## Chapter XVIII

# THE FALL OF JERUSALEM

In the year 36 A. D. an imposter represented to the Samaritans that he knew the spot where certain sacred vessels were buried, whereupon a group of Samaritans assembled in a village named *Tirathana* to follow him to Mount Gerizim. Pilate, having heard of the affair, sent a force of cavalry and infantry which attacked the assembled multitude, killing some and putting others to flight. The Samaritans sent a delegation to Vitellius, the legate, complaining that they had been maltreated. As a result, Pilate was relieved of his office and ordered to Rome. Eusebius relates that he was exiled to Gaul and committed suicide at Vienna.[1]

Soon after the removal of Pontius Pilate, Judea and finally nearly all the countries formerly governed by Herod the Great were given to Herod Agrippa,[2] the grandson of Herod the Great, who later was stricken and died at Caesarea.[3]

He left a seventeen-year-old son, named Agrippa,[4] but the Roman emperor, thinking him too young to govern his father's extensive domains, made Cuspus Fadus governor of Judea. After a short rule he was succeeded by Alexander Cumanus, Felix, Festus, and at length by the unprincipled Florus who used his office for rapine and plunder. His excesses so goaded and irritated his subjects that in 65 A. D. the Jews rose against their Roman rulers. They captured the strong fortress of Masada on the borders of the Dead Sea and put the Roman garrison to the sword.

Eliezer, governor of the temple and captain of its guard, placed himself at the head of a revolutionary group which took the name of Zealots — the same *in name* as the party organized by Judas Gamala in opposition to the census under Quirinius in 6 A. D. They attacked the castle of Antonia and after a two days siege captured it and executed the Roman guard. Soon many cities of Palestine assumed an air of independence.

Cestius, the Roman prefect of Syria, advanced against the rebels with an army of ten thousand Roman troops and thirteen thousand allies. During the feast of Tabernacles, in 66 A. D., Cestius pitched his camp at Gabao (*El Jeb*), about six miles north of Jerusalem.[5] After waiting three days to give the city time to consider his proposition to surrender, he advanced and seized the suburbs. The defenders drew back within the inner walls and hurled stones and javelins on the Roman legionaires who repeatedly attacked them.

As a means of protection the Roman soliders formed a roof of shields, each row fitting over the other like scales, under which they patiently worked away at the task of undermining the walls. Six months of the siege passed by and the fortunes of war seemed to favor the Romans. Cestius seems to have been disposed to follow up his advantage and force the walls, but was diverted from his purpose by one of his principal offiers at the suggestion of Florus, who is said to have wished to prolong the war.

The more considerate of the Jews were about to open the gates when, without any apparent reason, the army withdrew from the siege. The Jews, seeing the retreating columns, rushed out and cast their missiles of death on the legions as they retreated through the narrow passes. The Romans left behind six thousand dead, and immense quantities of war materials, which the Jews quickly appropriated; the Jews returned to Jerusalem confident of ultimate victory. The Christians, along with others who advocated peace, took advantage of the occasion and left the city "as from a ship that was going to sink."[6]

When Nero, the Roman emperor, heard of the strange retreat of Cestius, he sent Vespasian, one of the ablest of his generals, to take command of the forces of Syria and carry on the war against the Jews. Vespasian sent his son Titus to Alexandria in Egypt to bring the fifth and tenth Roman legions to Ptolemais where they were met by auxiliaries from the surrounding countries including a thousand horsemen and five thousand footmen which were sent by Malchus, the King of Arabia. The whole army, including the auxiliaries, numbered sixty thousand, besides the servants who followed in vast numbers.

With one hundred and sixty military engines and a famous battering ram, Vespasian advanced against the cities in Galilee. They first attacked Jotopata where Josephus, the governor, was in command. The Jews pored down boiling oil on the Roman soldiers, but the Romans built fifty strong towers near the walls whence, out of reach of the boiling oil, the soldiers could hurl stones and throw javelins. Jotopata held out forty-seven days; then, at early dawn of July 1, 67 A.D., the Romans made a surprise attack and took the strong city The women were reserved for slaves, fifteen thousand of the men were killed, and two thousand were sent to help cut the canal of Corinth.

Josephus and some of his leading men jumped into a dry well, and from thence went into an underground cavern. When they were discovered and asked to surrender on condition that their lives be spared, Josephus desired to do so, but his comrades argued that they should die together. Their death pact progressed until only Josephus and one comrade were left alive, then by mutual consent the two walked out and surrendered themselves to the Romans. Assuming the role of a prophet, Josephus advised them that Vespasian would soon become the emperor of the Roman empire. The Romans attached Josephus and thereafter used him as an advisor in the Palestinian campaign.

During the following months the other cities of Galilee fell to the Roman army. At the siege of Gischala the Jewish general, known as John of Gischala, feigned to accept the Roman offer of protection for surrender, but begged that the Romans would recognize the sacredness of the sabbath day and withdraw their army until the following day when terms could be formally concluded. When Titus, in all good faith, withdrew his troops for the night, John of Gischala and his band of Zealots marched out of the city under cover of darkness and made their way to Jerusalem. The Romans then went into winter camp at Caesaera.[7]

During the winter political affairs were unsettled in the Roman empire. A revolt broke out in Spain, spread to Gaul, and finally to Rome itself. Nero left the throne, attempted to escape for his life but met his death at the hands of assassins. Civil war ensued in which ambitious generals struggled for the throne. After one year of disturbance and turmoil, the army, which in those days held the balance of power, acclaimed Vespasian emperor, and soon he was away for Rome. To Titus was left the task of marching against Jerusalem.[8]

With a force of eighty thousand fighting men, the son of the emperor made his appearance before the city of Jerusalem in February of 70 A.D. fully expecting quickly to force the city into submission. He had brought with him a larger number of battering machines than had been used in the warfare of that time, and was accompanied by King Agrippa, Tiberius Alexander, and Josephus, the future historian.

Shortly before the passover many Jews came to assist in the defense of their city and still others came as pilgrims. When once they found themselves within the city they were obliged to take sides with one of three factions which fought each other because of disputes over war methods, temperament, and personal animosities. "One held the upper town, one the lower, and one the temple area in between. None cooperated with another; riots and assassinations were frequent, while the most powerful legions in the world waited at the gates."[9]

A few days before the passover, Titus took six hundred horsemen and rode about Jerusalem to survey the situation. The Jews attacked him with darts, javelins, and arrows. He managed to escape with a slight wound.[10] During the inaction which followed still other thousands of Jews flocked to Jerusalem to celebrate the *last* passover. Whether they knew or had any presentiment of the fate which awaited them no one can know, but they continued to gather until six hundred thousand, or as Josephus says one million, one hundred thousand, were crowded within the city.

Titus then appeared before the city with his legions, and summoned the inhabitants to surrender; the demand was submission, acknowledgement of the Roman rule, and the payment of taxes. His hope was to secure their submission without destroying the city. This he desired that he might return to Rome and enjoy the honors befitting his great position. Then, too, he was said to be devoted to a Judean princess, for whose sake he desired to spare the city.

The Judeans refused to negotiate with the Roman general. They had sworn to defend their city with their lives, and would not consider surrender. The siege began in earnest. The groves and gardens to the north and west of Jerusalem were destroyed.

The besiegers then drew nearer, encamped on three sides of the city and raised their engines against the outer wall. The operations were begun during passover (March or April, 70 A.D.) when Titus believed the Jews would not fight, but they rushed to the defense of their city, destroyed the battering rams, scattered the workmen, and brought alarm and confusion in the ranks of the Roman army.

The besieged threw massive stones and poured boiling oil upon the heads of their assailants, and even seized the ponderous missiles that were hurled into the city, and hurled them back as tools of destruction upon their enemy. In fifteen days the Romans had seized the outer wall and taken possession of Bezetha. Fighting continued for seventeen days during which the Romans succeeded in raising their banks opposite the tower of Antonia, but they stood for only a short time for some Jews succeeded in creeping through a subterranean passage and destroying them by fire.

The Jews, however, were in greater danger every day. Josephus pled with them to surrender, but his pleas only increased their anger. Titus crucified as many as five hundred Jewish prisoners a day, and cut off the hands of others and sent them back into the city. Yet there were no signs of surrender.

Titus settled down to a long siege. Famine stalked through the city, provisions failed and the situation within the city grew desperate. Houses and streets were filled with unburied corpses. Some pled for their fellow-men to surrender, but it was of no avail, the *Zealots* were determined to defend the city unto death. The disintegrating forces of party faction all but wrought havoc within the walls of Jerusalem while Titus' legions laid siege from without. Some of the inhabitants wrote accounts of the state of the city, tied them to arrow heads and shot them into the Roman camps.

In another month the earthworks were completed and the battering rams were again pointing at the tower of Antonia. Then soon the wall went down, but the Romans were surprised to find that they faced an *inner wall* which had been erected behind the one they had succeeded in destroying.

Then the daily sacrifices ceased on account of the scarcity of animals. Titus again summoned the people to surrender, but the mere sight of the man who bore the message enraged the Jews. The battering rams were raised against the sacred wall of the temple. The inhabitants were suffering cruelly from famine. Distinction between rich and poor was obliterated. Money lost its value for it could not purchase bread. They fought desperately in the streets over the most loathesome and disgusting food, a handful of straw, a piece of leather, or offal thrown to the dogs.[11]

The wealthy Martha, wife of the high priest Joshua ben Gemala, who had been accustomed to step on carpets from the house to the temple, was found searching the town like the very poorest for a morsel of food of even the poorest kind. One woman killed and devoured her own child.[12] Unburied corpses increased in the streets and houses until the sultry summer sun caused the populace to fall a prey to sickness, famine and the sword, but the army of the besieged fought on.

> He saw his sons by dubious slaughter fall,
> And war without, and death within the wall.
> Wide-wasting Plague, gaunt Famine, mad Despair,
> And dire Debate, and clamorous Strife were there,
> Love, strong as death, retained his might no more,
> And the pale parent drank her children's gore.[13]

Meanwhile the Romans began battering the outer walls of the temple, and Titus relinquished his hope of sparing the sacred edifice, yet determined to do all possible to save it. A council of war was called. This council consisted of six of the chief generals of the army; three advised the destruction of the temple, which if spared, would inevitably remain a focus for rebellion. Titus was opposed to this decision, partly on account of the feelings for Princess Bernice; and three of the council agreeing with their leader, it was decided to take the temple, but not to destroy it.

Twice did the besieged attempt to sally forth and drive back the Romans, but it was then too late. The doom of the city was inevitable. The hour of the City's doom was about to strike, and in striking, leave an echo that would ring through the centuries to come. The besieged attempted one more furious onslaught upon their enemies. They were again defeated, and again driven back to their sheltering walls. But this time they were closely followed by the Romans, one of whom, seizing a burning fire brand, mounted upon a comrade's shoulder, and flung his terrible missile through the so-called golden window of the temple.

The fire blazed up; "it caught the wooden beams of the Sanctuary, and rose in flames heavenward. At this sight the bravest of the Judeans recoiled terror-stricken. Titus hurried to the spot with his troops, and shouted to the soldiers to extinguish the flames. But no one heeded him. The maddened soldiery plunged into the courts of the temple, killing all who came within their reach, and hurling their fire brands into the blazing building. Titus, unable to control his legions, and urged by curiosity, penetrated into the Holy of Holies."[14]

The Jews became desperate in their death agonies, and closed wildly upon their assailants.

Their burning temple rose in lurid light,
To their lov'd altars paid a parting groan,
And in their country's woes forgot their own.
As 'mid the cedar courts, and gates of gold,
The trampled ranks in miry carnage roll'd.
To save their temple every hand essay'd,
And with cold fingers grasped the feeble blade
Through their torn veins reviving fury ran,
And life's last anger warmed the dying man!

Yet still destruction sweeps the lonely plain,
And heroes lift the generous sword in vain.
Still o'er her sky the clouds of anger roll,
And God's revenge hangs heavy on her soul.

The shouts of victory, the shrieks of despair, and fierce hissing of flames, making the very earth tremble and the air vibrate, rose in one hideous din, which echoed from the tottering walls of the sanctuary to the mountain heights of Judea.

There congregated clusters of trembling people from all the country round who beheld in the ascending flames the sign that the glory of their nation was departing. Many of the inhabitants of Jerusalem, unwilling to outlive their beloved temple, cast themselves headlong into the burning mass. But thousands of men, women, and children, in spite of the fierce onslaughts of the legions, and the rapidly increasing flames, clung fondly to the inner court.

The temple was burnt to the ground, leaving only a few smouldering ruins rising like gigantic ghosts from the ashes. A few of the priests had escaped to the tops of the walls, where they remained without food for some days, until they were compelled to surrender. Titus ordered their instant execution, saying, "Priests must fall with their temple." The conquering legions raised their standards in the midst of the ruins, sacrificed to their gods in the Holy Place, and saluted Titus as emperor.[15]

But the struggle was not over. The leaders of the rebellion had retreated to the upper city with some of their followers. John and Simon swore they would never lay down their arms nor surrender unless they were permitted to pass armed through the Roman camp. But Titus bade them throw themselves upon his mercy, which they refused. The Romans began to raise their embankment and after eighteen days of labor the siege of the upper city began. At last they were able to scale the walls and seize the fortresses; then spread through the city, plundering and murdering the wretched inhabitants.

On September eighth all resistance ended, and the survivors were driven into enclosures where they were assorted — some for death and some for slavery.[16] The walls of the Sacred City were entirely leveled, Titus leaving only the three fortresses of Hippicus, Mariamne, and Phasael to stand as lasting witnesses of his victory. "Under the ruins of Jerusalem and her temple lay buried the last remnant of Judea's independence." More than one million lives were lost during the siege. Jerusalem was left a heap of ruins, in charge of the tenth Roman legion.

Zion sat weeping in the midst of her ruins and fallen glories.

There still remained three fortresses that were not taken — Machaerus, Herodium, and Masada. Two of them were in the neighborhood of the Dead Sea, and the other between the Dead Sea and Bethlehem. Machaerus and Herodium soon capitulated to the Romans; but the fortress of Masada perched high on the almost impregnable promontory overlooking the strange waters of the Dead Sea remained unconquered and refused to yield — the defenders long resisting every onslaught of the Romans.

After two years, however, when their cause seemed hopeless, their commander called his men together and proposed that they should kill their wives and children, then kill each other until only one was left, who was to set fire to the fortress, then take his own life. Nine hundred and sixty persons perished in the carrying out of this gruesome death pact. And for the first century every semblance of Jewish military power ceased in Palestine.

## Chapter XIX

# THE DISPERSION OF THE JEWS

From the very beginning of the Jewish race there had sounded the voice of Jehovah through His prophets, telling of their wanderings and dispersions — that they would be scattered among the heathen.[1] And if ever the prophesies concerning any people have come true, this has certainly been the case with Israel.

The lure of adventure and the love of gain must have called many of Jacob's descendants from their fatherland while their national history was yet young. Some were taken away as captives; others were driven from their country by famine. Joseph's forced departure, being sold as a slave, was exceedingly significant.[2] The migration of Elimelech and Naomi, with their two sons, going to dwell in Moab in the time of famine is possibly but one case in many.[3] David's parents being cared for in Moab while he was hiding from Saul[4] and other such incidents cast much light on the manner in which Jewish people began to filter through the lines into other countries — some to return, it is true, but perhaps many of lesser importance never again to live in their homeland.

Israel and Judah were constantly in touch with foreign courts, and were often the victims of their greed and imperialism.[5] Their chief dispersions, however, are to be accounted for in their deportations, captivities, and colonizations. Their principal deportations and captivities are four in number: the Assyrian, the Babylonian, the Grecian, and the Roman. Their colonizations were many.

The Assyrian captivity began in 734 B.C. when Tiglath Pileser III carried away many of the Israelites, and was continued in 722 B.C. when the city of Samaria was taken and twenty-seven thousand, two hundred and eighty Israelites were deported into Mesopotamia and Media. The first part of the Babylonian captivity, in which the people of *Judah* were carried away by Nebuchadnezzar, took place about 605 B.C. (Some say 597 B.C.), and the second part came with the fall of Jerusalem in 587-6 B.C. when the city walls were razed to the ground and Solomon's temple destroyed. Zedekiah, the helpless king of Judah, was compelled to witness the excution of his own sons, was deprived of his eyesight, bound in chains, and carried captive to Babylon. Along with him were taken most of the leading inhabitants of Judah. Only enough were left to be vine dressers and husbandmen.

After this Jerusalem lay desolate until 536 B. C. when Cyrus, King of the Persians, conquered Babylon and permitted a remnant of people under Zerubbabel to return and rebuild the temple. Another part returned with Ezra in 458 B. C. and others followed under Nehemiah in 445 B. C.

It is usually estimated that about one-sixth of the Jews returned to Jerusalem. Those who did not return came to be known as "the *Dispersed.*" Many continued to live in Assyria, while some fled into Southern Arabia, settling in Yemen (Sheba). From this time forth little or nothing is known of the *Ten Tribes of Israel;* they came to be designated as "The Lost Tribes." It may be that they are not so completely "lost" as the annals of history would indicate, yet it is certain that many of them intermarried and merged with the people among whom they dwelt.

In Jeremiah's time (629-587 B.C.) a large company of apostate Jews went to dwell in Egypt where they hoped to "see no war, nor hear the sound of the trumpet, nor have hunger of bread,"[6] but to burn incense to "the queen of heaven, and to pour out drink offerings unto her,"[7] for which they had been rebuked in Palestine.

Seleucus I, fully aware of the aptitude of the Jews as colonists, invited them to come to dwell in the city of Antioch which he had so recently founded (300 B. C.). When his invitation received a ready response the Jews were granted their own governor and admitted to the same advantages as the Greeks.[8]

In 198 B. C., Onias IV, the son of the deposed high priest Onias III, was disappointed in his expectations of receiving the office of his father, and betook himself with a considerable number of his followers to Egypt, obtained a grant of land from Ptolemy VI and constructed a temple at Leontopolis similar to that of Jerusalem.[9] Jews from every part of Egypt attended the annual Passover feast held at this temple. The district between Memphis and Pelusium came to be known as the "country of Onias" and Ptolemy VII gave to Onias the revenues of this territory for the support of the temple. The sacred edifice remained until some time after the destruction of Jerusalem by Titus.[10]

During the wars of the third and second centuries before Christ, thousands of Jews were made captives and reduced to slavery. Often these captives were so numerous as to glut the markets. However, these Jews did not usually remain in slavery very long for as a rule they "clung with unswerving attachment" to their religion, which from the viewpoint of their masters, often made them inefficient servants. Then, too, because of the close federation of the Jewish brotherhood, which is one of their lasting traits, they often found fellow-Jews who were willing to pay the amount necessary for their ransom.[11] The Jews thus freed, usually remained in the land where they were released, and there in connection with their brethren established Jewish communities.

Philo tells us that the Jewish community in Rome owed its origin to released prisoners of war, even before Pompey carried his Jewish captives thither in 63 B.C.[12] Some few returned to Jerusalem as is evidenced by the "synagogue of the Libertines," which recent archaeological researches have revealed.[13]

According to tradition, Ptolemy I took some thirty thousand Jews with him to Egypt where they were used as a garrison for the frontiers. Some authorities consider the number too high, yet Josephus says that Ptolemy did make such use of "a great many" of the Jews, and that one hundred and twenty thousand Egyptian Jews were given their liberty by Phiadelphus Ptolemy.[14]

The Roman Senate, under Tiberias, sent four thousand Jews to Rome to wage a war in Sardinia. Many of them perished, but it is generally supposed that the survivors formed the nucleus of a Jewish community in that country.[15] Many other rulers made attractive offers to the Jews if they would come to settle in their country, for the simple reason that the Jews were industrious and aggressive, which usually meant that prosperity came to every locality in which they settled.

According to Josephus, Antiochus settled two thousand Jewish families in Lydia and Phrygia, in Asia Minor, granting to them the privilege of their own laws, extensive territorial possessions, and exemption from all tribute for ten years.[16] Their prosperity in one city opened the way for them in another until most of the larger cities of Asia Minor contained many Jewish inhabitants. From Asia Minor they crossed into Greece and on further into Europe. Philo, a well-known contemporary of Josephus, quotes a letter which was supposed to have been written by King Agrippa to Caligula. The letter gives one an idea of the extent of the Jewish settlements; it reads as follows:

> This sacred city, the Holy Jerusalem, is the metropolis, not only of the one country Judea, but of most lands, by reason of the settlements she has sent from time to time to the bordering lands of Egypt, Phoenicia, and the rest of Syria; also into the more remote Pamphylia, Cilicia, most of Asia as far as the recesses of Pontus; likewise to Europe, Thessaly, Boeotia, and Macedonia, Astolia, Attica, Argos, Corinth, as well as most

> of the best parts of the Peloponnese. And not only are the continents full of Jewish settlements, but so are the most famous islands — Euboea, Cyprus, Crete. I omit the lands beyond the Euphrates; for nearly all Babylon, and whatever other satraps have good land, have Jewish settlers. If, therefore, my fatherland obtain from you benefits, not one city, but tens of thousands are put under obligation, which are settled over every latitude of the habitable world — in Europe, Asia, Libya, in continents, islands, on seacoasts and far inland.[17]

Alexander the Great founded the city of Alexandria, and after his death a Jewish colony there was granted a charter by Ptolemy. These Jews greatly prospered until Alexandria became one of their greatest gathering places and centers outside of Jerusalem. Here their Sanhedrin was second only to that of Jerusalem. The Jews were excellent clerks and secretaries and the government made use of them in the work of administration. About 270 B.C., according to the so-called "Letter of Aristeas," King Ptolemy Philadelphus resolved to enrich his new library at Alexandria by the various sacred books. Since many of his citizens were Jews he became interested in their law and sent to the high priest at Jerusalem for translators. Seventy-two of these were dispatched to him, six from each of the twelve tribes, or seventy-two as corresponding to the number of the Sanhedrin. The fruit of their labors became known as the "Septuagint" version of the Old Testament.

Alexandria was a city of six hundred thousand Egyptian, Jewish, and Grecian inhabitants. It was divided into five sections; two of which were occupied by the Jews. Philo tells us that there were no less than one million Jews living in Egypt in his day.[18]

It has been estimated that, at the opening of the Christian era, there were some four million Jews living in the various parts of Europe, Asia, and Africa; and that only about seven hundred thousand of these lived in Zion. In speaking of this era, Graetz says:

> There was hardly a corner in the two great predominant kingdoms of that time, the Roman and the Parthian, in which the Judeans were not living, and where they had not formed themselves into a religious community. The shores of the great midland sea and the banks of all the principal rivers of the old world, of the Nile, the Euphrates, the Tigris, and the Danube were peopled with Judeans.[19]

In the book of the Acts the Jewish people are spoken of as being settled in large numbers in such cities as Philippi, Thessalonica, Athens, Corinth, and Rome. James addressed his epistle to "the twelve tribes *scattered abroad*."[20]

The destruction of Jerusalem by Titus, in 70 A.D., brought about the scattering of the Jews as had no event in all their history. From the burning temple ascended dark clouds of smoke trailing their way high into the heavens, informing the surviving Judeans and the inhabitants of all the surrounding countries that the city which had been set upon a hill was falling with a crash that would echo on the far-off shores of both time and eternity. The event spoke with a note of finality that assured the Romans that there would be a continuation of anything resembling a Jewish state.

Had the essence of the Jewish religion been wholly tied up with the temple it too would have vanished like the last streaks of day when night comes down with its chill; but Judaism, based on some principle deeper than outward symbols, was to survive even after its sanctuary and sacrifices had been taken away.

In terror did many flee from the sight of the fallen city; others deliberately took paths leading they hardly knew whither — only away from Jerusalem. However, the majority of the survivors were held as captives; and the account of their treatment at the hands of the Romans is a pathetic and sordid story. Many of the older people were slain outright or permitted to starve; the young men over seventeen were taken away for the Roman triumphs — to fight with wild beasts, to become gladiators, or to meet death in some other unnatural fashion. Thousands of young men were taken away to work out their lives in Roman mines, while thousands of young women, and children under sixteen, were herded together and driven away to the slave marts of the world.

This marching mass of Jewish captives so glutted the slave markets as to make it necessary for their captors to sell them at incredibly low prices. Thousands of the choicest Jews were taken with Titus and his conquering host to Rome. Along the way — at Caesarea, Beirut, and Antioch — many were done to death in the arena for no better reason than that the emperor and his friends should be entertained.

The victorious general entered Rome followed by a train of heavily chained, stalwart Judeans. This imperial city always kept high holiday on such occasions; and it was the custom to hurl the enemy leader from the Tarpeian rock, as a sacrifice to the Roman gods. Simon ben Giora, one of the most valiant and uncompromising of the Jewish leaders, was thus hurled to his death.

To commemorate the occasion Titus struck coins, and in his honor the Senate erected an arch of triumph. On the coins Judea was represented as a sorrowing woman sitting with fettered hands under a palm tree, while around the coin was the tell-tale inscription:

*"Judaea Capta"* ("The captive Judaea")

The arch which was erected still stands, and upon it are carved the reliefs of the Romans bearing the seven-branched golden candle-stick and the vessels of the temple.

The slave markets were not only glutted with Jewish slaves, and the proud Jew humiliated before Rome and all the world, but everywhere they began to be depreciated and legislated against as never before in the history of the world. Their humiliation was great; so great as finally to bring forth the uprising of the Jews of Egypt, of Mesopotamia, of Cyprus, and of Cyrene. The Egyptian rebellion was suppressed, thousands were killed in Mesopotamia, and Cyprus was drenched with blood and the Jews were forbidden ever again to set foot on the island of Cyprus. Even Jewish merchants who sought temporary refuge were done to death.

For decades after Titus destroyed Jerusalem the Jews who were permitted to remain in Palestine were not only submissive, but appeared grateful for the privilege of carrying on life and religion in the country so dear to their hearts. Hadrian, who ruled the Roman empire from 117 A.D. to 138 A.D., permitted the Jews to strengthen themselves in certain centers and showed them many favors at the beginning of his reign, but favors reflected their ruin in that they again felt their importance and became restless for revolt against Roman rule.[21]

In the year 130 A.D. — sixty years after Titus had destroyed Jerusalem — Hadrian laid plans to rebuild the Holy City.[22] The Jews petitioned him to rebuild their beloved temple, and he is said to have promised to do so, but on hearing of this the Samaritans protested and the Jews acted in such a way as to cause Hadrian to not only withdraw his promise but erect a temple to Jupiter on one portion of the temple area and drive a plowshare over the other portion and forbid the Jews to enter the heathenized city.

Such sad reverses and such flagrant desecration fanned into a flame the hope of a Messiah who should give the victory to the ancient people of God over all their enemies. The spirit of expectancy was so great that in 132 A.D. a daring young Jewish warrior named Bar Cochba arose and declared himself to be that "Star" that was to come out of Jacob and that "Sceptre" of Israel that should "smite the corners of Moab, and destroy all the children of Seth."[23]

Rabbi Akiba, a man of mighty influence among the Jews, not only accepted Bar Cochba as the Messiah but declared that the prophecy of Haggai was ready to be fulfilled when Jehovah would "shake the heavens and the earth, and . . . overthrow the throne of kingdoms, and . . . destroy the strength of the kingdoms of the heathen."

Insurrection broke out at once, and Bar Cochba became the "brain and sword" of the revolt. All who followed him were required to have one of their fingers hewn off as pledge of their determination to go through with the revolt. Some two hundred thousand enlisted with the young warrior. One victory followed another until fifty strong places and nearly one thousand villages were taken from the Romans. To many it seemed that another Maccabean had arisen, while others were certain that Bar Cochba was really the Messiah.

But the victories were not to last long for the Emperor Hadrian summoned the Fifth Macedonian and the tenth Claudian legions from the Danube and sent Severus, his most distinguished military leader, to lead these legions into Palestine. They reduced to submission city after city and district after district until in 135 A.D., during the third year of the revolt, Bar Cochba and his followers gathered at Bether (now called "Bittir" or *Khurbet el Yehud* — "Ruin of the Jews") an immensely strong Jewish fortress city six miles southwest of Jerusalem, where they purposed to make their *last stand.*

The Roman legions surrounded the stronghold, scaled its steep cliffs, effected a breach in its walls and butchered eighty thousand Jewish soldiers. Bar Cochba was slain and Rabbi Akiba, the standard bearer of the revolt, was taken prisoner and flayed alive, repeating as he died the grand words of the morning prayer of the temple, "Hear, O Israel! the Lord our God is one God."[24]

One-half million perished or were taken captive and the Bittir catastrophe spoke with a note of finality that even the Jewish mind could entirely comprehend. The pathetic incident went down in history as the last attempt of the Jews to recover their fatherland by force. Hadrian completed the rebuilding of Jerusalem and dedicated it under the name of *Aelia Capitolina,* in honor of the patron god of Rome, and issued an edict forbidding circumcision, the rite which distinguished Jews from other people.

Thenceforth the Jews were set adrift on the currents of the world's barbarism and civilization. They were all *supposed* to have been driven from Palestine, and were cursed and kicked and spit upon wherever they went. The proverbial "wandering Jew" had its rise in the minds of men as the descendants of Jacob were persecuted from country to country and from place to place. The Jews soon came to be despised in every land — the outcasts of the world.

> Tribes of the wandering foot and weary breast,
> How shall ye flee away and be at rest?
> The wild dove hath her nest, the fox his cave,
> Mankind their country — Israel but the grave.[25]

## Chapter xx

# THE PERIOD OF PILGRIMAGES

From the fall of Jerusalem in 70 A.D. to the triumph of Constantine in 312 A.D., the Roman rulers carried on a well-planned program to stamp out the rapid growth of the group known as "Christians." These all too human rulers were not only pagan in religion, but imagined themselves divine, therefore required each of their subjects throughout the vast empire to burn a pinch of incense to the ruler himself. The Christians were not only averse to anything that bore the semblance of paganism, but opposed everything that would in any way help on the pernicious practice or tend to connect them with worldliness in general.

They preached against pagan practices, opposed selling fodder for sacrificial animals, and banned the games and contests in the arena as well as the social functions of their day. The issue was clear-cut: the Christians could *tolerate the world and conform to it, or condemn it and seek to save it.* They chose the latter course with the result that they were dubbed "enemies of society." As such they were brought before magistrates, put through hurried "trials" and condemned to be thrown to the lions, gored to death by angry cattle, or banished to some lonely isle where death was more likely than life. Their minds were set on the salvation of men from sin, therefore they would not recant.

All over the empire — in almost every city and village — stalwart characters of both sexes had fallen as martyrs — the victims of pagan persecution. Yet the growth of Christianity was most phenomenal. Then in 312 A.D. Constantine proclaimed Christianity the state religion of the empire, ornamented the Roman eagle with the cross, and the dark night of persecution passed. The thought of Christians instinctively turned toward Bethlehem, Nazareth, and most of all, toward the Holy City of Jerusalem outside whose gray walls the dark tragedy of the crucifixion had set the precedent for deathless love.

Alexander, the friend of Origen, had made a journey to Jerusalem as early as 212 A.D. "for the sake of prayer and investigation of the places."[1] And Origen himself had gone in 216 A.D., but the waves of persecution had held the attention of the church until Constantine's bold move, then royalty itself led the way to the land of sacred memories.

Being an exceptionally keen politician, and desiring to show favor to his Christian subjects, Constantine supported a move to locate, recover, and adorn the tomb in which Christ's body had lain.

Helena, the royal mother of Emperor Constantine, came to the Holy Land and to the city of Jerusalem, in the year 326 A.D. to visit the sacred sites where prophecy had been fulfilled, and "pay the debt of pious feeling to God the King of all." On the way she delivered captives, relieved the oppressed, and adorned churches. With priests as her assistants she dug into a certain mound inside the present walls of Jerusalem[2] and found a sepulchre. Three crosses were located nearby — one for the Saviour and one for each of the thieves crucified with Him. In an attempt to ascertain which was Christ's cross we are told that these crosses in turn were taken to the bedside of a devout woman who was very ill. On beholding the first cross she grew hysterical, the second brought on spasms, but when the third was brought in, the afflicted woman was completely restored. This was therefore proclaimed the *True Cross* of Christ.

Proceeding to Bethlehem, Helena selected the cave in which Christ had been born, then to the Mount of Olives where the very spot, and even the last footprint previous to Christ's ascension, was 'fixed' once and for all. At Bethlehem, over the cave of the nativity, a basilica was built with rare columns said to have been once used in the temple at Jerusalem. The floors were of marble slabs and unusual mosaics which were uncovered during August of 1934 and found in a state of almost perfect preservation.

Another church was erected on the Mount of Olives,[3] and an oratory over the supposed site of the sepulchre, pending the time when a suitable church edifice should be erected. Helena spread the news, the Christian world rejoiced, and the emperor gave orders for Macarius, Bishop of Jerusalem, to erect an extraordinarily fine structure over the supposed place of Christ's crucifixion and burial.

Very soon after the recovery of these cities came a Christian pilgrim from Bordeaux, France, who visited Jerusalem and the various places of Biblical fame in Palestine. This was during the year 333 A. D. Soon afterwards he reduced the account of his pilgrimage to writing. His style was so vivid and the route and places he visited so minutely described that in the hearts of thousands there was created an unquenchable desire to follow his footsteps.

A beautiful and substantial building arose over the supposed site of Calvary. In fact, it was a duplex structure: one part over the small mound which they thought to be Calvary and the other over the tomb where they said Christ had been buried. In the year 337 this building was dedicated and called "The Church of the Holy Sepulchre." The pilgrimages began to be made. From almost all Christendom pilgrims came weeping, praying and worshipping.

Within a few decades, the desire to pray at the sacred places in the Holy Land became the *ruling* passion of multiplied thousands who classed themselves as followers of the Christ of Calvary. With persecution removed, the Christian church was soon 'lulled in the lap of comfortable popularity,' therefore grew weak and effeminate, and turned from repentance to penance, from the living Christ enthroned within the human heart to the meager comfort and strength derived from an empty tomb.[4]

Many a sinful soul longed for relief and finding it not in the mass administered in his home church, went to Palestine, where, he was assured, he would find that spiritual help which his soul so ardently desired. Many found better health and felt more religious, therefore returned to Europe, sold their property and returned to Palestine where they took up permanent residence. Some maintained private homes and others lived in monasteries. All this gave European Christians a great incentive to visit Palestine. The urge became so strong that the roads were thronged with believers of every rank, and almost every age.

The average pilgrim usually followed a well-marked road, paid the usual toll, and endured a variety of hardships and privations. If he ran the gauntlet of danger and disease and returned home safely he was looked upon as a superior person. He had trod the earth and breathed the air of Palestine, visited the Church of the Nativity at Bethlehem and the Holy Sepulchre at Jerusalem, walked the Galilean shores and bathed in the Jordan where Christ had been baptized. His sins were remitted, he could begin life over again, and at death wear his Palestinian shirt as a winding sheet and thereby be assured of heaven.

The fixing, without hesitation, of almost all the sacred rites recorded in the New Testament, increased interest among pilgrims, even though it militated against accuracy. Many pilgrims bore away water from the Jordan, earth from the sepulchre, and a splinter from the "true cross" that could ever replenish itself.[5] Pious frauds in the form of relics were common, and stories of unusual happenings were invented when it seemed well to stimulate further zeal. These, along with the real experiences, stirred Europe until pilgrims came from almost all quarters of the inhabited globe *to fulfill the cherished wishes of a lifetime.* Jerusalem became a prosperous city, and the Christians the foremost people of the day.

While basking in the sunlight of prosperity and popularity, the Christians forgot the teachings of their Lord and brought ignominy and shame on their heads by mistreating the Jews who resided in Jerusalem and Palestine. Decrees were issued against them, and they were despised and frequently persecuted. Then suddenly the tide turned when Julian, the "apostate", lifted the imperial scepter at Rome. His renunciation of Christianity led him to make a desperate effort to revive fallen paganism.

In Palestine his sympathies were for the Jews, and against the Christians. He annulled all legislation curtailing the rights of the Jews and promised to rebuild the temple as a means of disproving the prophecy of Christ.[6] The long line of Christian pilgrims thinned, and it seemed that a darker day had suddenly dawned.

The plan to rebuild the temple on Mount Moriah was frustrated, as is acknowledged by Christian and pagan writers, by fire bursting forth from the foundation, driving away the workmen and compelling them to abandon their work. It was supposed that this occurrence was brought about by supernatural power, but it is more than probable that the numerous subterannean passages had become heavy with inflammable gas which took fire from the workmen's torches, thus causing the mysterious explosion which frightened the workmen from the scene and caused the work to be suspended.

While Julian was vainly striving to check Christianity he was obliged to lead a campaign against the Persians, in which he met with many reverses. When the Roman rear guard was thrown into disorder by a charge of the new Persians, Julian rushed into the midst of the fray and was shot by an arrow. While he was endeavoring to draw it out, he was pierced by another in his fingers. Fainting and bloody he fell from his horse and was carried to his tent where on that night, in 363 A.D., he drew forth the arrow from his wound, and as the blood spurted forth he is said to have exclaimed, "There! Take thy fill, Galilean! Thou has conquered at last!"

His short reign of one year and eight months had been to the Christians as a bad dream that passed with the morning, but to the Jews as a rainbow that all too soon faded and failed to produce in subtance that which it had promised. If the influence of his reign brought an abatement in enthusiasm for visiting Palestine, then his early death and the flames reported to have burst forth from the temple site added fervor to the general enthusiasm for pilgrimages.

The dangers of the way were diminished as those who had formerly opposed the passage of the pilgrims had come to consider it more profitable to exploit them. Almost all the roads were opened to those who desired to visit Palestine and pray at the sacred places. Routes were carefully laid down for the pilgrims by various itineraries, but the plan most frequently used was that known as "the itinerary of the Bordeaux pilgrim."[7]

In 830 A.D. Gregory of Nyssa came to Jerusalem on some church affairs and remained. Jerome came to Bethlehem where he took up his abode in a small room within the church of the nativity, and labored for years on literary productions of a religious nature, his greatest work being the translation of the Scriptures into the vernacular of the western world, commonly known as the Vulgate version. His death occurred on September 30, 420 A.D., but long before this his influence had become so powerful that the number of pilgrims to Palestine was increased. Justinian erected on the south portion of the temple area a magnificent Christian church, of which a large portion is preserved in the present Mosque *El Akse.*

During the latter part of the fourth century Paula, accompanied by her daughter, Eudoxia, left Rome for Syria, where she landed at Sidon, came on down the coast visiting Caesarea and other places. Upon her arrival at Jerusalem the governor prepared to receive her with honors, but she declined the offer with the modest and significant words: "To these places we come, not as persons of importance, but as strangers, that we may see in them the foremost men of all nations. Whoever may be the first in Gaul, hasten hither. The Briton, separated from our world, if he has made any progress in religion, leaves the setting sun and seeks a place known to him only by fame and the narratives of Scriptures."[8]

After visiting the principle "holy places" she went for a short trip to Egypt, then returned to Bethlehem where she built a hospice for pilgrims, and there lived in prayer, devotion, and labor until her death — twenty-seven years later.[9] Women pilgrims increased. In fact pilgrimages among both sexes became so numerous and were accompanied by so many dangers to morals and good manners that certain conscientious churchmen felt obliged to use their influence to check the practice that had become so abused.

Augustine advised that God was approached better by love than by long pilgrimages. Gregory of Nyssa pointed out that the pilgrimage of itself aided nothing, and that the way to Palestine led through wicked cities of the East. Women, in particular, he said, would meet with many opportunities for wrong doing. Jerome declared that heaven might be reached as easily from Britain as from Jerusalem, that an innumerable throng of saints never saw the city of Jerusalem and the sacred places, and that these places had often been polluted.[10] But their words for the most part fell on heedless ears. What could be done about it when a decadent church regarded a pilgimage as an act meriting the very highest favor, and accumulating the greatest store of grace?

The downfall of the Roman empire and the Frankish conquest of Gaul brought a slight interruption, yet Gregory of Tours tells us that even during that period of sorrow and reverses the people in Europe were intensely interested in all that concerned Palestine. Many seemed pleased to escape the European arena of warfare and strife, to come to peaceful Palestine to seek out some quiet spot where, undisturbed, they could study and worship. Many of these were as earnest souls as ever sought higher paths, and they did receive spiritual benefit by retiring to a life of study and prayer.

The peace of Palestine, however, was not all that it might have been, for bishops quarreled over the supremacy of their sees, narrow-minded, untruthful monks sold spurious relics to superstitious people, and the "true cross," which was discovered to possess miraculous healing qualities, multiplied itself many times over until portions could be sent to all parts of the world, and yet the original cross remained to be displayed in the church of the Holy Sepulchre.

Superstition and corruption were occupying the center of the stage, when, in 614 A.D. Chosroes II, the Persian conqueror, advanced into Syria and marched on feebly-defended Jerusalem. In a bloody massacre he put thousands to the sword, destroyed the church of the Holy Sepulchre, and carried away the "true cross." Heraculus gathered an army, overtook the Persian conqueror, wrested the cross from him, and returned to his triumphal entry bearing the cross through the Eastern Gate. The city was not only restored to the Christians, but public subscriptions were taken in almost all parts of Christendom and the church of the Holy Sepulchre was rebuilt.

Pilgrims continued to arrive in Jerusalem almost every day, and pious frauds were perpetrated with such boldness as to bring disgrace to the very name of Christ. Jerusalem could not forever remain in the hands of its friends whose acts of pollution and refined paganism constantly increased the menace to these sacred spots. After a few years, there came the *Arab Invasion* which swept all before it. Pilgrimages — such as were made for the next few hundred years — were to take on a decidedly different aspect.

## Chapter XXI

# THE ARAB CONQUEST

In the midst of the shifting sands of the Arabian peninsula, during the latter part of the sixth century, a boy baby was born to one of the families of the *Kuriash* tribe. Bereft of father and mother at a very tender age, he became ward of an uncle, who used the boy as a sheep- and goat-herd near the city of Mecca, and in time permitted him to work among the camels. Eventually he became a camel driver, or a "camel boy" as commonly known in the Levant.

Young manhood arrived and an unusual opportunity was offered *Mohammed* — for such was his name. A wealthy widow, *Cadija* by name, needed a manager for her caravan which was to journey to Bosra, on the border of Palestine. Mohammed was entrusted with the caravan, and did so well that the wealthy widow offered him her hand in marriage. He became owner of the caravan and all the possessions of the widow.

On his trips to Palestine and Syria he came in contact with the religions of the Jews and Christians. Deep meditations engaged his fertile mind, and ere long he came to feel that there were not many gods as his fellow-countrymen had been taught, but that "God is one." *Cadija,* who so thoroughly believed in Mohammed, soon came to believe in his message as firmly as she believed in the man. A faithful servant believed, then a few others became his disciples.

The people of the city of Mecca soon came to depreciate his denunciation of their many gods; therefore he began to cast about for a more favorable locality. Then in the midst of his sincere efforts Cadija died, leaving Mohammed bereft of the nearest, dearest, truest, and most helpful person that was ever to come into his life. After this his keel was not to be so even; he lost his equilibrium, and manifested far more human weakness than heretofore.

One evening as the sun passed down over the western hills of Arabia and ceased to shine on the Gulf of Akaba; when twilight gathered on the Mediterranean Sea and darkness settled in on the city of Mecca, Mohammed was glad; he welcomed the darkness, for this was the night he was to forsake his home city for more congenial surroundings.

Accompanied by his trusted servant, he moved out of the city gate, mounted his camel and trekked northward four hundred miles to the city of Medina where he treated with the people and was received on the grounds that he and his "helpers" were to be protected and encouraged in the promulgation of the doctrine that "God is one."

The *Hegira,* or Mohammed's spectacular flight from Mecca to Medina, occurred in the year 622 A.D., and from that event the Moslems date time; and well they may, for from this date they began to do things that startled the world.

It was exceedingly fortunate for Mohammed and his followers that he lived in one of the most degenerate and disorderly periods of the world's history;[1] which made it possible for him to dream of, plan for, and carry on conquests which he could not have managed under normal conditions.

Soon after his rise to power, Mohammed thoughtfully cast his eyes far out beyond the barren rocks and shifting sands of Arabia and surveyed a system of things which had "waxed old" and was "ready to vanish away." From the summit of power Persia had sunk to the lowest depths of weakness and humiliation. Rome, so long the "mistress of the world," had grown weak, and while suffering from internal decay had been called upon to ward off the invading hordes of barbarians, but had failed. Ere long "the decaying fabric" had fallen asunder, leaving two empires — the East and the West.

The Western empire had but a brief and tempestuous history. Wave after wave of invading barbarisms swept across its sun-kissed soil until in 476 A.D. the empire ceased to exist, and "the darkness of universal barbarism" settled down over the Western empire.

The best that was left of the power and civilization of Rome was represented in the Eastern empire; known in history as the Greek or Byzantine empire; but it stood for very little in the way of religion, intellectual activity, and morals. There was no progress and no promise of a better day to come, but as Clark well says, "only a dogged holding on," "a steady sinking into hopeless decay."[2]

Mohammed's death occurred in 632 A.D., ten years after he began his rise to power. He had succeeded in uniting the countless wild and unrestrained clans and tribes of Arabia under one head, — he was that head. At first his death appeared disastrous, then it was seen that his closest followers had so imbibed his teachings and spirit that his genius led on as effectively as when he lived.

*Abu Bekr,* the first of his successors, was a man of simple life and profound faith. He not only believed and taught all that Mohammed believed and taught but thoroughly understood Mohammed's intentions regarding the invasion of foreign countries; and seemed really to believe that in spirit the Prophet would advance before the invading host as it plunged from the arid peninsula of Arabia into the more favored lands of the world.

As though hastened by an inner urge to accomplish some given task, Abu Bekr, soon after coming into his new position, sent armies out of Arabia. His goal was to take the often coveted "Fertile Crescent" by conquest. They first marched to the Euphrates valley, the country of the ancient Babylonians. The army was led by lieutenant *Khalid*, a young Arab who possessed a keen intellect, a daring spirit, an iron will, and a heart of stone.

He advanced with his army to the banks of the Euphrates where he captured the cities of *Anbar* and *Hira,* defeated and slew the last of the Mandars, sent the ruler's son a captive to Medina, and subjected the country to an annual tribute of seventy thousand pieces of gold.[3] Khalid was then ordered to Syria for the express purpose of assisting in the Syrian conquest, and lieutenant *Said* afterward led the army on into Persia.[4]

The success of Khalid, and the taste of Babylonian spoils confirmed Abu Bekr in the opinion that the Moslems would be victorious in their foreign conquests. Therefore he dispatched a circular letter to the tribes of Arabia:

> In the name of the most merciful God, to the rest of the true believers. Health and happiness, and the mercy and blessing of God be upon you. I praise the most high God, and pray for his prophet Mohammed. This is to acquaint you that I intend to send the true believers into Syria to take it out of the hands of the infidels. And I would have you know, that fighting for religion is an act of obedience to God.[5]

The messengers hastened to the people with the letter, and soon the Arabs were aroused until Medina swarmed with soldiers "panting for action."

Abu Bekr, at a given time, ascended a nearby hill, reviewed the army, then poured forth a fervent prayer for the success of the undertaking. In person, and on foot, he accompanied the army on its first day's journey, and ere they started on the second day, delivered that noted address to the leaders of the conquest:

> Remember that you are always in the presence of Allah, on the verge of death, in the expectation of judgment, and the hope of paradise. Avoid injustice and oppression, consult with your brethren, and study to preserve the love and confidence of your troops. When you fight the battle of Allah, acquit yourselves like men without turning your backs upon your enemies;

let not your victory be stained with the blood of women or children. Destroy no palm-trees nor burn any fields of corn. Cut down no fruit trees, nor do any mischief to cattle, only such as you kill to eat. When you make any covenant or article, stand to it and be as good as your word.

As you advance into the enemy's country you will find some religious persons who live retired in monasteries, and prepare themselves to serve God that way: let them alone, and neither kill them nor destroy their monasteries. But you will find another sort of people that belong to the synagogue of satan, who have shaven crowns; be sure you clove their skulls, and give them no quarter till they either turn Mohammedans or pay tribute.[6]

The first city in their road was the well-fortified city of Bosra. They found the Syrian garrison so strong as to discourage them, in fact they were being defeated, and a riot seemed near at hand when Khalid, "the inspiration of the Moslem army," restored confidence. After a short repose the Moslems performed their ablutions with sand, instead of water, recited their morning prayers, mounted their horses and prepared to move toward the fortress when they saw the gates of Bosra swing wide and the soldiers swarm out. Confident of their strength and certain victory, the people of Bosra had sworn to die in defense of their religion! But they were doomed to disappointment for the Moslem hordes met them with the frantic cry of "Fight! Fight! Paradise! Paradise!" and they were soon thrown into confusion.

In the midst of the uproar of the town the atmosphere grew tense with the ringing of bells and the exclamations of the priests and monks. The Arabs were gaining when Romanus, the governor, advised an early surrender. The people deposed him, then lifted holy crosses, waved consecrated banners and declared for victory, but the deposed governor obtained revenge by informing the enemy of a subterranean passage from his house under the wall of the city. The son of the caliph, with one hundred volunteers, passed through, and with the enemy on the inside and outside, the inevitable occurred — the city of Bosra fell to the sons of Ishmael; and Romanus, the apostate, stood before his former fellow-Christians and took the oath:

I renounce your society, both in this world and the world to come. And I deny him that was crucified, and whosoever worships him. And I choose God for my Lord, Islam for my faith, Mecca for my temple, and the Moslems for my Brethren, and Mohammed for my prophet, who was sent to lead us into the right way, and to exalt the true religion in spite of those who join partners with God.[7]

The Arab forces marched on to the plains of *Aiznadin*, (*Ajnadain*), where they encountered the Greek forces. These, after an engagement or two, offered to give the Arabian soldiers each a turban, a robe, and a piece of gold; ten robes and one hundred pieces to their leader; and one hundred robes and a thousand pieces to the caliph, if they would be at peace with them. The offer was met with scorn as the reckless Khalid answered:

> Ye Christian dogs, you know your option: The Koran, the tribute, or the sword. We people who delight in war, rather than in peace; and we despise your pitiful alms since we shall speedily be masters of your wealth, your families, and your persons.[8]

In the struggle which followed the Arabs won, and their spoil was truly great.

The sad tidings of another Mohammedan victory were carried to Damascus by swift messengers, but the messengers had not been long in the city when the watchers beheld long columns of Arabs approaching, as they were led by Amru with seven thousand horses and the rear brought up by Khalid in person. A patrol of two thousand horses was placed about the city and Arabian chiefs were stationed at their respective places before the seven gates of Damascus. The siege was on in earnest.

The people would soon have surrendered the city but for the encouragement offered by one, Thomas, a noble but fanatical Greek. There was fierce fighting day by day, and one or two engagements took place by night. Then at the hour of midnight on the seventieth day of the siege, one hundred chosen deputies of the clergy and people of the city were introduced to the tent of *Abu Obeidah,* the chief of the Arab command, who was known for his mildness as was Khalid for his harshness. He received and dismissed them with courtesy. They returned with a written agreement that all hostilities should cease; that all voluntary emigrants might depart in safety with as much as they could carry away of their effects, and that those who desired to stay as tributary subjects of the caliph might continue to enjoy their houses and lands and have the use and possession of seven churches.

On the following morning the gate nearest the general was opened and he and the soldiers under his direct command marched in, but a party of a hundred Arabs had opened the gate on the other side of the city, and at their head the hard-hearted Khalid burst in shouting, "No quarter to the enemies of the Lord." His trumpets sounded and a torrent of Christian blood flowed freely in the streets of Damascus. On reaching the church of Saint Mary he *appeared* astonished and provoked to find his comrades at peace with the citizens of the city.

Abu Obeidah, the venerable commander, saluted Khalid and said, "God has delivered the city into my hands by way of surrender, and has saved the believers the trouble of fighting." Whereupon Khalid replied:

"And am I not the lieutenant of the commander of the faithful; have I not taken the city by storm? The unbelievers shall perish by the sword. Fall on." But the commander calmed him, and the chiefs retired into the church of Saint Mary where it was agreed that the sword should be sheathed, and the citizens who cared to do so might remain. On this day of Arab victory, Caliph Bekr died, and was succeeded by Omar.

In a nearby meadow a large encampment was soon formed of "priests, and laymen, of soldiers and citizens, of women and children. They collected with haste and terror their most precious movables, and abandoned, with loud lamentations or silent anguish, their native homes and the pleasant banks of the Paraphar."[9]

The calloused Khalid was untouched by the spectacle of the people's distress, in fact he disputed the right of spoils and sternly declared that after the respite of three days he might pursue the emigrants and treat them as enemies of the Moslems. This he perhaps would not have done but for the passion of a Syrian youth whom historians charge with the ruin of the exiles. Long before the city had been taken a young nobleman named Jonas had been betrothed to a wealthy maiden; but her parents had delayed the wedding. The maiden being persuaded to escape with the man whom she had chosen, the pair reached the gate then called *Keisair* where they bribed the night-watchman and were in the act of passing without the gate when they saw that they were being encompassed by a squadron of Arabs. He exclaimed in the Greek tongue, "The bird is taken." This was a prearranged signal for his sweetheart to hasten back within the city; she obeyed, and he was soon arrested and taken before the lieutenant.[10]

In the presence of Khalid, and under threat of death, the unfortunate Jonas took the oath of the Mohammedan, and thus scorned the Christian faith. This occurred before the city was taken; then when victory turned the Moslems into the city Jonas hastened to the monastery where Eudocia had taken refuge; but her love for Jonas had died; the apostate was scorned. She preferred her religion to her country, and with the refugees left Damascus.

Four days later Jonas persuaded Khalid to follow the exiles. At the head of four hundred horses, in the disguise of Christian Arabs, Khalid pursued the fugitives and fell upon them in butchery. Vast sums of silver and three hundred loads of silk were taken. In the tumult Jonas sought for and found the object of his pursuit; but her resentment was inflamed by his act of treachery, and as Eudocia struggled in his hateful embrace she quickly drew a dagger from her bosom and thrust it deep in her own heart — suicide was sweeter than such captivity.

Another female, the widow of Thomas and the supposed daughter of Heraclius, was spared and released without ransom, while the other Christians were put to the sword. This rashness, coupled with that at Damascus, caused Khalid to be temporarily suspended as a leader of the Moslem army, yet soon he again resumed command and continued his daring warfare.

In one engagement after another the Arabian armies were victorious; then they fell back to a position south of the Sea of Galilee as the Christian forces were being marshalled against them in vast numbers. In the neighborhood of Bosra the Yarmuk river descends rapidly and finds its way into the Jordan. Here on the banks of this stream the vast host of Romans and Greeks engaged the Arabians in battle in the year 636 A.D. Though the imperial forces were much larger than those of the Arabs, the Arabs by strategy forced the imperial army into the lowland, then closed in on it and shut off every avenue of escape. The fighting became terrific. Then, in the intense heat of the Jordan valley, came a whirlwind of dust which gave the Arabs the advantage.

Most of the imperial soldiers were mowed down by the sword, others perished in the river, but a few escaped. The battle was decisive. The Arabs enjoyed the spoil, then returned to Damascus for a month's repose.[11]

After the bloody and decisive battle of the Yarmuk the Byzantine army was no longer in the field. Heraclius retired to Antioch and afterward bid an eternal farewell to Syria. The Saracens chose their own towns and took them at their leisure. In the year 637 the two chief forces of the Arabians met before Jerusalem, and the commander addressed his customary summons to the leaders of the historic city:

> Health and happiness to everyone that follows the right way. We require of you to testify that there is but one God, and that Mohammed is his Apostle. If you refuse this, consent to pay tribute, and be under us forthwith. Otherwise I shall bring men against you who love death better than you do the drinking of wine, or eating hog's flesh. Nor will I ever turn from you, if it please God, till I have destroyed those that fight for you, and made slaves of your children.[12]

Defended on every side by deep valleys and steep ascents, and having within the city the Church of the Holy Sepulchre which the Christians felt honor-bound to defend, the besieged fought the besiegers almost every day for four months. The walls of the Holy City were thickly planted with crosses and banners blessed by the prietsts. All fanatical zeal was unavailing, however, for at length the perseverance of the Arabs won the day.

The patriarch Sophronius appeared on the walls, and through an interpreter demanded a conference. After failing to dissuade the lieutenant of the caliph from his impious enterprise, he proposed, in the name of the people, "a fair capitulation," with this extraordinary clause: that the articles of security should be ratified by the authority and presence of Omar, the Caliph at Medina.

The messenger hastened to Medina, and there, in council, it was decided that since Jerusalem was the capital of Palestine, and after Mecca and Medina, was the most sacred of all cities, that the Caliph should grant the request. Mounted on a red camel, and carrying naught but a sack of corn, a bag of dates, a wooden dish and a leathern bottle of water, Caliph Omar came to Jerusalem in the simplicity of the Bedouin.

When he came in sight of the city he cried with a loud voice, "God is victorious. O Lord, give us an easy conquest." After pitching his tent of coarse hair, he calmly seated himself on the ground, signed the capitulation, by which he promised to permit the Christians of Jerusalem liberty of conscience in religious worship, and undisputed possession of the Church of the Holy Sepulchre, then arose and entered the city "without fear or precaution."

The inhabitants of the Holy City were impressed by the Caliph's simplicity. The patriarch, Sophronius, bowed before his new master, and visited with him in a rather free manner, but is said to have secretly muttered, in the words of Daniel, "The abomination of desolation is in the Holy place."[13]

Omar commanded the temple area to be prepared for a mosque,[14] and during his stay of ten days laid plans for future campaigns and for his present and future states of Palestine and Syria. To complete what yet remained of the Syrian conquest the Caliph formed two separate armies. The one under Abu Obediah and Khalid, and the other under Amru and Yezid. The latter remained in Jerusalem, and the former pushed forward northward and laid siege to Aleppo, which proved to be the hardest to take of all cities of the Syrian conquest.

In the midst of the city, on a large, lofty artificial mound stood the castle of Aleppo; the sides were not only precipitous, but were faced with freestone, and the mote below could easily be filled with water from nearby springs. In the earlier part of the siege the garrison lost three thousand men, yet remained exceedingly strong. When the siege had lasted for four or five months the Saracen commander despaired of taking "the impregnable fortress," but Caliph Omar sent him a message saying: "I charge you by no means to raise the siege of the castle. *Your retreat would diminish the reputation of our arms.*"[15]

Volunteers from all the tribes of Arabia soon arrived in the camp on horses and camels. Among these was *Dames,* of servile birth but of gigantic size. On the forty-seventh day of his service he proposed with only thirty men, to make an attempt on the castle. At his suggestion the army of the Saracens made a mock retreat while the huge Arab and his thirty men concealed themselves at the foot of the mound. In the darkest hour of the night seven of the strongest of the Arabs mounted on each other's shoulders. With the broad sinewy back of the gigantic slave sustaining the human column, the foremost man grasped the lowest part of the battlement, pulled himself up, and silently stabbed and cast down the sentinels. The men were drawn up by the long folds of their turbans.

Then with bold yet cat-like footsteps, Dames approached the palace of the governor, and beheld the people in riotous merriment as they celebrated their deliverance. Returning to his companions, they overpowered the guard, unbolted the gate, let down the drawbridge, and defended the narrow pass until the Saracen forces could make their way into the city and complete the conquest of Aleppo.[16]

Antioch soon capitulated, then the troops of Antioch and those of Jesusalem marched along the seacoast, taking one town after another until their banners were joined under the walls of the Phoenician cities of Tyre and Tripoli. No city dared dispute the will of the warriers from the desert. The tribes hostile to the Greeks went over to the victors. Soon all Palestine and Syria came under the rule of the Caliphs, and the land, first made sacred to the Jews, then to the Christians, was now to become the Holy Land to the Moslems.

This presented a somewhat unusual situation since the population of Palestine was composed largely of Christians, with a smaller number of Jews and other people domestic to the Near East. Jews and Christians were not considered full citizens, but in most cases were permitted to continue to practice their religion by paying tribute. Many inhabitants — especially Greeks — preferred emigration to Moslem rule. In such cases the conquerors confiscated their properties, but were pleased to permit others to retain their properties on payment of tax.[17]

In 638 a portion of the Caliph's army stationed at Gaza marched into Egypt, where they besieged and captured Al-Farama (Palusium), Memphis, Alexandria (A.D. 642). Later the conquest was pushed on across north Africa until Tripoli, Fez and Morocco were taken and Okbah, the famous Arab general, paused only when he came to the boundless ocean, where he is said to have spurred his horse into the waves, and raising his eyes to heaven, exclaimed: "Great God, if my course were not stopped by this sea, I would still go on to the kingdom of the unknown west."[18]

In the absence of adequate government the Arabs largely lost North Africa, but during the year 700 they recaptured it and in 711 invaded Spain, whence in time they overran the province of Aquitaine, planted their standard before the gates of Tours, France and forced men to ask if Europe and the world would become Moslem. Charles Martel (Charles, "The Hammer"), conscious of the impending danger, collected his troops and in the famous battle of Tours (A. D. 732) defeated and drove the Moslem forces back across the Pyrenees; much later they were driven from Spain.

As conquerors of the new countries the Arabs frequently found a more advanced civilization than they had enjoyed in their arid homeland, where the ways of the camels and cattle and desert lore, spiced ever and anon by wise maxims, constituted the small round of daily life. They enjoyed the adventure of conquest coupled with the privilege of sharing the wealth, prosperity, and culture of the conquered. This they evidenced by the "intellectual adaptability" with which they turned to profit almost everything they found.

Worship and war had loomed large in their thinking. The former was not to be diminished and the latter lessened only while they assimilated and developed the philosophy, science and art which they inherited from the Persian, Grecian, and Roman civilizations. In Palestine and adjacent countries they not only adopted many new administrative customs, revived languishing sciences, cultivated the arts, and encouraged industrial and commercial activities; but kept alive sage sentences and even brought into existence new wise maxims in harmony with the trend of the time. One of the proverbs said: "There are two creatures that are insatiable: the man of money and the man of science;" while another ran thus: "The ink of the learned is as precious as the blood of the martyrs."[19]

## Chapter XXII

# "GOD WILLS IT"

The middle of the eleventh century found Europe shrouded in the densest gloom of intellectual and moral darkness. Feudalism, licentiousness, and tyranny held brutal sway through the land. Ignorance, superstition, and degradation reigned among the masses that were subject to princes and barons who were held in check only by threats of the church, compunction of conscience, and the laws of chivalry; none of which served as a very effective safeguard against excesses. Seldom was there a chance for appeal from their judgment, and then by ordeal — the ordeal of combat or that of water or fire.

The princes and feudal barons were incessantly at war, and the deeds and valor of the knight were constantly heralded in the field and heard at the fireside. The people breathed strife-laden atmosphere, thought in military terms, and often saw service in wars waged between those who ruled parts of once great empires.

The church had sought temporal power for seven centuries, and was reduced to such intellectual and moral torpor that for the people it had little help to offer and no word of authority to speak. All save a few of its leaders were ignorant, licentious, and incompetent shepherds who were themselves such strangers to the regenerating grace of God as to regard it their chief duty to impress the people with their authority. Further confusion arose over the fact that there were *two* popes, and each claimed to be the genuine and only authority.

With such distorted views of life, and such woeful inadequacy among their spiritual guides, the people often lived extremely sinful lives and as a consequence were restless and uneasy. To atone for their wrongs they paid the church, did penance, or went on pilgrimages. These pilgrimages might be to nearby shrines, or to Rome; but the greatest of all pilgrimages was to Jerusalem, where they fully expected to look upon the place where the Lord had lain, receive absolution for all misdeeds of the past, and begin life anew.[1]

A pilgrimage to Jerusalem involved great expenditure of time, energy, and money; and not infrequently the supreme price — the life of the pilgrim. Those who were so successful as to make the pilgrimage and return to their home-land had much to tell of the sacred rites, of supposed miracles, and of the East with its gorgeous silks, heavy brocades, rich treasures of art carved in ivory or overlaid with gold; its fantastically carved weapons, its fine carriages, expensive carpets and luxurious homes. These they painted in glowing terms to their fellow-westerners who led rather monotonous lives, and were accustomed to so little that was beautiful and less that was luxurious.[2]

Aside from the Jews and Moors, there were none among the Europeans who were not nominally Christian; therefore the idea of a pilgrimage to the Holy City became exceedingly popular among the people. However, a change of masters in Palestine was to make affairs quite different for European pilgrims.

Aside from charging generous fees and inflicting mild abuse, the Arab rule, from 637 to 969 A.D. had been comparatively mild toward the Christian pilgrims who came to Jerusalem to worship. But in the year 969 the Caliph of Maez — of the Fatemite dynasty — ascended the throne of Egypt and began opposition to all that paraded under the name of the Christ of Galilee. Despite the fact that the Caliph's mother had been a Christian, he instituted many hardships on those who professed His name, and in a mad fit of anger ordered that the Church of the Holy Sepulchre be destroyed. Pilgrims who came from afar were often robbed or refused admittance to the Holy City. Many died in want and misery or were murdered by their cruel enemies.

Ere long, however, this situation was improved, and for a time it appeared that the Christians might continue to visit the sacred places unmolested, but it was not to be so, for a dark storm cloud was soon to arise from the northeast.

Togrul Beg, fierce and famous among the barbarious Seljukian Turks, overran Persia and proclaimed himself Sultan. In December of 1055 A.D. he entered Baghdad and assumed a protectorate over the Caliph. Two years later the Caliph appointed him "King of the east and west, Commander of the faithful." A "conqueror by nature and habit," Togrul Beg rested for but a short time in the fruitful Euphrates valley, then led his warriors westward on campaigns of further conquest[3]

In 1603 he died and was succeeded by Alp Arslan, his nephew, who, as "the Bold Lion," continued the warlike policies of his predecessor, met and defeated the Byzantines in the decisive battle of Manzikert (August 1071) and carried his victorious arms as far west as Antioch and the Black Sea. Malek Shah, his son and successor, extended the Seljukian dominion to the environs of the Bosphorus, and in 1076 the

Seljukes marched triumphantly into Palestine, wrested Jerusalem from the Arabs, and the Holy City fell under the dominion of the viceroys of Malek Shah.[4]

The natives opposed the Seljukes who retaliated by instituting measures of violence and outrage against both Christians and Arabs. Being Moslems the Arabs soon acquiesed, but the Christians who found nothing in common with the Seljukes, came to bear the brunt of the persecutions.[5]

Life became all but intolerable for the Christians who resided in the country, and unusual scorn was manifested toward the humble, defenseless pilgrims who came from foreign lands to pray at the tomb of their Lord. The Turk's attitude was irritating and his insolence ferocious. He despised both the places to which the Christians resorted, and the motives which led them thither. Many Christians were robbed or refused admittance. Some were imprisoned or murdered by their cruel enemies, while others died in want and misery.[6]

The newly arrived pilgrims were horrified at the humiliation to which they were subjected, and their fellow-Christians in Europe were shocked when the news was borne abroad that the Seljukian Turks were spurning and spitting upon the followers of Christ at His very tomb.

By 1083 the Seljukes controlled all Syria, and were soon joined by the Turkomans, a nomadic group from Central Asia, whose chief interest was pasturage and plunder. To further extend their rule the Turks took additional territory until Constantinople itself — the very eastern outpost of Christianity — was threatened. Simultaneous with this, the Moslems led campaigns into Spain and on October 23, 1086 overwhelmingly defeated the Christian army at the battle of Zallaca. Christian Europe took fright, while Alexius Comnenus, the new and vigorous emperor at Constantinople, hired mercenary troops, repulsed the enemy hordes, and took the offensive against the Seljukes for the recovery of Asia Minor. At the same time he began negotiations with the papacy to aid in raising recruits to ward off this barbarous people who threatened Christian lands.[7]

About this time Peter the Hermit, or "Peter of Picardy," as he is sometimes called, came into the limelight. He descended from a noble family of warriors who lived in Amiens, Normandy. Peter was small of stature and greatly deformed, yet his soldier heart was valiant and ambitious, even though it was housed in a body of a crippled dwarf. By diligent effort the physical handicap was largely overcome, and his marriage to a worthy woman added to his prestige. After her death Peter became a hermit, and finally decided to make the pilgrimage to Jerusalem.[8]

The Hermit's dwarfed body, impassioned soul, and eloquent voice attracted the attention of and made a tremendous impression on his fellow-pilgrims and on the Christians who lived in Jerusalem. After being badly used at the hands of those who controlled the holy places, he was permitted an audience with the Bishop of Jerusalem whom the Seljukes had imprisoned. There, in his cell, the bishop laid before Peter all the outrages suffered by the Christians at the hands of the Seljukes, and asked that he make an appeal to the Christians of Europe to come to the aid of those who had vainly endeavored to keep in their possession the places held sacred by all Christendom.

Armed with a letter from the Bishop, the Hermit began his return journey. On the way he is said to have had audience with Emperor Alexius at Constantinople, who also gave him a letter to Pope Urban II pleading for assistance against the barbarous hordes who not only desecrated the holy places but threatened the very existence of Christianity.

Arriving in Europe, the pious hermit recited with fervid and pathetic eloquence the story of the intolerable outrages to which the Christian pilgrims were being subjected[9]

Urban heard of the strange preacher and was singularly impressed. Happy indeed was he when the hermit hastened to him with letters from the Bishop of Jerusalem and the Emperor of Constantinople. With anxious tenacity Urban had clung to his papal throne, although he had been exiled from the Lateran, his word and authority discounted and his plans disrupted by the feudal barons who warred at will. The "Peace of God" had failed to bring spiritual life to the people and authority to the church, and the "Truce of God" was failing.[10]

Armed with appeals from those of high rank in both church and state and fortified by public sentiment, the shrewd but anxious pope saw a rare opportunity to unite all the fighting men of Europe under the banners of the church, thus restoring authority to the church and the papal throne to himself. Consequently in that same summer of 1905 there went out letters calling churchmen and lay lords to a special council to be held November 18 at Clermont, France. The purpose of the council was kept in strict secrecy.

In November, while the autumn breezes blew softly and men's hearts were thoughtful regarding the meager harvests of the year, there gathered at Clermont a great concourse of people, both ministry and laity. Urban had ridden across the mountains to keep the appointment, and he had seen to it that Peter the Hermit was present. Besides these there were 13 archbishops, 225 bishops, 390 abbots, a great company of priests and monks, thousands of knights and an innumerable multitude of people who crowded the valley and hillside about Clermont.[11]

On the eighth day of the council Pope Urban, accompanied by Peter the Hermit and followed by his cardinals and other high dignitaries, ascended a spacious platform overhung by a gorgeous canopy, and faced an immense multitude in the open field east of the little city of Clermont. Peter the Hermit prepared the way with one of his characteristic speeches, then on that momentous occasion, with the fate of millions in his hands, the eloquent Urban arose and began to speak in the native tongue of the French:

> Ye men of the Franks. God hath favored you in many ways, in your happy land as in your steadfast faith, and valor. To you our words are spoken, and by you our message will be passed on . . . Christ ordains it.
>
> From the borders of Jerusalem and the city of Constantinople evil tidings have come to my ears. . . . An accursed race, estranged from God, has invaded the lands of the Christians in the East and have depopulated them by fire, steel, and ravage. . . . These Turks have led away many Christians, captives, to their own country; they have torn down the churches of Christ, or used them for their own rites. In some they stable their horses, and befoul the altars with the filth from their own bodies.
>
> Even now the Turks are torturing Christians, binding them and filling them with arrows, or making them kneel, bending their heads to try if their swords can cut through their necks with a single blow. . . . They are ravishing Christian women. To speak of this is difficult, yet you have heard of it on the border of Spain. The time may come when you will see your wives violated and your children driven away as slaves.
>
> Pilgrims from our lands have been forced to pay toll at the gates of cities and at the entrance of churches. They have been accused and forced to purchase their freedom. Those who had no money were searched, even the callouses on their bare heels were cut to see if they carried money there. They were given scammony to drink, until they vomited, but finding no coins in the vomit, their bowels have been cut open with a sword so that if any treasure was hidden there it might be disclosed. Who can relate this without being deeply grieved? For they are your blood brothers — children of the same Christ and sons of the same church.
>
> Who will avenge these wrongs, unless it be you who have won glory in arms? You have the courage and fitness of body to humble these who have risen against you. And more must be said. Hear me! you are girdled knights, but you are arrogant with pride. You fight among yourselves, and kill your brethren. This is not the service of Christ, nor the way of life. If you would save your souls, then come forward to the defense of Christ. O ye that have carried on feuds, come to the war against the infidels! O ye who have been thieves, become soldiers. Fight a just war. Labor for everlasting reward.
>
> Let no obstacle turn you aside, but arrange your affairs and gather together supplies. Enter upon the journey when the winter is ended and spring is here again. You shall earn the right to absolution from all your

sins, and heaven is assured to any who may fall in this worthy undertaking. . . . The wealth of your enemies shall be yours; ye shall plunder their treasures and return home victorious, or purpled with your own blood, receive an everlasting reward. It is better to die in warfare than behold the evils that befall the holy places. Valiant knights, descendants of unconquered sires, remember the vigor of your forefathers and do not degenerate from your noble stock. Take up your arms, valiant sons, and go — God guiding you . . .[12]

Here the eloquence of the speaker was interrupted: many who had been weeping now buried their faces in their hands, and from the throng a voice rang out: *"It is God's Will!"* and the vast assembled host took up the shout that reverberated in a thunderous chorus through the valley: *"God wills it!" "God wills it!"*

Urged by the inspiration of the moment, Urban said: "Let this be your battle cry; when you go against the enemy let this shout be raised, 'God Wills It!' And those who vow to go shall take the sign of the cross."

Adhemar, Bishop of Le Puy, big of frame and earnest of soul, ran forward and fell upon his knees, offering his services. Knights of fame rushed up to him, threw their swords at his feet and pled for a commission in the army that should fight for the sacred cause. Men of wealth and those of poverty pushed through the crowd, sobbing as they came, "God Wills It!" Women wept and thrust their sons and husbands toward the earnest Hermit and the eloquent pope. Cardinals, bishops, and priests worked feverishly pinning on the shoulders of the volunteers little crosses of red cloth, sobbing as they did so: "God Wills It!"

When twilight stole in the people were dismissed with a papal blessing and the vast throng broke up into small groups — each planning for the holy war. Long into the night torch lights gleamed while the pope, the prelates, the barons and the knights laid plans for the mightiest military enterprise ever undertaken by the Christian church. Urban appointed Adhemar as the papal shepherd of the expedition, fixed mid-May of the coming spring as the date for assembling, designated Constantinople as the rendezvous for the pilgrims, and wrote Alexius to provide for them.

Once again France had found a worthy objective which challenged the best in her. Her people were happy; for said they: "God Wills It!

## Chapter XXIII

# THE CROSS AND THE CRESCENT IN CONFLICT

Following the Council of Clermont, couriers, envoys, and monks went forth to spread the news and urge the crusade upon the people. Urban empowered Peter the Hermit with a special commission to go everywhere telling the people what he had seen and heard and felt while on his pilgrimage to Jerusalem. He soon became by far the most effective advocate of the expedition to Jerusalem.

Clothed in a simple tunic, and riding a humble donkey, the Hermit went from town to town and from church to church, gathered the people and held vast audiences spellbound while he related the brutal insults which he received at the hands of the savage Turks, and the tales of horror which he had received from the venerable patriarch at Jerusalem. He made vivid to the European Christians the story of how the Holy Sepulchre was in ruins; Christ being put to shame, His name blasphemed, and His lowly followers beaten, mocked and spit upon by the base Seljukes who held possession of the sacred tomb where Christ had lain.

With impassioned eloquence he spoke of the foul desecration of the land hallowed by the Redeemer's life. When words failed him, he wept, he groaned, he smote his breast, and pointed to a crucifix which he kissed with fervent devotion.[1] He then challenged the warriors, all men able to carry arms, to hasten to the defense of their brethren, and to the rescue of the Holy Sepulchre from the infidel.

France took fire, and Europe was stirred wherever he went. Crowds followed at the Hermit's heels, they bowed down to kiss the hem of his garment, and plucked hairs from the mane of his mule as precious mementos. Tradesmen ceased to ply their tools, farmers left their fields, barons gave their lands to the church, freed their serfs, and all enlisted in the army which they verily thought would soon rescue the tomb of Christ from defiled hands.

The fame of Peter the Hermit spread throughout the continent; even in England the barons of William Rufus shared the excitement of their friends and relatives in Normandy. The actual number of those who, from the various ranks of society, rose up as if by a common impulse

if held at bay the Moslems could do no permanent injury, and if they did attack Saffuriya they would be at a disadvantage since they were far from their base of supplies and would possess no nearby water supply. "If we attack them," said Raymond, "then we will be unable to obtain water between here and Tiberias." No saner advice was ever offered military leaders, but suspicion, which is the characteristic of inefficient leadership, caused King Guy to ignore Raymond's advice, and without further consultation give orders for advance on the following morning.

At sunrise the poorly prepared Crusaders were beginning to take up the march. Three hours later the two armies met on the hills three miles west of Tiberias. The Latins endeavored to cut their way through to Tiberias, but the Moslems, with four soldiers to their one, surrounded them as completely as western cowboys ever corralled a herd of cattle. It was Friday — the Moslem's day of prayer and worship — and they seemed desirous of delaying the final struggle. The Latins milled about under the rays of an oriental sun, fought feebly and suffered from thirst. Then the sun hid itself behind the Galilean hills and all night long they heard the Moslem watch-cry, "God is great, God is great; there is no god but God." Dark forebodings beset the discouraged Latins.

Next morning Saladin ordered the battle with vigorous onslaughts. The dispirited Crusaders retreated up the hillside almost overcome by thirst. Raymond and his horsemen cut their way through and escaped, while the other leaders drew back onto the naturally fortified mountain known as "the Horns of Hattin," the traditional site of Christ's sermon on the mount. Here where Christ had said, "Blessed are the meek for they shall inherit the earth," His supposed followers gathered about "the precious wood of the true cross," and prepared to fight for their lives.[30]

The situation was pathetic, for the Crusaders were only nominal Christians, and many could not even qualify as being that. The motive which guided their forefathers when they captured those sacred acres had dimmed. Their valor and zeal had diminished and their loyalty to Christ had degenerated into a devotion for the "precious wood" which they had been taught to believe was a portion of the true cross.[31]

The Templars and Hospitallers as well as the foot-soldiers fought with great bravery until the Moslems fired dry grass. The smoke and fire swept up the mountain side completely disqualifying and exhausting the Latins. The grandmaster of the Hospitallers was mortally wounded, the principal leaders of the Christian army captured, and the footsoldiers put to the sword as sheep given to the slaughter.

King Guy, Reginald of Chatillon, Marquis of Montferrat, and a host of nobles and knights were led into Saladin's tent and seated before the victorious general. Saladin reproached Reginald for his treacherous conduct of breaking the truce and falling upon helpless and defenseless caravans and pilgrim bands. Reginald's only reply was a half-hearted appeal to the cruel customs of war. With the magnanimity befitting the spirit of hospitality and becoming a leader of the Orient, Saladin ordered refreshments, and with a smile offered King Guy a cup of cool, refreshing water. With the politeness becoming a Westerner, King Guy accepted the cup and passed it to Reginald of Chatillon. Saladin objected to this move saying: "Know that it is you and not I who give him drink; therefore it does not entitle him to his life from me." Saladin would be true to the Arab custom which reckons a prisoner's life safe if he has partaken of his captor's hospitality.[32]

For some hours the Sultan was occupied in giving military orders, then Reginald was again summoned to Saladin's tent where he was given the choice of embracing Mohammendanism or of dying like a dog. As unfaithful and avaricious as Reginald had been in other respects he spurned the conditions of escape by apostasy. Saladin drew his cimeter and with one blow struck off his head, thus fulfilling a previous vow to put him to death if he ever captured him. Later he presented the same alternative to each of the knights, and two hundred and thirty Christian knights stood fast in the Christian faith and were beheaded. Only King Guy was spared, and that with the understanding that he would never again lay claim to a Christian throne in the Near East. For a time he was held captive, but later was set at liberty.

Tiberias, Caesarea, Acre, Jaffa, Beirut, and every other town of any importance, with the exception of Tyre, was soon occupied by Saladin's troops. There were few to resist, for the flower of the Crusader army had been destroyed by a single blow at Hattin.

Within less than three months Saladin approached the walls of Jerusalem, where he attacked the city from the west. After five days he planted his siege engines on the north. Soon a breach was made in the wall, and the people of Jerusalem sent out envoys to ask for terms of surrender. At first Saladin suggested a merciless massacre, such as had been carried out by the Christian host eighty-eight years before, but changed his mind when the besieged announced their intentions to destroy the sacred places and take the lives of every woman and child to prevent their falling into Moslem hands. Terms were then fixed whereby each person might be ransomed, and be permitted to take away their movable belongings. The terms of this exceedingly reasonable contract were carried out on Friday, October 2, 1187, when the Christians left Jerusalem and the Moslems took possession.

The golden cross was taken down from the Dome of the Rock; the building was purified with rose water from Damascus, and the splendid structure became once more the great mosque under the Crescent of Islam.[33]

When the Christians of Europe heard of the fate of the Crusader army on the Horns of Hattin, the fall of Jerusalem, and of other strongholds in the Near East, the old Crusader spirit flamed up again, this time led by the barons and royalty of England, France, Germany, and Italy. The people themselves were so eager to go to the relief of the cross in the Near East that thousands became impatient with the slower preparation of royalty, and unable to restrain their ardor they hastened to the seaports of the Mediterranean and embarked for Palestine at their own expense.

So rapid was the accumulation of recruits that by the beginning of 1189 one hundred thousand men had gathered at the city of Tyre, the only stronghold that had been left the Crusaders. Uncurbed zeal caused the Crusaders to march out of Tyre and lay siege to Acre. Saladin sent a great army and the Christians soon found themselves opposed by forces from within and without the city. Their supplies failed and famine and disease took away more than the war, yet they held back the Moslem forces while others were coming to take their places. And those others were coming, for Europe was stirred more thoroughly than ever before. Philip of France, Richard of England, and Frederick of Germany were making preparations for Palestinian campaigns. All eligible men were to join their armies or pay the "Saladin tithe" — a scheme of taxation imposed on all those who did not take the cross.[34]

Frederick Barbarossa, Emperor of Germany, already a great veteran, flung himself into the breach with the enthusiasm of youth and prudence of manhood. His genius and generalship were unsurpassed in his day. Carefully weighing the perils of the great undertaking, providing against its hazards, he accepted only volunteers who could furnish means for their own subsistence for one year.[35]

Unwilling to entrust himself and his army to the mercies of the Venetian shipmasters, he marched his army of a hundred thousand by Constantinople and through Asia Minor. He was assisted by his son, the Duke of Suabia, together with the Dukes of Austria and Moravia. His great army of more than sixty thousand cavalry and fifteen knights and the additional footsoldiers was thoroughly disciplined and supplied. But few armies have ever moved forward with such a degree of regularity, such loyalty, and such wholesome subordination.

Refusing to countenance the double-dealing and treachery of the Byzantines at Constantinople, the careful old warrior passed by the city and made his way through heated deserts and dangerous passes where Turkish hordes watched every opportunity but were never able to take the old hero off his guard. Fighting his way through every peril, he came without disaster to Iconium, where he defeated the Turkish Sultan in battle and took the city by storm. Moving on with a steadiness and precision that caused the Turks to tremble, he came on June 10, 1190, to the little river Saleph in Celicia, where, while crossing the stream, he met with an accident and was drowned.[36]

The sad tragedy of Frederick's death spelled ruin to the great German host; they lost spirit and scattered. Many of his followers returned home in order to look after their own interests, others attempted to press on under the leadership of the Duke of Suabia, Frederick's son. But when the Moslems learned of Frederick's death, they charged and harassed the Christian army with such persistence that their death-dealing blows along with disease and famine wiped out all but a thousand men who fought their way through to the city of Antioch.

Antioch was then held by the forces of Saladin and the numbers far exceeded those of the Crusaders, yet the German knights fell boldly upon the Moslems and scattered all before them. Antioch was taken and the Saracens retreated to Damascus. The body of Frederick Barbarossa was buried in the Church of Saint Peter, after which the German Crusaders pressed forward to join the forces at Acre, but soon the gallant Duke of Suabia died and the splendid army of Frederick Barbarossa was reduced to a mere handful.

Just at this time there arose in England the most daring of all the Crusaders, Richard the Lion Heart, King of England. While Frederick was yet on his way to Palestine, and while the siege of Acre was in progress, Richard raised a large sum of money by the sale of castles and estates, and in the summer of 1190, joined Philip of France at Vezelay, where the two kings renewed their vows of friendship, reviewed their army of more than a hundred thousand men and set out on the march to Lyons. Arriving at that city they separated their forces with the understanding that they should meet again at the port of Messina in Italy.

Philip led his army from Lyons to Genoa and there took ship and arrived at Messina. Richard took ship at Marseilles and the two armies wintered at Messina. During the winter difficulties arose between the friendly kings. Richard had been engaged to marry Philip's sister, the Princess Adelia, but for some reason he ceased to care for her and ere the winter was over Princess Barengaria, daughter of King Sancho of Navarre, arrived in Sicily escorted by the queen mother, Eleanor of England. As a heart balm Richard paid Princess Adelia ten thousand marks and resorted to her all the castles which had been assigned as her dowry.[37]

With the opening of spring the two kings departed by ship for the Near East. Philip safely arrived in Palestine and joined his forces to the army before Acre. Richard suffered ill fortune. His squadron was struck by a storm off the coast of Crete and two of his vessels wrecked on the shores of Cyprus. The stranded crews were robbed and imprisoned by the people of Cyprus.

Disembarking his troops, Richard took the capital of the island by storm, put the governor in silver chains and levied a tribute upon the people. During the season of Lent, Richard celebrated his marriage with Barengaria and when the festivities were over he sailed for Acre, with his fifty war galleys, thirteen store-ships, and more than a hundred transports. On the way he captured a Moslem ship with fifteen hundred men and a vast store of "Greek fire."[38]

When King Richard came within sight of Acre on June 8, 1191, he was welcomed with huge bonfires and with great joy. Richard's courage, daring and audacity made him at once the favorite among all the Crusaders. And although he suffered from a siege of sickness, brought on by malaria which he contracted in the plain of Acre, yet he brought new life to the Crusader ranks. In fact, to his fellow-crusaders, the king of England became "Richard, the Lion Heart," "the Achilles of the host, whom nothing could resist or divert from his purpose."[39] His battering engines worked his will and the walls were broken on every side and the garrison so reduced in numbers as to give up in despair. Saladin at last gave assent and on July 12, 1191, Acre surrendered to the Crusaders.

In the hour of triumph Richard the Lion Heart took possession of the palace for himself, showed little courtesy to King Philip and the other leaders who had worked so faithfully to assist in the reduction of the enemy forces. Seeing that Leopold, Duke of Austria, had planted his banner on the wall, Richard seized the standard and, throwing it into the ditch, set up the banner of Saint George in its stead. The terms of surrender called for two hundred thousand pieces of gold, the liberation of certain Christian prisoners, and the restoration of the "true cross" which Saladin had captured at Jerusalem.[40] The Moslem camp broke up and the army withdrew toward Damascus. Richard, having detained five thousand hostages, permitted the remaining inhabitants of the city to depart in peace. But when Saladin failed either through negligence or inability to pay the stipulated ransom for the captives they were led out and all five thousand beheaded in cold blood.[41]

On hearing of the massacre, Saladin retaliated by butchering the Christian captives in his hands and seizing others for a similar fate. Thus the Cross and the Crescent were smeared with innocent blood that was wantonly shed.

The Christian world was pleased at the prospects in store for the Christian forces. It was verily thought that they would be enabled to retake Jerusalem, and it seemed that no reasonable victory would have been denied them but for the fact that Philip fell ill and, taking all of his soldiers but ten thousand men left under the Duke of Burgundy, he returned home.

The arrogance and disrespect of Richard has even been held as the chief cause of Philip's return. After his retirement the English king left Acre with about thirty thousand warriors and proceeded along the coast toward Jaffa. On the seventh of December, 1191, they were attacked by a large Moslem army, and the conflict which followed was one of the most remarkable of the Middle Ages. The vast forces of Moslems surrounded the Christians and pressed them from every side and showered arrows until the air was darkened with the rain of missiles. The knights were eager for the charge, but Richard calmly ordered all the warriors to stand fast until Saladin's host had emptied their quivers upon the army of the Crusaders. When this was accomplished, Richard gave the command and the knights made such a fearful charge that seven thousand of the noblest of the Turkish cavalry went down on the field and the rest of the army fled in all directions.

After this signal victory Richard marched on Jaffa and took it without resistance. The Moslem forces were so frightened that Richard might have marched on and recovered Jerusalem but for the fact that the French barons unwisely urged that they remain on the coast, rebuild their ruined fortresses, and take Jerusalem at another time.[42]

With the opening of the spring of 1192, Richard rallied his forces, took a solemn oath from his knights that they would not abandon the cause until the tomb of Christ should be recovered. He then forced his way to within a few miles of Jerusalem. The Moslem forces felt that they would be unable to hold the city, and were ready to yield it to the Christians; when lo, in a vale near *Neby Samwil*, the question was raised among the Crusaders as to whether they should undertake the siege of the city or defer it. Ten of the leading barons were called upon to decide the issue. These men concluded that it was not the opportune time for the prosecution of the enterprise. The Duke of Burgundy retreated with his men, and Richard was greatly mortified over the decision.[43]

While the Duke of Burgundy was retreating — supposedly for no other reason than that it should not be said that the English had taken the Holy City — the group stood speaking of the Duke's treacherous malice when one of Richard's knights cried out: "Sire, Sire, come but so far as this and I will show you Jerusalem!" When the king heard this he threw his coat-armor before his eyes, and in tears prayed, saying: "Fair Lord God, I pray thee, suffer me not to see the Holy City since I cannot deliver it from the hands of thine enemies."[44]

Richard returned to Acre and was preparing to return to England when he heard that the Turks had cut down the inhabitants of Jaffa and retaken the city, all but the fortress. Enraged at such an aggression, Richard took ship with a mere handful of knights and returned to Jaffa. With excessive recklessness the king jumped from his boat while yet in the shoal water, and wading to the shore swung the battle axe and led his men with such daring courage that the Saracens gave way and fled in terror, as though he were some evil genius.[45]

In future engagements he fought with such fury and seemingly in the height of his glory that the Moslem warriors developed a fear of him that was almost unparalleled. Even now his deeds are so well known that Syrian mothers sometimes frighten their unruly children with the mention of his name as a kind of "bogeyman." Saladin signed a truce with Richard which gave Tyre, Acre, and Jaffa, with all the sea coast between them to the Crusaders, and gave Christian pilgrims free entrance to the holy places of Palestine and especially of Jerusalem.

Saladin and Richard were beginning to understand each other and probably would have brought permanent peace, but for the fact that the long siege of illness and a conspiracy in England caused Richard to leave Acre in the autumn of 1192 and start on his homeward course. In a storm on the Adriatic his ship was wrecked and he was seized and held as a prisoner by the Duke of Austria, whom he had angered at the capitulation of Acre.[46] Emperor Henry VI of Germany took charge of Richard and compelled him to remain in prison for fifteen months.

Richard was released when he did homage to Henry and guaranteed the enormous ransom of one hundred thousand pounds. In order to make up this sum it is said that the English churches gave their silver-service to be coined, and that every man, woman and child in England and Normandy had to contribute toward the king's redemption. When in March, 1194, the king arrived in England, he had been absent from his kingdom for four years, the last fifteen months of which had been spent in prison.

Soon after Richard's departure from Palestine, Saladin announced his decision to join the pilgrimage to Mecca. But some of his followers advised him not to leave lest the Christians break the truce. This was his last opportunity to fulfill his desire to visit the city of Mecca, for within a few months he died and left his empire to his three sons, who established three distinct thrones at Cairo, Damascus, and Aleppo.

In the year 1198 a new pope came to the throne and exerted all his effort to inspire a new crusade. He wrote to all the Christian rulers of the West urging them to rally to the Cross and assist the holy work by enlisting themselves for the war in Palestine; and to give of their means for the enterprise. Great revenues soon came to the coffers of the pope. Foulque, an eccentric priest, took the place of Peter the Hermit and Saint Bernard, and vehemently preached to the people, calling on them to enlist for the holy war. Hundreds of knights and nobles assembled for the campaign.

Councils were held and soon a vast army, recruited largely from Flanders, France, and Italy, had gathered at Venice, where the leaders bargained for the use of Venetian ships for their transportation to Palestine. Eighty-five thousand silver marks were to be paid the Venetian's navy for its service in transporting four thousand five hundred knights, nine thousand esquires and men-at-arms, twenty thousand infantry with horses, and provisions for nine months. The fleet set apart for this service numbered fifty galleys, perhaps the best vessels then afloat in the Mediterranean.[47]

Bickerings and disputes among the barons brought delays until the zeal of many was abated and they returned home. Others became unwilling to pay and it was found that less than fifty thousand marks of the whole sum could then be secured. The Venetians, ever watchful of an opportunity to make merchandise of the Crusader cause, refused to depart with the soldiers of the Cross until the entire amount was paid. After some delay, however, the Doge offered to allow the Latins to postpone the remaining payment of thirty thousand marks on condition that they would assist in the capture of the town of Zara, which had revolted from the Venetian Republic. Though some were unwilling and returned to their homes and the pope entered a vigorous protest against the participation of any of them in an attack upon a Christian city, yet the majority assisted in the capture of the city and settled there for the winter, intending to go to Palestine in the spring.[48]

When the warm spring breezes began to blow, the Venetians, with a view to commercial concessions, induced the Crusaders to assist Alexis, the young Greek prince, to recover his throne at Constantinople. In turn he was to pay the Crusaders and Venetians two hundred thousand marks, and assist the Crusaders in taking and maintaining Palestine. When the city was stormed and the coronation service held for the prince, he paid over one hundred thousand marks, then refused to take further steps in fulfilling the terms of his contract. Friction developed which eventually led the Crusaders to storm Constantinople and put an end to the Eastern Roman empire for fifty-seven years, (1204-1261 A.D.).

On the ruins of this Greek empire the Crusaders founded a Latin empire under Count Baldwin of Flanders, the leader of the fourth crusade.[49] The empire was split up into a number of small states of which the Venetians received a large share. Thus the money, the manpower, and the inspiration of the fourth crusade was diverted from the original purpose, and fell upon the heads of the Byzantine Greeks instead of the warriors of the East who marched under the crescent.

## CHAPTER XXVI

# THE CHILDREN'S CRUSADE

THE FOUR GENERATIONS which had successively gone on crusades to recapture Palestine had ultimately failed to convey Palestine to Christendom as a realm over which they might continue to rule. Many who had gone had never returned, but those who had returned had much to say. Around every fireside thrilling tales had been told of the struggles to wrest the Holy Sepulchre from the grip of those who had long defiled it. Children heard these stories with deepest interest and in their minds was implanted the ideal service that one might render in life — that of a Christian warrior who would aid in delivering the Christian's Holy Land from the hands of those who had defiled it.

Emperors, kings, barons, and knights had given their wealth, their vigor, and even their lives in the common cause. It was only natural that the children should desire the day to come when they too might engage in such a service. Yet the outlook at this time seemed hopeless. The Christian peoples, with all their might and money and devotion, had failed to recover the central shrine of their beloved faith. Yet their mental attitude reflected a deep desire to do all possible to aid the Christian kingdoms in Palestine.[1]

Just at this time, in June 1212 A.D., when the mightiest leaders of the day had lost heart, Stephen, a shepherd lad from the village of Cloyes, not far from the Castle of Vendôme near Paris, was supposed to have had a vision in which Christ appeared to him in the guise of a poor pilgrim and commanded him to lead a crusade of children to the rescue of the Holy Sepulchre.[2] He said that the Crusaders had failed because their hearts were defiled and their hands unclean. "Innocent boys and pure virgins," he said, "shall wrest from the Saracens the Holy City and the Sepulchre." The Saviour was supposed to have accepted bread from him and to have given him a letter to the king of France calling upon the king to assist the cause.

The lad's influence was greatly increased by the report of the miracle which he was said to have performed at Saint Denis. He was returning one day from a procession organized in the diocese of Chartres to invoke God's wrath against the unbelievers when his sheep wandered from the road into the fields and began to graze the crops. Whirling his staff above his head, he entered the field to drive them off when, instead of scattering, they knelt down before him and prayed for mercy.

Stories of this kind grew and multiplied until the children of France were prepared to accept almost any wonder that was told about their twelve-year-old hero. His fame grew apace. Before long they not only believed that his mission was ordained of God but flocked to his standard from all parts of the country and regarded him as half-divine. The youth of France were thrilled with the prospects of following one of their number in the greatest of all enterprises.

Going on a crusade was so popular that parents suffered their children to leave, and where parents were unwilling to let them go many escaped from their homes by force or cunning, and in some cases by cutting holes through the walls of their homes. The majority of the young enthusiasts were boys under twelve years of age, but there were some who were older; also many girls were among them who were taken with the contagion of the day. Some of these girls followed their brothers, others small parties of their own, while a few attached themselves to lads of their choice and began a relationship that led some of them to deep regret.

Soon the children crowded the roads leading to Cloyes. The clergy joined in the exhortation and veterans of previous crusades gave the movement their blessing and provided the youthful recruits with a few practical points on Eastern travel. Self-nominated lieutenants of Stephen sprang up to rally the young of their village, fief, or dukedom and to lead them toward Cloyes to acknowledge the authority of the shepherd boy.

On their way to join Stephen the pilgrims gathered in numerous bands, and solemn processions marched in different directions through the various towns and villages of France, carrying banners, candles, and crosses, and swinging censers, while they sang in the vernacular "Lord God, exalt Christianity! Lord God, restore to us the true cross."[3] Some shouted the century-old watchword of the Crusaders, "God wills it."[4] Even old men, touched by the flames of this enthusiasm, joined their ranks as they passed by. And others of the population, interested, but hardly knowing what to make of it, gave them food and alms for their long journey. Many felt that the Lord was about to do some great and new thing through these innocents.

The sons and daughters of nobles set forth, accompanied by retinues of servants, the sons of soldiers carried swords much too heavy for them. Small girls waved perfumed censers; and many of both sexes bore the cross aloft as they marched.[5] The largest number of recruits came from the peasantry, many of the homeless waifs. In all, thirty thousand boys and girls ranging between the ages of eight and eighteen converged upon Cloyes during the month of July, 1212, prepared to take the Crusader's oath and embark for the Holy Land.

State and church were perplexed to know what to do. Many felt confident that the move was not practical, but the children and the mass of common people regarded the crusade as divinely ordered. King Philip Augustus, who had accompanied Richard the Lion Heart on the fourth crusade, sought advice from the University of Paris, and on the strength of it asked that the children return. Though the command was only partially obeyed, yet the king dared do little about the matter because many supposed the children's innocency would enable them to do what their sinful elders had been unable to accomplish.

The circumstances placed the leaders in an extremely awkward situation. They dared not forbid it by putting the forces of law and order into operation lest the people should charge them with being too confident to sit at home and when the children would go, aided by the angels of heaven, they had prevented them. Faced with this peculiar dilemma the leaders of state and church considered it best to do nothing but allow the movement to run its course as had previous crusades.

At length when the various groups had reached Stephen's headquarters at the Castle of Vendome the signal was given and the youngest army that ever marched set out along the highways for Marseilles — a distance of over four hundred miles. Such a sight had never been seen. With happy confidence upon their faces and utterly unconscious of the tragedies that were to overtake them, they sang with all their might: —

Lord help us to recover thy true and holy cross.

The began their march across Burgundy to the south. Stephen rode in a chariot-like cart hung with costly tapestries, and guarded by a group of his little followers who, to mark their special rank, were mounted on horseback and carried arms. Looked upon with veneration as a saint and admired hero, the shepherd lad received homage as sincere as ever did a military leader who led men. His followers and especially his bodyguard contended among themselves to obtain relics from his person — a hair from his head, a stray thread from his flowing robes. These they treasured as highly as their elders had valued portions of the "true cross."[6]

Whenever they came to the walls of any city they inquired, in their ignorance, if it were the Holy Jerusalem. Ere they reached Marseilles some ten thousand of these children were lost in the forest and arid wastes, or died of heat, hunger, or thirst, or dropped by the way from sheer fatigue.

Many thin forms wandered away from the group and strayed about the countryside inquiring for their leader, "until they dropped from sheer exhaustion; and long afterwards, in many a place, the puny bones were found where a child had crawled into the shelter of some bush or brake to die like a stricken animal, unnoticed and alone."[7]

When eventually they arrived at Marseilles after a month's journey, weary and travel-stained, they rushed up to the sea expecting to see a miracle. They had been told that the sea would open for them. But this miracle was unrealized, and the overland path which was to stretch itself before them to Palestine did not appear. Instead of this, their childish eyes looked upon vast expanses of rolling waters while nearer by the sailing vessels were roped to the quay and the sea-birds soared overhead and called to their fellows. Everything went on as it had before they approached the sea.

Disheartened and disillusioned, many of them gave up the struggle and set their faces homeward. But the return journey proved almost as disastrous as the journey forward. Many of the same merciless enemies beset their pathway and some who had been kind to supply their needs now turned upon them with scorn. Only a fraction of those who turned back from Marseilles ever reached their homes and loved ones they had so readily left only a few short months before.

The five or six thousand who remained on the coast at Marseilles were the strongest and most courageous of the great company that had set out from the Castle of Vendome. They now took a fresh oath that nothing should deter them from attaining the goal they had originally set out to win. After considerable indecision they were on the verge of discouragement when two men, Hugo Ferreus and William Procus, posing as substantial merchants, proposed that "for the sake of God and without charge" they would take them to Syria and the Holy Land.

Accepting the offer as from God, the army of children marched down to the docks and crowded into seven ships and put out to sea. At last it seemed they were really going to look upon the sacred soil of Palestine where their Lord had preached peace and loved children so well. With hearts overflowing with appreciation for those who were helping them to their journey's end, they gazed out across the sea, and chanted the hymn, *Veni Creator Spiritus,* as the vessels spread their sails and drew out of the beautiful harbor of Marseilles.

When only a couple of days out, a furious storm arose and two of the ships struck a rock off Sardinia and went down with their crews. The other five boats continued their way. Arriving at the African port of Bujeiah, the slave-dealing merchants sold a part of their captives, and then sailed on to Alexandria, Egypt, where the others were sold as slaves to the Saracens in the Mohammedan slave markets.

Some of them were transported to Bagdad, and among them were those who were hewn in pieces by the Saracen masters when they refused to deny their faith. Of the subsequent history of the rest we know practically nothing. During one of the later crusades, the Emperor Frederick II is said to have liberated some of the captives who in the meantime had become men; and one of the pilgrims who returned home after eighteen years of servitude reported that seven hundred of them had grown up as slaves about the palace of the governor of Alexandria, "No longer infants, but men of ripe age."[8]

Near the same date as the beginning of the Children's Crusade in France, there arose in the lower Rhine district of Germany a young peasant named Nicholas who was only ten years of age. It is not known if he received his idea from Stephen or received it independently. In any event, when he began to speak of a crusade the idea spread rapidly to many sections of the country. From the agricultural classes they left their ploughs, carts, or herds, and hastened to join the bands which were marching through the country. The sons of the noblemen hastened to join the marching masses. Within a short time their number increased to more than twenty thousand. Children of princes and those of the peasants united on a common basis, and the youth and the maid experienced the same rough task of a soldier's life.[9]

Nicholas bore aloft a flag on which was a Latin cross. Many of his followers wore long pilgrim cloaks, bore uplifted crosses and carried staves and leather purses. When it was known that they were about to start, undesirable characters of both sexes mingled with the excited children and marching away with them seized every opportunity to debauch and to spoil them.

Their journey up the Rhine Valley to the Alps was not so arduous, yet along the way they suffered from hardships, and some were robbed of the alms that had been given them. Some were kidnapped for ransom or immoral purposes, and a few were murdered outright. After having traveled three hundred and fifty miles they came to the foot of the Alps where many veterans of the best-disciplined armies had been unable to cross. But these high, snow-crested barriers failed to check the course of those German children. They penetrated the mountain passes, made their way over desolate, snow-covered ranges, and though their numbers grew less, they finally descended into the plains of Lombardy.

After a short rest the main body then marched down the Italian coast expecting a miraculous pathway through the sea to Palestine. At Piedmont the Italians refused the children entrance into their town. Some were captured and forced into slavery. The others pressed on until from a hilltop they beheld Genoa and the blue Mediterranean. Banners were raised and songs were sung. Nicholas regained the confidence of his young army, and on Saturday, August 25, 1212, they presented themselves before the gates of the city.

After careful deliberation the Senate of the city admitted the children, granting them a week's rest and refreshment. After contact with the self-reliant youths and observation of their habits, the elders of the city finally decided that the period of hospitality should end on the second day. An exception was granted in favor of a few of the boys and girls of noble birth who had made a favorable impression. These were allowed to settle down and to associate with the distinguished families of the city. The others were obliged to resume their pilgrimage.[10] The terrific heat brought on sickness which resulted in the death of many, yet the main force traversed the two hundred and fifty miles to Rome where they thought they would certainly receive aid from the Pope and the people.

Rome had received many armies — living hordes and tides of humanity from almost every corner of the earth — yet never had she seen such an army as these beardless boys and tender maidens; on their way from the north of Germany to wrest the Holy Land from the infidels. On hearing of their arrival Pope Innocent III sent for them and praised them for their ardor but endeavored to persuade them to abandon the enterprise and return home. The boys, he said, must keep their vows intact to the end that when they were old enough they should crusade again.[11]

The majority turned "silently and sadly" to make their way back to their homes. But the season was then far advanced and winter caught them staggering through the Alps. Some perished in the snow, more were taken into the mountain homes, and others were sold into bondage. A few, with emaciated forms and drawn faces reached their beloved Rhineland, but how different they were! Only the more vivid minds can imagine the difference which the experiences of those few short months had made in their appearance and outlook on life. Their elders became white with rage when they understood the full truth of the tragedy which had been enacted. Laying hold upon Nicholas' father, they accused him of being a villain and a slave-dealer and as a penalty hanged him in Cologne for trying to exploit the children for his own ends.[12]

But Nicholas and a remnant of his army were unshaken in their resolve to reach Jerusalem or died in the attempt. Leaving Rome with its pope and cardinals, they marched southward and after a tramp of three hundred miles reached Brindisi, which completed a march of about a thousand miles since their departure from Cologne. On arriving at the port they found that the bishop there had been instructed to prevent them from going further. Some were prevented from embarking for Syria but were given no assistance in obtaining shelter and provisions, or to return to their own country. Some of the braver souls boarded a vessel and sang their hymns as they set sail for Palestine.

"What ultimately happened to them is shrouded in mystery. From that moment the East seems to have swallowed them up, for although inquiries continued to be made, the little company of adventurers were never heard of again, with the single exception of Nicholas, the leader of the expedition, who was reported to have fought very bravely at Damietta against the Saracens in 1218, and to have eventually returned to Cologne. Whether their ship foundered, whether they were sold as slaves, or died of disease, or from any other misadventure, history does not say. The Crusade of the German youth was over and another fine ideal had been blotted from the world."[13]

The aftermath was more painful, for hope had been killed and agony alone remained. Limping along, barefoot, footsore, and ragged, in pitiable plight, this final contingent which attempted the return journey passed through the selfsame towns and villages in which they had so gallantly chanted their battle-cry but a few weeks before. Hundreds succumbed to disease. Many died by the roadside and were left unburied. What was even worse, many of the girls were led astray and afterwards wandered about with babes in their arms or in despair took to a life of shame. The picture was more pathetic than the human annals have before or since presented.[14]

A pall of apathy seems to have settled over Europe. All that the Pope could find to say, when he was told that the flower of the French and German youth had been decimated, was: "The very children put us to shame, for while we sleep, they go forth gladly to the defense of the Holy Land."[15]

## Chapter XXVII

# FATE OF THE CRUSADER KINGDOM

SOME HAVE SUPPOSED that the Children's Crusade "lit no torch and taught no lesson," but the pathetic sacrifice, coupled with the Pope's comment, had much to do in rousing the Christians of Europe to re-arm and redeem the rapidly disintegrating Christian kingdom of the Near East. In fact only three years had passed when Pope Innocent III responded to an appeal from Palestine and issued a letter to the Christian rulers of Europe, proclaiming the fourth Lateran Council. Before this great ingathering of the representatives of all Christian Europe he proclaimed a crusade for the following year, and called upon the leaders to unite and once more undertake the great work of subjugating the Moslems of Syria.[1]

This time the leaders of the expedition were King Andrew of Hungary and Emperor Frederick II of Germany. In addition to this there was a third army organized, consisting of a mixed multitude of Germans, French, Italians, and English. King Andrew set out with his forces in the year 1216, and was joined enroute by the Dukes of Austria and Bavaria. He arrived in Palestine, ravaged a few undefended districts, then for some reason gave up the enterprise, and re-embarked to Europe; having accomplished nothing.

The Germans, however, who had accompanied the expedition showed better mettle by joining themselves with the knights of Palestine to defend Antioch, Acre, and Athlit — the fragment of the crusader provinces. For some unknown reason the Christian soldiers fitted out an expedition and left Syria on a conquest of Egypt. Proceeding to Damietta, at the mouth of the Nile, the Christian forces laid siege to the double-walled city, and augmented by the constant arrivals from Europe, they finally burst into and took full control of this city which the Moslems had considered impregnable.

Coradinum and Al Kamil, two weak princes seated on the respective thrones of Damascus and Cairo, became greatly perturbed lest fresh forces from Europe make it possible for both Egypt and Palestine to be wrested from their hands. A bit later when about forty-six thousand Crusaders marched up the Damietta branch of the Nile toward Cairo,

Al Kamil took such fright that he offered to cede all Palestine to the Christians on the single condition that they should withdraw from Egypt. Such an offer had never been and never would again be made to Christians. Not only the Holy City, with the sacred sepulchre of Christ, but all Palestine was now theirs for the taking. King John of Palestine, the French and English barons, and the German knights eagerly favored the acceptance of such an offer; but the Templars and Hospitallers, along with the Italian leaders, and the stupid bigotry of Cardinal Pelagius, the legate of the pope, were so taken with the prospects of capturing the treasure-houses of Egypt that they let the offer go by unaccepted, and thereby lost the greatest opportunity of all Crusader times.[2]

One hot day in 1219, the Crusaders were resting when Francis of Assisi, a saintly monk and fearless preacher, walked into their camp and in his sermon took them to task for their outrages and massacres, condemned the moral corruption of the army, and informed them that they would surely be defeated unless wickedness were put away from them. Then going directly to the enemy's camp he preached "Peace and goodwill," then disappeared as quickly as he came.

The voice of the strange preacher had scarcely died away on the Egyptian air when the princes of Damascus and Cairo united their forces and marched against the Christians who were then encamped near Mansura. With the rise of the Nile the Moslems deliberately cut the channels, and overflowed the Delta surrounding the Crusaders. Without food and floundering in mud, the bigots who were responsible for the carnal clumsiness, sent an embassy to the Sultan offering him the city of Damietta for the privilege of retiring from Egypt. The Sultan readily accepted the offer and the crest-fallen crusaders took ship as quickly as possible and made for Acre.

The aftermath of discouragement was so great that large numbers of the warriors abandoned their fellow-crusaders and returned to Europe. Potentially the fifth crusade had offered more than any other, yet actually it accomplished virtually nothing. The papal legate had steered it to its ultimate fate!

The kingdom in Palestine became so shadowy and uncertain that the grandmaster of the Teutonic Knights and King John of Jerusalem grew so eager for help from Europe that they proposed to Frederick II of Germany that King John's daughter, Iolanta, should be given to Frederick in marriage if the German emperor would accept the Crusader province and lead an army to the Holy Land for the re-establishment of the kingdom planted by Godfrey in the city of Jerusalem. In the year 1225 Frederick II received thirteen-year-old princess Iolanta (Isabella) in marriage, and solemnly bound himself to lead an army to the Holy Land. But after the wedding was over he became enamoured of other affairs and delayed his Crusade to Palestine, although the pope often urged him to fulfill his solemn promise.

Finally Pope Honorius III died and Gregory IX succeeded to the papal throne. One of the first acts of the new pope was to send a letter to Frederick demanding that he fulfill his vow and lead an expedition to Palestine. Aroused by a sense of duty and the demands of the day, the emperor collected his army and in the autumn of 1227 took ships at Brindisi and departed for Palestine. The intense heat of southern Italy had already brought sickness and death to many of his men. Ship life brought such a wave of sickness and death that Frederick put back to port at Otronto.

Supposing him to be playing false in order to delay the fulfilment of his vow, the pope excummunicated Frederick and forbade his ever leading an army to Palestine. Astonished and stunned at such rigid measures, the emperor tarried until winter was past, then rallied sufficient soldiers to man twenty galleys and sailed away to Palestine in spite of the interdict of the pope. Veterans of former Crusades looked upon the move with contempt, and the pope followed him with anathemas and laid plans to defeat and cover him with disgrace. Nevertheless, the emperor made all speed and arrived at Acre with his handful of soldiers and prepared for the re-conquest of Palestine.

The masters of the Hospitallers and Templars, acting under the commands of the pope, refused to co-operate with Frederick and left him to lead his small army of thirty-five hundred German knights and ten thousand foot-soldiers. However, he prosecuted his campaign with such vigor that Syrian nobles loaned him money and many of their soldiers joined his forces. His first move was to write Al Kamil at Cairo that he had once offered to grant all Palestine to the Christians, and that it would be to his interest to do as much for him. The Sultan admired his frankness and diplomacy, but was reluctant to make any further concession than was absolutely necessary. In the meantime Frederick marched down the coast, took Jaffa, strengthened its fortification, then marching upon Bethlehem, Nazareth and other smaller cities, he drove everything before him. The people in Jerusalem and Damascus became so alarmed that Sultan Al Kamil advised that he was favorably inclined toward signing a peace treaty.

The terms of the treaty which was made on February 18, 1229, stipulated that henceforth Jerusalem and a strip of land from the coast to the Holy City should belong to the Christians; that the cities which Frederick had conquered should remain in possession of the Christians, and that the Mohammedan pilgrims should be permitted to visit the Mosque at Jerusalem; and that the peace should not be broken for ten years.

The pope's wrath knew no bounds when he heard of the victory of the excommunicated emperor. But acting as though there were no pope, Emperor Frederick entered the city of Jerusalem, followed by his train of German knights and soldiers, and going to the church of the Holy Sepulchre he knelt at the altar and placed the crown on his own head, for no churchman could perform the office.[3]

The victorious emperor returned to Acre and then set sail for Europe, where he was showered with honors by his own countrymen. The sixth Crusade had succeeded as signally as the fifth had failed, despite the fact that the pope, the Patriarch of Jerusalem, and the Templars and the Hospitallers had not only refused aid but had attempted in every way possible to thwart the plans of the man who succeeded.

The stupidity of those who remained in Palestine was so great that they did not enter in to occupy that which had been turned over to them. As for the pope, his efforts were turned to fighting Frederick rather than lending his influence toward the adoption of constructive and adequate measures for taking care of the partially restored kingdom in the Holy Land.

The persecutions which were directed against Frederick II not only brought bitter hatred in Europe but finally brought civil war in Palestine. After the strife had continued for a long while there was a measure of reconciliation effected between Frederick and the pope. But sad were the results in Palestine where more than half of the time of the truce concluded by the emperor with the Sultan had passed and little or nothing had been done toward securing the conquests made by Frederick in Palestine.

Learning of the division and bitter strife among the Christians the Moslem Emirs of Syria broke the truce, fell upon the outposts which had been established by Frederick and massacred a large body of Christian pilgrims on their way from Acre to Jerusalem. Then, as if that were not sufficient, they fought with the Templars and almost annihilated them. One disaster followed another until in 1244 Jerusalem was lost to Medieval Christendom.[4] The church which had been busy fighting Frederick found it necessary to turn its efforts toward the restoration of the Christian kingdom in Palestine lest every foothold in that country be lost. A council was called at Spoleto where it was decided that the holy war should be renewed and that the Franciscan and Dominican friars were to preach the Crusade in the various European countries.

Seven years had passed and it was discovered that the moneys which the monks had raised for equipping the armies had gotten no farther than the coffers of the monks and the papal treasury at Rome. There was no crusade — selfish greed had consumed its very potentialities.

In the meantime, the Sultan of Egypt had marched against Jerusalem with a large army, ejected the Christians and shut the gates of the city against them. The news of this proceeding stirred Europe until the barons of France and England, the Duke of Burgundy, and other nobles organized expeditions, independent of the pope and made their way to Palestine, where Richard of Cornwall, nephew to Richard the Lion Heart, took control and carried on an almost bloodless expedition which restored to the Christians the greater part of the territory which had belonged to them during the times of Baldwin I.

For two years the Christians enjoyed peace and prosperity. Then, in 1242 the Templars who had taken little or no part in the recent conquests offended the Emir of Egypt, which resulted in his influencing the Persian brigands, under the leadership of their chief, Barbacan, to march on Jerusalem and inaugurate one of the foulest massacres ever known in its history. Christians and Mohammendans were slain together. Churches were robbed, tombs rifled, and Jerusalem converted into a waste. In order to stop the carnage and destruction in Palestine the knights and the Syrian Moslems united their forces and fought with the Persians. Risking all on a single battle — the batter of Gaza — they lost, and the grandmasters of the Hospitallers and Knight Templars and the majority of the Christian soldiery of Palestine perished. The Persian victors seized the fortresses of Tiberias and Ashkelon, and swept on until only Acre and Athlit were left.

The Moslems of Syria and Egypt finally united their forces and defeated the Persian brigands and drove them from Palestine. But the position of the Christian kingdom was the most precarious it had been since the Crusaders first came to Palestine.

The loss of Jerusalem aroused all Christian Europe and caused Innocent IV who had recently come to the papal throne to convene a general council of the church at Lyons where he called on the secular princes of the west to suspend their hostilities toward each other for four years and combine their energies that they all might prosecute a great expedition in Palestine. This was in 1244.

In England the flame of Crusading enthusiasm burst forth with exceptional brightness. William Long Sword, the Bishop of Salisbury, the Earl of Leicester, Sir Walter Delacy, and many other knights and nobles armed themselves for the conflict. King Louis IX, the most saintly of all French medieval rulers, took the cross and rallied the forces in

France. Haco, King of Norway, took the cross and became an ardent exponent of the Crusades.

The Island of Cyprus was the place appointed where they all should meet. And although it finally developed that Haco, King of Norway, was unable to go, yet at the rendezvous there was a formidable host. The fleet contained eighteen hundred vessels and the army numbered two thousand knights, seven thousand men-at-arms, and about seventy-five thousand infantry. Strange as it may seem, unwise counsel prevailed and this great host, under the leadership of King Louis, set out to capture Egypt, arguing to themselves that Egypt was the gateway of Syria.

Arriving there, they leaped from their boats, waded to shore, routed the Moslem army and took Damietta.[5] Apparently the conquest was going to be easy, but it was not to be so, for Nejmeddin, the great nephew of Saladin, had come to the throne as Sultan, and his sterling soldier qualities would not admit an easy victory to the Crusaders. Putting to death fifty of his officers for having so cowardly fled from battle, he took command in person and convinced the Crusaders that they faced a real foe. After losing much time the Christian forces decided to march on to Cairo. When they had reached Mansoura the Count of Artois, brother of the French king, gathered about him the bravest of the knights of England and France and succeeded in driving the enemy across the canal and within the walls of the city. Acting indiscreetly, he refused the counsel of William Long Sword and rashly pursued the foe through the gates into the city. The other knights, not to be shamed by his valor, charged after him and when inside, the foe surrounded them and cut down the count, William Long Sword, and the grandmaster of the Templars. The grandmaster of the Hospitallers was taken prisoner and the Christians were able to hold the city only by the arrival of King Louis with the main army. But to them the city proved comparatively useless.

About this time Nejmeddin died and the Sultanate passed to his son. But almost before he had taken up the reins of government, the Mamelukes usurped the throne and began a new regime. The crusading army was trapped and almost annihilated. King Louis was captured and finally redeemed for four hundred thousand pounds in gold. He was permitted with the shattered remnant of his forces to take ship for Acre. The majority of the surviving knights, feeling that their vow had been performed, returned home. In 1245 King Louis took ship and sailed back to France, and the *seventh* Crusade, an ill-starred expedition, came to a conclusion.

As soon as Sultan Bibars was well in control of Egypt he led an expedition into the Moslem states of Syria and compelled them to submit to his sway. Then turning his attention to the Christian kingdom he began the sordid work of destroying the Knights Templars and Hospitallers. In 1265 he took the fortress of Azotus and in the following year that of Saphoury and put to death all the knights who defended these forts. In 1268 the Memelukes captured Antioch, inaugurated a bloody massacre and sold a hundred thousand Christians into slavery. By 1270 all the inland fortresses, as well as Laodicea and Jaffa, had been taken, and there remained no hope for the Christians unless they received help from Europe.

About this time Louis IX, moved by the conquest of Bibars, took the cross a second time, and began the *eighth* Crusade. Induced to believe that the bey of Tunis might be converted to Christianity he resolved to lead an expedition to North Africa. Joined by others, the vast Christian fleet sailed into the harbor of ancient Carthage. Learning that the bey was not interested in being converted, the Christians laid siege to the city, but ere long pestilence broke out and Saint Louis sickened and died, mourning pathetically, "Jerusalem! Jerusalem!" Almost all the army was destroyed by the pestilence; only a remnant were enabled to return to France. Prince Edward of England rallied his nobles, lords, and knights to the number of about a thousand, and arrived in Acre in the spring of 1271; and although he was enabled to gather only about seven thousand soldiers, yet after a residence of fourteen months, he succeeded in wresting from the Moslems a truce for a period of ten years.[6]

Eight years of this peace passed, when the Templars and Hospitallers, who had so far forgotten their vows and given themselves up to the mercenary and selfish spirit of the times, sallied forth and attacked Moslem merchants who passed in the vicinity of Acre. Then Khatil, the Mameluke Sultan, who reigned in Cairo, swore by the name of Allah that he would exterminate the last of the Christians within the limits of his dominions. Accordingly, in 1291 he gathered an army of two hundred thousand men and pitched his camp before the walls of Acre. Within the Christian fortress and the city of Acre almost every nation of Europe was represented. But all this diversity tended to weakness, for it brought division of counsel and little unity of purpose.

The ramparts of the city were well defended, yet the atmosphere tended to uncertainty and feverish excitement. A presentiment of doom seemed to hang heavily on the spirits of those who professed to follow the Christ who had said, "They that take the sword shall perish with the sword." When it became apparent that the noncombatants should make their escape by way of the sea, thousands hurriedly gathered their few belongings and hastened to the wharf. The harbor was soon crowded with ships and the process of embarkation went steadily on until only twelve thousand knights and warriors were left to the defense of the stronghold. For thirty-three days they held out, and then the Mameluke warriors effected a breach in the walls and began to pour into the city. The few inhabitants who remained were quickly butchered or seized as slaves. The knights sallied forth and fought until only *seven* were left to tell the tale of destruction.

The fate of the Crusader Kingdom in Palestine was sealed with the final fall of Acre. Only Athlit a small but strong fortress south of Mount Carmel, was yet untaken. Here the Christians gathered waiting for they hardly knew what; clinging to the last foothold until they saw all was lost; then on that last sad night they gathered in a large assembly room within the church, had prayers, then passed to their ships, hoisted sails, and the last of the Crusaders turned their backs upon Palestine and sailed away to Cyprus. Thus ended the drama which had lasted for one hundred and ninety-one years. The Crescent had triumphed over the Cross, and the Crusaders left behind only the ruins of their castles, their blood that coursed through the veins of the natives with whom they had intermarried and the memory of wars which they had waged and a kingdom which they had founded and lost.

## CHAPTER XXVIII

# THE REIGN OF THE MAMELUKES

THE "MAMELUKES"[1] is a modest title which history has bestowed on the rulers of Egypt and Palestine during the period between 1250 and 1517 A.D. These men were selected Turkish slaves — valiant cavalrymen — serving as the Egyptian royal bodyguard who slew the ruling monarch, usurped the Egyptian throne, and raised Bibars, their chieftain, to the position of *"Sultan."*

Since the Crusades had largely spent themselves and the Moslem forces were weakened almost beyond description, it is not at all surprising that the fierce Mamelukes, under Sultan Bibars, could overrun Palestine, capturing one city after another until the fall of Acre and Athlit in 1291 A.D., gave them almost undispited control of the country so sincerely desired by many nations and peoples.

During these two hundred and sixty-seven years of Mameluke rule in Palestine, little of consequence occurred and perhaps nothing that could be said to be constructive. To begin with, the Christian churches, built by so much Crusader sacrifice and toil, were demolished.

At times, the few pilgrims who came and those Christians who continued to live in the country were permitted to visit holy places with considerable freedom; at other times it was with difficulty, and usually by payment of a generous tribute.

During the reign of Nasir (1294-1341) grievous restrictions were issued upon both Jews and Christians. They were not only debarred from holding public office, but as distinguishing marks, the Christians were obliged by law to wear a blue turban and the Jews a yellow one.[2]

Twice was Nasir dethroned, and he reigned during *three* periods. On his first deposition, the Mameluke emirs chose Ketboga as ruler, and during these few years Palestine and adjoining countries suffered one of the most severe and prolonged droughts on record. Little food was to be found in the country, and it sold for fabulous sums, "Dogs, cats, vermin, and even young children were eaten."[3]

In 1363 the Christian king of Cyprus made a truce with the Sultan of Egypt, which gave him trading privileges in Beirut, Tyre, Acre, Jerusalem, and Damascus, and the opportunity of rebuilding the Christian churches in Nazareth, Jerusalem, and Bethlehem.[4] But Christians and Jews never knew when to expect kind or cruel treatment, nor when their buildings would be demolished. The state of uncertainty in which they were obliged to move was somewhat alleviated during the last century of Mameluke rule, but most of the improvement was for the Jew; the conflict of the Crusades could not be forgotten.

## Chapter XXIX

# FOUR CENTURIES OF TURKISH RULE

Selim I, "the Grim," of Turkey, and the Mameluke Sultan of Egypt, went to war in 1516 A.D. Their armies met for the decisive conflict in Northern Syria where the Turks triumphed and advanced southward along the coastal plain. Entering Egypt the following year they utterly routed the Mamelukes, hanged the unfortunate Sultan at the chief gate at Cairo, and assumed nominal control.[1] Thus, Palestine fell to the Turks in 1517 A.D. and their flag was destined to wave over the Holy Land until 1917 — exactly *four centuries.*

The Mameluke reign of evil had been so very unjust that the change of masters was welcomed as a boon by the people of neglected and abused Palestine. The people expected much, but for the first three years received little attention of any kind. Selim, the over-ambitious monarch, was occupied with plans to take yet other countries by conquest. His early death brought to the throne his son, Suleiman I, "the Magnificent," who systematized the laws, improved the lot of the poor, corrected many abuses aimed at Christians, and in 1537-41 rebuilt the walls of Jerusalem — which to this day stand as a monument to his memory.

During the splendid reign of Suleiman, or Solyman "The Magnificent," which lasted for forty-six years, the Ottoman Empire reached the zenith of its power and glory. The period has been known as the "Golden Age" of the Turkish Empire. His successor ruled fairly for a short time; then with the death of Suleiman II the sad and sorry rule of the "pashas" began, and continued with minor changes until the end of Turkish domination.

The "pashas" were provincial governors, of Turkish birth, who were appointed by the Ottoman government at Constantinople, to rule with all but unlimited power over certain outlying countries of which Palestine and Syria composed one. These pashas paid enormous prices to the Sultan for their annual appointments; they lived in almost regal splendor in their provincial capitols and made handsome presents to the principal officers of the court and government at Constantinople in order to enhance their prestige and to secure the support of powerful friends against intrigues which their opponents were constantly setting on foot about the royal court.[2]

Complaints of their mis-government frequently reached the court officials, and this necessitated additional gifts. All this, added to their private extravagance, caused them to often be in want of money, and to meet these expenses and bring enrichment to themselves, the pashas mercilessly taxed their subjects. Favoritism was showered upon those who responded and cruel oppression meted out to all who refused "allegiance." Thus the pasha often grew rich at the expense of his subjects.[3]

Native councilors, or "beys," were appointed to assist and act as a check on the pasha should he be inclined to act unjustly, but these native councilors were usually as corrupt as the governor himself, and quite as ready to get all they could for themselves out of their fellow-citizens.

Of course, these pashas and "beys" did little of the actual work but usually parcelled out their work to men of scant ability and too frequently of low morals. These native princes often grew rich at the expense of the populace, and oppressed the people under their jurisdiction until they were often regarded as no more than "petty tyrants" who were occasionally removed from office by public petition. Their successors righted no wrongs, restored no stolen property, and collected no less taxes.

Beside these there was in the provinces an ancient hereditary feudal aristocracy known as the "Effendi." These consisted of old families, the ancestors of which, as a recompense for their faithfulness to the government, had received certain portions of land which they had helped to conquer. The effendi frequently owned whole districts, held the peasants as their subjects, and kept soldiers to execute their commands.[4]

Sheikhs exercised a measure of authority over every village, yet the manner of rule was extremely hazy, for law and order could hardly be said to exist in Palestine at this time. Each sheikh or other person of importance paid tribute or gave gifts to some higher authority, and aside from this was a law unto himself. Blood feuds and petty wars among the Arabs were frequent. Robbers infested the roads, brigands extorted generous "gifts" from travelers while Turkish guards feigned helplessness.[5]

Every youth was subject to military call. Those who wished to be exempt had to pay fifty gold pounds each — which few could afford. Every Turkish war called for its toll of the local population, which, if they ever returned home, were often broken and invalid. Infant mortality was desperately high, plagues were common, and sanitation was very little known.

Rulers took what they pleased from whom they pleased and the people dared say little about the matter. Gifts were always in order and taxes were taken from the people until the cultivation of the soil was ground down by tax collectors and oppressors. No encouragement was given to agriculture, while on the other hand artificial terraces were permitted to be broken down and the soil to wash away. Fertile valleys were impaired by centuries of wasteful cultivation while water resources were affected by the destruction of forests. In case a man planted more olive trees, improved his farm and increased the yield of his land, the tax gatherers "came down like a wolf on the fold," and "the last state of that man was worse than the first."

With their own implements, the peasants worked the land owned by the effendi and used seeds which they bought with money usually borrowed from the landlord against a rate of interest for which the term "usurious" was very mild. At harvest time the tax collectors flocked to the villages to collect their taxes *in kind.* They were no sooner away than the effendi appeared on the scene to collect his rent of from twenty-five to fifty percent of the crops. If the peasant had further debt the money-lender appeared and collected his money plus exorbitant interest. Thus the peasant was often left with a few piles of grain, some primitive tools and equally as poor prospects of the coming season. Many lost hope and became spiritless under such "hard bondage and oppression, usury and violence."[6]

Ever and anon affairs became intolerable and the people revolted, but their lot was not long improved, for at best they only received a new pasha, who in all probability soon sank to the level of his predecessor. The Port at Constantinople not only tolerated such unjust government but permitted the population to decline in numbers, the soil to be destroyed, and the resources of the country to lie undeveloped.

In 1807 Ali Bey complained that "the want of books and masters to instruct the people in the physical sciences and the innumerable discoveries of the last ages keeps from them those interesting acquirements which could not fail to give elevation to the mind."[7] In a further comment he designated the Turkish Empire as "a nation in which hardly one individual in a thousand knows how to read and write."[8]

Thus, for four centuries Palestine was ruled by an alien race which had no interest in the development of the country, its institutions, or its ideals. Complacency, intrigue, and a touch of romanticism so characterized these strange and sordid centuries as to suggest a carry-over in governmental affairs from the "Dark Ages." The chief thought of government at Constantinople seemed to be to receive revenues; therefore pashas, princes, and sheikhs had no incentive to rule justly, but heaped upon the country heavy taxation, neglect, and mal-administration until not only was the land cursed from Dan to Beersheba, but the entire Turkish Empire from Cairo to Constantinople.

Some suppose the Turks spent a long time in doing *nothing* with the country — if indeed, misusing, abusing, and bringing it to ruin can be so generously evaluated. But the Turk was not *all* to blame. He was suspected of evil designs from the first. For centuries there had been a feeling which was often expressed in semi-prophetic phrases that the "Turkish scourge" was to last for but a limited time, then God would break his power of rule in the Near East; that "within a certain time best known to God, his divine majesty, opening the eyes of his clemency upon the Christians, will unite the wills of their Princes, kindle their affections with holy zeal, and blessing their arms, will make them victorious over the Turk, whom he will banish out of the east, and chase into Scythia, from whence they came to be a scourge unto Christendom."[9]

Vast reserves of energy, resourcefulness, endurance, and persistence are necessary factors for success against great odds. The Turk, being a bit short on these essentials, finally failed — as many prayed for and every one expected — and after salvaging his vast empire had only the heart of the carcase left as a residue for favorable display before the eyes of a greedy Western World.

The complacency of these four centuries was interrupted by a few adventurous and dynamic characters who, entering the Palestinian stage, played rather dramatic roles, and at least left something of which the historians may write. These characters were: Fakr-ed-Din, Omar Zahar, Jezzer-Pasha, Napoleon Bonaparte, and Mohammed Ali.

## Fakr-ed-Din

Fakr-ed-Din of Beirut was appointed chief of the Druzes and ruled as Emir from 1595 to 1631 A.D. During this time he drove back the Bedouin Arab tribes which so often crowded into the fertile plains of Syria and Palestine, and extended his rule over southern Lebanon and upper Galilee. He expelled the Turkish representative, then quieted the Ottoman government by paying a heavy tribute. In time, however, as the powerful Sheikh became stronger he endeavored to become independent by shaking off the Turkish yoke. The central government at Constantinople became alarmed and sent an expedition to crush him.

Fakr-ed-Din fled to Italy where he remained a few years at the court of the Medicis at Florence. His son, Ali, repulsed the Turks and held his territory. On his return from Europe, the Sheikh, having imbibed an appreciation for Christianity and justice and Western ways, endeavored to introduce Western innovations in his dominions. His kindness and favor to the Christians aroused his Mohammedan subjects and Sultan Murad "availed himself of the hatred" of these Moslem subjects against the Emir by ordering the Pasha of Damascus to attack Fakr-ed-Din. His son, Ali, who led the Druze forces, was defeated at Safed. Beirut was captured and the Emir taken to Constantinople, where he was strangled in 1631, and his followers, especially the Christians, were disappointed in their hope of a better day.[10]

## Omar Zahar

Soon after the middle of the eighteenth century an Arab Sheikh of one of the Bedouin tribes from the Hauran, east of the Sea of Galilee, arose to power and apparently did the reverse to Fakr-ed-Din, who had arisen to spectacular heights during the previous century. The Emir (Fakr-ed-Din) had been of the more civilized group which continually guarded the *status quo* against the hordes of Bedouin Arabs which at certain seasons swarmed in from the desert and grazed their herds in the Jordan Valley. That the leader of one of these Bedouin groups should come in to restore peace and make portions of Palestine prosperous is a bit of irony which goes to make up the history of the country.

Zahar planted himself in the mountain fastness at Safed, took Tiberias from the Pasha of Damascus, then seized Acre and firmly established himself there. He put to death all rivals to the throne, built forts, restored the defenses of the city of Acre, and erected for himself a strong castle on the hills about nine miles to the northeast. He subdued the other Arab tribes, put down the lawless element, restored peace, made the land more productive, and brought such prosperity and contentment that the people from far and near were glad to place themselves under his protection. Becoming master of all the Galilee district, he built a splendid port at Acre, where he received merchant ships from various European countries.

In 1768 he asked the government at Constantinople to confer on him and his heirs the title of "Sheikh of Acre, Prince of Princes, Governor of Nazareth, Tiberias and Safed, and Sheikh of all Galilee" — a rather *modest* title for a Bedouin Sheikh, yet his accomplishments were such as to make him extremely popular with the people of Palestine and correspondingly feared by the Port at Constantinople.

In 1769, while Turkey was engaged in war with Russia, Ali Bey, ruler of Egypt, made an alliance with Zahar. In carrying out the terms of the alliance, Mohammed, Ali's general came to Palestine and assisted

Zahar in the defeat of the Pasha's army, then returned, leaving Zahar in sole possession. In later life he became so very rich and indolent as to neglect his people and the affairs of his district. Bad management culminated in an investigation by the Sultan during the year 1780. Feeling sufficiently independent, he quarreled with the Sultan and refused him further tribute.

Incensed at the rebuff, the Sultan dispatched a fleet from Constantinople to bring the inefficient but haughty rebel to his senses. Calling at Beirut, the fleet took on board an official named Ahmed Bey, and then proceeded to Acre, where they bombarded the forts to such good effect that Zahar, accompanied by two of his Moorish slaves, fled from the town across the plain eastward. However, the two affrighted dependents, having no desire to be on the losing side, fell upon their master and having cut off his head, returned to greet the conqueror. "Whose head is that?" asked the admiral. "It is the head of Omar Zahar, late ruler of this place," was the reply. "And who are you?" continued the admiral. "We are two Moors, the personal servants of Omar. We have cut off his head, and thus should die all who dare to oppose you." The admiral motioned to his executioner, who was near by, and in a very few moments, the two servants of Zahar paid for their unfaithfulness by having their heads struck from their shoulders.[11]

## Jezzer Pasha

During the time Zahar had ruled in Acre, an Albanian slave named Ahmed, had become efficient at the Egyptian court in carrying out the orders of the ruler and getting rid of inconvenient rivals, for which service he received the title of el-Jezzer ("the butcher"). On getting into difficulty with his master, Mohammed Bey, he had taken refuge with Zahar at Acre but returned to Egypt five years later, on the death of Mohammed Bey, where as a Turkish official he was known as Ahmed Bey. When Zahar revolted, the Turkish government had him come to Beirut and join their fleet, and direct the campaign against the insurrection at Acre. His success and Zahar's defeat and death caused the Turkish government to install him as governor of Acre, a position he held from 1780 to 1802.

During these years he was known to the people as Ahmed Pasha el-Jezzer. He taxed agricultural enterprises, banished the French factories, and cruelly put many out of the way by death. No one doubted his right to the title — ("the butcher"). A typical case of his cruelty is found in the following: The Pasha one day met a Christian banker, an exceedingly handsome man, to whom Pasha el-Jezzer owed a large

sum of money. Resolving to spoil the banker's good looks, the governor ordered that his right eye be put out. This was done, but a few months afterwards the butcher met him again, and to his amazement and rage the Christian looked no less handsome than before, for he had pulled a fold of his turban over his sightless eye. The Pasha ordered that his other eye be put out, and in a short time the unfortunate man also lost his head, and the Pasha's debt to the deceased Christian was not paid.

Yet despite all his cruelty there was an aggressiveness that helped to counterbalance his heartlessness. Since the city of Acre needed a better water supply, he set his men to work to construct a splendid aqueduct that has stood until this day. He so improved the city from within and fortified it from without that he was enabled to successfully withstand the siege of 1798 conducted by Napoleon Bonaparte the great French military leader.

## Napoleon

Following brilliant victories in Europe, there came a brief season of peace. Then Napoleon Bonaparte's military turn of mind caused him to survey the field and turn his attention to Egypt. Supported by a well equipped fleet and an army of thirty thousand, he sailed away from Toulon in May of 1798. After twelve days at sea Napoleon and his men landed at Cairo, conquered the Mamelukes and took charge of the country "with the easy sweep of a wave over level sand."[12]

"Under the spell of the forty centuries which regarded him from the pyramids,"[13] he announced his design to conquer Palestine and restore the Jews to their fatherland. Lloyd George thinks that Napoleon had in mind to "take Europe in the rear"[14] by gaining Egypt, Palestine, and Constantinople; then proceeding to attack Austria. Others think he had in mind to march on eastward until, like Alexander, India and the east should lay at his feet. Be that as it may; he marched along the Maritime plain and with comparative ease took Gaza, Joppa, and Caesarea, then marched on northward as many a general before him had done.

Once on the brow of Mount Carmel, he overlooked the bay, and pointing to Acre, said to Murat, "The fate of the East depends upon yonder petty town, Constantinople, and the Indies; a new empire in the East, and a change in the face of the whole world." Eight times he led his veteran soldiers to the assault, and eleven times he withstood the desperate sallies of the Turkish sabers, but Acre stood, being defended by "the bloody Butcher" within and protected by English and Austrian warships from the sea.

Hearing that a Turkish army of thirty-six thousand were marching to attack him in the rear, Napoleon sent a detachment of troops under General Jean Baptiste Kleber across the plain of Esdraelon to take Nazareth and Tiberias. The Turks surrounded Kleber's small army at the foot of Mount Tabor, but when about to strike, heard the French soldiers cry out: "Here comes the little Corporal," and indeed, Napoleon did come. Three hundred of his troops surprised the Turkish camp and set fire to their tents. The Turks fell into a panic and retreated in confusion, part toward the Jordan and part toward Nablus; their losses were heavy.

Napoleon returned to Acre and rejoined his small force of one thousand men which was besieging an army numbering eight thousand, supported by two British men-of-war. Soon after his arrival a Turkish fleet with twelve thousand reinforcements and abundant stores arrived in the harbor. Seeing that the situation was hopeless Napoleon made an eloquent speech to his small army, then turned his back on Acre and marched away to Egypt, and from thence sailed to Europe where within a few years he made a record which caused him to go down in history as the world's greatest military genius.

## Mohammed Ali

Jezzer el Pasha died in 1802 and was buried in the great Mosque of Acre and was succeeded by his son, Suleiman. The weakness of Suleiman made a number of petty independent chiefs to spring up, who not only disregarded Suleiman, but defied the Port at Constantinople. Suleiman died in 1814 and was followed by Abdulla Pasha, who strengthened the fortifications, and built the citadel and repaired the present aqueduct extending northward from the city of Acre.

The wickedness and deceitfulness of Abdulla caused him to have his Jewish secretary murdered. The Jew had anticipated just such an event and had secretly arranged that after his death an inventory of Abdulla's property should fall into the hands of the government — knowing that the latter had claims on the estates of el-Jezzer and Suleiman.

The government accordingly pressed its claims; — Abdulla refused to pay and was besieged in Acre. He called for the intervention of Mohammed Ali who sent twenty thousand men under the command of his son Ibrahem Pasha and settled the dispute, but when, in 1831, Abdulla refused to properly remunerate the Egyptian leader, he laid siege to Acre, took and plundered it. The Turks were expelled and Mohammed Ali ruled over Palestine. He increased taxation but outwardly showed a tolerant spirit toward religion. "While arraying himself in the cloak of European civilization he was crushing the inhabitants of the Holy Land under a heavy yoke."[15]

On the twenty-fifth of June, 1839, a battle was fought at Nezib, where whole Turkish regiments with their officers, bought with Egyptian money, went over to the Egyptians. The Turkish forces were routed and the Ottoman fleet was treacherously delivered into the hands of the Viceroy. The European powers intervened. A fleet representing the allies attacked the Syrian coast and Mohammed Ali was obliged to sign a treaty in London on July 15, 1840. Palestine and Syria were restored to the Sultan, and Mohammed Ali and his successors were obliged to remain hereditary rulers of Egypt under the nominal suzerainty of the Port.

After this the European nations began to take a more active interest in Palestine. Protestants, Catholics, and Jews founded missions or colonies, or sent their representatives to the land of three faiths. The German Kaiser visited Palestine in 1898, and lent almost unlimited encouragement to German commercial and religious enterprises. The people were led to believe that Germany would be glad to control the entire Levant. But she was not alone in her ambitions, for France had held claims on Syria since the days of the Crusades, and the British longed for Palestine more than for any other country which might come into her possession.

The "Port"[16] — as the power and authority of the Turkish government at Constantinople was called — was occasionally faced with depleted finances and needed loans to replenish her exchequer and make possible her continued existence. These loans, during the later periods preceding the world war, were made by governments with the throttling threat that no more help would be forthcoming if Turkey charged beyond *ten* per cent port duties on incoming merchandise.[17]

With little encouragement for agriculture, and less for the development of her natural resources, the Turkish empire teemed with many a doubtful and hazardous tax situation; yet the Port at Constantinople sat in luxurious sublimity, "fared sumptuously every day" and lacked sufficient energy to rise and "shoo" away the powers that peacefully penerated the Levant by means of commercial aggression.

These "Great Powers" gradually tightened their throttling cord about the Turkish neck. Yet the desires of foreign nations were not to be gratified until the Turks should occupy Palestine while the sands of four centuries told out their full tale of time.

## Chapter XXX

# THE REVOLT OF THE ARABS

The Arabs have ever chafed under restraint and rejoiced in liberty and outdoor life as few people on the face of the earth. Arab feet and Arab fortunes have moved and been blown willy nilly over the vast, sandy, arid peninsula of Arabia while the sands of time have told out the tale of more than three millenia. During the last century Turkish despotism extended its direct sway over certain larger towns in which strong Turkish garrisons were soon established. Roaming tribes and outlying districts were kept more or less in fear by the heartlessness and ruthlessness occasionally practiced by these foreign garrisons.

The Arabs never acquiesced to this galling yoke, but persistently resented it and saw to it that Turkish authority never entirely robbed them of all rights and never extended over all their beloved peninsula. Any rule, however, was extremely irksome, and there was an occasional rebellion.

In 1904, a kind of "Arab renaissance" got under way. It was supported by two very effective secret revolutionary societies which hastened its spread; and deepened the desire for national freedom and for the unity of all Arab peoples in an Arab state with officials of their own choosing. However, it soon became apparent that self-release was impractical if not impossible. They then began to look for help from outside seources.

In 1912, Turkey's discontented element organized a movement known as the Young Turk revolution. In this the Arabs thought they saw the dawn of a new era when at least a greater measure of freedom would be granted them; therefore they joined the Young Turks in their effort to overthrow the old regime. However, their hopes were soon dispelled, for when the Sultan was overthrown and the new Committee of Unity and Progress set out to Ottomanize all the peoples and races which made up the Turkish Empire, the Arabs saw that a deliberate attempt was being made to suppress their culture and traditions, and to substitute for them that which was purely Turkish. Even their beautiful language — "the tongue of angels," as they call it — came near being displaced by the Turkish.

The disillusioned Arabs fell back discouraged but not entirely hopeless. Great Britain was a neighbor and friend which had long held India and had been interested in every important land and water route to that country. As early as the seventeenth century a British concern known as the East India Company had established trading posts along the shores of the Persian Gulf. Britain had virtually owned and controlled the Suez Canal since 1875 and her navy had cleared the Gulf of pirates, made it safer for commerce by buoys and beacons, and had not only cultivated the friendship of the Arabs but had seen to it that no other power established itself in sections lying immediately off these waters.

Once or twice Britain had helped certain Arab tribes and there was a kind of gentleman's agreement that more substantial help would be forthcoming when the day arrived for the Turkish yoke to be thrown off. When Turkey entered the World War on September 8, 1914, the British representative in Egypt immediately sent to inform the Arab leaders that British assistance would be forthcoming if they desired to throw off the Turkish yoke, join the Allies, and actively participate in the war against the Central powers.

The Sheikh of Koweit hesitated to take sides openly, but Ibn Saud of the Nejd, and Hussein, the High Sheriff of Mecca, were disposed to throw off the yoke and declare themselves at war with Turkey at the earliest moment such a move seemed wise.

Captain Shakespear was sent into Central Arabia where, in behalf of the British Government, he negotiated with Ibn Saud, the great Arab leader of modern times. Soon the revolt was on and arms were clashing, but in the first engagement Captain Shakespear lost his life while operating a machine gun in the front ranks of the desert phalanx. This unfortunate incident brought to an end Great Britain's efforts to deal through Ibn Saud. He and his men of the Nejd lost their opportunity to distinguish themselves in the great world conflict. Britain's attention was now turned to Hussein, High Sherif of Mecca and ruler of the Hejaz.

On June 9, 1916, the Grand Sherif of Mecca, aided by his four sons, raised the revolt against Turkish imperialism. As the ruler of Mecca and head of the prophet's family he carried most of the Arab tribes of the Hejaz with him in the revolt. Soon after the signal was given, the swarthy Arabs easily crushed the Turkish garrisons of Taif, Mecca, and Jidda, and opened up communication with the British fleet in the Red Sea so that the arms and food needed for the desert men might be brought to their coast.

At Medina, where Sherifs Feisal and Ali raised their father's flag on June 13, events were less fortunate. The Turks had expected hostility and had brought down large forces from Syria; and although Feisal raised all the tribesmen and villagers about Medina and occupied the suburbs yet he was unable to take the Holy City itself. The wanton massacre of the Arab women and children and the bursting shrapnel and artillery fire caused Feisal and his Arab forces to fall back from the level plains about Medina into the hills where he tried to hold his disheartened men together while he sent messenger after messenger to Rabegh, their sea-base, to beg that fresh stores, money, and arms might be sent them. They seemed slow in coming for his father was dependent on the British for these supplies.

At this juncture began one of the most thrilling chapters of Arabian history and of the world war. Thomas E. Lawrence,[1] a former archaeologist and at that time an attaché of the British war office at Cairo, boarded a naval vessel on the way down the Red Sea, supposedly on a "joyride" with Sir Ronald Storrs, the confidential assistant of the British High Commissioner. Sir Ronald was making an official trip to Jidda where he was to meet Sherif Abdulla, second son of Hussein, Grand Sherif of Mecca, to discuss future plans of the war, and especially the possibility of British aid in a measure which had not thus far been extended.

During the interview Abdullah laid the need before Sir Ronald Storrs and begged that a British brigade, composed of Moslem troops if possible, be mobilized at Suez and rushed to Rabegh in order to strengthen Ali and Feisal and turn the tide of battle in favor of the Arabs. Storrs urged the importance of full and early information from a trained observer for the British Commander-in-Chief in Egypt, and suggested that Lawrence be permitted to take ship for Rabegh and from thence ride up the Sultani road toward Medina as far as Feisal's camp to talk over the needs and prospects with Feisal, then report to the British command in Egypt.

This presented no small difficulty, for Christians had long been forbidden to enter Arabia. Both Abdullah and Storrs talked to the Grand Sherif over the phone and gained his permission for Abdullah to write Ali, who was then commanding the Arab forces at Rabegh, to suggest that Lawrence be mounted at Rabegh and conveyed safely and as quickly as possible to Feisal's camp.

On seeing Feisal, the thirty-seventh descendant of Mohammed, dressed in his long white silken robes, standing in the doorway of his black tent, Lawrence fancied he looked upon the Arab leader who would assist him in bringing the Arab revolt to a successful issue.[2] After the formalities were over Feisal asked Lawrence how he liked his camp, and was astonished to receive the reply, "Well, but it is far from Damascus."

On making his report at Cairo he was furnished with men, money, up-to-date artillery, and a large battle cruiser; the latter to lend prestige, back up the land forces, and use as occasion might require. When the steamer put into port at Rabegh there was great rejoicing among the Arab forces.

Lawrence, the quiet-mannered blond Britisher, donned native clothing and was presented with a ceremonial dagger and placed on a level with the Grand Sherif's sons.[3] After this, he loaded his camels with sacks of gold and plunged into the arid peninsula, where he sought the sheikhs and fighting men of western Arabia.

Throughout the Hejaz he rode the grey limestone hills, the black besaltic steeps, and the sandy wastes of that arid country in search of Bedouin encampments where with gold, promises of priceless freedom and potential Arab nationalism, he enlisted from among the scattered tribes of western Arabia an army of two hundred thousand Bedouins for the Allied cause.[4] These swarthy, backward, yet keen-witted sons of Ishmael were elated over money, modern rifles, and the privilege of going to war with great nations as their allies and paymasters.

Lawrence mounted his "irregulars" on camels or horses, and with these intrepid desert men he wrecked trains, blew up the tracks of the Hejaz railway, shut up the Turks in Medina and cut them off from their base of supplies.

They cleared the country of enemy groups and trekked northward, until within fifteen months they were working just east of the Dead Sea, in direct co-operation with the Palestinian forces under General Allenby. Passing through the enemy's line, Lawrence organized resistance among the northern tribes, cut the Damascus railway near the vital junction of Deraa, and contributed materailly to the demoralization and defeat of the Turkish battalion. Within a few more months Lawrence and Feisal marched into Damascus along with the allied forces and assisted in hoisting the Arab flag which fluttered over Damascus — the immediate goal of Lawrence's dream.

## CHAPTER XXXI

# THROUGH GAZA TO THE GATES OF JERUSALEM

DURING THE LATTER PART of the nineteenth and the early part of the twentieth centuries the various European powers — England, Germany, France, Russia, Italy, and others of lesser importance — engaged in a race for power and supremacy in the Near Eastern countries which, for the most part, helped to make up the potentially disintegrating Turkish Empire. Astute diplomacy coupled with enticing loans, commercial investments, engineering projects, secret intrigues, a little propaganda, and an occasional "punitive expedition," were measures whereby these powers sought to obtain a "lion's share" of Turkey — long known as "the Sick Man of the East."

The World War broke in and around Flanders Fields, and the hardest and most stubborn fighting took place there, yet there was another arena in which the fighting was to prove more interesting, and in some respects more decisive. Statesmen, diplomats, and militarists maintained an unflagging interest in Near Eastern developments.

The war was only well under way — only two months had passed — when, on November 5, 1914, Turkey joined the conflict on the side of the Central Powers. This was as many had expected, for the Turkish army had been trained by German officers, and they could influence Turkish opinion. The "complacent" German staff had an intense interest in the Bagdad railway, the Suez Canal, and other commercial-political projects in the Near East, yet it feigned interest in assisting the Turks to regain lost portions of their rapidly disintegrating empire — in Egypt, it said the Turks should be restored to complete supremacy.[1] And this promise — as it may have seemed — was to prove a deciding factor in the Palestinian campaign in particular and in the world conflict in general.[2]

Egypt had long been regarded as the "half way house"[3] of the British Empire — midway between England and India. The Suez Canal, which ran along the border of Egypt, was veritably the "great artery of the British Empire." It not only connected England with her Overseas Empire, but was the direct route by which she brought her troops and provisions from India and Australia. The Germans regarded it as the "jugular vein" of the British Empire. They were correct in such a view, for it had long served Britain and since the outbreak of the war there had constantly passed through it troops and supplies on the way to the battlefields of France.

To cut this "jugular vein" seemed to be one of Germany's chief objectives from the beginning of the war. The British, backed by their allies, were bent on keeping it open and defending it against attack lest their troops be delayed, the great Canal be lost, and they be shut out from the Levant and from the direct passage to their vast overseas possessions.

For more than three decades Britain had maintained a peacetime garrison of some five thousand men to secure the country in general and the Canal zone in particular from invasion by a foreign enemy,[4] but this small force began to be augmented soon after the outbreak of the war. By November 16, Indian troops destined for the defense of Egypt reached Suez, and battalions were moved as quickly as possible to Ismailia and Port Said.

Contingents from Australia and New Zealand were brought to Egypt for military training. The intention was to send them later to France, but temporarily they would be available as reserves in Egypt.[5] An average of four warships — British and French — were stationed sufficiently near to be used in case of emergency.

On November 20, twenty miles east of Kantara, a patrol of twenty men of the Camel Corps were attacked by two hundred Bedouins who approached the Canal under a white flag. One half of the patrol lost their lives, but the attack was the only one which occurred that year (1914).[6]

By January of 1915, English and French air service had been established in the Canal zone, warships had been prepared to act as floating batteries, a Camel Corps to act as reserves and some thirty thousand troops (largely Indian) guarded the Canal, while about forty thousand yeomanry from Australia and New Zealand were in training near Cairo.

The organized effort for the defense of the Canal had not been completed any too soon, for by mid-January some fifteen thousand Turco-Arab troops, with five thousand camels for carrying water and a like number for transporting supplies and ammunition, moved out of Beersheba and started across the Sinai desert. The well-ordered march brought the enemy near the Canal by the first day of February. The British troops expected the attack at any moment, and having had ample warning of its approach, and being reinforced by an armoured train and the New Zealand infantry, awaited it with confidence.[7]

Before dawn, on the morning of February 3, loud shouting and howling broke out just south of *Tassum* Post. The enemy was beginning the attack on the Canal, and "the Champions of Ismal" were calling upon Allah, and adjuring each other to die for the faith.[8] Light pontoons which the Turks had brought with them were launched on the waters of the Canal. These were loaded with troops while other Turks crouching on the eastern bank opened fire to cover the crossing. The British troops defending this portion of the Canal opened fire upon the pontoons, resulting in the sinking of many of them. Only two or three of the pontoons reached the western bank, and the surviving members of their crews, numbering about twenty, surrendered to the British.

There was almost continuous fighting throughout the day, but no further crossing of the Canal was attempted. The next day the French and British warships all but swept the east bank, with the result that many of the enemy were killed or captured. By the tenth of February the only enemy reported in the neighborhood of the Suez Canal was a body of four hundred at *Rigum.* Some two thousand had been either killed or captured, and the others had marched back to Palestine.[9]

Soon after this abortive Turkish attempt on the Canal the British government reached a decision which for the time being diverted attention from the Canal zone to the Dardanelles. None too great success had attended Allied efforts on the European battle front. The conflict had largely settled down to trench-warfare. The battle lines west of the Rhine were so well defended and offered so little at such great cost that it was thought best to break the enemy's morale by attacking at some less carefully guarded point — at some distant unexpected place. An expedition against the Dardanelles was thought to offer unparalleled opportunities.

Victory in such an undertaking would not only make inroads on the Central Powers by eliminating Turkey, but would give the Allies control of the Dardanelles, the Bosphorus, and the Black Sea; thus affording passage for arms and ammunition from the Allies to Russia in exchange for wheat.[10] Many battleships and vast numbers of soldiers were sent to participate in the Dardanelles campaign, but due to a lack of co-ordination in command and other minor causes the advance met with bloody defeat and dismal failure. After losing three battleships and more than two thousand men, the campaign was abandoned and the major portion of the forces were transported to Egypt for rest, reorganization, and complete re-equipment.

The evacuation of Gallipoli, or "The Dardanelles," had the effect of liberating large forces of Turkey's best troops for operations against Mesopotamia and Egypt. Their thought was to organize the *Yieldrium,* or "Flying Squadron," at Damascus, and hasten to the Euphrates valley to stop the advance of the British who were pressing their way northward under the direction of British headquarters in India, and to use the rest of their forces for Palestine, Egypt, and Arabia.

In the meantime, however, the British had decided to abandon their former protection for the Suez Canal. The former method of maintaining a defense line extending practically the entire length of the Canal was proving expensive in men as well as in material. Consequently four hundred thousand British troops were organized into the Egyptian Expeditionary force under the command of Sir Archibald Murray. Their new objective was to secure control of the entire Sinai desert, which could be effected by an advance to *El Arish,* near the Palestinian border. No longer were they to be on the defensive; they were to take the offensive.

The first step was to prepare for the advance across the desert. The Turkish army had crossed this desert with little difficulty, but British military officials knew that their soldiers could not withstand the heat nor the hardships incident to desert life, unless they were supplied with water and munitions and had a constant connection with the Egyptian base. Consequently they adopted the wise plan of carrying a water main — pipe line — and a broad gauge railway from Kantara eastward as they advanced across the desert.[11] Waterworks were constructed at Kantara, the water was taken from the Sweet Water Canal (which came directly from the Nile river), purified and pumped into the large main and thus was available for the troops as they advanced with the railway.

The first objective was to reach and occupy the *Qatiya* oasis, twenty-five miles east of the Canal, and thus deny the enemy the only district within striking distance where a sufficiency of water permitted the assembling of a large force. On the tenth of March (1916) the first load of rails and sleepers arrived at Qatiya and within a short time the railroad and water main were well under way. The workmen were protected by permanent posts. Toward the end of April the Turks made a raid on the Qatiya oasis and surprised and captured some advanced posts of the Yeomanry. There was much fighting in this section, and at times the British lost their positions, but later regained them by the effectice service of the mounted divisions from Australia and New Zealand.[12]

By July, 1916, the railway had reached the village of *Romani* — marking the western end of a scattered group of oases extending for some fifteen to twenty miles. With the beginning of August a strong Turkish force of about sixteen thousand men, under the direct command of Kress Von Kressenstein, entered the eastern end of the oasis. At dawn on the morning of August 4, it attacked the British force of about thirty thousand men under Lieutenant General H. A. Lawrence. The Turks made a determined assault but were heavily repulsed as far as *Bir el Abd.* They left behind three thousand prisoners[13] and their total casualties amounted to nearly half their original force.

They may perhaps be accounted fortunate to have escaped at all, for intense heat and lack of water prevented the more vigorous action in pursuit, which might have made possible the annihilation of the Turkish force. The British losses amounted to about eleven hundred in all, most of whom were of the Anzac Mounted Division.[14] This advance against Romani marked the last determined attempt of the Turks to invade the Suez Canal Zone. Henceforth their efforts were confined to opposing the British offensive.[15]

The defeated Turks retreated to *El'Arish,* leaving a small detachment at *Bir el Mazar* till the middle of September, when it was dislodged by the Anzac Mounted Division. There was no further fighting till December. The progress of the British force towards El'Arish was governed by the rate at which the railway and its accompanying pipe line could be laid — about twenty miles per month. The water supply available in Sinai was too brackish for constant drinking by troops, — even the railway locomotives could not use it long without loss of efficiency.[16] The water used came through twelve-inch pipe to the end of the line in the desert.

The "Desert Column" under Lieutenant General Philip Chetwode, assisted by a flying column under General Chauvel, cleared the province of Sinai of all enemy forces and permitted the main army to occupy El'Arish by Christmas. The troops had crossed the desert with success attending their every move. At last they had set foot on the "Promised Land." Mine sweeping operations were at once commenced in the roadstead of the small harbor. A pier was erected and on the twenty-fourth the supply ships from Port Said began unloading stores and supplies. Thereafter the army availed itself of supplies coming both by land and sea routes.[17]

The commander, Sir Archibald Murray, had reached his original objective. But his troops were not yet well settled when he received instruction from the war cabinet to the effect that though the defense of Egypt was still to be the main consideration, an *offensive campaign was to be made into Palestine.*[18] The Turks — now definitely on the defensive — retreated and took up a position between Gaza and Beersheba. These were the two natural gateways into Palestine from the south, therefore theirs was a strategic position.

By early spring (1917), the British forces had extended their railroad and pipe line to Rafa, some twenty miles from Gaza. On March 26, the British rushed Gaza from three sides, and had in reality won the victory. The garrison, as was afterwards known, was on the point of surrender, but owing to a breakdown of communications the British knew not of the good fortune that was really theirs for the taking. One division after another was withdrawn, then the British realized that they might have stabled their horses in Gaza that night.

Since they had thrown away a victory already won they resumed the attack the next morning, but reinforcements had reached Gaza during the night and the British were obliged to forego the prize for the time. The Turks closed the gap between Gaza and Beersheba by a series of fortifications and greatly strengthened the defenses of Gaza.[19]

The British brought up some war tanks (never heretofore employed in Near Eastern warfare) in which they placed great confidence. Hoping to gain a better position, the British attacked on the seventeenth of April. In this they were successful, but the decisive attack on April 19 failed with heavy loss; the tanks developed mechanical defects in the heavy sand or were put out of action by the well placed Turkish guns; and the weight of artillery supporting the British attack was insufficient to demolish the formidable defenses of Gaza. The British casualties were seven thousand,[20] many of them lay unburied for days.

There came a long pause in active operations. Then in July General Sir Edmund Allenby succeeded Sir Archibald Murray, with instructions to report on the conditions under which offensive operations could be undertaken against the Turkish forces on the Palestinian front. The new general of the Palestinian forces was no novice at leading men — especially cavalry forces. He organized his forces and prepared to advance.[21]

## Allenby's Advance

From July to October the enemy's force on the Palestinian front has been increasing. Large supplies of ammunition and other stores had been moved in. It was evident that the Turks meant to make every effort to maintain their position in Southern Palestine. The Turkish army held a strong position extending from the sea at Gaza, roughly along the main Gaza-Beersheba road to Beersheba. Gaza, their strongest fortress, was heavily entrenched and wired, and offered every facility for protracted defense. The remainder of the enemy's line consisted of a series of strong posts from one to two miles apart, and finally the fortifications about Beersheba.

Since the weakest part of the enemy's thirty mile front was the left flank extending to Beersheba, General Allenby decided to attack the enemy's left at Beersheba. However, by superior military strategy he combined the sea and land power and kept the enemy in doubt up to the last moment as to the point of attack.

A bombardment of the Gaza defenses by land began on October 27 and on the thirtieth a warship of the Royal Navy assisted by a French battleship began to co-operate in this bombardment. A feeble move was made as though Gaza was to be taken, then with thirty thousand pack camels to furnish food, water, and supplies, the eastern force — the strongest of the British forces — concentrated some miles south of Beersheba on the evening of October 30. That night they marched to their appointed positions.

Early on the morning of the thirty-first the divisions moved into action and soon Beersheba was being attacked from the south, east, southeast, and northeast. The day's fighting climaxed with a cavalry attack by the Australian light horse, who rode straight at the town from the east, surprising and entering the city at about seven o'clock in the evening. The Turks were surprised by the dash of the London troops and yeomanry supported by their artillery, and the result was that the British took the ancient city of Beersheba with two thousand prisoners, thirteen guns, and five hundred dead. This proved to be the first of a series of brilliant victories in the Palestinian campaign.[22]

At eleven o'clock on the night of November 1, the British army took Umbrella Hill just a bit more than a mile south of Gaza and at three o'clock the next morning those brave Britishers charged Gaza. The bombardment and fighting continued with success until on the sixth the Turks were seen moving along the north road from Gaza. That night they evacuated Gaza and the British took possession of this ancient stronghold of the Philistines.

Position after position along the Gaza-Beersheba road was taken until the Turkish army was retreating all along the line. The Turkish rearguard fought stubbornly and offered stiff opposition, but near *Huj,* on the eighth, a splendid charge was made by the Worcester and Warwick yeomanry in which twelve guns were captured and the resistance of the hostile rearguard broken. The Royal Flying Corps attacked the retreating columns with bombs and machine-gun fire and brought in the report that the enemy was retiring in considerable confusion, and could offer no serious resistance if pressed with determination.[23]

Instructions were accordingly issued on the morning of the ninth to the mounted troops, ordering them to press the enemy relentlessly. In the afternoon one section of the enemy began organizing for a counterstroke, and by the tenth and eleventh the Turks had formed a general line along the *Wady Sukereir.* A detachment which had retreated toward Hebron returned and prolonged the enemy's line toward *Beit Jibrin.* The Royal Flying Corps reported the hostile forces numbering about fifteen thousand. By the morning of November 13 the enemy's forces had increased to some twenty thousand and presented a front twenty miles long — from *El Kubeibeh* on the north to *Beit Jibrin* to the south. The right half of the enemy's line ran parallel to and about five miles in front of the Ramleh-Junction Station railway; thus the Turks hoped to protect their main line of supply from the north.[24]

During the British drive on the thirteenth the fifty-second (Lowland) Division assisted by a dashing charge of the mounted troops broke the enemy's center, captured his strongest position and on the morning of the fourteenth occupied Junction Station. During the drive the enemy's army had been broken into two separate parts; the one retired north along the Plain of Sharon and the other east toward Jerusalem. Each of these consisted of small scattered groups rather than well formed bodies of any size.[25]

The mounted troops pressed on northward. *Naaneh* and *Ayun Kara* were taken, then at the site of ancient Gezer, a hostile rearguard was captured on the morning of the fifteenth in a brilliant attack by mounted troops who galloped up the ridge from the south. One gun and three hundred and sixty prisoners were taken. By the evening of the fifteenth the mounted troops had captured *Ramleh* and *Ludd,* and pushed patrols to within a short distance of *Jaffa,* (ancient Joppa). The following day *Jaffa* was occupied without opposition.

Biblical scenes and events of bygone days crowded the minds of the British soldiers as they fought for and gained place after place of which they had heard from the lips of their parents, Sunday School teachers, and ministers. It was not unusual for the officers to inform their men regarding the historic significance of the places before they were taken, and General Allenby often consulted the Bible, the Apocrypha, Josephus, and George Adam Smith's *Historical Geography of the Holy Land,* as well as the annals of the Crusades. This he did because each of the works contained accounts of military successes and failures on these very hills and plains. No other sources offered such a store of exact information regarding Judean topography and military strategy.

## The Advance on Jerusalem

Knowing that the narrow passes from the Sharon plain to the plateau of the Judean range had seldom been forced, and that they had often been fatal to invading armies, General Allenby naturally thought to march on Jerusalem when he could make use of his entire force, but an advantageous opportunity presented itself. The enemy forces failed to entrench themselves in the narrow mountain passes and hastened through the hills in a state of disorder. Fearing lest they should see their mistake, reorganize, and defend the lower passes, Allenby decided to march on Jerusalem at once.

It was a bold decision, since he had only three infantry and two mounted divisions immediately available, and the supply of these strained the resources of his transport to the utmost; the troops had already done much hard marching and fighting; little was known of the present state of the hill country save that it was very difficult and that only the main road which ran through the valley of Ajalon was fit for wheels.[26]

The Anzac Mounted Division and the fifty-fourth division were left to hold the Turkish eighth army in the Plain of Sharon, while the remaining three divisions advanced into the hills, the seventy-fifth up the main road, the fifty-third on its left and the Yeomanry Mounted Division on the left of the fifty-second. The last two divisions were to depend entirely upon pack transportation. The plan was for the seventy-fifth division to lead the way along the main road from *Ramleh,* through the *Beth-horans* and penetrate within a few miles of Jerusalem; when the other two divisions, forming the left, were to swing across the Jerusalem-Nablus road ten miles north of the city. It was hoped by this plan to compel the surrender or withdrawal of the Turkish army in Jerusalem, and if the latter result were achieved to prevent its joining with the Turkish forces in the north about Nablus, on the plain of Sharon and in the Esdralon valley.[27]

On the seventeenth of November long lines of Yeomanry began to move from Ramleh through the mountain passes by way of the valley of Ajalon and Lower Bethhoran. By the evening of the eighteenth one portion of the yeomanry had reached Lower Beth-horan, while another portion had occupied *Shilta.* On the nineteenth the infantry commenced its advance. *Latron* and *Amwas* were captured, and the narrow passes from the plain to the plateau of the Judean mountains were cleared of small bands of the enemy. Neither time nor opportunity was given for the enemy forces to fortify themselves in these narrow passes, lest the conquest prove slow, costly, and perhaps fatal, as it had proven to many invading armies.[28] However, there was sharp resistance, and once on the Judean mountain ridges the Turco-German forces swarmed out and offered bitter opposition.[29]

On the twentieth and twenty-first there was hard fighting for all three divisions of the army. The seventy-fifth division captured the crest of the ridge at *Enab* in a fog on the twentieth, and at mignight on the twenty-first stormed the heights of *Neby Samwil* — the traditional home of Samuel the prophet. This gave the British the most commanding position in the environs of Jerusalem. The fifty-second division captured some smaller towns farther north, and the yeomanry penetrated to within a short distance of the Nablus road, but was unable to take the well-fortified heights of *Bireh.*[30] Winter rains set in and the hillsides were rendered slippery. It became apparent that they could not take the city without reinforcements.[31]

Having splendid positions west of Jerusalem, orders were issued to consolidate the positions, reorganize the forces, and prepare for an advance on the Holy City — Jerusalem. By December 7 these plans were complete.

At dawn on the eighth the armies swung into action with the specific understanding that every risk to the Holy City should be avoided! The three divisions northwest of Jerusalem held their positions, while the sixtieth (London) division, assisted on the left by the seventy-fourth division and on the right by the fifty-third division, which had been brought up from Gaza and Beersheeba, advanced on Jerusalem from the south, along the Hebron road. Midst the rain and mist the Turks fought the forces south of the city, but one day of it was enough for them.

Near sunset the British troops passed *Lifta* and came within sight of the city. A sudden panic fell on the Turkish cavalry west and southwest of the city; they broke ranks and "galloped furiously" cityward along the Jaffa road. In passing they alarmed all units within sight or hearing, and the weary, bedraggled infantry rose and fled. Confusion rose high in the ranks of the Turks, but hope rose higher with the Jews. At the close of that sad week, with the setting of that Saturday evening's sun, the Turk, after four centuries of misrule, was leaving the Holy City in the bitterness of defeat.

This was the day of the Jewish feast *Hanukkah,* which was in commemoration of the delivery of the city by the Maccabees. Jewish joy was not easily curbed. "The Turks are running, the day of deliverance is come," shouted many a Jewess as she ran to and fro calling to her father and brothers who concealed themselves from the eye of the Turkish police who had sought them for arrest and deportation. The nightmare was fast passing but the Turk still lingered. While the shades of night hung fantastically about the Holy City the Turkish guns fired continuously, perhaps to hold back the British forces, but more probably to cover their own retreat. Or perhaps, as some have thought, they fired their guns to frighten away the *jinn*.[32]

"Toward midnight," says a reliable eyewitness, "the Governor, Izzet Bey, went personally to the telegraph office, discharged the staff, and himself smashed the instruments with a hammer. At two o'clock on Sunday morning tired Turks began to tramp through the Jaffa gate from the west and southwest, and anxious watchers, peering out through the windows of the Grand New Hotel to learn the meaning of the tramping, were cheered by the sullen remark of an officer, '*Gitmaya mejbooruz.*' ('We've got to go'), and from two till seven o'clock that morning the Turks streamed through and out of the city, which echoed for the last time their shuffling tramp."[33]

By seven o'clock Sunday morning the last of the Turkish soldiers were passing out through St. Stephen's Gate on the east and making their way along the Jericho road. The governor was the last official to take his departure. He left in an unrequisitioned cart which he had "borrowed" from Mr. Fred Vester, of the American Colony Store. Near dawn the governor hastened down the Jericho road, leaving him a letter of surrender, which the Mayor,[34] accompanied by a few frightened policemen, set forth to deliver.[35] With the flag of truce he walked toward Lifta hill, and just after sunrise was met by two British Tommies (Sergeants Hurcomb and Sedgewick, of the 2/19th Batallion London Regiment) who received the white flag and were photographed.

Various divisions took positions on the roadways leading to and from the city. British patrols approached the gray walls, passed through the gates and took charge of the ancient Jerusalem — the most famous city on the face of the earth, and the religious capital of the world.

Two days later, on December 11, General Allenby made his official entry, *walking* into Jerusalem by the *Jaffa* gate, followed by his staff and by representatives of the French, Italian, and American governments. A proclamation was read from the steps of the Tower of David in English, French, Italian, Arabic, and Hebrew announcing peace and toleration for all races and creeds within the Holy City. The proclamation ran as follows:

> To the inhabitants of Jerusalem the Blessed and the people dwelling in the vicinity. The defeat inflicted upon the Turks by the troops under my command has resulted in the occupation of your city by my forces. I therefore here and now proclaim it to be under martial laws, under which form of administration it will remain so long as military considerations make it necessary. However, lest any of you should be alarmed by reason of your experience at the hands of the enemy who have retired, I hereby inform you that it is my desire that every person should pursue his lawful business without fear of interruption.

> Furthermore, since your City is regarded with affection by the adherents of three of the great religions of mankind, and its soil has been consecrated by the prayers and pilgrimages of multitudes of devout people of these three religions for many centuries, therefore do I make known to you that every sacred building, monument, pious bequest, or customary place of prayer, of whatsoever form of the three religions, will be maintained and protected according to the existing customs and beliefs of those to whose faiths they are sacred.[36]

The name "Allenby" fell upon the ears of the inhabitants of Jerusalem with singular force. To them it sounded like the blending of the two Arabic words: *Allah* (God) and *Neby* (prophet), the Prophet of God. And his modest yet fearless entry through unpretentious *Jaffa* gate and his forceful yet considerate proclamation from the steps of David's Tower was in harmony with the spirit of the prophets of old. To the people he was the twentieth century prophet of God sent to deliver them from the Turkish yoke. Jewish and Arab joy knew no bounds.

Crowds thronged Jerusalem streets, covered the walls, and rejoiced in the fulfillment of the Arab prophecy that when the waters of the Nile flowed into Palestine the prophet *al Neb* from the west should drive the Turks from Jerusalem. Christianity the world over put on her garments of praise. Songs were sung, poetry was recited, prayers offered and sermons preached. No Allied victory touched the heart of the religious world, awakened sentiment, and inspired confidence more thoroughly than did the taking of Jerusalem.

Here the Bible had its beginning, David built up a mighty kingdom, Solomon reigned in regal splendor, and Jesus Christ opened up a fountain "in the house of David." Here the mighty Maccabees defended their religion against Hellenism, Herod constructed the beautifud temple to win the good will of the Jews, and Titus destroyed it to humble their haughty descendants. Here Peter the Hermit caught inspiration for the Crusades, Godfrey of Bouillon ruled without a crown, and mighty Saladin "flung aloft the flag of Islam." How very fitting that this, the twenty-third fall of the City of Peace, should have been effected peaceably, though after a fierce campaign, and returned to the Christians, the Jews, and the Mohammedans. Many hailed it as the first piece of genuine political reconstruction that had taken place during the war.

## Chapter XXXII

# ACROSS ARMAGEDDON WITH ALLENBY

The theory that the war could be won by the elimination of Germany's weaker allies had gained in favor because of the partial victory in the Near East. The "Yieldrium Army," which had been organized to rescue *Bagdad,* had of necessity been used in Palestine. On the theory that one more telling blow would force Turkey to sue for peace, General Allenby, with the assistance of the Arabian army under Lawrence and Feisal, planned to strike that blow.

The divisions of Indian troops were moved from Mesopotamia to reinforce Allenby's army, and all prepartions for a huge drive were being made when German successes in France caused two complete divisions, twenty-four additional British battalions, nine regiments of yeomanry and five and one half batteries to be withdrawn from Allenby's forces and dispatched to France. Undaunted by the seeming set-back the General set to work and gradually replaced all these with Indian cavalry from France and fresh units from India. By the end of the summer the new forces were trained and the great cavalry leader was ready to execute plans for the final drive which would send the Turks from Palestine forever.

Every possible means was employed to lead the Turco-German forces to believe that General Allenby meant to employ the same plan that he had so effectively used against them in the Gaza-Beersheba battle, whereas the plan was in fact the reverse of the Gaza-Beersheba battle. *Then* he struck at the Turkish left flank while pretending that his intention was to break through along the coast. *Now* he proposed to break through on the coast while causing the Turk to apprehend a blow at his left flank. The steps taken to mislead the enemy as to the real point of attack formed one of the chief features of the preparations for the battle.

Three complete divisions, many batteries and other units were encamped in the deep trench of the Jordan valley. These in conjunction with the Arabian forces under Lawrence and Feisal had made two raids east of the Jordan, cut the railways and tantalized the Turks generally. Agents were dispatched by Lawrence with instructions to bargain for a large supply of forage in and about Amman. Everything indicated that Allenby would use his strong right, when with all possible secrecy the divisions began to be moved by night from the Jordan valley and the Judean hills to the coastal area.[1]

The olive woods and orange groves north of Jaffa were used to hide the increase of troops. The units normally encamped behind the line in this section had during the summer been cantoned somewhat widely and disturbed in such a way that additional troops could be accommodated without any increase in tentage or bivouacs. Thus battalions in reserve had for some time previously been disturbed between two half-battalion camps. When the time came, each of these camps was occupied by a whole battalion, and so the force in the area was doubled without any change being visible from the air. But it was above all the dominance secured by the British Air Force that enabled this concentration to be so concealed. So complete was the mastery it had obtained in the air by hard fighting that by September a hostile aeroplane rarely crossed the British lines.[2]

On the other wing everything possible was done to suggest the preparation of a great attack. The camps in the Jordan valley vacated by the cavalry were left standing and new ones were pitched. Fifteen thousand dummy horses, put together of sticks and canvas, filled the deserted horse lines. A constant stream of horses was led to and from the brink of the historic Jordan river. It was the same few hundred horsemen that went back and forth from early until late, yet the Turco-German lookouts away on the mountains of Gilead saw it as a great army — so vast that diligent and continuous effort from morn to night was necessary to get all the animals to water.

Sleighs drawn by mules raised clouds of dust to make observation difficult and to feign activity. The British West Indian battalions on several days marched from Jerusalem down to the valley, returning by lorries at night to repeat the march the next day. Additional bridges were thrown across the Jordan. Wireless traffic was continued from *Talaat ed Dumm* long after the headquarters of Desert Mounted Corps had left that place for the Coastal Plain.[3]

These demonstrations were an important part of Allenby's plan. He meant that the enemy should take cognizance of the supposed concentration in the Jordan valley and move his forces thither to ward off the attack. The scheme worked with clock-like precision. One third of the enemy's forces was moved east of the Jordan, with the corresponding weakening of the forces along the Plain of Sharon.

Every night Allenby moved masses of troops and transport into the apricot and nectarine orchards of Ludd and Ramleh and the orange groves of Jaffa and Sarona. On the great evening of September 18 fresh divisions of infantry, cavalry and artillery gathered until the orchards, cactus hedges and hills of the fertile Plain of Sharon were covered with men of war who panted for action. After midnight orders were given and thousands of khaki-clad soldiers left their tents to move nearer the firing-line. On reaching their places they spread out their stretcher for a rest before the battle began, but there were few who slept. The night air was full of excitement. Horses champed at the bit and pawed the dust, while men waited for the battle to be ordered.

Exactly, at four-thirty, on the morning of the nineteenth, the hills and valleys shook, thunder and flash came from every side, from back and front. The big guns hurled their shells over the plain, others barked and shrieked in front. Behind the rolling barrage the infantry crept forward against the enemy. For two hours the fighting was terrific, and then the big guns stopped and the battle moved away over the plains — the enemy broke rank and retreated in wild disorder. The guns and infantry had smashed the enemy's defense. The British command unleashed masses of cavalry and by seven-thirty the leading cavalry divisions were through the Turkish lines and a general rout was on.[4]

At the "Pass of Megiddo," near the ancient city of Megiddo, — now called *El Lejjun* — the Turks made a stiff stand against the British cavalry but too much had already been lost. Resistance clearly became hopeless, and the Turks fled across the ancient plain of Megiddo — the world's greatest battlefield. Carrying out General Allenby's instructions, the horsemen hurried to *Affule, Jenin, Nazareth,* and *Beisan* where they blocked the Turkish lines of retreat and cut off communication with the main army.

A Turkish plane droned in and landed in the midst of the plain. The place had changed hands so quickly that the Turkish pilot knew not that he was landing on enemy territory. On seeing his plight, he quickly set fire to his plane and submitted to arrest.

The infantry "shepherded the straggling remains of the Turkish seventh and eighth armies into the hands of the mounted troops. The Royal Air Force, with bombs and machine gun fire, caused havoc in the bewildered Turkish transport, penned in and crowded on narrow hill roads."[5] Disorganized bodies of troops, masses of transport wagons, guns, lorries, in unutterable confusion were pressing forward on the roadways. Some of the troops had thrown away their arms in the mad flight for safety. Through the narrow defiles streamed the flying army doomed to disaster, without respite and without hope, only dimly imagining as yet the horrors in store for it. Men knew little of what lay before them. They fled every man in terror from the winged scourge that darted from the sky and hurled destruction and death upon their broken ranks.

Only a few of the most determined Turks and some of the better fed and disciplined German units managed to break out to the east and cross the Jordan. These spread the news and soon British forces crossed the Jordan and the entire Turkish army was on the retreat toward Damascus.

The Arabs under Lawrence not only cut the railways and all lines of communication but threw themselves across the pathway of the retreating Turks and captured, harassed, and delayed them until on September 30 the Australian Mounted Division succeeded in getting astride the Damascus-Beirut road just outside the city, thereby cutting off the remains of the Turkish fourth army. On the following day Damascus was occupied, and the Union Jack and the Arabian colors fluttered over the world's oldest city with a continuous history.

After some delay, due to malaria and influenza and disorganization, two columns advanced northward to complete the occupation. One moved along the coastal region, while the other advanced from Damascus and easily took *Homs* and *Hama,* and occupied Aleppo on October 26. The last fighting took place north of the city on the twenty-eighth. On the thirtieth the Armistice of Mudros was signed by terms of which the entire Turkish army ceased hostilities against the Allies and placed all her ports and strategic points at their command.

The advance of which the people had dreamed and talked for months had been achieved within a few days. Samaria and Galilee, with their clusters of Jewish colonies, were relieved, and all Palestine was again united. Men, women, and children were wild with excitement. The Turkish army had disappeared from the whole country both west and east of the Jordan, like chaff driven before the wind, a fact which seemed akin to the miracles of the Bible times.

Care was banished and the long pent-up spirits became free again. As the news of the victory spread, each day had its celebrations and feastings. One night two thousand of the most orthodox people of the Jewish community, the Hasidim, gathered around Governor Storr's house and serenaded him with Hebrew songs, to which, to their great joy, he replied with Hebrew thanks. Another day the Jewish Council of the city organized a procession of the children and representatives of every section, which waved flags and palm branches and sang as they went to express their gratitude to the authorities.

Great crowds gathered daily in the streets. Some ardent spirits were for sending a telegram to the king; others were for collecting money at once to erect a monument to General Allenby. Every night there was singing and dancing in various parts of the city.

The Arabs marched in processions, danced their sword-dances, chanted their songs in ecstasy, maneuvered in fantastic style to express their gratitude, and formed deputations to convey their thanks to the authorities. For all the population — Moslem, Christian, and Jew — the words of thanksgiving of the Psalmist expressed their spontaneous feeling:

> This hath come from God; it is wonderful in our eyes. It is a day which the Lord hath created. Let us rejoice and be glad in it.[6]

The British Expeditionary Force had fought its way along the most ancient, the most interesting, and the most familiar highway known to men, — the "Dareb es Sultani" — the Royal Road, as the Arabs delight to call it. It had passed through a remarkable variety of soil, climate, and scenery and had fought valiantly where the tides of thought, trade and war had flowed between Asia and Africa since the dawn of history. Almost every place through which they passed awakened memories of some well-known person or some deed of renown.[7]

By two short, quick, well-directed drives General Allenby and his gallant men had not only defeated and pushed back but completely driven the Turco-German forces out of the country and compelled them to sign an armistice. He had annihilated the enemy and ended the war with Turkey then and there. Allenby and his men had done what the Crusades, backed by all the medieval poyer of Europe, had failed to accomplish. His campaign has gone down in history as one of the best planned and most effective military campaigns of all time. It seemed fitting that the subjects of descendants of Richard the Lion-hearted who participated in the Crusades should have ended the dominion of the Crescent in the land of sacred memories.

* * * *

*As I dream, it seems to me*
*I have ridden with Allenby!*

On a day, in the time long gone,
I rode into the heart of the dawn
Out of Gaza. My desert steed,
Son of a sire of the Nedjid breed,
Took the breath of the morning sun
With never a pause till we had won
O'er rocky sweep and o'er sandy swell
To the riven House of Gabriel.
Then, ere the shut of the eve, we came

Where the last red streamers lit with flame
The mosque of Hebron set in the vale,
With its towering minarets, and its tale
Of Isaac's and of Abraham's tombs,
Where only the Faithful in the glooms
May bow, while faintly the cressets flare,
And the swart muezzin calls to prayer.
Thence on to Bethlehem we sped,
With the dome of Allah overhead,
And never a sign of a cloud in view
To blur the breadth of its gold and blue.

*So he marched, and it seems to me*
*I have ridden with Allenby!*

Then Jerusalem, and the hill
Of Golgotha, and the sacred, still
Church of the Holy Sepulchre!
The Vale of the Mount, and the ceaseless stir
Of Pilgrim feet where the Christ once strayed,
Under the cruel Cross down-weighed!
I rode by Jenin with its palms
Clear-cut against the noon-day calms;
I rode by Nablus, I rode by Nain,
And over the wide Esdraelon plain
Up to the slope of Nazareth,
Where out of the dim bazaars the breath
Of shaven sandalwood was blown.
I skirted the snow-crowned mountain zone
Of Hermon, and saw the morning star
Silver the roofs of Kefr Hawar.
And then I looked on the lovely loom
Of orange, pomegranate and citron bloom,
(A bower that to the Prophet's eye
Was a prescience of Paradise)
And came to Damascus by the gate
That leads to the ancient Street called Straight.

*So he marched, and it seems to me*
*I have ridden with Allenby!*

Never again the Turkish blight
On all this land of lure and light!
Never again the brutal ban
From far Beersheba unto Dan!
Rather the beam of His promised Peace
In this home of holy memories!
His peace for all men under the sun
From Nebo north to Lebanon;
His peace through the hand that set them free!

*I have ridden with Allenby!*

## Chapter XXXIII

# THE BRITISH IN BIBLE LANDS

The peace that came to Palestine as a result of General Allenby's masterfully directed campaigns heartened the Western Allies and set the precedent for other well-directed drives which culminated in Armistice and peace on the European battle front. The idea that the tide of victory could be begun to be brought in by forcing peace on battle lines far removed from the European front was justified, and perhaps exceeded the expectations of those prosecuting the war on the Allied front. Palestine, which had given the world the Bible and the "Prince of Peace," led the way in bringing peace to a troubled world that seemed to have caught the war spirit wherever men were found.

The problem of the government of the country of Palestine incited deep interest among peoples of many lands. However, the record of the British as colonizers lent hopefulness to the West as well as to the destitute, disease-ridden population of Palestine.

On retiring from the country the Turks had removed the coin from the banks, carried away the government registers, and deliberately wrecked the administrative machinery and economic foundation of the country.[1] But with manly concept of the gravity of so challenging a prospect as ruling over a country enshrined in the sacred memories and traditions of many nations and peoples, General Allenby established military administration headquarters in the German Hospice on Mount of Olives, and undertook the task of bringing order out of chaos. Sir Arthur Money was appointed Chief Administrator of Palestine, Sir Ronald Storrs as military Governor of the city of Jerusalem, along with other capable men who completed the personnel of the administration. It was a happy circumstance, if not divine providence, that brought together such stimulating people as Allenby, Money, Watson, Storrs, Popham, and their associates. They were honest, imaginative, and effective, and their purpose was to help the people of Palestine "come into the full fruits of justice and freedom."[2]

The Jerusalem Relief Laundry, with W. D. McCrackan, an American, at its head, employed many native women who went about the task of de-lousing and cleaning the people's clothing; the Y. W. C. A., under the efficient supervision of Mrs. Watson, went forward with relief work on a gigantic scale.

Governor Storrs organized and became the president and moving spirit of the Pro-Jerusalem Society, which raised some seventy-five thousand dollars and set about the task of restoring and beautifying the city. The ancient and medieval walls and towers, which had fallen into a sad state of decay, were repaired, and the rampart walk around the upper portion of the walls was completed so that for the first time in centuries one could "walk about Zion, and go around about her," and "tell the towers thereof."[3]

Trades, industries, and farming were encouraged and a more adequate water system inaugurated when, through the reorganized municipality of Jerusalem, the British cleaned, repaired, and restored Solomon's Pools, along with the splendid aqueduct, installed a modern pumping plant, and brought millions of gallons of water into the vast reservoirs located under the Temple area on Mount Moriah.

In due time departments of finance, law, and justice, health, agriculture, public works, and education were established. With the assistance of the American Red Cross, the Hadassah Organization of Jewish Women in America, and the English Protestant Syria and Palestine Relief Committee, the administration was able to bring about a substantial improvement in the sanitation and health conditions of Palestine. Infectious diseases were checked, a scavenging system introduced, and hospitals and clinics were opened in Jerusalem, Jaffa, Hebron, and in smaller towns.[4]

For two and a half years the Administration carried on with varying degrees of success. It was then reorganized on a more permanent basis under the Mandate. But the people of Palestine were not destined to live in the quiet enjoyment of a country so sparsely populated. The deep interest of a world-wide movement known as "Zionism" was converging on Palestine. Prophecy and destiny, coupled with a people's undying love of Palestine, would form into mighty, persistent, human tides which would bring wave after wave of Jewish men and women, young and old, into the Promised Land.

## Chapter XXXIV

# UNDYING LOVE FOR PALESTINE — ZIONISM

The Jewish people have been attached more devotedly to Palestine than have any other people to their fatherland. With deep passionate love and strong tender affection, they have throughout the ages spoken of the country as the "Land of Israel." When they lost their country, and their Temple was destroyed by Nebuchadnezzar in 586 B. C., they sorrowed as they went on their way to Babylonia. There they never could feel quite at home, but hung their harps in willows, and said, "How can we sing the Lord's song in a strange land?"[1]

When again they lost their country with the destruction of Jerusalem in 70 A.D., and in the fatal rebellion under Bar Kochba, culminating in the grievous battle of Bitier in 134 A.D., they were scattered to every country on the face of the earth. But wherever they went they carried with them an undying love for Palestine. To them Palestine was permeated with sacredness and a spirit of holiness as was no other land. They dreamed about it, and knew its rivers and mountains better than those of their native country. They gave their money to keep some of their people there. To live even in the dry thirsty desert areas of Palestine they considered equivalent to fulfilling all the commandments of the law, and more satisfying than all other experiences of life.

Because of their unwillingness to dry up the fountain of love for their fatherland, turn their backs on the past, and become part of the social order in the several countries where they resided, they often fared badly at the hands of their fellow men. Their books were frequently burned, their feasts derided, their synagogues plundered, their cemeteries desecrated, and their shops pillaged.[2] Although entire communities were forced into ghettoes, or prisons, or exile, yet the ideal of their race remained.

The inquisitions, expulsions, massacres, and all else that befell the Jews only bound them more passionately to their traditions, their laws, and their beloved Zion. In fact, persecution went far toward wedding them to their ideals and toward confirming their belief that their proper home was Palestine, where, if they could only go, they would find peace and happiness. From the wild wastes of Andolusia to the gloomy recesses of the ghettoes of Europe they stretched out their hands to Palestine, sang of it, prayed for it, wept for its fallen majesty, and patiently waited the hour of redemption.

> Give me leave, O Lord, and time, release me from that which Thou hast me bound, so that I may go to Thy Land, which calls to me.[3]

As the Jew has wandered from place to place, he has been comforted by reading God's promise made through Israel's early leaders:

> When thou art in tribulation, and all these things are come upon thee, even in the latter days, if thou turn to the Lord thy God, and shalt be obedient unto his voice . . . he will not forsake thee, neither destroy thee, nor forget the covenant of thy fathers which he sware unto them.[4]
>
> And it shall come to pass, when all these things are come upon thee, the blessing and the curse, which I have set before thee, and thou shalt call them to mind among all the nations, whither the Lord thy God had driven thee, and shalt return unto the Lord thy God, and shalt obey his voice according to all that I command thee this day, thou and thy children, with all thine heart, and with all thy soul; that then the Lord thy God will turn thy captivity, and have compassion upon thee, and will return and gather thee from all the nations, whither the Lord thy God hath scattered thee. . . . And the Lord thy God will bring thee into *the land which thy fathers possessed,* and thou shalt possess it; and he will do thee good, and multiply thee above thy fathers.[5]

The city of Jerusalem, with its Temple, held large place in Jewish affections. It was to them the focal point of religious interest and religion held first place in their lives. They loved to be in the city and to worship at their Temple. They face the Holy City when praying to God in foreign lands. With vivid reality the land, the city, and the Temple perpetually entered almost the entire round of their lives.

The belief in the ultimate restoration of Palestine has long been so intimately connected with the daily life of every conforming Jew that every morning, wherever he is found throughout the world, he rises, puts on his Talis or prayer shawl, and sends up this plaintive appeal:

> Blow the trumpet of our deliverance, O Lord God, set up our banner to assemble our scattered brethren, gather them from the four corners of the earth, come back full of loving kindness to Thine own City of Zion and reign over it, as Thou hast promised us. Build it up again and establish it forever. Be praised, O Lord, Thou wilt set up Jerusalem again.[6]

Yearly, since the destruction of Jerusalem and the fall of the Temple, faithful Jewish families scattered around the world have gathered in their homes on April 15 to commemorate the Passover season. During the meal of remembrance the entire family eats bitter herbs to recall the hardships of Egyptian bondage, and then partakes of unleavened bread in token of the unraised dough which was yet in the ovens when God commanded them to hasten from Egypt. Before the guests of the household they set the gullet of a fowl in semblance of the lamb which was killed, and whose blood upon the door post stayed the hand of the Angel of Death. In remembrance of the destruction of the Temple they partake of a hard-boiled egg and salt water. In the corner of the room they have a traveler's staff and a little bundle, items intended to serve as perennial symbols of Israel in exile, a wanderer among the nations.

At the conclusion of the Passover Feast, which lasts until midnight, the eldest child arises from the table and opens the door. The head of the house recites:

> Thou God of Abraham, Isaac, and Jacob, long have we waited for Thy promise. We beseech Thee now to send Thine anointed whom thou hast promised, the Son of David. Have mercy upon thy people Israel. Gather us according to Thy Word and we shall be Thy people and Thou wilt delight us as of old. Behold all things are ready and we wait.[7]

After a few minutes of waiting the door is closed and the head of the house recites:

> How long, O Lord, how long? Will thine anger not be turned away from Thy people and wilt Thou have mercy and restore us to Thy favor? Behold our suffering. We are scattered among the heathen. They mock us, saying where is thy God, where is the promise of His coming? We grow faint, yet we hope. Lord our God, may it please Thee to gather Thy people speedily. Restore us Thy favor, *at least next year may we celebrate this feast with Thee in Jerusalem, Thine own habitation.*[8]

Then by arising and exchanging the salute, "NEXT YEAR IN JERUSALEM," they express the persistent hope which gives Jewish history its poetic grandeur and makes of it a drama unique in the world.

> Oh, city of the world, with sacred splendour blest,
> My spirit yearns to thee from out the far-off West,
> A stream of love wells forth when I recall thy day,
> Now is thy temple waste, thy glory passed away.
> Had I an eagle's wings, straight would I fly to thee,
> Moisten thy holy dust with wet cheeks streaming free.
> Oh, how I long for thee! Albeit thy King has gone.
> Could I but kiss thy dust, so would I fain expire,
> As sweet as honey then, my passion, my desire.[9]

When centuries had passed and the fond hope seemed no nearer fulfillment, some of their leaders endeavored to console them with the thought that God had purposely dispersed them among the nations that they might fulfill a mission. To the majority this preachment often seemed impractical when they were face to face with the stern facts that they were not wanted, and, if wanted at all, then not as Jews.

A few — a very few — were willing to banish thoughts of their past, and leaped into the stream of humanity to take their chances along with the millions who seemed unconscious of any special mission in life. Yet that vast majority who were unable to forget past history or banish hopes for the future were unable to do more than be pushed and goaded along in time's stream. They had no Moses to lead them out.

Both Christians and Jews often suggested that something should be done to enable the Jews to return and possess homes in their mother country. In the course of the centuries there were numerous schemes for the settlement of Jews in Palestine, but none of them seemed to materialize. During his invasions of Egypt and Palestine in 1798 and 1799, Napoleon issued a proclamation promising the Holy Land to the Jews and the restoration of the glories of Jerusalem. During the siege of Acre, on April 20, 1799, he invited the Jews of Asia and Africa to rally under his banners in order to re-establish ancient Jerusalem. Designating them as the "rightful heirs of Palestine," he broadened his appeal to all Jews, and concluded his appeal with the word:

> Hasten! Now is the moment which may not return for thousands of years, to claim the restoration of civil rights among the population of the universe which has been shamefully withheld from you for thousands of years, your political existence as a nation among the nations, and the unlimited natural rights to worship Jehovah in accordance with your faith.[10]

The proclamation was accompanied by a letter from Aaron, "the first Rabbi and priest of Jerusalem," who appealed to his brethren to "rebuild the walls of the orphaned city and a Temple to the Lord . . . Let all men of Israel capable of bearing arms gather and come to us."[11]

A month later Napoleon lifted the siege of Acre and returned to France. When in Paris he assembled the Jewish leaders and conferred with them regarding their future welfare; however, with two-thirds of Europe at his throat, Napoleon was unable to assist the Jews in the attainment of their age-old desire.

One year later, just across the English Channel, James Bicheno wrote a book on the *Restoration of the Jews — The Crisis of all Nations.* In 1804 Thomas Witherby wrote a plea for the removal of all prejudice. Lord Shaftesbury and others urged the British Government to secure facilities for Jewish colonization under an international guarantee. These proposals received extremely favorable comment from the press, especially from the *Times,* for on political as well as sentimental grounds they commanded considerable support. The British Government appointed a consul at Jerusalem and showed its good will by instructing its representatives to take the Jews then present in Palestine under their special protection, but the British seemed to feel that a further move was unwarranted at the time.

Then, about 1860, a rather strange and unexpected person known as Moses Hess began to voice the sentiments of the majority — he dared to advocate the feasibility of the Jews' actual return to Palestine. Hess was born in Bonn in 1812, of orthodox parents, but while pursuing higher studies in a German university he had become skeptical, and had thus brought a barrier between himself and his kinsmen. Being set adrift, he was on the lookout for something to which he might anchor his mental and social urge. In time he became intimate with Karl Marx and adopted his social doctrine, but soon afterward he left Germany and settled in Paris where, with fewer acquaintances, he reconsidered life — especially Jewish life in its many ramifications — and returned to Judaism.

Hess carried his socialistic and nationalistic ideas over into Judaism, and when the three were compounded he had a form of Jewish nationalism. The tenor of his teaching was that, for the best interest of humanity, each people, like each individual, should develop natural qualities to their maximum power; that if this applied to other races, it was true in the case of a people like Israel who had so well served the cause of civilization; and that the salvation of no other race seemed more important than that of Israel.

Adjusting his telescope for a view along the vistas of the tomorrows, Hess argued that if the ancient genuis of the Jew was to be recovered, and if Jewish influence was to affect the destiny of the world, then the Jewish people must group themselves, restore a national unity, and establish themselves in a country where they could again take up the natural life that had been suspended for centuries. And when this was done those Jews who for any reason cared not to leave their adopted countries for the new Judea would nevertheless be greatly blessed, encouraged, and fortified by the feeling that they were a people among other nations of the earth.

His plain declaration was that, whether the Jews like it or not, they are a nation; and that, like every other nation, they have their allotted place in the scheme of things — their mission being to translate their religion into terms of a better social order. But, being scattered and oppressed, so he argued, their creative powers were sterilized and they were rendered incapable of fulfilling their mission so long as they were in exile.

> It is only with the national rebirth that the religious genius of the Jews will be endowed with new strength and again be reinspired with the prophetic spirit. "Therefore," said the nineteenth-century Moses, "as soon as the political situation in the East takes a favorable turn, the establishment of Jewish colonies in Palestine must at once be begun, as a first step towards the resettlement of the Jews as a nation in their historic home.[12]

Writing in 1862, he quotes more than one French publicist in support of his prediction that "France will help the Jews to found colonies which may extend from Suez to Jerusalem and from the banks of the Jordan to the coast of the Mediterranean."[13]

In the same year Hirsch Kalischer, an orthdox Rabbi, born in Prussian Poland, definitely proposed the immediate establishment of a Jewish Society for the colonization of Palestine. The time had come for them to redeem the soil of Palestine by their own exertions. They should pass, he insisted, from passive expectance to active endeavor. Five years later, in conjunction with Rabbi Gutmacher of Graetz, he issued an "Appeal to our Brethren," in which the Jews of England in particular were passionately urged to support "the colonization, cultivation, and improvement" of the "abandoned, devastated, sacred soil."[14]

Kalischer's appeal made a favorable impression on the Alliance Israelite Universelle, which had been founded in Paris in 1860 in the interests of oppressed and persecuted Jews in all parts of the world. In 1871, the Anglo-Jewish Association was founded in England. These organizations, augmented by Christian sentiment, went a long way toward arousing general interest in re-establishing the Jews in their ancient father-land.

Penez Smolenskin, a Russo-Jewish nationalist, founded the Hebrew review, *Ha-Schochar* (The Dawn), in 1869, and for sixteen years carried on very effective propaganda. His principal thesis was that the Jews had a more important mission than the merging of themselves as rapidly as possible into their environment. The Jews, according to his views, were not a sect, but a people — a people bound together by common traditions and common ideals, of which Palestine was the historic symbol. Their first duty was to be themselves and to cherish their own distinctive heritage.[15]

In the litetrary sphere the idea was popularized in the *Hebrew Melodies* of Lord Byron, who gave poignant expression to the homelessness of the Jew in the famous lines:

> The white dove hath her nest, the fox his cave,
> Mankind their country, Israel but the grave.[16]

Benjamin Disraeli, in his romance, *David Alroy* (1853), revealed his sympathy with the ideal of Jewish restoration to Palestine when he made his hero say:

> You ask me what I wish: my answer is a national existence, which we have not. You ask me what I wish: my answer is the Land of Promise. You ask me what I wish: my answer is Jerusalem. You ask me what I wish: my answer is, the Temple, all we have forfeited, all we have yearned after, all for which we have fought, our beauteous country, our holy creed, our simple manners, and our ancient customs.

In 1876, George Eliot's *Daniel Deronda* appeared. It was no less than a passionate plea for the foundation in Palestine of a model Jewish State on the order of the old, yet containing elements of modern democracies.

> There is a stone of wisdom among us to found a new Jewish policy, grand, simple, just like the old — a republic where there is equality of protection . . . Then our race shall have an organic center, a heart and a brain to watch and guide and execute; the outraged Jew shall have a defense in the court of nations . . . and the world will gain as Israel gains.

Stein observes about such passages:

> These glowing visions were again and again translated into concrete proposals by men like Lord Shaftesbury and Laurence Oliphant and by a long line of half-forgotten pamphleteers. The British Government was not prepared to commit itself to any new policy in Palestine, but it continued to show a benevolent concern for the welfare of the Jews, and when Oliphant went to Constantinople in 1879 in the interests of a proposed Jewish settlement east of the Jordan, it gave him every encouragement and support.[17]

The Russian monarch, Alexander II, was assassinated in 1881, and with the ascension of his son, Alexander III, the minorities, especially the Jews, suffered grievously. During the Easter season an orgy of murder and pillage was inaugurated and hundreds of Jews were killed and thousands rendered homeless. In May, 1882, an order was issued which restrained Jewish privileges and made their lives almost unendurable. Romania followed the Russian example, and the Jews in various European countries were made to feel that they were not wanted.

This move of anti-Semitism caused Leo Pinsker, a doctor from Odessa, to lift his pen and suggest the adoption of constructive measures. In his pamphlet entitled *Auto Emancipation* Pinsker said:

> We do not count as a nation among the other nations, and we have no voice in the council of the people, even in affairs that concern ourselves. Our fatherland is an alien country, our unity dispersion, and solidarity the general hostility to us, our weapon humility, our defense flight, our originality adoptability, our future tomorrow. What a contemptible role for a people that once had its Maccabees!
>
> The civil and political emancipation of the Jews is not sufficient to raise them in the estimation of the peoples. The only remedy would be the creation of a Jewish nationality, of a people living upon its own soil.
>
> The international Jewish question must receive a national solution. Of course, our national regeneration must proceed slowly. *We* must take the first step. *Our descendents* must follow us in measured and not overhasty time.
>
> A way must be opened for the national regeneration of the Jews by a congress of Jewish notables.[18]

Though written in the concise phrases of a physician diagnosing a case rather than in the glowing accents of a prophet envisioning a great dream, that little pamphlet readily became the Bible of Zionism and set in motion currents that were to have considerable influence on others who were to take up the cause later.[19]

Leaders among the scattered Jews felt the need for actual organization among those who supported the ideal that the Jews must return to Palestine. Hermann Schapira, who through unusual genius had come to outstanding professorship, had greater dreams than teaching at Heidelberg. His ambitions had early turned toward the founding of a Jewish university in Palestine to serve as a spiritual center for the agricultural colonies which were being established. And while doing everything in his power to promote such an idea he, along with Pinsker and Lilienblum, succeeded in organizing a "Lovers of Zion" society in Odessa. Its object was the establishment of agricultural settlements in Palestine.

By the latter part of the nineteenth century the movement got well under way and was taken up in different parts of the world. Among the first to espouse the movement to return to Zion was the Jewish student youth. Particularly in the universities throughout Russia, small, enthusiastic groups banned together to promote the richer and more wonderful life that seemed to be opening to them. In 1884, Schapira conceived the idea of creating a Jewish National Fund for the purpose of purchasing Palestinian land for the Jews. He firmly believed that the land should belong to the Jewish nation rather than to private individuals. "But the times were not yet ripe for such undertakings and his words were like those of a voice calling in the wilderness."[20]

The Zionist movement, in its modern form, and the Zionist Organization which controls and is responsible for all the organized work in the making of the Jewish National Home, began with the appearance in Jewish life of Dr. Theodor Herzl. He was a brilliant, resourceful, handsome, and influential correspondent of the Vienna *New Free Press,* who frequented literary, political and journalist circles throughout Europe. Herzl was a Jew, but one that had been long detached from his people.

In the year 1895, Herzl was sent by his paper to Paris to report the Dreyfus trial which was to shock such a large portion of the world. He said that to him the case was "like a blow on the head." No longer did he speak of the Jews as "they" — he came to feel for the first time that he, too, was a Jew, and that his former reasoning was unsound. While the anti-Jewish feeling raged in France, Herzl wrote a booklet entitled, *Jewish State,* in which he analyzed the source of the Jewish trouble as "homelessness." He contended that the only solution to the Jewish problem was to provide a land for the people without one. Herzl recognized the efforts of the "Lovers of Zion" and others of like sentiments, but his foresightedness caused him to see that there could be no permanent, large-scale colonization in Palestine until there was some recognition of Jewish rights there, or perhaps until some kind of a Jewish State would be created by the consent of some of the stronger nations and influential individuals whose opinion went far in deciding international affairs.

Immediately upon the publication of his booklet, Herzl came to be regarded as the leader of the "Homeless." He had injected an ardor, an inspiration, and a sense of something new into the old familiar desires of the Hebrew people. The Jewish masses hailed him enthusiastically, and he communicated with leading Jews in all parts of the world. In August of 1897, just two years after he had adopted the idea of Zionism, he called into session the world's first Jewish Congress. There, at Basel, Switzerland, gathered the representatives and leaders of the Jewish people throughout Europe, and under the guidance of Herzl's deft hand the World Zionist Organization was established and its program formulated. The Congress was unanimous in its adoption of the following:

> "The aim of Zionism is to create for the Jewish people a home in Palestine secured by public law.
>
> In order to attain this object the Congress adopts the following means:
>
> 1. The systematic promotion of the settlement of Palestine with Jewish agriculturists, artisans, and craftsmen.
>
> 2. The organization and federation of all Jewry by means of local and general institutions in conformity with the local laws.
>
> 3. The strengthening of Jewish sentiment and national consciousness.

4. Preparatory steps for the procuring of such Government assents as are necessary for achieving the object of Zionism."[21]

Immediately Herzl launched into a program of ceaseless diplomatic efforts and negotiations with ecclesiastical and government leaders throughout Europe and Western Asia. He went to St. Petersburg in an effort to overcome the opposition of the Russian Government to the Zionist movement. About that time he also wrote an utopian novel, *Old Newland,* depicting the life of the Jews in their revived state. Shortly after his negotiations in Russia he was invited to testify before the British Royal Commission on Alien Immigration, and through that appearance won a number of very influential friends for the cause of Zionism.

He interviewed the Italian King, the Pope, the Kaiser of Germany, and then went to Turkey to ascertain the possibilities of securing Palestine direct from the Sultan. For months he sought the privilege of a personal interview with this great ruler. Then one day while Herzl sat waiting in the outer office, one of the Sultan's many slaves entered and beckoned the distinguished-looking man to follow him. They walked through the long and spacious corridors and finally arrived at the throne room. The room was decorated with many precious gems, and the Sultan's throne was of pure gold.

Tall, dignified, handsome Theodor Herzl made a low, respectful bow and began to speak as only Herzl could speak.

The Jews, he said, were persecuted everywhere in Europe, and could not seem to find a home anywhere but in America, which could not take them all. Would the Sultan consider letting them return to Palestine, their ancient Homeland? While the small, round, gorgeously clothed Sultan sat on the soft pillows on his golden throne and listened, he was sufficiently impressed with his tall, handsome, eloquent visitor that he decorated him for his personal heroism and offered to permit the Jews to return to Palestine for twenty million dollars.

For the first time in many years, Herzl was thoroughly happy, for he felt confident that many Gentiles would help and that certainly all the Jews of the world would contribute money to purchase Palestine. On presenting the matter, however, it soon became evident that his task would not be so easy. He tried to interest almost every chancery of Europe as well as those high in financial circles. Government heads received him courteously but did nothing, and the financiers offered him little or no assistance. Baron de Rothschild was interested, but had already sent all of the Jews to Palestine that he could hope to maintain, and Baron de Hirsch was not especially attracted to the soil of Palestine. He rather chose to offer opportunities for his Jewish brethren to settle on the fertile lands of Argentina, where he had already sent large groups to farms whose soil he thought better than the rocky lands of Palestine.

Being unable to raise the money to buy Palestine was quite disheartening to Herzl, but he wisely took the position that if Palestine could not be had then Israed must have quarters elsewhere.

Joseph Chamberlain, the Minister of the Colonies, assisted Herzl in contacting the Egyptian Government about Jewish settlement on the Sinai Peninsula, adjoining Southern Palestine. When this charter failed to materialize, the English came forward with an offer of Uganda, Africa. Herzl was ready to accept, but few Jews would move in any direction save to Palestine; none would accompany him to Uganda. No country would satisfy but the Holy Land of their fathers.

The controversy over the Uganda project aggravated a serious heart affection and on July 3, 1904, while in the prime of his life, Herzl died.[22] He had devoted his talents as an orator, writer, and politician, as well as his great personal charm, to the cause of changing the dreams of his people into a reality. Though he himself saw but little of the fruitage of his efforts, he had set Jewish imagination and affection in motion, and had gathered Israel in a kind of congress which would not break up until the rolling waves multiplied and thousands of Jewish pilgrims were firmly planted on Palestinian soil.

## Chapter XXXV

# ENTERING THE PROMISED LAND

For long centuries the Jewish people had sung, and prayed, and wept, and seized every possible opportunity to return to Palestine. Scholars, saints, and fair-sized groups of exiles had trekked back in every generation for more than eighteen hundred years.

When the Jews rebelled under Bar Cochba and were defeated and driven from Judea in the second century A.D. an influential remnant found refuge in Galilee, where Tiberias became their headquarters. The people tilled the soil and worked at manual labor, while their Sanhedrin worked to complete the Jerusalem Talmud and wielded their rabbinical authority. They were driven from Galilee during the fifth century, but were permitted to return near the middle of the seventh century and replant their rabbinical schools.

After the terrors of the Inquisition and the expulsion of the Jews from Spain at the end of the fifteenth century, many found homes in the villages of Galilee. Large numbers of these refugees were distinguished for their education, scholarship, business enterprise, and deep piety; therefore their villages became centers of scholarship and mystical speculation as their sages "sought to hasten the advent of the Messiah by pondering on the mysteries of the Word, and penetrating the secret wisdom of God's law."[1]

During the seventeenth century Shabbatai Zevi of Smyrna posed as the Messiah and revealed the ever-present readiness of Jews to abandon what they regarded as their merely temporary homes, relinquish their material possessions, and embark on the perilous journey to the land of their destiny. But Zevi proved false.

In the middle of the eighteenth century, a movement was started to establish schools of rabbinical learning in the Holy Land and to support the scholars by the contributions of the Jews throughout the world. This succeeded in that it sent a steady trickle of pious Jews to the four cities of Jerusalem, Hebron, Tiberias, and Safed, which were their "Holy Cities."[2]

All the early Zionist leaders laid stress on not merely the return of the Jews to Palestine, but on the return to the soil. It was accepted as axiomatic that agriculture must be the basis of a regenerated Jewry in Palestine. Despite all these teachings, the first Jews who returned formed local Jewish communities in Jerusalem and other cities of Palestine where they found little means of self-support and had relief from want and misery only as funds were sent in by sympathetic world Jewry.

In 1861 a Palestine Society was formed with the object of effecting the purchase of large tracts of land in Palestine, to be parcelled off in small holdings. However, no "Back to the Land" movement was actually experienced until in 1870, when a representative body of French Jews known as The Alliance Israelite Universelle, led by Carl Netter, founded an agricultural school known as "Mikwek Israel" ("the gathering of Israel") on the Sharon Plain some four miles southeast of Jaffa. Here, under competent teachers, Jewish young men began to study the soils, plant trees, in general to inform themselves about all experiment with seeds, raise dairy cattle, and branches of agriculture and horticulture. Before long, orange groves, orchards, and avenues of eucalyptus and bamboo trees impressed all who traveled along the nearby Jerusalem-Jaffa road. Those who took time to look over the place found various orchards of fruit, a splendid dairy herd, and many well-planned fields of grain and produce. The fact that this large tract of barren and sandy soil had been transformed into a flourishing settlement proved an inspiration and impetus to others.

Orthodox Jewry hoped for, and expected, the Divine Messiah to appear and relieve them of their oppressions and lead them back to their fatherland. However, during the later part of the nineteenth century their persecution became so intense in parts of Europe that thousands of Jews came to feel that God would be with them in their endeavors if they proceeded forthwith. Therefore, leaving all behind, they turned their backs on Russia, Poland, and Romania, and took the road to Palestine. The spirit of return seized Jewish people in other parts of the world, and small bands made their way from Baghdad, Aleppo, and Bokhara, and from Arabia, Persia, Morocco, and Turkestan. Many came from the Yemen district of southern Arabia "where Jews were settled since the destruction of the kingdom, living as an inferior caste under the Moslem rule, but intensely cherishing the hope of a return to the home of their ancestors."[3]

The Jewish Colonization Association established a number of Jewish settlements in Lower Galilee in 1901, and gave every settler a considerable area of land for the cultivation of wheat. Only nominal success accompanied this venture, as had been the case with the other colonies; however, valuable experience had been gained, trying conditions overcome, and some success achieved, even though the methods had been somewhat haphazard.

The Zionist Organization, which came into being in 1897, had not thus far officially aided the work in Palestine. Herzl and his associates had maintained that they were obliged to first secure a political status in Palestine before proceeding with a colonization program. However, in 1901 they established the Jewish National Fund for the purpose of purchasing land in Palestine as the inalienable property of the Jewish people. By 1908 the Fund had grown sufficiently to enable the purchase of considerable land on which they founded five or six Jewish settlements, one of which was Tel Aviv. The policy pursued in their colonies was somewhat different in that it was based on mixed farming, that is, farming which involved corn, dairy produce, vegetables, poultry, and plantations; and all the work was to be done by Jewish labor.

The work of the Zionist Organization struck a new and encouraging note in the field of colonization, and made possible fairly steady progress, at least when one considers the severe restrictions which the Turkish Government imposed upon the Jews.

Jewish immigration to Palestine increased steadily up until the World War. In 1845 Palestine had had but 12,000 Jews; by 1882, 24,000; by 1890, about 47,000; and by 1914, something like 85,000 inhabitants. Of this number only 12,000 were located in forty-four colonies comprising 440,000 dunums or 110,000 acres of land.

Some of these entered Palestine with the hope of leaving poverty behind, others came to avoid oppression, while still others were actuated by religious motives. But before long they were working to maintain themselves, redeem the soil, rebuild the Jewish fatherland, and thus make Zion once more a reality upon the earth. Palestine was impoverished, disease-ridden, and disordered; therefore these early settlers had almost insurmountable difficulties before them. They drained swamps and suffered from want of almost every kind. Many died of malaria and other dread diseases. A few survived, the noble spirits of the deceased lived, and others kept coming to take their places.

When the World War broke out in 1914, both the Allied and Central Powers desired the moral and financial support of the fifteen million Jews throughout the world. Each of them, therefore, endeavored to make capital of Zionist ambitions. There were more Jews in Russia than in any other country on the face of the earth. And there had been more Jewish persecutions there than had pleased the sons of Abraham. Their sympathies, therefore, were to a great extent anti-Russian, and in favor of the Central Powers. The Germans had extensive plans for the Near East. The Kaiser had visited Palestine in 1897, religious colonies had been planted there, and the Berlin to Baghdad Railway was almost completed. As the war advanced, members of the German General Staff publicized their proposals for Jewish restoration to Palestine under an arrangement to be made between the Zionists and Turkey. Herr Von Dobbeler urged action in the following terms:

> The Jew is a born colonist; he understands more than any other man upon earth how to utilize all the advantages available. With his spirit of industry he will open up the treasures of the Palestinian soil, plant forests, discover wells, and draw the finest fruits from the land; and even if he is not a farmer himself, he will find sufficient labor-power among the Fellahin. The commerce of the whole of Turkey will advance with the compact Jewish element within her empire, and there will come a day when Turkey will recognize her wealth and realize that she will be in a position to arm herself against foreign foes like her allies in Central Europe.[4]

Major Karl Franz Enders, of the General Staff, said:

> The establishment of a Jewish state would endow the restless people of the Jews with fresh cohesion, and with a positive — and no longer disintegrating — strength. As an industrial and commercial State it would become the hinge between the empires of Europe, Asia and Africa; as a people of colonists it would infuse a considerable amount of fresh blood into enfeebled Turkey. As the Jews, politically, are mostly inclined to be Republicans, they ought to be presented with a Republic upon their ancestrial soil. But a Jewish Republic should for all time form a constituent of the Ottoman Empire.[5]

But the Allied Western Powers were by no means idle in regard to the Jewish question. Many of the world's most influential Jews lived in England, France, and America, and were in most cases both loyal and patriotic. Large numbers of these who were Zionist worked for the defeat of the Central Powers with the thought that such an accomplishment would in some way "aid in giving reality to the age-old yearning of the Jewish people" to return to their beloved Palestine. Certain outstanding Jewish leaders sought to influence great political leaders to this end. As early as September, 1914, President Woodrow Wilson, together with the British and French ambassadors to Washington, held conferences with Mr. Louis D. Brandeis, the great Jewish jurist, about facilitating Jewish settlement in Palestine in return for general Jewish assistance in the war.

In England, Mr. C. P. Scott, Editor of the *Manchester Guardian,* introduced Dr. Chaim Weizmann to Mr. Lloyd George and Mr. Herbert Samuel, who were leading members of the British Cabinet. Dr. Weizmann, lecturer in Chemistry at the Manchester University, was not only an effective chemist; he also possessed an active mind, an eloquent voice, and unbounded energy. His personal magnetism, joined to his impressive mental ability and great driving power, commanded the respect of British officials as well as of his fellow Jews.

Early in 1915 a proposal was submitted to the British Cabinet recommending that Palestine be made into a dominion "into which the scattered Jews would in time swarm back from all quarters of the globe, and in due course obtain Home Rule." The matter was viewed with favor by such members as Gray, Samuel, Crewe, Lloyd George, and Lord Reading, but no action was taken. The Zionist leaders then carried forward a vigorous campaign to enlist other responsible Jewish leaders, and thus strengthen Zionism from within. Many Jewish writers joined, among whom was Major Norman Bentwich.

In October of 1916, the Zionist leaders submitted to the British Government a formal "program for a new administration of Palestine and for a Jewish resettlement of Palestine in accordance with the aspirations of the Zionist Movement."[6]

As the war progressed there came about a serious crisis due to a shortage of acetone, a vital ingredient used in the manufacture of shells and other ammunitions of war. Germany's continuing victories gave great concern, and sent the allies in search of some chemical that would replenish their stock pile of explosives and improve their striking power. When Mr. Lloyd George, Minister of Munitions, explained the situation, Dr. Weizmann entered his laboratory and undertook a series of experiments where by care, prayer, and painstaking effort he perfected a formula for the production of actone, which made possible an effective anti-zeplin bullet and the high explosive known as TNT — an achievement which helped the Allied forces to eventually win the war.[7]

After the effectiveness and great value of Dr. Weizmann's discovery became apparent, Mr. Lloyd George said to him, "You rendered great services to the State, and I should like to ask the Prime Minister to recommend you to His Majesty for some honor."

"There is nothing I want for myself," said the great chemist.

"But is there nothing we can do as a recognition of your valuable assistance to the country?" asked the Minister of War.

Thereupon Weizmann replied: "Yes, I would like you to do something for my people." Then he explained at length his desire to see the Jewish people return to the sacred land of Palestine which they had made famous. Lloyd George listened, and went away to think.[8]

In the spring of 1917, Mr. Balfour, British Foreign Secretary, visited America, and among other things he discussed Zionist aspirations with President Wilson and Associate Justice Louis D. Brandeis of the Supreme Court. President Wilson was not only sympathetic, but allowed his sentiments to be made known. Then, on November 2, 1917, Mr. Arthur J. Balfour, Secretary of State for Foreign Affairs, formally announced the sympathy of the British Government with Zionist aspirations and its favorable attitude toward the establishment of a national home for the Jewish people in the following letter which afterwards became known as the Balfour Declaration:[9]

Foreign Office
November 2, 1917

Dear Lord Rothschild:

I have much pleasure in conveying to you on behalf of His Majesty's Government the following declaration of sympathy with Jewish Zionist aspirations, which has been submitted to and approved by the Cabinet:

"His Majesty's Government view with favour the establishment in Palestine of a national home for the Jewish people, and will use their best endeavours to facilitate the achievement of this object, it being clearly understood that nothing shall be done which may prejudice the civil and religious rights of existing non-Jewish communities in Palestine or the rights and political status enjoyed by Jews in any other country."

I should be grateful if you would bring this declaration to the knowledge of the Zionist Federation.

Yours sincerely
(Signed) Arthur James Balfour

The success of the British Expeditionary Force under General Allenby during the autumn of 1917 and the spring of 1918 brought Palestine within the orbit of the British Empire, and increased their potential for implementing the Balfour Declaration.

In April of 1920 the Supreme Council of the Peace Conference met at San Remo and resolved that the Balfour Declaration should be incorporated in the treaty of peace with Turkey and that the Mandate for Palestine should be assigned to Great Britain. Shortly afterwards it was announced that Mr. Herbert Samuels, who for some time had been serving General Allenby and the British Government as special consultant in Palestinian affairs, was appointed as the first High Commissioner of Palestine.

At eleven o'clock, on the morning of June 30, 1920, with a day that was fine, hot, and clear, a British destroyer, grey and trim, anchored outside the rocks which shelter the port of Jaffa. Governor Storrs of Jerusalem rowed out to the ship, went aboard, and shortly afterwards returned with the High Commissioner. Sir Herbert Samuel "was dressed in white from head to foot, wearing even a white helmet. Against this whiteness, the purple scarf of the order thus conferred upon him before leaving England, which he wore over his shoulder and fastened at his side, presented a startling and brilliant contrast," to the kahki uniform of his escort. The destroyer thundered with its guns from the sea and the Royal field artillery, stationed on the beach, replied with a round of firing. A guard of honor presented arms, and an airplane circled overhead like a watchful eagle.

Sir Herbert Samuel was conducted under the large field tent where the Mayor of Jaffa welcomed him with the words:

> I beg to welcome you and to express to you our congratulations on your safe arrival in the Holy Land. This country is in great need of a British High Commissioner who will justly, firmly, thoroughly, and ably investigate the conditions and needs of the country in all respects. Therefore, from the depths of our hearts we desire the happiness of this town and country, with its inhabitants under the shield and protection of the British Nation, the foundation of whose governments throughout the world is based on justice, freedom, and equality for all sects and denominations. May Almighty God help us all in our efforts to do what is right and peaceful. . . .[10]

After replying in appropriate terms, the High Commissioner proceeded toward the motor-car which was to take him to Jerusalem. Colonel Donald Grey stepped forward and performed the simple, yet significant act of placing a small Union Jack on the front of the car in which the Commissioner was to ride. This act marked the first official display of the British flag in Palestine, and denoted that Great Britain had assumed responsibility of the mandate over the country.

In 1922 a resolution was passed in the League of Nations which officially placed Palestine under British Mandate, and this resolution was fully ratified on September 29 of the following year. This Mandate for Palestine imposed on Great Britain the obligation of re-organizing the country in such a way as to secure the establishment of a Jewish national home, facilitate immigration, and provide for close settlement of the land. It also provided for a Jewish Agency to advise and cooperate with the Palestine administration in these matters.

The Balfour Declaration, the Allied victory under Allenby, and the Palestinian Mandate indicated the world's willingness to encourage and facilitate Jewish immigration to Palestine. To the Jew, they constituted an invitation to him to return to his ancient fatherland. The Jews, who, in general, were quite ready to accept the invitation, therefore began to leave almost all countries and to throw themselves in waves on Palestinian soil.

From 1919 to 1924 an average of almost ten thousand Jews entered the country annually. In 1925 this number increased to thirty-four thousand. They came from Poland, Russia, Rumania, Lithuania, and Germany, with a sprinkling from the United States and other remote points. The country was not prepared for them, and none of the leaders knew how to cope with so large a tide of Jewish humanity.

There were two classes of immigrants: the "capitalists" and the workers. There first came a great boom, while the money was being spent. Tel Aviv mushroomed out at a fantastic rate. Its population almost doubled in one year. But a rapid recession came. Its first signs were already perceptible in the later part of 1925. Many of the Polish immigrants had left some of their possessions behind, to be liquidated gradually. But there was a financial crisis in Poland, and the expected funds never came. The little stores that had been opened were in frantic competition with each other — so much so that one customer sometimes would mean the difference between survival and extinction. The long lines of well-stocked, yet almost unpatronized shops and stores became the wry symbol of the economic unhealthiness of too many immigrants entering Palestine in the absence of wise planning and adequate financial assistance.

During the next three years the volume of incoming immigrants diminished. They were, nevertheless, good years from the standpoint of wise planning for the coming decades. Dr. Ruppin and other Zionist leaders not only made better and more far-reaching plans for close-settlement of the immigrants on the land, but Zionism reached westward and took in American industrialists and financiers who would henceforth furnish prestige and executive ability, together with large sums of money for the settlement of Israel's dispersed sons and daughters who would return to the fatherland.

In the years immediately following the riots of 1929, Palestine was getting set for the fulfillment — at long last — of the mass return. And in 1933, 1934, 1935, the miracle came to be accepted as a commonplace thing. By the end of 1936 there were 404,000 Jews in Palestine. Some came legally, others came "illegally," but come to Palestine they did.

As the pressure increased in Nazi Germany and other places in Europe, there were increases in the tides that drew the Jewish people to Palestine. So many came that the Arabs sensed that there would soon be no place for them; therefore they protested, called special strikes as protest measures, attacked Jewish settlements, and petitioned the League of Nations and other world authorities to stop the Jews from coming to Palestine. They put pressure on the Government, and assassinated individual Jews and many Arabs who favored the Jews, until in 1939 the British sent a commission to investigate. As a result, the British issued an official "White Paper" restricting Jewish immigration, and asking that it be stopped altogether by 1941. However, by 1941 there were 502,000 Jews in Palestine.

## Chapter XXXVI

# TROUBLE IN THE HOLY LAND

The *Arabs* rather liked to have the earlier Jewish colonists in Palestine. They gave the Arabs work, respected them, and often purchased their produce. The Arabs supposed they would be glad to have more Jews come, but became uneasy when they saw the Jews returning in such large numbers, not entirely on their own initiative, but by the help of the British. This spirit of uneasiness increased when it was whispered around that a powerful British official by the name of Balfour had given their country to the Jews, who would take full control when they had attained a majority of the population.

Their feelings seemed confirmed when, in 1920, they heard that Sir Herbert Samuels, a Jew, was coming to Palestine as the British High Commissioner, and that Mr. Norman Bentwich, another Jewish gentleman, would serve as Attorney-General for the Government. Apprehensive of a threat to their supremacy, the Arab ruling class instigated among the Arab population a violent hostility toward the incoming Jews. In that same year rioting broke out in Jerusalem and Jaffa, and attacks were made on Jewish settlements in upper Galilee.

It was rumored that a second uprising was scheduled to take place with the arrival of Sir Herbert Samuels, but great precautions were taken by the Government and nothing came of it. On finding that the Arab population suspected the British authorities of intending to expropriate their holdings for the sake of turning them over to the Jews, Sir Herbert Samuels obtained from the British Government an official interpretation of the Balfour Declaration. This statement explained that the Balfour Declaration did not point to the creation of a wholly Jewish Palestine, nor did it point to either the disappearance or the subordination of the Arab population, language, or culture. Neither was Palestine as a whole to be converted into a Jewish national home. Rather, it stated merely that a Jewish national home was to be founded in Palestine, in order that the members of the Jewish community should know that they were in Palestine by right and not on sufferance, and that they were to have ample opportunity for the full development of their capacities. The Palestine community was to become a center in which Jews as a whole might take, on grounds of race and religion, an interest and a pride.

In spite of this explanation, the Arab inhabitants, influenced in large measure by outside forces, refused to recognize the Balfour Declaration or to assent to the Mandate so long as it contained articles guaranteeing the creation of a Jewish national home in Palestine. Moslem and Christian Arabs sent deputations to wait upon the British authorities and presented petition after petition to the League of Nations.

These deputations asserted that the Balfour Declaration sacrificed the rights of the majority already in the country for the sake of a minority not yet arrived, namely, Jewish immigrants who were still to come. To safeguard only the "civil and religious rights" of the Arab majority in Palestine was to treat them as though they themselves were the minority. The Balfour Declaration, they affirmed, was therefore inconsistent with the League Covenant, and Great Britain, they contended, should have been forced (in accordance with Article XX of the Covenant itself) to repudiate the Balfour Declaration before being permitted to acquire membership in the League.

So bitterly did Moslem and Christian Arabs resent the Balfour Declaration that they refused to cooperate with the authorities when the latter attemped in 1922 to establish a national Legislative Council in Palestine. This body was to have been composed of ten appointed officials and twelve elected members — eight Moslems, two Christians, and two Jews.

The Arabs boycotted the elections on the ground that they could not be sure that the rights of the majority would be guaranteed unless the Arab members of the proposed Legislature outnumbered Jewish and official members combined. The boycott being effective, the High Commissioner was forced to give up the plan for a legislative body. After that time the government was carried on by the High Commissioner in consultation with his immediate subordinates and a small advisory council made up entirely of officials. Proposed ordinances were published in the official gazette before promulgation, a procedure which gave interested persons an opportunity to make representations to the authorities before the measures were actually put into force.

Arab grievances were, for the most part, inspired by neither religious nor racial feeling, but by economic, social, and political matters. In these they were so displeased that they came to dislike both the British and the Jews.

They objected to what they considered the artificial division and subdivision by foreign powers of the territories of the Near East, practices which, so they argued, occasioned barriers and political boundaries detrimental to the economic, social, and political interests of freedom-loving peoples. They objected to the Balfour Declaration on the ground that it would tend to separate Palestine from the other territories should the Arab countries become unified later on.

Then, too, the Arabs objected to certain attitudes too often assumed by the "new Jews" who came to Palestine during the 1920s. The earlier Jews had purchased the land at generous prices and had settled quietly. Moreover they not only purchased what the Arabs had to sell, but employed the Arabs to do much of their work. The "new" Jews came with money, machinery, and determination, and told themselves continually, "We are a homeless people returning to a land without a people" — a refrain which acted like a patent toxin indeed. And when there, the "new" Jew too often left the impression that he was the man of the hour — one who had just returned home, disregarding the fact that the Arab far outnumbered him, and that their ancestors had lived there for thirteen centuries.

Envisioning himself as a man with a mission to rebuild his fatherland, many a young Jew with an inflated sense of self-importance showed bad manner by elbowing his way past waiting lines and presenting himself to be served before those who waited in order. Then, too, the Arab sense of modesty was shocked by the familiarities of scantily clad young men and women of the Kvutza colonies, who threw to the wind altogether too many conventional, social, and moral restraints, paraded the roadways arm in arm, and lived careless of appearances.

Moreover, the Arabs were nettled by the "superiority complex" of some of the British administrators who were arrogant and blustery, and who let it be known by their mannerisms that they expected everyone to look up to them with "envy, admiration, and obedience." In too many cases the "natives," as they were called, were unable to air their grievances or reason with officials. They therefore soon came to feel that their only recourse was violence. In this attitude they were too often encouraged by outside forces, such as Nazism and communism.

At various times during the 1920s there were protests, strikes, and riots. Then came the year 1929, when, during the month of August, on the Jewish Day of Atonement, the inflammatory situation was further aggravated by the incident of the "Wailing Wall."

## The Wailing Wall Incident

For some three millenniums the high-roads and by-paths of orthodox Jewish history and sentiment have ended in Jerusalem, and for more than fifteen centuries the terminus there has been a grim, gray wall known as the "Wailing Wall." Marking the western boundary of the Temple area and separating this sacred area from the city proper, the wall towers some 60 feet above a 98 by 24 foot long, stone-paved courtyard leading out of the windings of David Street. Its lower courses are made up of huge, yet strikingly beautiful, marginal-drafted "Herodian" stones which are some of the finest and most venerable in the world.

Like an imperishable symbol of the eternal race, this inscrutable religious fragment, known to the Jewish people as the "Western Wall," had stood as an unobtrusive testimony to a great past, and had remained inviolate while the sharp claws of time had mangled one empire after another.

The wall was holy, and could never be destroyed, according to a legend of the rabbies, because it had become the dwelling place of the *Shekinah* presence of the Divine Majesty that was forced out of the Temple at the time of its destruction. The Jews believed it to be the point nearest to where once stood the Holy of Holies, and to be made up of all that remained of their ancient Temple; therefore, on the city side of the wall, they had lamented Israel's departed glories, and had prayed and worshipped there since the fourth century. The Wall took a deeper hold on Jewish religious affection during the eighteenth century when it became a frontispiece of every Jewish prayer book and a theme of decoration in synagogues and homes. Those who could not pray at the actual wall in Jerusalem had, through recent centuries, paid others to do it for them. And there had always been a small Jewish population who lived here on *Haluka,* a religious dole, sent in by devout Jews from all over the world to insure such prayers being said at this great stone symbol of their most ardent hopes.

The wall and its narrow pavement was the property of the Moslems. They made the Jews pay dearly for the privilege of praying there. From time to time feelings had been ruffled, and minor difficulties had arisen over the use of the wall. Yet nothing overly serious happened until Chief Rabbi Cook appointed a Polish Jew as *shammas,* or beadle, at the Wailing Wall, where only a Sephardic Jewish beadle had served before. The latter resented this, for the tourists who came to pray at the wall usually gave him tips or gifts which he now would have to share with the new beadle. However, the two finally agreed that the Polish beadle should receive what the European and American Jews would give while the donations of the Oriental and Sephardic worshipers should go to the old beadle!

All went well until August of 1929, when there came to Jerusalem a famous Polish rabbi who, from time to time, had been the honored guest at the Wailing Wall. The rabbi was accompanied by many admirers, most of whom usually tipped the Polish beadle. His colleague demanded a new division of the gratuities, but his demand was refused.

Just before the Jewish Day of Atonement the visiting rabbi expressed the desire for a screen to separate the men and women worshippers at the Wall. Although such a screen was not customary, the Polish beadle, influenced by a particularly generous gift, hastened to fulfill the wishes of the honored guest. Being refused a share in the generous gift, the long-established Sephardic beadle went — on the eve of the Day of Atonement — to the Arabs and told them of the "new wall," fixed to the pavement by an iron bolt, which the new beadle had erected there. Evidently he wished to intimate that nothing of the kind would have happened "had he been the only one to serve at the Wailing Wall." The Mufti, or chief religious leader of the Mohammedans, had little concern who served at the wall, but he was very definitely interested in advising the British authorities that the Jews had exceeded their rights, and that he was protesting on the ground that the screen, fastened to the pavement by an iron bolt, interfered with Moslem rights of ownership, and that trouble would accrue if it were permitted to remain.

The Deputy-District Commissioner, while visiting the Wall on the eve of the holy day, viewed the transgression, and directed the Jewish beadle at the wall to have the screen removed before the morning service. Morning came and the beadle had not removed the offense, but had gone with a deputation to ask for a stay of execution. The stay was not granted, and the Commissioner directed a British police officer to take action.

On arriving at the Wailing Wall, the police officer found the Jews deeply absorbed in fasting, praying, confessing, and seeking forgiveness of God, in harmony with their sacred custom on this their Day of Atonement. Waiting until there was a silent interval in their prayers, and in ignorance of this moment of solemn devotion, the police officer moved in among the worshipers, seized the screen, and forcibly removed it amid protesting, scrambling, and weeping fathers of Israel. In the melee the Jews suffered considerable damage of prayer books, scrolls, and paraphernalia incident to their worship. But greatest of all was their deep humiliation at being offended at their holiest site on their holiest day in their holiest city where they constituted a two-thirds majority. Their reaction was a storm of indignation, a rash of meetings, and a flood of protests — one of which was sent to the League of Nations. But nothing in the way of satisfaction came to the Jews, other than an expression from the Government saying they "regretted" the incident, and the issuance of a "White Paper" which was a feeble attempt to state the rights of both parties and the position of the Government.

In the meantime the Arabs began to stress their rights to the Wailing Wall, and to raise the cry that the Haram (Dome of the Rock) and the holy Aksa Mosque were in danger, and that Jewish agression aimed at the restoration of the Temple on the site. Furthermore, the Arab religious officials proceeded to emphasize their legal rights of ownership by building an extension upon the northern part of the wall, and constructing a doorway and steps leading from the Temple area through the Wall to the praying place of the Jews. And here, beside the Wall, from a newly created minaret, the Muezzin "called the faithful to prayer with resounding song — while the Jews worshipped before the nearby Wall." Jewish protests only brought further Arab provocations, a reaction which quite disgusted the Jews. Yet they clung tenaciously to the Wailing Wall, lest they seem to betray the pious Jews of all the world, to whom that Wall symbolized everything they loved in Palestine. The more the Jews clung to the Wall, the more the Moslems felt that the Jews wanted to take something from them. They were beginning with the Wailing Wall — they would end, surely, with the Dome of the Rock.

Arab sentiment was further verified when on the ninth of Ab, the memorial day of the destruction of Solomon's and Herod's Temple, (events which had transpired 2515 and 1859 years ago respectively) the Jews, ten thousand strong, marched in solemn procession to the Ancient Wall, beside which stood the lay worshippers lamenting the fall of their temples.

Later in the afternoon three hundred Jewish youths marched by the Wall, carrying a banner veiled in crepe and singing the Jewish National hymn. In quick response two thousand Arabs "visited" the holy site of the Jews, where "by the pressure of the crowd" the Torah table was broken; chairs, wash bowls, and towels destroyed; and sacred books such as the Psalms and Lamentations were torn and charred by fire.

The following day was the Jewish Sabbath but its sacred atmosphere was rent with rumors of Arab plans for another attack at the Wailing Wall. Feeling that there was no protection from the Administration, a division of the Jewish Brith Trumpeldor marched to the Wailing

Wall and blockaded the place of worship to prevent any disturbance of Jewish prayers. The police cooperated with the Trumpeldors and guarded the narrow winding street leading to the wall. Being so carefully guarded, a quiet calm prevailed there, but no such good fortune was to prevail in certain other unguarded sections of ancient Jerusalem. Out in the Bokharian quarter, inhabited by Oriental Jews, the Arabs came into conflict with a group of Jewish boys and inflicted wounds on many of them. One, being seriously wounded, was taken to the government hospital, where, on Tuesday night, August 20th, 1929, he died — the first Jewish victim of the Jewish-Arab disorders. Desiring to keep the death a secret, the Administration and the Zionist Executive begged the parents to let their child be buried the same night, that there might be no excitement. The parents not only refused on the grounds that they wanted an honorable burial for their son, but they capitalized on the event, and circulated the death notice widely so as to arouse the wrath of the Jews against the Arabs.

On the following day, Jewish Jerusalem was filled with an unparalleled eruption of accumulated wrath against the British and the Arabs. Three thousand Jews followed the corpse to the cemetery, and the procession was both preceded and followed by armoured cars and mounted police. Jews who desire to do special honors to the deceased usually direct the funeral procession out of old Jerusalem through Jaffa Gate and thence around the city, by the way of Gethsemane, to the cemetery on Mount of Olives, overlooking the vale of Kedron.

On attempting to go this route and show honor to the martyred lad, the procession found the road suddenly blockaded by Arab and English police. With aroused determination the Jews threw themselves against the police lines, only to have the police drive against them from three sides with their clubs, wounding twenty-seven in the procession — two so severely that they were sent to the hospital. At last a semblance of order was restored and the funeral cortage took the route through Damascus Gate to the cemetery on Mount of Olives, where the burial was made in a shallow grave. The Jews returned with their hatred and indignation deepened and their fury knowing no bounds.

Having observed that an almost unlimited amount of energy had been displayed by the police against the Jews, and almost nothing had been done to protect them, the Arabs were encouraged to undertake what eventually became on orgy of anti-Jewish riots. Various sections and suburbs of Jerusalem were attacked and were saved from utter destruction only by the organization of Jewish self-defense units. At Hebron, on August 23rd, a Jewish student was murdered, and on the following day a wholesale slaughter of the Jews of that city took place. After this came an entire week of massacring and looting throughout the country, the violence culminating in the burning of the city of Safed. Hundreds of Jews were killed, thousands were forced to evacuate their homes, other thousands lost all their possessions — houses, farms, cattle, crops and personal property. Relief organizations took care of the refugees, but the government remained almost passive until September 2nd, when Sir John Chancellor, High Commissioner of Palestine, issued a proclamation which placed considerable responsibility for the trouble on the Arabs.

The Arab executive replied with a telegram of protest, and called a special emergency meeting of the Executive Arab Congress in Jerusalem to decide what further steps should be taken. Fiery anti-Jewish speeches were made, and the Committee of Holy Warriors of Palestine issued a pamphlet urging the Moslems of the entire world to rise up against the Jews. Many high-thinking Arabs deplored the atrocities perpetrated upon the Jews, and Emir Abdullah of Transjordan gave out a statement declaring that peace had been restored in Palestine, and warning the Arabs of his country against crossing the Palestinian border.

A Commission of Inquiry was appointed. In time many Arabs were prosecuted, and a reasonable measure of peace and security was restored; yet the inquiry was limited to the immediate emergency and did not extend to considerations of major policy. Neither the Arabs nor the Jews were satisfied. The majority of the Arabs felt that the Jews had aspirations, strengthened by action taken at the Zurich Congress, which would eventually displace the Arabs, or at best relegate them to the status of a minority group. When speaking of the British Administration policy, they called it the "British Zionist policy," for they were confident that the British favored the Jews. But the Jews, generally speaking, were, in turn, quite dissatisfied with the way in which the British had permitted affairs to drift from bad to worse. They were sure that the majority of the British officials were pro-Arab in their leanings. Thus, the Arabs and Jews were prejudiced against each other, and they were both mildly set against the British.

During the months and years which followed, many dark storm clouds blew into Palestine's political sky. In 1934 Jewish immigration figures soared to a new high and Arab uneasiness increased accordingly. Moderately serious disturbances came in 1935, and exceedingly serious strikes and riots in 1936.

On May 18, 1936, the Secretary of State for the Colonies announced that a Royal Commission of Inquiry would be sent to Palestine to "investigate the causes of unrest and the alleged grievances of either Arabs or Jews without bringing into question the terms of the Mandate." The Commission was headed by Mr. Earl Peel, and was afterwards known as "the Peel Commission." On arriving in the autumn of 1936 they made their investigations, and, after styling the mandate "unworkable," they recommended a partition of Palestine into an Arab state and a Jewish state, with a British Mandate over a corridor beginning at Jaffa and widening to include Jerusalem and Bethlehem with their holy places.

The British Government issued a White Paper in which it expressed agreement with the partition plan, but both the Arab Higher Committee and the Zionists staunchly opposed the plan. On January 4, 1938, however, the British Government issued another White Paper which announced the appointment of the Partition Commission whose task was "to recommend boundaries for the proposed Arab and Jewish areas under British mandate . . . . " On arriving in Palestine this Commission soon became so discouraged with its efforts that it concluded that any plan for partitioning Palestine was impractical.[2]

In the same year the British Government proposed a round-table conference between the representatives of the Palestinian Jewry and the Arab leaders of Palestine and the neighboring Arab states. But when both Jews and Arabs objected, the Government was obliged to conduct separate negotiations with the two groups in February and March of 1939. Seeing the weakness of the British Government in the Near East, the Arab leaders virtually demanded "the immediate stoppage of Jewish immigration into Palestine and the formal repudiation of the Balfour Declaration."

In the wake of three years of serious and sustained Arab pressure and demonstrations against Jewish immigration, and under the influence of the recent demands, the British decided that as an empire they could not well afford to bring down on themselves the wrath of the entire Moslem world of 350 million souls. Therefore, on May 17, 1939, Great Britain issued a White Paper stating that within ten years Palestine was to become an independent state under British Military protection. It proposed a maximum of 75,000 Jews to be admitted at an annual rate of ten thousand over the five-year period from 1939 to 1944, with an additional twenty-five thousand Jewish refugees from Germany to be admitted as the High Commissioner considered best. After that time, Jewish immigration was to be permitted only by the consent of the Arab majority and British approval.[3]

Sensing that this official document carried the note of finality, and feeling that they could expect little or nothing more from the Mandatory, the Jews formed themselves into more closely-knit secret organizations whose purpose was to aid Jewish immigration, protect the Jews from Arab aggression, and encourage the British to administer the Mandate more equitably, or else force them to give up the Mandate and get out of Palestine altogether.

These secret organizations, known to the outside world as "The Jewish Underground," were well-organized military groups, each separate from the other. They were the Haganah, the Irgun, and the Stern groups.[4]

The first of these, the *Haganah,* had already been organized as the militant arm of the Jewish Agency. It had been the Jewish people's army, organized with the express purpose of defense against Arab raiders or any other force hostile to the general or specific interests of the Jewish people. Its plan had ever been to act under orders from the Jewish Agency, but always for the defense of the Holy Land.

Its aim of defending the Holy Land captured the imagination of thousands of Jewish youth, who panted for the kind of action which carried with it the atmosphere of adventure and romance. Girls as well as boys — some in their teens, others in their early twenties — rallied to the common cause for the safety of their people. Yet the leadership of the Haganah was sufficiently well advanced in years to make it dependable and trustworthy.

Although there were only slightly more than 60,000 trained members of the Haganah, their general support was so consistent and steady that it was generally felt that Palestinian Jewry would accept Haganah orders in almost any emergency. The British Government was sufficiently sympathetic toward the aims of the Haganah to allow, and even to issue arms for use in protecting the Jewish people from unwarranted raids.

The Haganah had exercised unusual restraint during the 1935 strikes and riots, because of the non-retaliation policy set up by the Jewish Agency. The British lauded them for their fortitude and for the splendid discipline which they had exercised. But within the ranks of the Haganah was the belligerent Vladimir Jabotinsky, former leader of the nationalist Revisionist Party, with a following of some five thousand. Bent on revenge, Jabotinsky and his followers broke away from the Haganah and formed a new group which they called the *Irgun.* Organizing a campaign of counter-terror against the Arabs, they hid land mines in the Arab meeting places, and carried out the bloody policy of "an eye for an eye," one which resulted in scores of Arab deaths. The British prosecuted certain individual members of the Irgun as murderers, whereupon the Irgun proposed to make life so miserable for the British that they would have to leave the country.

However, following the outbreak of the war in 1939, the Irgun, like the Haganah, joined forces with the British against Germany. Their announced intention was to "fight the war as if there were no White Paper, and the White Paper as if there were no war." With that move, however, a third group made its appearance. From the ranks of the Irgun stepped Abraham Stern and three or four hundred followers who refused to ally themselves with the British on the grounds that they were the arch-enemies to the cause of Jewish national independence. Calling themselves "Israel's Freedom Fighters," this "Stern Gang," as they came to be called, pledged their lives to murder, arson, and destruction of the British and their facilities. British censorship prevented the publication of most of the Stern's activities, but their measures of sabotage were highly successful and at times almost crippled British defense. Stern himself was soon killed by the British police when he was trapped unarmed in his hideout, but his followers continued against the Government.

The experience and background of the Haganah and the Irgun made these Jewish youths valuable underground fighters for the Allies in their struggle to destroy Nazism. Many of the young Jewish fighters trained as commandos by British military experts raided installations in North Africa and Syria. Other young people, girls as well as boys, were actually parachuted into Nazi-occupied Europe where they caused uprisings and engaged in sabotage against the Germans. Meanwhile, choice young Haganah fighters were formed into the *Palmah* or Hebrew commandos. The British carefully trained them for partisan work in Palestine lest Rommel's forces should rush in from North Africa. The close co-operation between the British and the two illegal formations made possible effective warfare against the Nazis.

However, by late 1943, government and underground relations became rather tense. The danger of enemy occupation had passed and the date was approaching when, according to the White Paper of 1939, Jewish immigration would cease completely. News of the wartime Nazi persecution of Jews in Germany had filtered through into Palestine and had caused the Jews to redouble their efforts to bring their fellow Jews to Palestine where they could rebuild their shattered lives. Although the Jewish Agency had the legal power to combat British restrictions, the Haganah engaged in faster and more effective action. Members of the Haganah, a number of whom operated in Europe as British commandos during the war, supervised European emigrant embarkation upon ships bound for Palestine. Then, going still further, armed formations guarded the Palestinian beaches during the unauthorized landing to prevent interference from the government. In such operations as these the Haganah had the solid support of Jewish public opinion in Palestine. But on learning of these successes, the British effectively closed the doors of Palestine and brought anguish, distress, and suffering to thousands of would-be immigrants by turning back shipload after shipload from the very shores to which they most fervently desired to disembark. These they interned in concentration camps on the island of Cyprus and less desirable places. Three Jewish refugee ships were sunk at sea, and another was turned back to Germany. All of this irked the Jews and worsened their relationship with the British.

Fearing action from the underground, the High Commissioner sent the British police to disarm the Haganah. A searching party was sent to the agricultural colony of *Ramat Hakovest,* on the Plain of Sharon, where they expected to find stores of military arms and munitions. In order to gain entrance they told the settlers that they sought Polish deserters, but when they began to tear down walls and dig in the fields, the farmers realized the true motive and attacked the police with fists, stones, and furniture. In striking back, the British killed one Jew and left him as a fuse for a still greater outrage throughout Palestine and Great Britain.

After Sir Harold MacMichael was recalled, a milder position was taken toward the Haganah by the new high commissioner, Lord Gort. And Alan Cunningham, who replaced Gort, also seemed kindly disposed toward the Haganah. However, Sir John Shaw and Mr. Robert Scott, second and third in command, influenced Cunningham to undertake searches for the Haganah arms. In the spring of 1946 they issued a warrant for the arrest of Dr. Moste Sneh, who was alleged to be the head of the Haganah. These efforts proved to be useless, however, for the seaches failed to disarm the Haganah and Dr. Sneh slipped out of the country. At a later date the government made an attempt to legalize the Haganah, but that effort, too, was futile, for the Jews were well aware of the fact that such an arrangement would entail the centralization of their arms in government-controlled armories.

Relationships between the Haganah, the Irgun, and the Sternists varied from time to time. Members of the Haganah generally subordinated themselves to the government and regarded the two dissident groups with displeasure. Once, when Winston Churchill made pledges to the effect that Jewish aspirations would be satisfied after the war, the Haganah actually co-operated with the Palestine Police to restrain activities of the extremists. But when Foreign Minister Bevin stated that he could not allow some 100,000 more Jews to enter Palestine, their attitude began to change. Momentarily the Haganah swung to the extremist position, but later realized the shame of its destructive activities and turned to prevent further trouble from the Irgun.

The terrible demolition of one corner of the King David Hotel in August of 1947 was said to have been an act of vengeance by the Irgun as a counter-action against provocation given by the Haganah, as well as a thrust at British military officialdom. On one occasion the Haganah learned of the Irgun's plan to blow up Citrus House, Great Britain's civil and military headquarters at Tel-Aviv, and sent scouts who discovered a 45-foot tunnel that the Irguns had dug under the streets to the building. Immediately fourteen men were assigned to cement up the entrance, but as they worked, a booby-trap exploded and one young man was killed. The British were not notified of that sacrifice until some time after it had passed. Many such plots were foiled by the Haganah, and many British lives and much valuable property were saved by Haganah action, but the British never learned of them until after the dissidents had escaped. Therefore, the British never seized any Jew who had been denounced by his fellow Jews. For a time there was considerable talk of civil war between the Haganah and the extremists, but neither side really wanted war and no such serious threat materialized.

Refusing to submit themselves even to Jewish leaders the five or six thousand members of the Irgun Azai Leumi continued to harass the British government with sabotage activities. They seemed firmly convinced that the only way in which Palestine would ever belong to the Jewish people was for them to take it by force. As targets for their subversive activities they chose symbols of British authority in Palestine. Police headquarters, income tax offices, immigration department offices, railway stations, and other property of the Palestine government were mined. Even though notices were usually given for the evacuation of each building before an explosion, almost inestimable losses were suffered every year. The big blaze of arson could usually be extinguished, but the same old fires smouldered underground.

The still more extreme group of Sternists hated the British as much as they despised the so-called "war-mongers" of Europe. To them, every Britain in Palestine, by his mere presence in the country, constituted a threat to Jewish aspirations. Therefore their activities frequently took the form of assassination. The extremists admitted that they were a minority, but they would not be discouraged. Every revolutionary movement was started by a minority, they claimed, and they were determined to make some changes which they felt should be made.

Affairs grew worse towards the close of 1946 and in the beginning of 1947 as the tempo of terrorism was stepped up by both Jews and Arabs. Underground warfare became the vogue as the Arabs fought both the

Jews and the government in an effort to stop Jewish immigration; the Jews retaliated in kind for all damage done them by the Arabs, and at the same time devoted vast energies, money, and manpower toward blasting the British out of Palestine. Life and property became cheap and were sacrificed in a profligate manner as boycotts, bombing, burning, and sniping became so widespread that death and destruction became the common perils of every day.

The British augmented their military forces and placed the entire country under martial law, measures which, however, met with little success, for the British fought against enemies which they could not see. Therefore with "studied caution" they withdrew behind barb-wire protective screens as they fought a losing battle. Many British parents back in England and Scotland came to wonder why the lives of their sons should be sacrificed for such a muddled issue. They not only wondered but sometimes sided with other forces in influencing world opinion.

Feeling that a thorough and exhaustive effort should be made to understand the Palestine problem and to arrive at a fair and equitable settlement impartial to both Jews and the Arabs, the United Nations appointed a Special Committee on Palestine on May 13, 1947. This Commission went directly to Palestine and made an exhaustive study of the situation. On August 31 they recommended an end to the British Mandate over Palestine, and a division of the country between the Arabs and Jews so that each of the contending parties would enjoy independence. Their recommendations, along with their well-mapped plans for the division, were adopted by the General Assembly of the United Nations on November 29, and their suggestions became the groundwork for the establishment of the Jewish State.[5]

The Jewish people accepted the decision of the United Nations and began at once to prepare the groundwork for their state in harmony with the directives given them by the United Nations Assembly. The Arabs not only objected to the partitioning of Palestine, but announced their intention of resisting it by all means possible. They demanded that the country be left intact, and that the Jewish immigration be brought to an end. To make effective their demands, the Arabs set fire to the Jewish commercial center of Jerusalem and began a program of violence, bloodshed, and destruction that not only taxed the ability of the British and Jewish authorities to keep order in Palestine, but also kindled the fuse of a war of aggression by Arab States against Israel. Some members of the United Nations Assembly came to feel that they had made a mistake in ordering the country partitioned. The British Government announced its intentions of terminating the Mandate.

## CHAPTER XXXVII

# A NATION BORN IN A DAY

FOR EARTHLY SPLENDOR and moral grandeur, history assigns the ancient Hebrew nation first place in the annals that record the significant achievements of nations. But the glory of that far-famed nation began to fade with Solomon's latter days, and passed entirely with the destruction of Jerusalem by Titus in 70 A.D.

Then, for almost nineteen centuries, the Romans, the Byzantines, the Persians, the Arabs, the Seljak Turks, the Crusaders, the Sarcens, the Mamelukes, the Mongols, the Ottoman Turks, and the British governed Palestine as an outlying province. At times the Jews were oppressed, at other times they were either tolerated or befriended, but there were always some Jews who remained in Palestine, and they ever held tenaciously to the faith that they would survive those who ruled them, triumph over tyranny, and some day again enjoy national unity.

Small success was achieved by other peoples who undertook the rule of Palestine. It was as if the country waited for its ancient sons and daughters to awaken and return, and certainly the Jewish people waited patiently and hopefully through the centuries for the day when, by the grace of God and the help of others, they would again enjoy the security of statehood and the glorious heritage of national life.

The reality of that age-old vision became heavy with possibility when, during the early days of the year 1948, the British reached the decision to yield up the Mandate and evacuate Palestine at a given date in the then not distant future. Later the date was revised, and, shortly after sunrise on May 14th, Great Britain's flag, the Union Jack, was hauled down from its staff over the Government House in Jerusalem. Sir Allen Gordan Cunningham, the British High Commissioner, drove to the airport in his bullet-proof Daimler, and flew to Haifa in an RAF plane, where he boarded the British light cruiser, *Euryalus,* which precisely at midnight (the deadline for Britain's mandate over Palestine), passed the three-mile limit of Palestine's territorial waters. Thus, after thirty years, the British rule in Palestine ended.

On the sunny afternoon of that very day, while the atmosphere of quiet satisfaction filled the flag-decked streets of Tel Aviv, a multitude gathered at a roped-off, guarded section of Rothschild Boulevard near the white, modern, two-story Art Museum. Within the exhibition hall of the Museum, at a long table, on a dais under a huge portrait of Theodor Herzl and a large Jewish flag, sat sixty-one-year-old David Ben-Gurion, with white bushy hair, wearing an expression of strength and confidence. Twelve colleagues occupied places about the table. Before them, in the main hall, sat the thirty-seven members of the People's Council and other political, social and religious leaders of the community. The two chief Rabbis of Tel Aviv, Rabbi I. M. Unterman of the Ashkenazi community, and Rabbi Jacob Moshe Toledano of the Sephardic community, were present, along with many representatives of the local and foreign press, some four hundred in all. Both inside and out, everyone waited with unabated interest.[1]

At exactly four o'clock Mr. David Ben-Gurion called the meeting to order. The assembly rose and sang the Jewish National Anthem, "Hatikvah," while in an adjoining room the Palestine Symphony Orchestra played. The music had hardly ceased when Ben-Gurion rose, and in firm, strong, and emphatic voice read in Hebrew the Declaration of Independence which had been previously prepared for the occasion. It spoke of "The Land of Israel" as the place where Israel was born, where it had obtained independence and achieved a culture of universal as well as of national significance," as the place where it had written the Bible and from which it had given it to the world. It spoke of exile and dispersion, of faithfulness in prayer, and of desire to return to the land of their fathers and attain statehood. It spoke of Herzl's vision of a Jewish State, of the First Zionist Congress, of the Balfour Declaration, of the heroic sacrifices of the Jewish people, the Mandate, and the resolution of the United Nations General Assembly calling upon the inhabitants of Palestine to take steps to establish an independent State. Accepting these, and the "self-evident right of the Jewish people to be a nation, as all other nations in its own sovereign State" it concluded:

> ACCORDINGLY WE, the members of the National Council representing the Jewish people in Palestine and the Zionist movement of the world, met together in solemn assembly today, the day of termination of the British Mandate for Palestine, by virtue of the natural and historic right of the Jewish people and of the Resolution of the General Assembly of the United Nations,
>
> HEREBY PROCLAIM the establishment of the Jewish State in Palestine, to be called *Israel.*[2]

The entire assemblage rose and applauded, and many among them wept. Mr. David Ben-Gurion concluded the Declaration of Independence. He then read the first official decree, which abolished the White Paper of 1939 and removed the legal barrier to unrestricted Jewish immigration and to the free purchase of land by the Jews anywhere in Palestine.[3] The Declaration of Independence was signed by the members of the National Council, which, by proclamation, immediately became the Provisional Government that should administer the affairs of the State of Israel, "with trust in Almighty God."[4] At 4:38 P.M., Ben-Gurion struck his gavel on the table and said, "I hereby declare this meeting adjourned. Our State has been established."

Near the close of the session there was a stir of excitement when a soldier in uniform pushed through the crowd and summoned Israel Galilli, secret commander of the Haganah, for conference on the near-by stairway. On returning, Galilli approached the table with a smile and handed a note to Ben-Gurion. When the session was over, it was learned that the news brought by the soldier was that Western Galilee was now in Jewish hands. This added to the jubilation. Old friends from many parts of the world greeted each other warmly. Many pushed forward to shake the hands of Ben-Gurion and other officials. Outside, crowds cheered. Cameras clicked as the heads of the new Jewish State took the salute of the Guard of Honor and entered their cars. The crowds had only begun to disperse when the news came that President Truman had recognized the Jewish State. Other nations followed his example shortly.

The allocation of portfolios was completed by May 30, when the thirteen Ministers divided among themselves the sixteen Ministries, as follows: Agriculture, Communications, Defense, Finance, Foreign Affairs, Health, Immigration, Interior, Justice, Labor and Building, Minorities, Police, Religion, Trade Industry and Supply, War Victims, and Welfare.

The re-establishment of a Jewish State in the land of Israel became a reality because "a single-minded and stout-hearted minority, willing to venture everything in the pursuit of an idea" had returned to Palestine and defended themselves while they labored to rebuild their beloved fatherland with their own hands.

There were many thousands of British troops in Palestine when London decided to give up the Mandate. They began going home on May 15, and in June the last five thousand withdrew from Haifa like an army leaving a battlefield on which it had been humiliatingly defeated. In the harbor were nine British ships, protected by an aircraft carrier, a cruiser, and four destroyers, with all their guns unlimbered for action. Spitfires patrolled the sky. Every half-hour during the night British depth charges were exploded in the harbor to discourage any saboteur who might try to attach limpet mines to the hulls of the British ships. As the troops moved from the top of Mount Carmel and through the city streets, the Royal Marine Commandoes protected their flanks and their rear while they entered the waiting ships. They used a pier nicknamed *Via Dolorosa,* so named because the British had often rounded up Jewish refugees who had been smuggled illegally into Palestine, and shipped them *via Dolorosa* to the Island of Cyprus in steel cages. When the British ships were fully loaded with the five thousand troops and with nearly fifty thousand tons of their equipment, the Commando commander made a final inspection of the port, handed the keys to the harbor installations over to Jewish officials, and took a small boat for the *H. M. S. Phoebe.*

As the last British ship left the quay, the Union Jack was lowered slowly from the staff on top of the Port Authority Building. The Prime Minister of the new Jewish State of Israel made a brief address to an all-Jewish crowd of soldiers, sailors, and civilians. Among other things he suggested that the Jews of Palestine had friends among the British and that the Jews would be willing to be friends with Britain on condition that she abandon the war she was waging on the Jewish State through Arab mercenaries.

The blue and white flag of Israel was raised on the public buildings of Haifa, on the few corvettes in the harbor which comprised the Israeli navy, and on the masts of forty-six small vessels of the once "illegal fleet" of boats which had brought so many loads of European refugees in defiance of the British Navy. That night the Jewish citizens celebrated their new freedom.

On May 17, 1948, three days after the birth of the nation, Dr. Chaim Weizmann, the famous Jewish scientist, received a message in Manhattan's Waldorf-Astoria in New York that the Provisional Government of Israel had elected him its first President. In due time he returned to Palestine, and on September 30, 1948, at Tel Aviv, he attended his first meeting of the Provisional Government of the State of Israel. In his initial address he said:

> I have come home to Israel many times. On four such occasions I have returned at significant moments in our history. I came in 1907, after the Hague Congress, after the fight for the synthesis between political and practical Zionism. I came in 1918, after we had achieved the Balfour Declaration. Despite all we have since experienced, that declaration marked our first political attainment. I came in 1944, at the close of the Second World War, which ended the dominance of our arch-enemy in Europe. With it ended a savage period which brought into relief the indispensability of the land of Israel to the very existence of the people of Israel. During that period the Land of Israel was transformed into a veritable state, a political fact acknowledged by world opinion to the extent that we were able, since then, to look forward to a decisive development in the history of our nation.

This time I come, with that development already a milestone on the historical record. I come after the political struggle at the United Nations forum, which led to the recognition of the justice of our claims. I come after the struggle on the field of battle; after the creation of our State; I come as a citizen of the State of Israel. These achievements we owe to the great work done in this land during the past thirty years, on foundations laid by the early pioneers who came to this country three generations ago paving the way for their successors.

This is a great and sacred moment for me. And I think it is a fitting moment to pay tribute to the memory of all who fell, that Zion might be rebuilt, and of all who fell fighting in its defense. Let us also pay tribute to the memory of the millions who were massacred in Europe, and who, in their death, sanctified the Holy Name.

The great honour that you have paid me brings with it a great responsibility on my part. I shall endeavour to the best of my capacity to carry out the great political principle I adopted as my guide many years ago: "With justice shall Zion be redeemed and with righteousness they who return unto her."

War has been forced upon us. We shall defend the State with all our resources. We are fighting for the existence of our nation. At this moment it is fitting that I stress yet once again that the Jewish people are a peace-loving people, and that we are all anxiously looking forward to the day when we can convert the sword into the ploughshare. I hope and pray that that day is not far off.

To David Ben-Gurion, the Prime Minister, who has stood at the helm during the darkest hour, to Eliezer Kaplan, the Minister of the Exchequer, to Yosef Sprinzak, the Chairman of the State Council, to Moshe Shertok, the Minister of Foreign Affairs — to all who, at this fateful hour are responsible for the future of the young State, I extend my sincere wishes that they may be strong and of good courage. May they be favoured with wisdom and understanding.

Whatever political experience I may have gathered during the course of my life, I place unreservedly at the service of the State.

We have no illusions that at the beginning our path will be smooth and clear. But this is not the first time that we shall show our ability to overcome obstacles. This time, moreover, we have reinforcements from all over the Diaspora, from among world Jewry, which takes pride in our gains and maintains close ties with our State.

The best guarantee of our success is the desire to carry out our obligations wholeheartedly and to the best of our ability. Only the best is good enough for the people and State of Israel. I congratulate you on the first steps you have taken. May they bring the State to greatness and to peace.[5]

The new State of Israel took a major step toward establishing itself on a permanent basis when on January 25, 1949, it held a public election in which all persons, without distinction of race, creed, color, or sex, who were within the boundaries occupied by the Israeli armed forces, were allowed to vote on whom they would of the 1,288 candidates who presented themselves, on twenty-one party lists, for a possible membership in the permanent assembly of one hundred twenty members.

The total number of votes cast was 440,095. When this number was divided by 120 it gave a unit number of 3,600, which meant that any political party was entitled to as many delegates in the assembly as the votes pooled by that party divided by 3,600.

When the votes were counted it was found (1) that David Ben-Gurion's right-wing labor party, known as "Mapai" had won forty-six seats in the assembly; (2) that "Mapain," a party of left-wing leanings, but thoroughly Zionist, had won nineteen seats in the assembly; (3) that the "United Religious Block," a cartel of four parties which emphasizes Jewish religious tradition, won sixteen seats; (4) and that the "Herut," a political party which was the outgrowth of a terrorist military organization, was fourth in the returns. Other minor parties were the General Zionists, three Arab parties, Oriental Jewish parties, and the Communist party, which polled 3.5 percent of the entire vote and won four seats.

On February 14, 1949 the members of the Constituent Assembly, the first parliament of Israel, met in Jerusalem. High above the ancient shrine of three faiths, a Zionist banner proclaimed: "Our feet shall stand within thy gates, O Jerusalem." It was a day of triumph in the city which, for centuries of their exile, had been the symbol of the Jews' lost homeland. The choice of Jerusalem, the ancient capital of the Jewish State, as well as of the date, were of symbolic significance. At the time of the Assembly, Jerusalem held the status of Israeli-occupied territory, administered by a military governor, Dr. Bernard Joseph, formerly the legal advisor of the Jewish Agency.

February 14 was also the day on which the Jewish festival of the Feast of the Trees, celebrating the first signs of spring, had fallen. During the more peaceful years the children would have hiked into the fields to plant new trees and to pick wild flowers.

The Arab-Israeli war was at a standstill, and sunshine bathed the Holy City, Israel's "Eternal Capital," when the delegates walked through the flag-bedecked Herzl Street, the city's main thoroughfare, toward the Jewish Agency Building. The high spot of the day was the stirring address by Dr. Chaim Weizmann who, weeping as he faced them, opened the Israeli Constituent Assembly with these words:

> It is with a feeling of deep reverence and consecration that I rise to open the Constituent Assembly of the State of Israel — the first Knesseth Israel (Assembly of Israel) of our time, in this, our eternal city of Jerusalem.
>
> This is a great moment in our history. Let us give thanks and praise to the God of Israel, who, in His mercy, granted us the privilege of witnessing the redemption of our people after centuries of affliction and suffering . . . . It is our people who once gave the world the spiritual

message fundamental to civilization. The world is watching us now to see the way we choose in ordering our lives, how we fashion our State. The world is listening to hear whether a new message will go forth from Zion, and what that message will be.

A new message is not born without some sore travail of the creative spirit. The creative force of our nation will soon meet a new and serious challenge. The constitution which this Assembly has been called upon to frame will be the supreme test . . . .

Today is a great day in our lives. Let us not be thought too arrogant if we say that it is also a great day in the history of the world. In this hour a message of hope and good cheer issues from this place, from this sacred city to all oppressed people and to all who are struggling for freedom and equality — From this place we send fraternal blessing to our brethren throughout the world. We stretch out our hand in peace to the neighboring countries and extend friendship to all peace-loving peoples of the world . . . .[6]

Having opened the Assembly with such a memorable address, Dr. Weizmann remained for a time, then returned to his home at Rehovot.

Three days later,the Knesseth elected Chaim Weizmann, then seventy-four, Israel's first President (his office so far had been provisional). Twelve members of the Israeli Parliament, representing the twelve tribes of Israel, formed a delegation and met Dr. Weizmann at his home in Rehovot to escort him into Jerusalem. He was given a ten-inch silver key to the city and a pair of seventeenth-century scissors to cut the ceremonial ribbon across the road to Jerusalem. For Dr. Weizmann, who had traveled much and made many human contacts, and for his Zionists, it had been a long road.

The delegation escorted him to the Zionist Executive Building where an honor guard of officers of the armed forces led him to the rostrum of the Assembly, as the delegates and the diplomatic corps rose in silent tribute to the scientist-statesman who had devoted a lifetime to the cause of his people. The Shofar (ram's horn) was sounded, and the flag of Israel was raised over the building. Solemnly raising his right hand, the man who was to head the first Jewish state in two thousand years, said,

I, Chaim Ben Ozer Weizmann, as President of the State, pledge allegiance to the State of Israel and to its laws.

I thank you for the great honor bestowed upon me by my election as first President of the State of Israel. With all my soul and with everything within me I shall strive to fulfill the sublime mission for the benefit of our people, and to raise the prestige of our State. The duty bestowed upon me is a great one.

At this great moment in my life, in all our lives, I extend heartfelt greetings to all citizens of Israel and to the Jewish people the world over. I am aware that whatever is done or not done in this country will cast its light or shadow upon our whole people. I assume my duties as the President of Israel with full knowledge of the responsibility that devolves upon me.[7]

At the close of the ceremony the speaker of the house exclaimed "Yehi Hanassi" (Long live the President). For the first time in two millennia, the traditional benediction for a Jewish head of state was pronounced. A white-bearded rabbi declared: "Blessed be our Father in heaven who has shared His glory with His faithful." The audience cheered, wept, and broke into singing "Hatikvah," the Jewish national anthem of hope.

President Weizmann called on David Ben-Gurion to form a cabinet in order to replace the provisional State Council which had been created when the new State was formed on May 14, 1948. This important task was accomplished, and the new Cabinet was formed on March 3, 1949, consisting of seven representatives of Mapai, three representatives of the Religious Bloc, two from the Oriental Jewish parties, and one from the Progressive Party. With the Mapai coalition and four minor parties in the newly formed cabinet, the new state bore the impress of Mapai's secular, social-democratic, and on the whole, pro-Western program.

In establishing the State of Israel, the Jews had, for a second time, accomplished a task which in itself was unique and without a parallel. For at no other time in world history, so far as is known, had a people other than the Jews, been destroyed and then come back after a lapse of time to re-establish themselves.[8]

The drama of rebirth, accomplished in such swift and spectacular style, gave affirmative answer to the age-old prophetic question, "Shall the earth be made to bring forth in a day, or shall a nation be born at once?"[9]

## Chapter XXXVIII

# WAR BETWEEN ISRAEL AND THE SONS OF ISHMAEL

The Arabs had made up a majority of the population of the Fertile Crescent for nearly thirteen centuries, and had long regarded it as a very important part of the Arab world. Palestine was not only a part of this area, but contained Jerusalem, which to them was "the Holy City," second only to Mecca and Medina. To face the prospect of any part of Palestine being taken from them was a just cause for "Jihad," or holy war. Therefore, when the top leaders of the Arab world saw the determination of the United Nations Assembly and the Jews to partition Palestine, they called a special meeting in Cairo for the early spring of 1948.

They denounced the Partition Plan and talked of war in open defiance of the authority of the United Nations. After long deliberation, they decided to invade Palestine with the termination of the British mandate. However, there was among the Arab chieftains a lack of cohesion and unity. They deeply desired to defeat Zionism and the Jews and to make all Palestine Arabic, but there was so much mutual distrust that they could not agree on a unified command nor even on a single headquarters from which to direct the invasion. They left Cairo, consequently, with the understanding that each would rally his own army to attack Palestine and the Jews as might seem best to him.[1]

While Arab war preparations went forward in surrounding states, the Arab irregulars in Palestine engaged the Jews in sporadic conflicts as the British progressed with their plans to yield the mandate and evacuate the Holy Land by May 15. Some rather desperate and decisive fighting took place in such cities as Mishmar Haemek, Haifa, Jaffa, Safed, and Jerusalem. In most of these places the tide of conflict turned in favor of the Jews. During the last day of the mandate, the Arab irregular forces, aided by armored cars and volunteers from Transjordan, attacked and overran four Jewish settlements near Hebron known as the Etzion Bloc. More than six hundred Jewish soldiers and settlers were killed or captured, and the central mountain region from Bethlehem to Hebron fell to the Arabs.

Then, on the morning of May 15, when the British had departed and the infant Jewish state of Israel was but one day old, the hills and valleys of Palestine echoed the war chants of Arab soldiers from seven Arab states. With colorful *kaffiyehs* draped around their heads, belts of ammunition around their waists, and rifles in their hands, they crossed the boundary lines and opened their offensive against Israel from the north, the east, and the south.

The initial coalition of forces invading Israel numbered between 30,000 and 40,000 and behind these were such reserves as might be drawn from a population of some forty million who made up the participating Arab states. The Lebanese invasion army moved into central Galilee, the Syrians north and south of the Sea of Galilee, the Iraquis took up positions in the central hills of Judea, while the British-trained Arab legion from Transjordan, aided by a small contingent of troops from Saudi Arabia, ascended the Judean hills by way of the Jericho road, and sent one column north to Ramallah and thence on to Latron.[2]

The main army drove for ancient Jerusalem, where there stood in the Temple area the highly venerated "Dome of the Rock" and the sacred Mosque of *El Akse.* The Temple area, along with the Arab and Christian quarters, was soon taken, and the ancient Jewish quarters besieged and fired on from three directions. The Jews fought for their lives and their sacred synagogues, but within less than two weeks they were shelled into submission, and the survivors taken into captivity. The New City of Jerusalem, with its beauty of architecture and landscape and its 100,000 Jews was entirely surrounded and placed under siege, but spared actually being taken at the first onslaughts only by sham defenses, bold defiance, and frantically brave fighting by a few hundred Haganah soldiers and thousands of elderly men and young Jewish patriots. Nevertheless, the city was siege-ringed and threatened with submission by thirst and starvation.

The Egyptian army crossed the Sinai desert and took over Beersheba, Hebron, Gaza, Mijdal, Faluja and Ashdod, which placed it within twenty miles of the new Jewish capital of Tel Aviv. Lydda and Ramle were held by local Arab forces.

With 100,000 Jews under siege in New Jerusalem, the Arabs in control of the central mountain region from Jenin to Beersheba, Galilee invaded by two armies, and the Israeli capital with its nearby colonies threatened by enemy armies, affairs looked dark indeed for the Jews. The crisis grew even more grave as the siege-ring was tightened about New Jerusalem, and its inhabitants marooned without an avenue to obtain food, water, and adequate munitions of war with which to defend themselves. If the historic city was lost, the disaster would obviously appear an ill omen for the Jews. Its fall would echo and re-echo around the world.

But Israel was not inactive, as it might seem to the uninformed observer. The people were readying themselves for the struggle that would decide the fate or fortune of their cause. Imbued with a consciousness that their homes, their families, their lives, and the very nation they themselves had fashioned was at stake, and borne on by a full tide of determination and enthusiasm, they linked themselves with the victorious armies of biblical days as they courageously prepared to defend their own cause with a deep sense of divine destiny from which there could be no retreat.

Four exceedingly important goals lay before Jewish military leaders: first, to defend to the utmost every Jewish settlement in the path of the invading armies; second, to create a navy to lift the blockade and bring in men, munitions, and immigrants by way of the sea; third, to lift the siege of Jerusalem; and, fourth, to take the offensive and save Israel.

## Defense of Settlements

The stubborn stand made by the Jewish defenders of every settlement was far more than static defense. It not only checked the enemy's initial onslaughts, but was the means of converting every settler into a soldier, and many colonies into a network of trenches and subterranean fortresses which for the time became strongholds of defense and later, in combination with the newly-raised field armies, as springboards for counter-attacks. The advance of the Syrian troops in the Jordan Valley, for example, was halted at the boundary line of the Degonia A and B settlements, when these troops were repulsed and their tanks destroyed in close fighting by small arms and homemade hand grenades and explosives. This operation was soon followed by daringly conceived raiding operations undertaken by Jewish forces on the enemy's flank and rear. The Syrians were routed and came no more into the valley immediately south of the Sea of Galilee. Similar exploits were repeated at other settlements.

## Israel's Navy

On the first full day of Israel's independence, a large crew of engineers, carpenters, fitters, and painters walked briskly into Haifa harbor and along an out-of-the-way quay, where they located five dismantled Hagana ships ("Hagana," "Wedgewood," "Medinat Hayehudim," "Hatikva," and "Hanna Seneh"), which had been intercepted by British patrols, brought to Haifa, and confiscated. Swarming aboard, these faithful men worked night and day until in June all five of these former "illegal" refugee ships were on duty. A fishing trawler sent up from Africa, an ex-icebreaker, the *Elath* and these five ships formed the nucleus of Israel's navy, but they were manned by men who had manned the "illegal" refugee ships, and men who had served in the merchant navies of the Allies during World War II. The rest were fishermen and yachtsmen.

One of the first jobs of this youngest of the world's navies was performed on May 27, 1948, when four Egyptian ships appeared off the coast of Tel Aviv. The only Israeli ship ready to attack them was the *Elath,* equipped with two actual twenty-millimeter guns and two dummy six-inch guns designed in cardboard to deceive the enemy. One writer describes the ensuing action as follows:

> The Egyptians, who had not expected Israel to have any navy, were taken by surprise when their decks were raked by shells from the 20mm. guns, while through their binoculars they could make out what they took to be two 6-inch guns swinging in their direction. They began to retract with all guns firing and the *Elath* in hot pursuit."[3]

When Israel's tiny navy was complete, it patrolled Palestine's coast line, broke the blockade, and functioned as a protective force for the unarmed immigration ships which poured into Israel from May 15 onward. It bombarded the harbors of Tyre and Gaza, prevented the Egyptian-held Gaza strip from receiving supplies from Alexandria, and attacked and blew up enemy coastal installations, railways, and trains. Moreover, in a naval engagement on the 21st of October, it sank the *King Farouk,* flagship of the Egyptian navy.

## Efforts to Lift the Siege

Every available soldier was pressed into service, and thousands were hustled off the immigrant boats at Haifa harbor, hurriedly armed and trained, then packed into buses and sent to lift the siege of Jerusalem. Many died at Latron or elsewhere on the way, but they all fought so courageously and with such frantic zeal that large numbers of Arab soldiers who formed the ring around new Jerusalem were drawn away to fight the Jews who frantically charged towards Jerusalem to aid their besieged compatriots.[4]

A Haganah brigade, composed of members of various formations from all over the country, crossed miles and miles of hills and defiles, and three times broke through the siege-ring to escort huge supply convoys to Jerusalem.

Meanwhile under constant fire from the enemy, the Israeli command sent its crack Palmlch shock troops to battle the Arab legion at *Bab el Wad,* and Latron, while Jewish engineers and infantrymen, aided by thousands of civilians, old and young, secretly carved the "Burma Road," a narrow one-track route many miles long, running across the limestone hills of Judea, a road which by-passed Latron two miles to the south and linked the Tel-Aviv front to Jerusalem. Over it went caravans of pack-bearing donkeys, herds of cattle, and ant-like armies of Jewish civilians who trudged on with loads of flour and ammunition. Then soon there came hundreds of heavily-laden jeeps and trucks bearing signs "If I forget thee, O Jerusalem!" loaded with food, fuel, ammunition and other essentials to stave off starvation, thirst, and annihilation during the months of siege and bombardment of the Holy City.

### The Counter-Offensive

The first moves resembling an offensive taken by Israel against the Arab armies were commando raids — sudden night attacks, infiltration tactics, and sabotage action by small detachments striking at enemy key points. These were tiny attacks, but important.

Moves more akin to a counter-offensive, however, were taken in eastern Galilee when the Jewish forces captured Safed, Tiberias, and Samakh, and broadened the Jewish holdings in the Jordan Valley both north and south of the Sea of Galilee. In other sections Israeli fighting forces were mounting sufficient strength for what promised to be an offensive, when on June 11, 1948, with the war less than one month old, the United Nations Security Council ordered a four-week truce in the war between the sons of Ishmael and the sons of Israel.

The four-week truce — June 11 to July 8 — was used to very great advantage by the Israeli armies. They not only completed their training and consolidated their positions, but enacted one of the most startling operations of the war. The terms of the truce banned the reception of all military supplies by either the Arab or Jewish armies, but the ban was not very effective, for both Arabs and Jews found ways to bring in supplies at certain ports not covered by United Nations observers. The Jews merely did the better job of it.

Supplied with millions of good American dollars raised by the United Jewish Appeal, the Israeli representatives went among the nations seeking one sufficiently sympathetic toward the Jews to sell them munitions and supplies. In need of cash, and having the nod of assent from the Kremlin, Czechoslovakia quietly opened its bulging munitions stores, and a secret airlift operated night by night across the Mediterranean, bringing, as Bilby reports, "a steady stream of pom-pom guns, Mauser rifles, crated airplane engines and tank parts, armoured cars, and half-trucks into the outstretched arms of the Israeli Army and Air Force. The military stores of the new state increased enormously and within a few nights a formidable air force for such a small state was created."[5]

When the Arabs renewed the battle at the end of the truce, the newly-armed Israeli army aimed a pincer movement at the nearby twin cities of Lydda and Ramle. With infantry and armor working in close partnership, and with the Air Force bombing and strafing ahead of the ground forces, the Jews not only encircled and overran these two large Arab cities but pursued the fleeing Arab army into the Judean heights, and overran a long string of hill villages east of Lydda and Ramle. Then, turning northward, they captured *Ras el Ein,* drove a wedge north of Latron, and entirely removed the threat to Tel Aviv and other important Jewish cities on the Sharon plain.

In Galilee, the Israeli armored columns, with their newly acquired equipment, in a two-day "blitz" campaign launched simultaneously from three directions, dealt such a stunning blow to the Arab forces that the whole northern front collapsed, and the Jews not only took control of almost all Galilee but carried their offensive across the Lebanese border.[6] Then, on July 18, came the second cease-fire deadline ordered by the Security Council at Lake Success.

## The Second Truce

Stunned and demoralized by the heavy losses on two battle-fronts, the Arabs readily accepted the truce. At least it gave respite from the swift-moving, hard-hitting war machine so effectively wielded against them. The Jews, on the other hand, were so elated over their recent victories and so pleased with themselves and their military organizations that they reeled with the wine of war. They were now very sure that on the battle-field they could sweep everything before them. Impatiently they waited to know what would be done, but most of all they wanted to fight again.

Count Folke Bernadotte, Mediator for the United Nations, came forth with a proposal that peace and final settlement be reached on the basis that all the Negeb be awarded to the Arabs in exchange for all Western Galilee for the Jews, and that the Arab and Jewish States form an economic union in accordance with the original Mandate as including Trans-Jordan. Immigration within its own boundaries would be "within the competence of each member," provided that "following a period of two years from the establishment of the Union, either member would be entitled to request the Council of the Union to review the immigration policy of the other member and to render a ruling thereon," this ruling to be binding on the member whose policy was at issue.[7] The plan apparently appealed to many interested powerful personalities, and some think it possible that even the Arabs might have accepted some such plan rather than take further risks in war. But Israel was in no mood to cede Western Galilee, which it had taken by dint of such strenuous battles. Nor was Israel interested in foregoing the possibility of gaining the Negeb for Jewish settlement and development. Nor, again, was she content to permit others to control her immigration policy. The Israeli press, therefore, actively encouraged by government officials, carried on an "intense and caustic" campaign against the peace proposals. Then, on September 17, 1948, when the Bernadotte Plan was gaining favor, the Swedish nobleman was assassinated in Jerusalem by two members of the Stern gang.[8]

The murder was brutal — a dastardly deed which instantly and rightfully elicited the indignation of the civilized world. Ben-Gurion, Israel's Prime Minister, ordered the arrest of all members of the Stern gang, offered $20,000 reward for the murderers, and put a law through Parliament making membership in a terrorist band a criminal offense. But the murderers were never apprehended, nor did the Bernadotte Plan gain either Arab or Assembly approval.[9]

## The Last Round

During the month of October frequent clashes occurred between the Israeli and Egyptian forces in the south. Seeing these offered an opportunity to settle the Negeb question once and for all, the Israeli military command secretly moved the best of its troops, artillery, and armored cars southward in a skillfully planned military preparation. Meanwhile, Dr. Walter Eytan of the Israeli Foreign Ministry wrote the truce commission that, in accordance with the terms of the truce, Israel intended to send a motor convoy through with food supplies for its isolated settlements in the Negeb.

On October 15, while moving southward, a sixteen-truck convoy was fired on by the Egyptian forces. Two trucks were destroyed, the convoy withdrew, and the Israeli government then not only announced its freedom to act as a result of the Egyptian truce defiance, but proposed to renew war immediately.[10] That night Israel unleashed its military machine in a well-coordinated blow at the Egyptian forces occupying the Philistine Plain, the Shephela, and the Negeb of Southern Palestine. In the vanguard of the fight, the Air Force sent out wave after wave of B-17 bombers, British Beau Fighters and Spitfires, and German Messerschmitt fighters. The armored columns and the infantry attacked in an extremely daring pattern of frontal and flanking movements. Even Israel's small Navy hurried along the coast and bombed enemy installations. The Air Force was especially effective in support of ground forces — attacking troop concentrations, airfields and lines of communication, blowing up railways and transport convoys on the roads, and destroying ammunition dumps. It tied down the enemy and developed the offensive on a broad front. At El Arish it struck with such persistent and repeated bombings that Egyptian planes on the ground were destroyed and installations and runways damaged until the air field was virtually put out of use. The repeated bombings of Gaza, Rafa, Faluja and other targets demoralized the enemy, and prepared the way for the Israeli army to go forward.[11]

After three days of widespread air, land, and sea fighting, the Jews had smashed the Egyptians' east-west line of entrenchments and opened up a wide land corridor to their settlements in the Negeb. After a full week of fighting, the Israeli forces succeeded in destroying the Egyptian coastal positions at Ashdod, Majdal, and Beit Hanun, and in unbalancing the whole defensive structure of the Egyptian army. The crowning blow came on October 21, when the Israeli Navy sank the *King Farouk,* the flagship of the Egyptian Navy, and a Jewish mechanized column, with the aid of bombers, fought its way into ancient Beersheba, the communications hub of the Negeb.[12] Israel columns advanced southward in a whirlwind campaign through the Negeb to the ancient sea-port of Elath, and at one stage by a turning movement the offensive was carried across the Egyptian frontier toward El Arish. When all fighting was brought to a halt by a final cease-fire order from the Security Council of the United Nations, the main body of the Egyptian forces was bottled up in the Gaza-Rafa coastal strip, and the Israeli forces held the larger portion of Palestine from Dan to Elath. Israel had not only cleared its own territory of invading forces, but also occupied a part of the territory alloted to the Arabs in the Partition Plan.

By this time the Arabs had become somewhat disillusioned as to their strength and ability to defeat the Jews and wipe the Zionist National Home off the map. In the initial stages of the conflict they possessed a semblance of unity and had prosecuted a colorful and apparently effective campaign, but when, with close unity, bold strategy, and superior skill, the Jews had inaugurated a war of swift movement, it had been too much for the Arabs with their lack of a unified military command. They did not like to quit with the scales of military conquest balancing so heavily in favor of the Jews, but for the moment they were at least half willing to listen while the United Nations representatives made suggestions.

The first move to end the Jewish-Arab conflict was made by the Egyptian Government, when on January 6, 1949, it notified Dr. Ralph J. Bunche, U. N. Acting Mediator, that it was ready to discuss an armistice with Israel. Later in the month the Israel and Egyptian leaders, under the chairmanship of Dr. Bunche, met for peace talks.[13]

On February 24, after protracted negotiations, Dr. Walter Eytan for Israel and Colonel Seif ed Din for Egypt signed an armistice agreement whereby Israel received 700 additional square miles of the Negev area, and Egypt retained a coastal strip of about 135 square miles from its border to Gaza — afterwards known as "The Gaza Strip." This was a crucial event in the history of Palestine, but also marked a significant turn in the relations between Israel and the Arab States, for it marked the first definite Arab acceptance of the fact that Israel was an established state.[14]

Lebanon, Jordan, and Syria afterwards signed individual armistice pacts with Israel. But final peace terms have never been signed between Israel and its neighboring states. The principal bars to peace are the following: (1) Disunity within the Arab League; (2) the resettlement of the 700,000 to 800,000 Arab refugees who fled their homes because of the fear of war, or on the advice of Arab leaders who promised to restore them to their homes after victory, or who were frightened into leaving by Jewish atrocities and threats during the Jewish-Arab conflict; and (3) the bitter and perpetual anti-Jewish propaganda which forces an overwhelming majority of the peoples of Middle-Eastern countries to boycott the Jews of Israel and of the world. This spirit of hatred and revenge, perpetually fanned, constitutes a veritable build-up for the fateful, frightful, and culminating Battle of Armageddon.

## CHAPTER XXXIX

# ISRAEL'S RETURN ON "MAGIC CARPETS"

> Fear not: for I am with thee: I will bring thy seed from the east, and gather thee from the west; I will say to the north, give up, and to the south, Keep not back: bring my sons from far, and my daughters from the ends of the earth. . . .
>
> . . . thy sons shall come from far . . . All they from Sheba [Yemen] shall come . . . Who are these that fly as a cloud, and as the doves to their window? Surely the isles shall wait for me, and the ships of Tarshish first, to bring thy sons from far, their silver and their gold with them . . .[1]

ALONG WITH THIS Biblical prophecy of Israels return from the four corners of the globe are to be placed those significant words contained in Israel's Proclamation of Independence given forth to the world at Tel Aviv, Palestine, on May 14, 1948. This proclamation read:

> The State of Israel will be open to the immigration of Jews from all countries of their dispersion.[2]

Therefore, the first act of the Provisional Government of Israel, after proclaiming the indpendence of the State, was the repeal of the White Paper of 1939 of the British Mandatory Government, the document which severely restricted Jewish immigration and the acquisition of land in Palestine.

This proclamation, along with the first official act of the independent State of Israel, not only symbolized Israel's dedication to the primary task of "The Ingathering of Israel," but also brought tidal waves of immigration which converged on Israel from every part of the globe. It was no longer an immigration of individuals, or a movement of young pioneers coming ahead of their families, but it was obviously the return of a nation, a torrential inflow of whole communities and families embracing three or four generations, complete with their patriarchs and babes in arms. In a number of cases the entire surviving Jewish population of a country came to Israel, bringing with them all their institutions, synagogues, and the inmates of their hospitals and asylums.

The mass inflow into Israel began with the evacuation of the deportation camps in Cyprus, and later, of the Displaced Persons Camps in Europe. No less than 104,000 Jewish immigrants were allowed to leave for Israel from Poland, where the great Jewish population had been almost annihilated by the Nazis and Communists. Immigrants from Romania, numbering 96,000, were next in importance among East European arrivals. The first community to be transplanted to Israel almost in its entirety was the Jewry of Bulgaria, next came the survivors from Yugoslavia and Czechoslovakia. Almost all the Jews living in Tripolitania and Lybia, and many from Morocco, Tunis, and Algeria, also came to Palestine.

In 1949-50 one of the most colorful and significant events connected with the return of the Jews to Palestine was enacted in Yemen (ancient Sheba), when hope broke through the darkness of centuries and the entire Jewish settlement of 52,000 was transported to Palestine on "Magic Carpets."

These Jews had migrated to Yemen sometime after the exile of the "Ten Tribes" (722 B.C.) and after the fall of Solomon's temple in 586 B.C. In the first century of their stay in Yemen, they prospered exceedingly and came to live so contentedly that they ignored Ezra's call, in 458 B.C., to return to their fatherland in Palestine. Subsequent generations realized the error and acquired a deep desire to rectify the error which their fathers made in not going up to Palestine when Ezra went from Babylon with a community of the exiles and called them to come up from Yemen. The messianic hope, gained from a study of their Hebrew prophets, begot in them an assurance that the Day of Redemption and release would come just prior to the coming of the Messiah. Therefore, throughout the long night of their exile they kept alive the flame of their longing for the Promised Land, seizing on this hope to lighten their darkness. False Messiahs came and went, persecutions and oppressions were often bitter; yet, faithful to their religion, they brought up their boys to read the Torah in the traditional manner, wore beards and earlocks, sent their important dead to be buried in Palestine, and clung tenaciously to the belief that the day of their redemption and release would come when they would be miraculously returned to Palestine where they would help "rebuild the old wastes," make the "desert blossom as a rose," and await the imminent coming of the Messiah.[3]

Palestinian emissaries, continuously sent to all the countries of the Dispersion, reached Yemen from time to time and spread the news of the Jewish communities which existed in the land of Israel. A group migrated in the fifteenth century by way of Aden, and one of their number, *Saadya ben David Adoni,* settled in Safed and engaged in copying ancient manuscripts. In 1561 a Yemenite sage, Rabbi Joshua ben David Adoni, became author of a commentary on the Mishna, and one of the greatest sages of the land. In 1567 the Yemenite poet Zechariah el Dharhar arrived and wrote a book describing his journeys in the country, and especially his visit to the Safed rabbinical college of Rabbi Joseph Caro. During the eighteenth century Rabbi Shalom Mizrachi came from Yemen and headed the "Beth-El" Synagogue and school of Jerusalem. He was succeeded in this post by his son and later by his grandson.

Exaggerated reports reached Yemen of the land purchases by Baron Rothschild and of the activities of Lawrence Oliphant, a non-Jewish Zionist. Rumors had it that the Sultan had granted permission to all Jews of the world to proceed to inhabit the land of their fathers. Shaw and Capa describe the effect of these reports in these words:

> All the Jews of Yemen rejoiced exceedingly, and thought that the destined redemption had indeed come and that they would be redeemed in that very year, or in the following year. All the Jewish inhabitants of Yemen were stirred by a great enthusiasm to sell their property and to go and live in Jerusalem. It was as though a new spirit had entered the heart of every single Jew, the like of which had not been since the day of the Exile.[4]

Two aristocratic families set out for Jerusalem in the spring of 1881, and others, on receiving the news of their safe arrival, traveled on foot to the port of Hudaida, from there by sea to Alexander, on another ship to Jaffa, and from there they walked to Jerusalem. Within two years one thousand Yemenites reached the Holy Land, but the expedition fared badly. Much sickness, poverty, and privations attended their way, and they found no land awaiting them. When the news of these misfortunes reached the Jews of Yemen, their ardor was temporarily cooled. In time, however, the Yemenite Jews in Jerusalem built a small colony near Siloam on the slopes of the Mount of Olives, and not only organized themselves into a special community, which enabled them to preserve their own traditions and lead their own way of life, but also printed and sent special prayer books, and described their new life in letters to Yemen. This stimulated others to follow.

By 1902 there were 2500 Yemenites in Jerusalem and Jaffa. In 1907 large numbers came to live in the settlements and villages of Palestine, where they became excellent agricultural laborers. About 1500 Yemenites immigrated to Palestine and settled in the villages of Judea, Samaria, and Galilee during 1911 and 1912. Following World War I, the ruler of Yemen renewed oppressive and humiliating anti-Jewish laws, of which the most intolerable one was the edict issued in 1921, which ordered the compulsory conversion to Islam of every child orphaned by the death of its father. The Jews did all in their power to resist this harsh measure and to save their orphans by getting them out of the country, but their lot was made more difficult still when the

Imam ordered the confiscation of the property of any Jew who went to the land of Israel.

In 1929 immigration from Yemen was forbidden altogether, yet the Jews escaped secretly to the British-held port of Aden, and came into Palestine by the slow process of receiving immigration certificates from the Mandatory government. At the end of the Second World War, there were approximately 22,000 Yemenite Jews in Palestine; however, there were more than 50,000 in Yemen whose lot grew progressively worse. Yet they waited their release with unswerving faith in the coming of the Messiah.

When the news of the establishment of the Jewish State reached Yemen, the Jews felt certain that the time of redemption was approaching. When told of the victories of the Israeli armies, they exclaimed, "The pangs of the Messiah — there is war in Israel." Among themselves the people began to say, "Come, let us go up to the Land of Israel." Yet from their leaders came the word, "Wait, for the vision is yet for the appointed time." And they did wait, many of them with their possessions rolled up in sacks, waiting for the sign.[5]

Then, upon a day, there came an official letter from the Land of Israel saying:

> "Arise, brothers, and arouse yourselves. The proper hour has come. Our country awaits the sons and builders for its redemption and yours for raising its ruins and settling its waste places. Surmount the suffering and travail of the way, because without you Israel will not be redeemed. Delay not, nor lose the proper hour lest you be late. Dare to come up at once and do not leave behind you the ancient culture in writing and garb. . . ."[6]

At once they sold their homes and possessions for what little they could get out of them. Going to their synagogues, they performed memorial services for their dead, read their Bibles, prayed for forgiveness for their sins, took with them the Scrolls of the Law and other holy objects, and buried in the ground what sacred objects they could not take with them. They provided themselves with dried meat, cakes, butter, flour, spices and coffee, and set out on the way for Aden. The women gathered sticks along the way, and baked bread over a tin in the fields or wrapped the dough about stones and laid them in the fire.

All the roads leading toward Aden were so crowded with tumultuous companies of Jews that the authorities closed the borders and barred the way of thousands. Baffled but not defeated, they turned to the waysides, where they sat weeping and praying under the canopy of heaven. Their sacred days of Rosh Hashanah and Yom Kippur came, and they "prayed exceedingly much, broken-hearted, and weeping on the ground."

Their most frequent plea was "O Lord, when will we merit to enter Israel's gates?"

As they waited, their food supply dwindled away until there was no bread for the adults and not a drop of milk to keep the infants alive. They stood and raised their prayer to God on high. And while they were still praying, Arabs came and brought them food and milk, and said, "Give us money, and you will get bread."

One day messengers from Israel came and strengthened their hearts and cheered them with this message:

> "Do not worry. No man will remain in the Exile of Yemen, and the State of Israel will not forsake you. In a little while an end will come to your troubles. There is a Jewish heart in Israel. Let there be no hunger among you."[7]

The Jewish Agency's representatives brought food and supplies and obtained permanent passage through the Protectorate at a price of six dollars for each person. Thus the borders were thrown open, and the Sultans of the regions under British protection, which lay between Yemen and Aden, no longer forbade them to pass through their territory.

A sigh of relief was given, praises went up to God, and tens of thousands of the sons and daughters of Israel moved across the borders, crowded the roadways, and moved on toward their goal. Great companies came from every section of Yemen, and followed on with great enthusiasm for their fatherland. The urgency was so great that sickness and trembling of the body could not stop them. Women gave birth while riding donkeys, and after fulfilling the appropriate religious ceremonies, they moved on. Bilby narrates this episode in this passage:

> And thus we came to Aden as long as there was breath in our nostrils, bruised and robbed, weary and bereft of everything. After a way of travail, sometimes lasting two months, and sometimes three, there was not a penny with us nor any possessions. Also the rich among us came, most of them without money, in the same position as we, bereft of all.
>
> And they gathered us into the great camp which was near the city, and it was on the sands of the desert, and the place was too small for us all, and we lay in large numbers on the sand, under the bare sky, next to one another, each family together, and mighty sand-storms raged about us, and in our hearts we prayed for *aliyeh*, to fly "on eagles' wings" to our country.[8]

There was room in the transit camp at Aden for one thousand people, but the stream of immigrants coming into Aden grew each day until the flood reached a peak of thirteen thousand in one month alone. For the most part they possessed nothing but a single piece of clothing. Eighty percent had malaria. They came sick, weary and emanciated — the average weight of a male adult was eighty pounds — and many two- and three-year-olds weighed less than new-born infants. Yet they were expectant, for the Day of Redemption was being ushered in, and they were on their way home.

Streams of immigrants kept coming into Aden each day, and, according to the promise given to the British Administration in Aden, the Jews had to be transported to Israel as fast as possible. The sea passage was closed to the immigrants because the Egyptians, who controlled the Suez Canal, were at war with Israel. It was therefore necessary to send them by air. Six great Skymasters were hired, and these, each carrying 130 immigrants, flew regularly from Aden to Lydda. Thus the exodus from Yemen, known to the world as "Operation Magic Carpet," was in progress. By March of 1949 some 5000 had been transported to Israel from the Aden camp, in November of 1949, 28,000, and by March of 1950 the number reached 40,000. Within a few more weeks 52,000 had been flown to Israel and not a Jew was left in Yemen.

"And I bore you on eagles' wings and I brought you unto myself." There was never a truer expression of the marvel of Jewish history than the noble ritual that took place on the airfield at Aden, for as the Yemenite Jews went into the modern American planes and the pilot prepared to take off, the Shofar — ancient ceremonial horn of the Hebrew people — was solemnly blown, for the Skymaster was "Messiah's Magic Carpet," and the airfield at Aden was the threshold of Redemption.

## Air Lift from Iraq

Since the days of Nebuchadnezzar (586 B.C.), Jewish families and communities had lived in, and usually been an integral part of, the commercial, social, and political life of Iraq, or Mesopotamia. They had "seen conquerors come and go, watched plagues and pestilences devastate the inhabitants, lived through massacres and civil war," and yet they had overcome temporary setbacks, grown in power, wealth and culture, and manifested a constantly renewed vitality.

On assuming office at the close of the First World War, King Feisal II proclaimed:

> "There is no meaning to the words 'Jews, Moslems, and Christians' in the terminology of patriotism. There is simply a country called Iraq, and all are Iraqis. I ask my countrymen, the Iraqis, to be only Iraqis because we all belong to one stock, the stock of our ancestor Shem; we all belong to that noble race, and there is no distinction between Moslem, Christian, and Jew."[9]

And thus they lived and prospered in Iraq until during the late 1920s when so many Jews returned to Palestine as to apparently threaten Arab supremacy in the Fertile Crescent — particularly in Palestine.

Following the 1929 Arab uprisings in Palestine, there developed a systematic and widespread propaganda campaign throughout Near Eastern countries. Arab Nationalism grew rapidly, and the Palestine Problem became a major issue in Iraqi politics. For a time there was only slight discrimination against the Jews, but by July of 1937 the smouldering inner hostilities broke out when tens of thousands of Arabs marched the streets of Baghdad in violent anti-Jewish demonstrations. Jewish merchants sought safety in the privacy of their homes. In 1938 terrorist acts were committed, and then in June of 1941 there were bloody days, when one hundred and ten Jews were killed and two hundred and forty wounded, when eighty Jewish enterprises were looted and nine hundred and eleven Jewish homes were destroyed. Material damage was officially estimated at near three million dollars. Insecurity and fear of life characterized Jewish life in Iraq during the years which followed.[10]

The Jewish situation in Iraq was definitely worsened when, on May 15, 1948, Iraq, together with Egypt, Syria, Lebanon, and Transjordan went to war with the new State of Israel. Martial law was declared in Iraq, Jewish homes were searched, property was confiscated, and arrests, trial, imprisonments, and executions were carried out. Jews who were Zionists, or were even sympathetic toward what was going on in Israel, were sought out, tried, sentenced, fined, and in many cases lost both their lives and their property. Not only immigration but even visits to Palestine were strictly banned. On October 18, 1948, all Iraq Jews living outside the country were ordered to return by the end of the month. Failure to do so, they were told, would lead to confiscation of their property. Some who did not return were tried in absentia and lost much of their money and property through fines and confiscation.[11]

Seeing that liberty, prosperity, and even life itself hung so precariously in the balance, many thousands of Jews slipped across the eastern border into Iran (Persia), with Palestine as their ultimate destination. Smuggling operations soon became common and Iran swarmed with Jews on their way to Palestine.[12]

On March 4, 1950, the Iraqi Senate passed a bill which permitted Jews to leave Iraq if they wished to do so. The authorization required that all who cared to take advantage of this legal exit should do so within one year and stipulated further that they lose their Iraq nationality. There were then about 130,000 Jews in Iraq, and of these, one-half or more desired to emigrate to Palestine.

It being unlikely that Syria and Lebanon would allow the free passage of Jews through their territory, and the sea route being virtually closed, the trip by air seemed the only alternative. The situation imposed a heavy responsibility on the State of Israel and on all Zionist and Jewish organizations throughout the world. Yet the authorities made an appeal for extra funds, prepared housing accommodations, employed a fleet of air liners as they had done in the "magic carpet" operation from Yemen, and began the air lift. Realizing that they were working against time, the planes shuttled back and forth with a rapidity that was amazing. Month after month pilots flew these Skymasters night and day to save thousands of Jews from oppressive exile. Sixty million dollars was spent, and when the allotted time was up they had succeeded in bringing more than seventy thousand Jewish men, women, and children from Iraq to Israel where, with more than a million others, they felt they had come home not only to enjoy a pattern of culture which was their very own, but also to aid in rebuilding their fatherland. They joined that mighty host who are giving tangible shape to prophecy, awaiting the imminent coming of the Messiah, and entering into the great destiny of Israel, a phenomenon which has no precedent and no analogy in human history.

> Tribes of the wandering feet and weary breast,
> Now can ye homeward flee and be at rest;
> The wild dove hath her nest, the fox his den,
> Mankind their country, Israel — his land again!

## Chapter XL

# REBUILDING PALESTINE

The story of Jewish effort in rebuilding their Fatherland is one of courage, heroism, and extreme sacrifice. Their principal achievements are represented in the restoring of the Hebrew language, reclaiming waste lands, replanting forests, preparing for transportation and communication, receiving and absorbing Jewish immigrants, expanding agriculture, founding an industry, exploiting natural resources, building an educational system, promoting health, and planning for the religious welfare of the people of Palestine.

### Restoring the Hebrew Language

The one single unifying force which was absolutely necessary in repeopling and rebuilding Palestine was a common language which could be readily comprehended by all who returned to their fatherland. Yet, half a century ago a dozen million Jews scattered throughout the world conversed in almost every known language, except the Hebrew. That language was the language of prayer. To use it in everyday life was considered a sacrilege by Jewish authorities. And yet no other language would do for the Jews. Hebrew was to be introduced, even though it would take many years and be accomplished only at great cost.

The basic work involved in the rebuilding of the Hebrew language was a mighty miracle born of a noble ideal, wrought and realized by the enthusiasm, poverty, and persistence of a short, slight, yellow-complexioned young Russian Jew whose name was Eliezer Ben Yehouda, Son of Judea.

Born of poor parents, he left home at an early age and joined nineteen other young men who lived in a poor thatched-roofed building, begged their daily bread from house to house, and studied the Talmud under famous Rabbis. The Rabbis usually knew Hebrew, and in time they taught it to their students, but all commentaries on the Biblical text were in Yiddish. To use the sacred language of Hebrew, even for religious teaching, was considered very wrong. Yet Ben Yehouda became deeply interested in Hebrew, learned its grammar, reveled in its beauty, and finally came to use it for ordinary purposes.[1]

One day while preaching in a synagogue to a group of orthodox Jews who wore their greasy caftans, their fur caps, their beards, and their side curls, a Moscow merchant on business in the village entered the group, was carried away by Ben Yehouda's eloquence, and offered to take him into his own home and pay for his education.

In Moscow Ben Yehouda went for three or four years to the academy in preparation for entering the University. In the evenings, after dinner, he gave Hebrew lessons to Deborah, the eldest daughter of the merchant, who was about his own age.

One day in the spring of 1877 while Ben Yehouda was yet a young man in his late teens, a crisis arose in the merchant's home when he took a rigid stand in favor of all Jews standing by their fellowmen. All laughed at him, except Deborah. On reaching a decision to go away, he confided in Deborah. She gave him money, and when he crossed the threshold for the last time, she put her hand over his head, and said "Goodby, God bless you, Eliezer, I'll come to you whenever you call for me."

Set adrift as a wanderer, he went to Warsaw, Lemberg, Berlin, and within a year arrived at Paris. One night while yet on the way, sleeping in a barn and alone with his thoughts and his Maker, a vision of his life's work came to Eliezer. Discarding his gaberdine cloak, his fur cap, and his Yiddish language, he christened himself Ben Yehouda (son of Judea) and consecrated his life to restoring the ancient Hebrew language and reviving Palestine.

In Paris he found himself penniless, but was soon befriended by a Pole who became so fascinated with Ben Yehouda and his vision of a revived Palestine that he introduced him to Paris, and accompanied him to Algiers, Tunis, Carthage, and back to Southern Russia, where he met the novelist and journalist Perez Smolensky, whom Ben Yehouda kissed and told of his plans to go to Palestine and revive the life and language of the Jewish people. Smolensky suggested that he collaborate with him on the *Dawn,* and for a time, forget the hazardous work in Judea. But Ben Yehouda would not be disobedient to the vision of the mission to which his life was consecrated.

Soon Deborah joined him. They were married and took a boat down the Danube, bound for the City of Zion. On that romantic voyage, Ben Yehouda solemnly pledged Deborah that henceforth he would speak to her only in Hebrew. And although Deborah knew only the Hebrew he had taught her, yet from that time on, for the sake of the cause for which they lived, they always exchanged their thoughts in the Hebrew language which had been lost for centuries.

After a twenty-day voyage across the Black Sea, through the Bosporus and over the Mediterranean, they landed at Jaffa and traveled for twelve hours on donkeys until they beheld the city of Zion, about which they had so long dreamed.

On their arrival in Jerusalem they found about twenty thousand Jews, mostly older people who had come there to pray at the Wailing Wall, to study the Torah, and to be buried in the sacred burial grounds on the Mount of Olives. Almost all of these Jews had one thing in common: they were supported by *Halouka,* or gifts from Jewish people sent to support the pious who lived in Jerusalem and prayed at the Wall for the restoration of the temple and Judea to the Jews.

But there was so much that these Jews did not have in common that they dwelt separately in small ghettos according to the country from which they had come. Those from Germany, Hungary, Russia, Poland, Romania, Austria, Caucasus and from Bokhara usually spoke Yiddish and were known as the *Ashkenazim.* Those from Morocco, Tunisia, Egypt, Yemen, Salonica, and Smyrna usually spoke Spanish, and were known as the *Sephardim.*

Into this conglomeration of Semitic peoples come Ben Yehouda talking Hebrew and endeavoring to unite the people by their accepting the one language. The Jews blew the shofar and heaped curses on Ben Yehouda, who dared degrade the sacred tongue by using it in ordinary speech. But he remained steadfast in the belief that the Hebrew language would be the basis for unifying Israel.

The Ashkenazim drove him out of their synagogue. He went to the Sephardim, but, being persecuted, he soon gave up going to either of the synagogues. Poverty reigned in the home. The twenty francs which he received as assistant editor of *The Rose of Sharon* was quite insufficient. Poor Deborah, accustomed to the ease of a well-to-do family, was permitted only the barest necessities of life. The Pole who had stood by Eliezer Ben Yehouda suddenly disappeared, either through discouragement or by foul play. And to climax affairs, the editor of the *Rose of Sharon* discharged Ben Yehouda on the grounds that he was ruining his paper. Thus, in the very city of Jerusalem, where he had come to resurrect their lost language, the people were deaf to his voice and adamant to his needs. Only Pines, a well-read Lithuanian Jew, shared Eliezer's views, and stood by him in his days of dire need.

When Deborah became the proud mother of a son, Pines got a Sephardim rabbi to perform the rite of circumcision, and gave the son the name of Ithamer. Pines said to Deborah, "Persuade your husband to let him learn a living language so that he won't be an idiot." But Ben Yehouda would permit only Hebrew spoken to the child. When three years had passed the child had not spoken a word. It seemed that Jehovah had given Ben Yehouda a mute son. Then one day a billy-goat ran near the child, whereupon Ithamer ran to his mother shouting, "Mama! Mama!" in perfect Hebrew. Five children followed the birth of the first. Each in its turn learned to speak only Hebrew.

In *Glory,* a small paper that Ben Yehouda founded, he attacked the Jews for their willingness to live merely from *Haluka,* rather than exercising industry. An attack against this pious group led to the lighting of black candles wrapped in black cloth in the great synagogue of the Ashkenazim. This was the ancient formula for excommunication. A curse was pronounced upon him, his family, and his future prosperity.

On the next day following his excommunication Ben Yehouda wrote an article in *Glory* with these opening words: "I am dead, but I still live!" Deborah pleaded with him to ask for pardon, because with such a curse pronounced upon them at death they could only hope to be buried like donkeys. Through the kind intervention of Pines, Ben Yehouda was not excommunicated by the Sephardim.

Deborah was aware that she did not have much longer to live, so she sent for her mother to come from Moscow. Arriving in Jerusalem, the mother was appalled to find her daughter poverty-stricken and dying. Deborah's last request to her mother was that her younger sister be sent to Jerusalem to marry Ben Yehouda and carry on with him the work that was so dear to them.

No one attended her funeral except their good friend Pines. On their way to the burial grounds a group of infuriated Ashkenazim's men saw them and not only stoned the casket but refused to let them proceed further. They did not want their holy ground contaminated by this unholy person. The pallbearers, frightened by the mob, dropped the coffin and fled. A few of the Sephardim, taking pity on Ben Yehouda, picked up the coffin, and, quieting the mob, proceeded to a lonely spot in a far corner of the cemetery and there buried the last remains of faithful Deborah. Upon her tombstone, Ben Yehouda wrote "To Deborah, the first Mother of the newly-reborn Jewish people!"

A few months later Ben Yehouda married Deborah's sister in Constantinople. Returning to Palestine, persecution was once again directed towards him and his new wife. On one of the anniversaries of the Maccabees, he wrote an article asking that this land of many martyrs be given back to its rightful owners, the Jews. This was the opportunity for which Ben Yehouda's enemies were looking. They reported him to the Turkish officials. He was arrested on the day of the birth of his second wife's first child. In order to stay out of jail while waiting his trial, he had to put up a bail of two hundred pounds. But who would post bail for him? By chance or providence, a pilgrim from Morocco was there who, though a perfect stranger to Ben Yehouda, yet out of pity for him paid the two hundred pounds. That set him free. At that very moment the rain that had been looked for began to fall. The people, already sorry for betraying a Jew to the Turks, thanked God for his deliverance.

While Ben Yehouda continued to write articles and work day by day to form and write a Hebrew dictionary, his writings and influence leaped across oceans and his all-absorbing idea caught fire in other hearts and minds. Theodore Herzl and his followers imbibed his teachings and soon became thoroughly converted to the idea that Hebrew should be the spoken language of Israel. Ben Yehouda became their her, one to whom they looked with a deep sense of gratitude. They wrote to thank him for his persistent efforts, and requested that he continue his work in writing a dictionary of the Hebrew language.

Once the great Theodore Herzl was won over, the battle became easier. Others followed, until it became apparent that the use of Hebrew as a spoken language would link up the Jews with their Hebrew-speaking forefathers in Bible days, and that it would provide a common medium of expression and a unifying bond for the Jews coming to Palestine from all parts of the world.

The German Jews of Jerusalem inaugurated Hebrew as the medium through which all their courses should be taught. The idea met with such approval that on the anniversary of the Maccabees the children of the school sang Israel's "Song of Hope" in Hebrew and presented to Ben Yehouda a seven-branched candle-stick with all the candles lighted.

Ben Yehouda's final contribution was his Hebrew dictionary of eight volumes, in which he not only listed the Hebrew words of the Bible, the Talmud, and other Jewish books, but also coined many new words and filled it with modern ideas and feelings. These met the needs of modern life, and made Hebrew a living language.[2]

Hebrew became the official language of the Jewish Agency and of the Jewish educational system during the British administration. And the language of the Old Testament has also become the language of the Israeli Government, of its Parliament, of its courts, its press, radio, shops, trades, and schools.

Famous scholars teach in the Hebrew language at the Hebrew University. The people speak it on the streets and in their homes. Small boys and girls learn by heart the alphabet of Moses, chatter Biblical Hebrew in their games, and write school compositions that echo the language of the ancient tablet and scroll. A dead language has come to life. It is "a deliberate, romantic, and religious revival unprecedented in history."[3]

### Reclaiming Waste Lands

In ancient times Palestine was an exceedingly fertile country, but through many centuries of neglect and maladministration, much of the country has become barren and waste. Its forests had been destroyed, its hillsides eroded, its drainage clogged, its irrigation ruined. Terraces had been permitted to sink, and about three feet of soil had washed downward to the lowlands and had been carried out to the ocean, where the blue of the Mediterranean had been turned to a dirty brown as far as the eye could see. Large lowland areas, once extremely fertile, had become veritable marshlands which bred deadly disease, while other areas had been turned into fields of sand which blew hither and yon at the will of the winds. Gaunt, hungry hillsides mocked many sections of the uplands, while heaps of ruins dotted the land from one end to the other. Yet the sons of Israel loved their fatherland and soon envisioned themselves fulfilling Isaiah's prophecy:

> And they shall build the old wastes, they shall raise up the former desolations, and they shall repair the waste cities, the desolations of many generations.[4]

Individual or collective right to the land was one of the first necessities, and to secure this right the Jews purchased more than half a million acres of land at fabulous prices. Fifty percent of this land was bought by the Jewish National Fund, was held collectively by the Jewish people, and leased to worthy families on forty-nine year hereditary leaseholds at two percent of the land's cost. The other was purchased by individuals or by organizations; still other vast tracks were to be taken later by conquest during the Arab-Jewish war.

In order to rebuild the wasted land as rapidly as it was recovered, farseeing minds of the Jewish National Organization and the Jewish Agency made long-range plans whereby large numbers of returning Jews could be located in agricultural settlements. Young men and women, and older ones as well, moved in and undertook the enormous task of reclaiming and rehabilitating dearly purchased land which to them became "home." With poor housing and equipment, small capital and little encouragement, these noble souls were often confronted by privation, uncertainty, the dragons of disease, and by the elements of nature at their worst. Yet with zest they terraced hillsides, leveled sand dunes, drained swamps, set out eucalyptus trees, plowed, planted, cultivated, and expended loving care and increasing toil upon acres once tilled by their forefathers. In the process many sickened and died, but others came to take their places and continued until they won.

On the Plain of Armageddon and in the Valley of Jezreel they drained, reconditioned, and turned into flourishing colonies some forty thousand acres of land — land where men and women work and children play; and where vegetables, fruits, grain, fodder crops, cattle, and poultry are produced in surprisingly large quantities.

The great Plain of Acre, with its many thousands of fertile acres, had long lain undeveloped — its splendid springs and abundant rainfall fomenting marshy wastes to breed mosquitoes and malaria, and its uplands going to sand and ruin. But the Jews drained the swamps, promoted sanitation, built roads, constructed factories, and changed the appearance of the worn, sandy wastes and marshy acres into a paradise of green where village after village and grove after grove have sprung up during the last four decades.

The shifting sands along the coastal Plain were utilized and stabilized by locating cities and villages on them, and by transforming them into fertile lands by adding organic fertilizers, plowing under green cover crops, and adding clay to the unruly soil. Tomatoes, squash, sorgum cane, peanuts, and various forage crops have been grown with such gratifying results that many have been astonished to see the success encountered in reclaiming this kind of soil.

Near the Dead Sea, at an altitude of 1250 feet below sea level, the Jews established a test colony they called Beth-Haarana. The salt-saturated soil of this area had been void of all growth for centuries, but they leveled the earth and divided it into beds which they then filled with water for a period of three or four months. As the water circulated through the soil, it tended to carry away the salt in solution and settle the soil into the lower strato. The land was then flooded with fresh water and each section stocked with fish, which after a two-year period produced a coating of organic fertilizer on the land. Tons of other fertilizers were then mixed with the soil, after which trees and crops were planted. After seven years of faithful work this community of more than two hundred people produced large quantities of fine fruits, vegetables, and dairy products.

Firm in their resolve to rebuild the land, the Jews have taken over various hilly sections in the Galilean and Judean mountains, reterraced the hillsides, rebuilt the soil, and planted olives, figs, grapes and other deciduous fruits, as well as great varieties of vegetables.

The Negev, or Southland, which consists of some forty-eight percent of modern Palestine, is, roughly speaking, a huge triangle, with Beersheba at the center of the base and the port of Elath on the Red Sea coast forming the apex. During patriarchal times it was a vast pastureland and the home of Abraham, Isaac, and Jacob.

Later, under the Nabateans, the Romans, and the Byzantines, the Negev developed a population of 100,000 people, who enjoyed improved roads, highly developed irrigation systems, and a flourishing trade. It declined during the sixth century A.D. and fell into decay with the Arab conquest in 636. Its uneven, arid, sand-blown acres have for centuries been inhabited by a few Bedouin tribes who live in tents, farmed small patches of ground, or wandered from place to place in search of scanty grazing for their cattle and camels.

In 1942 a committee of experts from the Land and Afforestation Department of the Jewish National Fund explored the Negev and carried out tests to ascertain its water resources, weather, soil and flora. Of the 2,875,000 acres comprising the area, they advised that 400,000 acres were suitable for cultivation and another 400,000 suitable for afforestation. In 1943, therefore, the Jews established three experimental settlements in widely separated sections of the Negev. Then, on October 6, 1946, three years after the establishment of the three test settlements, one thousand veteran settlers set up eleven new villages in one night in the famous "Operation Negev."

By 1948 there were twenty-six settlements in the Negev. Then, with the coming of statehood, and the large influx of immigrants looking for living space, the way was open for large-scale settlement in this great southland. Planning for the Negev was no longer on the piecemeal order, but became a part of a concerted all-embracing effort to bring the entire area back to fertility and usefulness.

Armies and crews of khaki-clad young men and women, along with others who were not so young, moved into the Negev; and, working under experts, they made surveys, operated bulldozers, built houses, bored wells, dug ditches, laid pipelines, constructed huge stone and concrete catchments, planted trees, arranged gardens, drilled grain, and put in forage crops. Within two years, 1,077,000 tamarisk and eucalyptus trees were planted in the forest areas, and tree-shelter belts (for windbreaks) were planted in criss-crossing rows for a total length of some five hundred miles. The cultivated area in the Negev rose from 62,500 acres in 1948 to 275,000 acres in 1956. Scores of new colonies have been established, and the work of creating new settlements, arranging new farms for new families, laying concrete conduits for bringing water from the Yarkon (AUJA) River, and restoring the wastes of the great southland of the Negev goes forward with Zionist zeal that is without parallel in modern history.

Urban development in the Negev has kept pace with other forms of development. Beersheba has taken on the aspects of the true "Capital of the Negev," and the city of Migdal Aza, a former Arab center, has become the scene of bustling life. Housing developments for new immigrants have been rising almost everywhere, and the area is humming with activity. Since 1948 enthusiastic Israel had poured nearly $7,000-000,000 into the development of this great southland. And now with its agricultural, mining, and port possibilities the Negev faces an exciting future. The shortage of water and security are its only deterrents, and the water shortage is rapidly being overcome. The $40,000,000, sixty-five mile Yarkon-Negev pipeline, which diverts the waters from the river Yarkon to the Negev, was completed in 1955. This supplies 100,000,000 cubic meters of water annually. A second pipeline of the same size is scheduled for completion in 1958.

One of the most dramatic of the present reclamation projects is the drainage of the Huleh Valley, where more than 18,000 acres of swamps are being transformed into a rich agricultural area where some 2,000 families are being settled.

In almost every section of Palestine except the Judean wilderness the Jews have tried or are now in the process of trying their hand at rebuilding the soil and making agriculture a reality. Where there have been marshes they have drained them; where land had been ridden with disease they have cleaned it and made it healthful; where hills have been steep they have terraced them, where there have been stones they have cleared them; where there were no wells they dug or bored them; where there were no houses they have built and inhabited them. All in all the Jews have founded more than 800 agricultural colonies, have spent billions of dollars, and by their loving care and unceasing toil have done and are yet carrying forward a marvelous job of reclaiming the land — a monumental work of colossal proportions which is little less than a large-scale miracle.[5]

## Replanting Forests

In olden times Palestine's hills and valleys were beautified and enriched by acacia, oak, pine, cedar, cypress, fir, olive, myrtle, carob, box, and plane trees. But these have long since perished, except for remnants here and there.

In the early years of Zionism the Jews sensed the value of trees of every kind. Therefore, the Jewish National Fund organized the "Tree Fund" and set out to accomplish a national re-forestation program. In its infancy the organization sought funds for the Herzl Forest, as a memorial to the founder of the Zionist movement. On the Plain of Armageddon, at Ginegar, they planted the Balfour Forest of 80,000 trees. At Mishmer Hemek they planted 3300 pine and fir trees, then branched out and planted many forests and groves of from 1000 to 10,000 trees in the names of illustrious personalities such as King George, Dr. Albert Einstein, Justice Brandies, and many others.

The B'nai Jeshurun Sisterhood of New York planted a forest of 1000 trees and their splendid example was followed by other societies, synagogues, and clubs. The usual cost of planting a tree was officially set at one dollar and fifty cents. Thereafter organizational efforts were exceedingly effective, as appeals were made to societies, groups, and individuals to plant trees in honor of friends or loved ones, and as tokens of appreciation for special events such as wedding anniversaries, the birth of a child, or the safe arrival after a journey. Jewish Arbor Day, a unique festival in the Jewish calendar, is a spring festival when the blossoms of fig, carob, dates, and other fruit trees are brought into the Jewish home to shed the aroma of the fields of Zion. This ancient festival is now celebrated each year in Palestine by planting trees. And wherever Jews reside outside Palestine, Arbor Day is celebrated by making contributions to the Jewish National Fund for replanting trees in the soil of the Jewish homeland. The trees usually planted are the carob, eucalyptus, tamarisk, cypress, oak, olive, cedars of Lebanon, and various varieties of pine, including the Jerusalem and Stone Pine.

America has long shown great interest in reforesting modern Palestine. In one year the Tree Fund campaign netted almost $100,000, a sum which was added to the National Fund and used to bring the George Washington forest up to almost one hundred thousand trees, a forest, incidentally, which is to have perpetual care by the Forestry Department of the Jewish National Fund. In 1952 the Martyrs' Forest, a memorial to the six million Jewish victims of Nazi terror, was started in the hills and mountains near Jerusalem. It will cover 7,500 acres, will be subdivided into ten woodlands, and will be the greatest afforestation project undertaken in Israel. Likewise, the Children's Memorial Forest — to serve as a memorial of the children massacred in Nazi Europe — is now being planted in Galilee. It will provide a brighter future for the tens of thousands of children in Israel today.

Between two and three million trees had been planted in Palestinian soil up to the Declaration of Statehood in 1948. Since that time more than 25,000,000 saplings have been planted, covering an area of 80,000 dunems or 20,000 acres. A Forestry Department has been created and given jurisdiction over 140,000 acres of land reserved for forest. It is now producing vast quantities of saplings each year, and is placing them along the main highways of the country, along railway right-of-ways, and wherever they are most urgently needed.

Some of these trees will provide a source of food. The pods of the carob tree, for example, provides concentrated fodder for cattle, as well as a form of honey sugar for human consumption. Other kinds of trees produce a variety of fruits, nuts, and oils which the Jewish and Arab people use and export. In the main, however, the highways, the hills, vales, sandy swells, and plains of Palestine are being reclothed with trees so that as they grow they will prevent erosions and preserve moisture in the hill countries, increase the absorption of the land in swampy areas, serve the purpose of sand fixation in sandy areas, act as windbreaks, raise the level of underground water, create new soil, provide a ready supply of limber, create new industries, provide work for new immigrants, and make for a more healthful, invigorating climate for all who live in or visit the Holy Land. And, too, these millions of trees springing up at so many places in Palestine give meaning and fulfillment to Isaiah's prophecy:

> "Instead of the thorn shall come up the fir tree, and instead of the brier shall come up the myrtle tree: and it shall be to the Lord for a name, for an everlasting sign that shall not be cut off."[6]

## Transportation and Communications

Under the British administration one of the largest most commodious ports of the eastern Mediterranean was constructed at Haifa. On falling heir to these port facilities, Israel repaired and extended the main quays, added space for mooring of harbor craft, installed new equipment such as huge floating cranes, weigh-bridges, cargo trollies, tractors and fork-lift trucks to facilitate speed and efficient handling. The port's annual cargo-handling capacity is now one and a half million tons. Further expansion is taking place at the mouth of the Kishon river where a modern and well-equipped auxiliary port, extending two miles along the canal, takes vessels up to 3,000 tons draught.

At Tel Aviv and Jaffa splendid new ports have been constructed which have a combined capacity of 500,000 tons a year.

At Elath, Israel's "window to the East," on the shores of the Red Sea at the head of the Gulf of Akabah, port facilities have been constructed for exporting minerals mined in southern Palestine, and for receiving cargoes from East Africa, Aden, and the countries of the Orient.

Israel-owned shipping has been rapidly augmented until her merchant fleet of thirty-four vessels shares a total gross tonnage of 137,000 tons. Three of these are passenger steamers, including the newly-acquired

SS. *Jerusalem,* which has a displacement of over 15,000 tons, and twenty-eight freighters, including five fruit-carriers.

A special school, offering training courses in seamanship, is now held for ships' masters, mates, engineers, and marine radio operators. Twelve hundred officers man these ships, and the Israel flag is now carried by Israel vessels to most ports of the world.

Airfields have been constructed at Lydda, Haifa, Tel Aviv, and Elath. The field at Lydda is in the International "B" class, ranking with London, Paris, and Zurich. Its equipment includes modern electronic navigational and approach aids. This airport is now used by ten international airlines which together operate fifteen different routes to or through the airport to all parts of the world. In 1953, 1,568 planes of the international class entered this field carrying 60,517 passengers and vast quantities of cargo and mail.

The Israel-owned airline, El-Al, has established a network of routes to four continents — Asia, Africa, Europe, and North America — reaching London, Paris, Brussels, Amsterdam, Zurich, Vienna, Rome, Athens, Johannesburg, Nicosa, Istanbul, and New York. It maintains its own repair shop at Lydda and operates its own fleet of passenger transport planes. Local internal air services are operated by Arkia, a company established in 1950, which carries passengers and freight from Jerusalem to Lydda, Haifa, Tel Aviv, Nazareth, Tiberias, Beersheba, Elath and other parts of Israel.

Road construction has gone forward at so rapid a pace that a most excellent highway system now links almost all important points in Israel. This work entailed major engineering feats through rugged mountainous terrain, the blasting of millions of tons of rock, and the construction of hundreds of bridges spanning yawning chasms. This was especially true in building the splendid highways linking Jerusalem, Tel Aviv, Beersheba, Kurnub, Sodom, and Elath. It is all paying off, however, in the movement of passengers and cargo, and in shortening the distance to potash works, phosphate and kaolin quarries, and potential oil fields.

CHAPTER XLI

# REBUILDING PALESTINE
*(Continued)*

## Receiving and Absorbing Jewish Immigrants

During the thirty years the British administered Palestine there were 484,000 Jewish immigrants who entered the country. This was an average of 16,133 per year.

On the very day on which the people of Israel declared themselves independent, they flung the gates of the new State wide open for Jewish immigration from the four corners of the earth. And during the three and a half years that followed — from May 15, 1948, to the end of 1951 — immigrants poured into the country in a vast tidal wave that more than doubled the Jewish population. They came from most every country under the sun, and came at the rate of twenty-three per hour each hour of the day and night for three and a half years.[1]

This period of mass immigration began with the rescue of 40,000 from the detention camps of Cyprus, and 100,000 from the displaced persons camps of Germany, Austria, and Italy. Simultaneously, immigration began from all those countries in which the Jews were persecuted or were in imminent danger of maltreatment. They had to be saved and without delay. The entire population of Bulgaria and Yemen, and almost all the Jews from Iraq, Libya, Tripolitania, Yugoslavia, and other countries came to Israel. Other thousands came because of the inner urge to return to their Fatherland. They arrived in Israel from seventy-four different countries and all five continents.

The homecoming reached such proportions that from May 15, 1948, to the end of 1953, 717,923 Jewish immigrants and 4,531 tourists entered the country and took up permanent residence — the greatest homecoming in medieval and modern times. But it was the realization of the highest aim of the young State. It was, in fact, the basic reason of its creation. The inalienable right of every Jew to immigrate to Israel had been embodied in the Declaration of Independence, and was one of the most fundamental laws of the State — "The Law of the Return." Two million souls were to reside in Israel by 1957, of which 1,800,000 would be Jews.

Life in Israel meant a tremendous personal revolution for the vast majority of the new arrivals. In their countries of origin, they had been craftsmen, petty traders, middlemen, merchants, and members of the free professions. When they arrived in Israel, they were arbitrarily settled in cities, towns, urban, and rural settlements. They found employment in the ever-expanding industries, such as building construction, workshops, factories, and on farms.

Realizing that a people rooted in the soil would link the nation with the country as their homeland and recapture for Israel that union of native land and native culture which characterized it in olden times, the Government adopted a master plan aimed at balancing the population and developing the country as a whole. They established new urban centers in out-of-the-way places and fostered a "Back to the Country" movement which, by December, 1956, resulted in the establishment of some 830 rural settlements throughout the country. These agricultural colonies usually followed one of four distinct patterns: the *Moshava,* the *Moshav Ovdim,* the *Kvutzah,* the *Moshava Shitufi.*

The Moshavim (singular, Moshav) are rural villages or settlements based on private land-ownership and private enterprise. Each inhabitant works his own land according to his plan, owns his own house, buildings, tools, cattle and equipment, and makes as much money as his industry may determine. If he chooses, he may employ Arab or Jewish labor to work his farm or groves. And though these colonists frequently avail themselves of the benefits of cooperative irrigation, marketing, and buying, each still lives under his own vine and fig tree. Most of the earlier colonies were of this type, Petah Tikvah and Rishon le Zion being worthy examples. Among the new colonies of this type are Benyamina, Hersaliya, Raanana, and Kefar Aaron. In 1938 there were seventy-nine Moshava colonies, and when the state of Israel was established there were approximately one hundred and seventeen, many of which rated as the more stable colonies of Palestine. In 1953 alone, 1,535 families settled in agricultural settlements of this type.

The Moshav Ovdim is a settlement of small farmers who do not own the land as their private property but hold it under hereditary lease. The land is national property, owned by the Jewish National Fund, and is leased to the settler for a forty-nine year period. Each settler receives only the amount of land which he and his family can cultivate and may not permanently employ outside labor. He enjoys full property rights of plantation, livestock, buildings and farm equipment. The settlers practice cooperation in all matters affecting the colony as a whole, such as the acceptance of new members, the purchase of livestock, seed and necessities, and the sale of the produce, as well as in the maintainance of the necessary institutions. Long-term loans, when needed, are advanced by the Jewish public agencies. Nahalal, Athlit, and Kfar Felix Warvurg are examples of the Moshav Ovdim settlements, of which more than three hundred have been established.

The Kibbutz is a strictly communal agricultural settlement located on nationally-owned land. The land is granted to the settlers as a group according to the terms of the Jewish National Fund, and the entire estate is worked in common. They live as one common household, eat in one large dining room, purchase supplies from one common purse. Every one draws his clothing from the common stock. The land when under crop cultivation, the living quarters, the buildings, and public institutions all are owned in common by the community. The members of a Kibbutz have, in theory, completely divorced from their minds all thoughts of private ownership of money and property. Money as an individual possession does not exist. Each man is supposed to work as much as he can and receives what he needs. His daily round of life is directed by the common will of the community. If children are born, they, too, belong to the community, and are placed in large dormitories or communal nurseries where oversight is the responsibility of nurses who carry out the wishes of the community. This being considered the more economical form of operation, a conscious effort is often put forth to establish new colonies after this pattern. Genegar, Kfar Giladi, and the Deganiyas are examples of these collective colonies. At the end of 1954 there were 223 of these settlements with a combined population of 76,115.

The *Moshava Shitufi* are settlements based on collective ownership of property and collective work as in the Kibbutz. Each family, however, has its own home and is responsible for its own domestic affairs, such as feeding, laundry, and care of the children. Each family receives money according to its size and needs. These settlements develop industrial enterprises alongside its agricultural activities. At the end of 1953 there was a total population of 5119 who live in thirty colonies of this type.

More than 50 Maabarot, or "transitional villages" were established for the absorption of new immigrants. In these there lived from 100 to 1000 families who were constantly being absorbed into permanent settlements. The majority of the Maarbarot have now been converted into agricultural colonies like one or another type of the established settlements.

There are 104 Arab rural villages with a population of 116,500. These own their own homes, work their own farms, and live simple yet colorful lives, as did their forefathers in past generations.

## Expanding Agriculture

Agriculture has played a unique and striking role both in Jewish history and in the years of settlement which preceded the Jewish State. In their dispersion the Jews had been driven from the land, and in most cases had been forced to become town dwellers. Through the centuries, however, many had thirsted for the soil, and in modern decades the land of Israel became a central symbol of the Zionist dream. Modern settlement formally began with the establishment, in 1870, of an agricultural school at Mikveh Israel, a few miles from Jaffa. Some thirty-three agricultural schools and training farms have been established since, and at this time (January 1, 1957), some 400,000 Jews are engaged in farming almost 1,000,000 acres of land in Israel. In addition there are more than 40,000 "Auxiliary Farms," of about one-fourth acre each, on which as many householders produce vegetables, fruit, poultry, and eggs in their spare time.

Israel's Jewish population now numbers nearly 1,800,000. Her non-Jewish population (mostly Arab) numbers 200,000 persons, of whom 140,000 are directly or indirectly employed on the soil. There are some 14,500 Arab-owned farms, excluding the Bedouin, whose farming activities represent perhaps another 3100 units. The Arabs have followed the same methods of farming for many centuries, but the Ministry of Agriculture employs eighteen instructors and experts who work exclusively among the Arab population to aid them in terracing, soil conservation, and improved methods of farming.

The domestic and industrial crops thus far produced in Israel are in short supply, but are increasing from year to year. The following table based on 1952-53 yield will convey a fair idea of what is produced on farms.[2]

### PRODUCTION OF MAIN CROPS

|  |  |
|---|---|
| Wheat | 29,500 tons |
| Barley and oats | 66,000 tons |
| Hay | 110,000 tons |
| Fodder | 640,000 tons |
| Pulses | 3,700 tons |
| Oil seeds | 9,000 tons |
| Peanuts | 7,000 tons |
| Corn (maize) | 15,000 tons |
| Tobacco | 1,800 tons |
| Potatoes | 55,000 tons |
| Vegetables | 205,000 tons |
| Citrus | 11,140,000 cases |
| Table grapes | 12,500 tons |
| Wine grapes | 9,500 tons |
| Bananas | 11,000 tons |

| | |
|---|---|
| Olives | 13,500 tons |
| Fisheries | 3,100 tons |
| Fish ponds | 4,600 tons |
| Cow milk | 128,000,000 Liters |
| Sheep Milk | 21,000,000 Liters |
| Eggs | 370,000,00 Eggs |
| Honey | 700 tons |
| Sugar Beets | 40,000 tons |
| Flax | 7,500 tons |

Other crops, such as cotton, flax, ramie, agave, kenaf, maize, carob beans, apples, plums, avocados, bananas, dates, figs, flowers, and flower bulbs are produced in varying quantities. In most cases they are being rapidly expanded. For example: in 1956 Israel produced about one quarter of the country's needs in soft wheat, and produced and exported 5,000 tons of hard wheat suitable for macaroni manufacturers.

## Citrus Fruits

The scientific production of citrus fruits, such as oranges, grapefruit, and lemons, has long since become one of the most outstanding achievements of Palestinian agriculture.

These fruits enjoy most favorable natural conditions for growth, and through the use of modern irrigation facilities, large mechanical plows, and scientific care, the quality of the fruit has been improved and the quantity increased. In 1939, 75,000 acres were producing citrus fruit. In this year, citrus exports reached the highest figure on record, with fifteen million cases sent abroad, of which ten million was the Jewish share.

But the war, which soon followed, monopolized shipping, and permitted oranges to rot and plant pests to multiply in neglected groves.

The Arab-Jewish war contributed to further neglect and destruction, but with the signing of the armistice, the Israeli authorities began the rehabilitation of the citrus industry. The citrus export in the 1949-50 season totalled 4,222,703 cases, and has been enjoying a healthy increase every year since that date. In 1953-54 more than 8,000,000 cases were exported along with vast quantities of citrus by-products, juices and concentrates, with a total income of $21,200,000. Palestine is now the largest exporter of citrus fruits outside America, and the "Jaffa" orange enjoys world fame.

## Sheep and Goats

From the time that Israel became a people and up to the Great Dispersion, sheep raising was one of the most important branches of agriculture in Palestine. The Patriarchs were shepherds. Moses tended the flocks of his father-in-law in Midian, and David was a shepherd lad. In the golden age of Israel the land simply teemed with flocks which gave of their milk, their meat, and their wool. Sheep raising left its mark not only on the economic life of the people but upon its spiritual life as well: its holidays and festivals, its ceremonials, the songs of its poets and seers, its legends and its stories. Thus, long after the Hebrew shepherd's flute fell silent, and the Jews wandered in distant lands, they longed for their ancient homeland and for the pastoral activities common to shepherd life.

Therefore it is little wonder that with the first sparks of national awakening the figure of the Jewish shepherd should become the symbol of the return to nature and work, and to the conquest of the country.

At first the various colonists kept a few sheep, none of which could have been more than small herds. But in time it became apparent that the coveted life and legend of the Jewish shepherd, with their tradition of heroism and devotion, would be restored only when Jews lived with Bedouin shepherds in order to cultivate the shepherd's heart and learn how to raise sheep.

A few of the younger Jews donned Bedouin garb and became shepherds with the Bedouin. Their daily provisions consisted of one Bedouin flat cake, the grass of the field, and parched wheat which they themselves prepared. After one year they returned to Galilee, where they undertook to pasture the flocks owned by some of the settlements and soon to organize The Shepherd's Association, whose members were determined to acquire and tend their own flocks. At first these men lived in the pen together with their charges, with only a partition of mats separating them from their sheep. But this was not enough, for meager provision, intermittent illness, and lack of funds caused the project to fail.

However, the seed had not been sown in vain, for after a few years a number of shepherds in the Jewish Legion dreamed of sheep raising as a part of the economy of the country. But they, too, needed funds, and met with small success. Then, in 1920, the Jewish National Fund came forward with capital to finance the industry, and colonies acquired flocks both in Upper and Lower Galilee. But for a long time the sheep were inadequately housed and improperly fed, and little effort was devoted to scientific breeding. Mortality soared because of diseases and neglect. At times it seemed that the modern Jew would never grasp the know-how and regain the true shepherd's heart; yet they envisioned themselves as pioneers, and persevered therefore until they mastered the shepherd's art.

In recent years the Jewish Sheep Association has introduced scientific methods, improved pastures, imported new varieties, crossed the native "fat-tailed sheep" with the Caracul sheep of Central Asia, and improved the sheep and goat industry to the point where it is now one of the most honorable and beneficial of all Israel's economies.

In 1931 the Jews possessed only four flocks of 2213 head of sheep and goats, but by 1945 their number had increased to eighty flocks of 21,360 head. Today Israel's sheep flocks number 90,000 head, and their goat herds total more than 100,000 — 30,000 of which are of the famous Zaanen breed. These produce milk, cream, butter, cheese, leben, meat, and wool.

## Cattle

For many long centuries cattle of Palestine have been of inferior quality and have produced very little milk. The first Jewish settlers found the native cows to be a very inferior breed. Year after year they had been left without supplementary feeding during the long dry summer months. Cattle of such poor stock were of practically no value to the struggling colonists. Therefore special investigation and experimentation were conducted in conjunction with the Agricultural Research Station at Rehovot.

At first, cattle were imported from the Netherlands to replace the native milk cow, but, despite the fact that these were good milk producers, they could not survive Palestine's climate and disease. Finally, Holsteins from Holland and Jerseys from England were crossed with Syrian and Lebanese breeds — these latter being superior to the native cow of Palestine. Soon the experiments developed a strain of milk cow that could survive under Palestinian conditions and yet yield a satisfactory quantity of milk. Whereas the Arab cow gave only about 700 quarts of milk a year, the new hybrid has increased the average to something over 4000 quarts. Some prize specimens are said to produce 5000 to 8000 quarts yearly.

Since the natural increase of farm livestock does not suffice for the need of the growing population, the Department of Agriculture, jointly with the Jewish Agency, is each year importing thousands of milk cows from the United States, Holland, Switzerland, Australia, and neighboring countries. Experts attached to the cattle-breeding section are aiding in the selection and improvement of stocks by artificial insemination and the pooling of pedigreed champion bulls. Studies have been made and experiments carried out regarding grazing lands, the production and storage of silage, and the use of citrus fruits for feed.

Labor, patience, energy, and scientific knowledge have together worked a modern miracle in Palestine. Large-scale modern dairies are now being operated throughout Upper and Lower Galilee, the Plain of Esdraelon, the Jordan Valley, in Rehovot, Tel-Aviv, and Haifa, near Jerusalem, and, more recently, in the Negev. From these dairies come increasing supplies of liquid milk, butter, cream, cheese, and other milk products. The annual milk production reaches the amazing and almost unbelievable figure of 150,000,000 liters — an amount sufficient to cover all domestic needs. And now a start is being made in the breeding of cattle for beef production. Vigorous efforts are also being made to develop natural pastures in the south and in the Negev, and herds of Herefords have been imported to form the nucleus of future herds.

## Fishing

In ancient times fishermen held a place of great importance in Palestine as producers of food. From the Mediterranean, Lake Huleh, and the Sea of Galilee fishermen made great hauls of edible fish. Today, fish constitutes a valuable part of the diet and serves as a protein source in the place of meat.

Fishing in Israel is subsidized by the Government and is divided into three branches: sea fishing, lake fishing, and pond fishing. The Israeli fishing fleet is a part of Jewish navigation and operates along the eastern coast of the Mediterranean and in the Gulf of Akaba near Elath. In the Mediterranean the catch is largely the Triton sardine. The Gulf of Akaba is proving one of the richest fishing-grounds in all the world, not only in terms of human nutrition, but also as it has given rise to a whole series of industries, such as the production of fish-oil, fish-glue, fish meal, and other products.

Fishing in Lake Galilee and Lake Huleh and in artificial lakes has long been a thriving business, but is now being expanded. Some 9000 acres along the coastal regions and in the valleys have been made into ponds for breeding carp. The fishing companies have recently sent nearly two million dollars in purchasing boats, in constructing harbors, and in extending their business in general. They are now catching more than 8000 tons of fish annually, and bid fair to increase this catch year by year.

## Irrigation

Israel's basic agricultural goal is to render the country as nearly self-sufficient as possible. Under prevailing weather conditions, this can be accomplished only by widespread irrigation. During recent years the

Government, aided by Dr. Walter C. Lawdermilk, has adopted a comprehensive national irrigation plan whereby the Jordan river and its tributaries, other rivers and springs, rain and flood waters, and Palestine's vast underground water resources will be utilized.

Regional irrigation schemes have been vigorously pressed forward in various parts of the country. The Lake Huleh project is now about complete; this enormously rich Basin of 18,000 acres is being irrigated by the waters from the huge fountains at Hesbeyiah, Dan, and Banyas. In Galilee a 1500-foot dam has been constructed across the Beit Natufa Valley which will constitute a lake impounding 250 billion gallons of irrigation water. Work is also going forward on the Jordan Valley Scheme, a project which will irrigate 25,000 acres in the Jordan and Beisan Valleys and which, by means of the larger canal on the upper Jordan, will bring water into Galilee, the Plain of Armageddon, the plains along the Mediterranean coast, and then link up with the large sixty-six inch concrete pipeline which carries water from the Yarkon (Auja) river to irrigate 50,000 acres of cotton, grain, and fodder in the vast semi-desert regions of the Negev. A second pipeline will be laid to another section of the Negev this next year.[3]

All over the country are sprouting the sharply-edged shapes of derricks and drills. Israel is drilling for water, which is the earth's greatest treasure. A chain of reservoirs and artificial lakes is being set up to store the rain water, and terraces are being built on the hillsides to keep floods from washing top soil away. The Soil Conservation Service and the Forestry Department have been established within the Ministry of Agriculture, and vast acres of land in Israel are now being surveyed and classified as to soil, slope, and rockiness. Measures are being taken for contour cultivation terracing, drainage, flood control, stream bank erosion control, and pasture improvement.

At a cost of approximately $140,000,000, the water resources of the country are now being integrated into a vast nation-wide network of pipes and reservoirs which will collect water wherever it is available and distribute it to areas where it is needed. Much of this system is now in operation, and within a short time more than one million thirsty dunams will be irrigated and the domestic and irrigational needs of almost two million people in the state of Israel be served with "the elixir of life," known to the people of Palestine as "the gift of God."

## Industry

In the beginning years few settlers had capital, and were unable to borrow sufficient funds for any more than small-scale industrial operations. Skilled labor was difficult to obtain, raw materials were in short supply, and domestic consumption was extremely limited. Yet, as the country grew, its industrial needs became apparent. Farmers had to have machinery, pumps, and irrigation pipes, and their products had to be processed in flour mills, bakeries, and canneries. Every line of endeavor, in order to progress, had its specific needs. Individuals, therefore, as well as public and private institutions, came forward with capital. Factory and warehouse buildings were constructed, power and processing plants erected, and plans laid for the development of many major industries.

Favorable industrial progress was made during the British administration, but a new day dawned for industry when the new State of Israel was set up and the population doubled. Many newcomers brought with them equipment, tools, industrial skill, and experience. Others brought capital, a resource augmented by the millions upon millions of dollars advanced by American investors and philanthropists.

In a brief time new and larger industrial plants sprang up and industrial output was doubled, and within six years the number of workers employed in industry increased from 300,000 to 590,000. Natural resources were discovered, and the wheels of industry turned as they had never before turned in the Holy Land.

In 1950 the Parliament passed the "Law for the Encouragement of Capital Investments." Then, an Investment Center was set up to guide prospective investors — particularly those from abroad. The law was designed to insure that encouragement be given all economic initiative and capital investment which might enhance Israel's productivity, or enable Israeli goods to compete in world markets. It offered various privileges and facilities to approved undertakings, including exemption from payment of customs duty on imported goods, exemption from payments of Property Tax on new buildings or additions to existing buildings for five years, relief from local taxes, and generous concessions on income taxes.

By March 31, 1954, 1750 enterprises, representing capital investments of $220,000,000 and IL 105,000,000 had been "aproved" or "recommended" by the Investment Center. No less than 695 of these enterprises had already started production and these going concerns had invested $133,500,000 of foreign capital and IL 86,200,000 of local capital.

Large, beautiful, and well-ventilated industrial plants, equipped with the latest machinery for the production of almost every kind of consumer goods, were soon operating at astonishing speed. A fairly adequate idea of the variety of goods produced may be gained by glancing at the following table listing the products which are manufactured, processed or finished by Israel's industry.[4]

*Textiles* — Spinning and weaving (wool, cotton, silk), finishing and dyeing, clothing articles (including knitwear, interlock, fashionwear, etc.), rayon.

*Leather* — Tanning footwear, fancy goods, etc.

*Plastics* — Bakelite products.

*Nylons.*

*Foodstuffs* — Millings, canning, fruit juices and concentrates, jams, chocolate, biscuits, olive oil.

*Chemicals* — Pharmaceutical products, paints and dyes, waxes, soap, fertilizers, chlorine, caustic soda, and trichlor-ethylene.

*Building Materials* — Building hardware (nails, screws, locks, doorknobs, etc.), cement, concrete blocks, tiles, bricks, plywood, wire.

*Sanitary Equipment* — Pipes, baths, porcelain fittings, etc.

*Glass and Ceramics.*

*Furniture and Household Goods.*

*Tools and Machinery.*

*Diamonds* — cutting and polishing.

*Handicraft* — Religious articles, metalwork, filagree work, etc.

*Newsprint and Paper*

*Printing and Bookbinding.*

*Refrigerators, Radios and Washing Machines.*

*Other electric appliances* — Electric bulbs, stoves, fans.

*Automobile Assembly* — Trucks, passenger cars, jeeps, bus bodies, spare parts.

*Railway engines and equipment.*

*Irrigation Pipes.*

*Tires and Rubber Products.*

*Watches and Precision Instruments.*

*Steel*

However, the table gives but a faint picture of the total industrial picture. It tells nothing of volume. Many of these companies are small. Others are large, even according to European and American standards.

In the building materials industry three cement companies produce 1,000,000 tons annually. All local cement requirements have been met, and substantial quantities exported. During 1953 cement was shipped to a number of countries, pre-eminently Turkey, at a total value of $1,477,000. Among outstanding orders for 1954 was 1,000,000 tons for use in the construction of United States bases in Spain.

The metal industry employed 16,509 workers in 1952, and has an annual output of about $30,000,000. The textile industry, even as early as 1950, employed 10,223 workers. Food processing concerns employed 20,000 in 1952. In the same year the chemical industry employed 3,500 workers, and enjoyed an annual production value of about IL 15,000,000.

During 1953 the diamond industry cut and polished and exported 146,804 carats valued at $12,723,000.

Three large paper manufacturing concerns supply the country with various kinds of paper including two-ounce bond, kraft, wrapping paper, and cement bags. The newly-opened Israel-American Paper Mills, capitalized at $2,250,000, covers some 80,000 square feet, employs a labor force of one hundred, and expects to turn out 20,000 tons of paper a year.

Two large tire factories, the Alliance Tire and Rubber Company and the General Tire and Rubber Company, with their five hundred employees, manufactured 116,000 tires during 1953 to help revolutionize the country's transportation system. The Kaiser-Frazer plant at Haifa had been in operation only six months when the one thousandth car rolled from its assembly line. In a brief time production was stepped up until the plant, with its five hundred workers, was turning out trucks jeeps, trailers, station wagons, limousines, and 4-door Aero Passenger cars at the rate of three hundred vehicles per month.

The Palestine Potash Company rebuilt and enlarged its plant at the southern end of the Dead Sea. A splendid highway linked it up with Beersheba, and the plant resumed operations in the autumn of 1953. With its new equipment, machine shops, warehouses, and loading facilities, the output has been increased to 180,000 tons per year. Two of the largest chemical engineering concerns in the world — the Chemical Construction Corporation of the United States, and the Powell Dufferin Corporation of the United Kingdom — have constructed large chemical works at a combined cost of $35,000,000 for the extraction of salts, phosphates, gypsum, and pyrites of the Dead Sea and southern Palestine areas. The utilization of the vast storehouse of wealth in the Dead Sea and he Negev are playing an important role in the industrial development of the Holy Land.

## Natural Resources

In Bible times Palestine was known not only as a "land flowing with milk and honey" but also as a land "whose stones are iron, and out of whose hills thou mayest dig brass." King Solomon exploited these mineral resources heavily, and remains of his copper mines and smelting foundries may still be seen in the extreme southern Negev.

During the British rule in Palestine, only 15,000 tons of sulphur were mined, and known deposits of minerals in the Dead Sea were extracted. But soon after the State of Israel was established, comprehensive survey of Israel's mineral assets was ordered. An initial report, submitted in May of 1949, indicated the presence of various minerals and declared that the possibilities for their successful exploitation was favorable. As surveying continued throughout 1950 the list of minerals became "increasingly impressive."

Encouraged by this report, the Government, in March, 1951, established the Israel Mining Corporation which was to direct further geological surveys and recommended measures to utilize the country's mineral wealth.

The Company turned its attention to phosphate, ball clay, glass sand, and iron in Mahtesh Hagadol (The Great Crater), south of Beersheba; it worked on copper and manganese at Timna, twenty-five miles north of Elath; on the bitumen-bearing rocks of Sodom at the southern end of the Dead Sea; on the peat deposits of Lake Huleh; and on the mica and felspar of the Elath region.[5]

The initial work in each of these fields proved that they would be profitable beyond expectation. The copper deposit north of Elath, for example, is sufficiently large to yield 100,000 tons of extracted metal, and an expected extension of the area will give an additional 300,000 tons. This year, 1956, the company plans to process 1000 tons of copper ore per day, and from 4500 to 6000 tons of metallic copper during the year.

Since copper sells for about $650 per ton, some $2,000,000 a year will be saved for Israel, and a like amount for iron and steel from the iron ore discovered. This should care for at least a third and possibly half of all the iron and steel requirements of Israel.

During the autumn of 1953, Dr. Dov. Joseph, Israel minister of development, invited a well-known Swedish geologist to come to Israel to help with geological surveys. Previously only three deposits of ore, containing a mere 35% of iron, had been discovered in the Negev. One day the Swedish geologist suggested that there was geological strata in Galilee identical with the Negev strata. When other geologists, somewhat skeptical, were dispatched to the Galilee area they found deposits of ore of an even more substantial iron content than the Negev deposit. Moreover, this area was located less than sixty miles from Haifa, Israel's main seaport, on a principal road, with plenty of water and plenty of labor easily available for mining operations. Mining operations are already under way there, and iron content is estimated at several million tons.

Galilee is within the ancient boundaries of the tribe of Asher, one of the twelve among whom the land was divided before Moses' death. In blessing the twelve tribes, Moses' blessing to Asher was, "Let Asher be blessed with children. Let them be acceptable to his brethren. Let him dip his foot in oil. *Your bars shall be of iron and copper*. As your days, so may be your strength." Here is the iron of which Moses spoke; once more, a Biblical reference to mineral wealth was proven factual.

Phosphates have been found in far greater quantities than iron and copper. Twelve fields of phosphate rock have been found in Israel, and plans have been completed for a calcination plant to enable the quality of the phosphate to be enriched. This, it is hoped, will produce 600,000 tons of calcined phosphate a year when operations in the new plant are under way. Quantities of manganese have also been discovered. This extremely rare, black mineral is vitally needed by the big steel producing countries as an alloy to produce hard-wearing metal.

There are unlimited quantities of gypsum in the Negev. Glass sand from the Negev is supplying all the requirements of Israel's glass industry.

The chemicals of the Dead Sea remain far out in the front ranks of natural resources of Palestine for both the Jews and the Arabs. Before the Jewish-Arab war, the Palestine Potash Company operated extensive plants at both the north and south ends of the Sea. The northern works were destroyed during the war, but the southern works, located at Sodom, fell to the Jews, yet stood idle from the beginning of 1948 until in 1952, when a new company, known as the Dead Sea Works, took over and began preparations for the renewed exploitation of these vast chemical deposits.

A splendid highway from Beersheba to Sodom was constructed and opened for traffic in March, 1953. The works resumed production during the following June. This unique reservoir of chemical wealth contains the following:[6]

| | |
|---|---|
| Potash<br>—used for making soap, fertilizer and nitrates. | 1,300,000,000 tons |
| Bromine<br>—used in medicines, synthetic chemicals and color agent. | 835,000,000 tons |
| Salt<br>—table, bath, and commercial. | 11,900,000,000 tons |
| Gypsum<br>—used as dressing for soils, and plaster paris. | 81,000,000 tons |
| Calcium Chloride<br>—used as drying agent. | 6,000,000,000 tons |
| Bitumen or Asphalt<br>—used for paving roads, sealing ships and embalming. | unknown quantity. |
| Magnesium Chloride<br>—the lighter than aluminium metal of the future. | 22,000,000,000 tons |

The Dead Sea is forty-seven miles long, nine miles wide, and from three to thirteen hundred feet deep. Israel possesses a thirty-five-mile shore line, and therefore has ready access to these riches which are beyond the dreams of the most avaricious.

This remarkable composition of chlorides and bromides are extracted and manufactured by the energy of the sun, prevailing winds, and fuel necessary for the generation of electricity. Before 1948, the Sodom plant had an annual production of 60,000 tons of potash. Recent production figures stand at 100,000 tons in 1954 and nearly 150,000 tons in 1955. The company is now working on plants which will produce bromine, calcium chloride, and magnesium chloride. All these minerals benefit the country, in that they develop industries, reduce imports, and expand exports. According to official forecasts based on present production plans, within two years (by the middle of 1958) a gain of $100,-000,000 dollars per year may accrue to the national economy from this almost untapped and practically inexhaustible concentration of chemical riches.

## Oil

The presence of oil in the Holy Land was suggested by Moses more than 3300 years ago, when in Deuteronomy 32:13 he prophesied that Israel would pump or "suck oil out of the flinty rock." Little was thought about the matter, however, until in 1885, when a German scientist reported oil in the Dead Sea area. Then, in 1912 the Standard Oil Company shipped piping and equipment to the Near East in preparation for the first test drillings, but these efforts were brought to a standstill by World War I, and the pipings and fittings were actually used by General Allenby in bringing the Nile water across the Sinai desert as he pushed his expeditionary forces toward Gaza.

In 1950 the Israeli government employed Messrs. Max and Douglas Ball, oil and gas consultants of Washington, D.C., to examine Israel's oil geology. Their optimistic report, delivered to the Government at the beginning of 1952, led the Israeli Parliament to pass the Israel Petroleum Law, a measure which made it clear that the Government desired to open her oil resources to free and competitive enterprises, both local and foreign. Duty-free importation was to be allowed each operator for anything required by him in his operations, including machinery, equipment, installations, fuel, building materials, and transport facilities. The royalty payable to the Israel Treasury was to be one-eighth of the oil produced.[7]

Nine companies applied for licenses, eight of which signed oil leases on 2,500,000 acres of land. Oil soon became the target of a feverish scientific research throughout Israel. The search advanced from the exploratory stage to test borings when, by the middle of 1953, four different companies erected derricks and began drilling operations in the

Dead Sea area, in the Negev, on the Plain of the Philistines, and on the Plain of Sharon.

For two years five giant drills pounded away on a round-the-clock schedule — twenty-four hours a day, seven days a week — probing the earth's secret hiding places of the "black gold" that could revolutionize the life and industry of Israel. More than $5,000,000 plus 1,500,000 Israeli pounds were spent by the searchers for oil. The Israeli population became increasingly oil-conscious as newspapers were scanned daily for reports of an oil strike. Around the world, and especially in the Western world, many people waited to know if there was indeed oil in the Holy Land.

Then, within certain official circles, hints began to be dropped that the drill site of Heletz near Migdal Askelon and thirty miles south of Tel Aviv, might be the right site. On Thursday evening of September 22, in anticipation of what could happen on the morrow, Mr. Y. Federman, one of the directors of the Lapidoth Petroleum Company, retired early so that he could arise before dawn the next morning to get to the drill site of Heletz. He did arrive at the site early — just in time to see a gigantic shaft of greenish black substance gush from the borehole and spurt more than a hundred feet in the air. And the shout went up, "Oil! Oil! Oil!" The Holy Land's first oil well had come in at 5:37 A.M. Friday morning, September 23, 1955. The well blew in for 1200 barrels of high-gravity oil that first day, and then was set at from three to four hundred barrels a day. When news of the strike reached Tel Aviv, Jerusalem, and other Israeli cities, the people went wild with excitement. When the news reached the New York Exchange, demands for shares in four oil companies, with interests in Israel, was so great that their opening on the market was delayed for two hours. When it did open, shares sold from four to eight times the usual price.

This one producing oil well, however, had little more than symbolic significance, for its production is less than two percent of the young nation's current oil requirements of approximately 1,100,000 tons a year, valued at $34,000,000. Yet it augured well for future exploration. Having had its first big boost in oil, the Israelis intensified the search for oil in many areas.

Geologists suggested that the structure of the Heletz field alone was capable of supporting up to fifty wells. Acting on this advice, the operators began to drill other wells. By March of 1956 another producing well was brought in, and by September 14, 1956, oil from Israel's seventh oil well spurted into the sky. By Jan. 1, 1957 a dozen oil wells were yielding approximately six per cent of the country's needs — a saving of some $2,000,000 annually. Since that time other wells have been brought in and nine private oil companies are drilling in Israel — five with United States capital, two financed by Canadian capital, and two by domestic capital.

Israel's first oil was transported to Haifa in trucks, but now a pipeline has been completed from Heletz to Ashkelon, and the oil is shipped by train from Ashkelon to Haifa refineries. The gasoline is then sent to various sections of the country. Some 32,000 tons of fuel gas, a by-product of oil purification, were also produced this past year in Israel.

## Building an Educational System

Among the early Jewish colonies in Palestine, the schools which they organized did not adhere to any given standards, nor were there text books in Hebrew. But textbooks gradually evolved, and about six months before the outbreak of the First World War, the Palestine Office of the World Zionist Organization set up the first Jewish Schools Education Committee, bringing under its supervision and direction the Jewish schools already in existence in the country. The greater part of the education budget for that year was covered by the Zionist General Council in Berlin, while in the following war years it was met by the Provisional Executive Committee for General Zionist Affairs in New York. Following the British occupation of Palestine, a Department of Education, collaborating with the Education Committee, was set up in 1918 by the Zionist Executive in Palestine, and during the years 1921-1922 a uniform system of education was introduced.

During the British administration of Palestine (1918-1948), the mandatory government operated and supported Arab schools and recognized the educational autonomy of the Hebrew school system, but placed it in the category of privately maintained schools. Only nominal grants of aid were made annually for the support of Jewish schools. This entailed great sacrifices on the part of the World Zionist Organization and of the Jewish Community, which had the continuous responsibility of absorbing large numbers of immigrants, many of them destitute refugees. But the Jewish people gladly supported their educational institutions, for were they not definitely Jewish? In those days, however, the Jewish schools in Palestine were divided into so-called educational "trends," of which there were four major divisions:

1. The "Mizrachi," or religious schools, which educated the youth to a strictly orthodox way of life. The textbook was the Torah, and other studies counted for small worth.
2. The network of "Labor" schools, which aimed to educate their youth in the ideals of labor, co-operation, equality, the pioneering life,

and Zionist socialism. These schools possessed few textbooks, preferring to spend their time studying such subjects as seeds, soils, insect control, poultry, and animal husbandry.

3. "Agudat Israel," an institution which represents a distinctly religious approach to Jewish education and all aspects of Jewish life.

4. The "General' trend, which was both secular and non-political. It represented an earnest atttempt at merging the more desirable aspects of the American, British, German, and Palestinian systems, and was, on the whole, a most excellent way of education. However, it could wield only small influence over the "Mizrachi," the "Labor" and the "Agudat Israel" systems.[8]

This system, which had arisen out of peculiar circumstances of Jewish settlements in Palestine prior to the establishment of the state of Israel, no longer met the requirements of the new modern state. Many felt that the "trend" system had gradually developed into a situation characterized by vested interests, undue political influence, and partisan strife. While the parent was free to choose the trend he preferred for his child, the choosing turned more and more into an annually recurring fight over children, since each trend naturally attempted to recruit as many pupils as possible.

The trends, though under the over-all supervision of the Ministry of Education, and though bound by a minimum curriculum prescribed by the Ministry, were largely administered by their own particular organizations.

Thus, the Mizrachi Religious Party controlled the religious schools, the General Federation of Labor controlled the labor schools, and the center and right wing parties exercised control of the 'general' type of schools.

The "State Education Law," passed by the Parliament in August, 1953, abolished the "trend" system, and set up a unified state education in kindergarten and elementary schools subject to the supervision of the Ministry of Education and Culture, with a view "to base fundamental education in Israel on values of the heritage of Israel and the achievements of science, on the love for the country and loyalty to the State and the people of Israel, on training in agriculture and manual labor, on pioneering, and on striving toward the creation of a society built on freedom, equality, tolerance, mutual help, and love for mankind."[9]

Parliament provided for State religious education with the understanding that such institutions should only be religious with respect to curriculum, way of life, teachers, and inspectors.

The new system provides for free choice of the parent between two types of schools — a religious type and a secular one.

The Compulsory Education Act passed by the Israeli Parliament in 1949 provides for compulsory and free school attendance of every child between five and thirteen years of age, and for youths age fourteen to seventeen who have not completed their elementary education. This extends as a matter of course to all children in the country, irrespective of race, creed, or sex. When the new school year commenced in Israel in the autumn of 1953, the nation's public schools opened their doors to the unprecedented number of some 380,000 children.

Not attending government schools are more than 7000 pupils between the ages five to eighteen in Jewish religious parochial schools. (Yeshivot and Talmudei Torah). These schools are recognized as meeting the requirements of the compulsory education law with regard to the obligatory curriculum. Also not included in the total figures are some 7000 children in private kindergartens, and another 7000 students in missionary non-governmental schools.

On the adult level a network of evening classes, reaching out literally into every settlement and transition camp, has been designed to meet the urgent demand of the immigrants for the study of Hebrew as well as their need for civic and general education. Professional and skilled immigrants, such as lawyers, engineers, teachers, doctors, technicians, are provided with intensive courses in Hebrew in special schools, including room and board. These courses last five months. They provide thirty hours a week instruction, and the rest of the time is devoted to self study. These schools, called "Ulpanim" (houses of learning), have proved to be very effective means for the speedy absorptions of the more educated among the immigrants and at the same time have helped to provide the country with badly needed skilled personnel. Almost all of the Ulpanim graduates are sure to find immediate employment with government or private agencies. In little more than four years, more than 10,000 have taken seventy Ulpanim courses.

In order to train a skilled community of farmers, the Government maintains thirty-nine agricultural schools which give instruction to 6000 students.

Other educational institutions include 48 vocational training schools with more than 5000 students, 250 evening schools for working youth with 12,000 in attendance, 24 teacher training colleges with 3400 students, and a network of adult educational schools and classes all over the country.

In the 1953-54 school year, about 26,000 were enrolled in 107 Government Arab schools, and were taught by 700 teachers. About 80%

of the total Arab population of school age now attend school, and a higher percentage will be attained as soon as more Arab teachers are trained. These schools are supported by the Israeli government, and are operated not only in towns and villages but also in many Bedouin encampments.

At the top level, there are four institutions of higher learning: the Institute of Technology at Haifa, which provides the technical and scientific personnel so urgently required in the building of the country. This school is attended by some 1400 students in its several departments: Civil Engineering, Architecture, Mechanical Engineering, Electrical Engineering, Chemical Engineering, Agricultural Engineering, and Science.

The School of Law and Economics in Tel Aviv has about 1000 students who study law, economics, political science, and auditing. Extension courses are offered to some 200 students.

But the greatest institution of Hebrew education and culture in Israel is the Hebrew University of Jerusalem. Its academic staff for 1954-55 consisted of 510 professors, lecturers, and instructors. It had six faculties, with the following enrollment in the same academic year.[10]

| | |
|---|---|
| Humanities and Social Sciences | 1196 |
| Mathematics and Sciences | 560 |
| Agriculture | 172 |
| Law | 617 |
| Medicine | 356 |
| Dentistry | 34 |
| Pharmacology | 23 |
| Total | 2,958 |

In addition, 305 graduate students did research for their doctoral degrees at the Weizmann Institute of Science at Rehovot.

The aims of Jewish national education are to imbue the youths of the land with (1) *training in physical labor* "either for tilling the land or some other work — not as a class ideal but as a national ideal, not as a bitter necessity, but as the proud and honored mark of a nation that desires an upright life and a share in the work of creation." Work is a fundamental and obligatory element in the education of youth; (2) training in the pioneer way of life so that "children of the exile" may be transformed into "builders of the Homeland, town-dwellers into tillers of the soil, unproductive idlers into productive toilers." Only by fostering "this daring, creative and enterprising pioneering spirit among the youth as an organic part of our education shall we be able to continue carrying out our labor of redemption, which is barely beginning;" and, (3) to impress upon students the *great human ideals promulgated by the Hebrew prophets* — "justice and lovingkindness, human brotherhood, and the love of human-kind." Israeli leaders are confident that by being true to these aims they can transform the ideals of Eliezer Ben Yehuda into an entirely completed reality, consolidate the unity of Israel, and shape the character of the people as they desire.

All education, therefore, is to be based jointly on the Bible and the achievements of science. Every boy and girl in the State must be taught that their history did not originate with the founding of the State of Israel but that behind them lie four thousand years of effort and achievement, years which have set their stamp upon the history of humanity, and moulded the spirit, destiny, and purpose of Israel — and that the richest period of their great past — so rich in spiritual heroism, unique masterpieces, and outstanding personalities — was during Bible times, "from the days of Moses to those of Ezra when we were fashioned into a people — into the people of the Book." "Our progress," said Prime Minister David Ben-Gurion, "will be transformed into a decline if we do not pass on to youth the spiritual heritage of all our past generations; and, in particular, the mighty heritage of ancient times . . . the heritage of the Bible. . . . It is impossible to imagine any education in Israel that is not solidly based on the Bible."[11]

## Health

For many centuries the health conditions of Palestine have been atrocious. Pilgrims, soldiers, tourists, immigrants and those who have resided in the country have too frequently suffered from malaria, dysentery, typhoid, smallpox, and even the Black Plague. The mosquito, the sandfly, and other harmful and deadly carriers went almost unchallenged; swamps went undrained, and the bravest of men quailed before enemies against which they did little to destroy.

Many brave men and women have made contributions toward a healthier Holy Land, but none have done so nobly as recent Jewish organized effort. In this momentous fight, the *Kupat Holim,* the *Hadassah Medical Organization,* and the *Malben* have made memorable contribution.

Kupat Holim is a voluntary health insurance organization based on the principal of mutual aid. It was established in 1912 by the Jewish agricultural workers of Judea. Although it started with only 150 members, it has grown into an extensive health organization so that at this writing (1956) it boasts of 352,000 registered members, who, together with their dependents, represent a total membership of over one million insured persons. Kupat Holim operates a wide network of medical institutions in various parts of the country. These include 810 dispensaries, 14 general and special hospitals (capacity 2000 beds), 860 medical centers, 12 convalescent homes, and 183 infant welfare stations. These institutions are staffed by 1300 doctors and 1600 nurses, in addition to scores of dentists, pharmacists, and technicians.

*Hadassah,* the Jewish Women's Zionist Organization of America, first sent a medical mission to Palestine in 1913. These fourteen doctors, nurses, and medical workers began to teach Jews and Arabs the fundamentals of public health — what to do with sewage, how to protect the water supply from contamination, how to guard expectant mothers and new-born babies from infection. Other Hadassah teams followed, healing and teaching, establishing health centers, draining swamps, and destroying mosquitoes and other carriers of deadly disease. Through the past forty-three years they have been the most active and most effective force for the health of Jews and Arabs throughout Palestine. Today the Hadassah Medical organization provides most of the curative and much of the preventive services in the Jerusalem area. It maintains three hospitals (capacity 701 beds) in Jerusalem, Beersheba, and Safed, 35 medical centers, and schools for nurses. Hadassah jointly with the Hebrew University established and maintains the Hadassah-Hebrew University Medical School. On the western outskirts of Jerusalem Hadassah is now erecting a new ten-million-dollar medical center which will comprise the University Hospital, the Hebrew University-Hadassah Medical School, the Nurses' Training School, and the Outpatient Department.

Malben Institute, sponsored by the American Joint Distribution Committee, is responsible for the handicapped and hard-core cases among immigrants. It has built eight hospitals (capacity 1558 beds), a Post-Tuberculosis Rehabilitation Center, out-patient clinics in Tel Aviv and Haifa, fifteen old-age Homes for more than 2000 aged persons, a village for one hundred blind persons and their families, a home for retarded children, and twenty-three sheltered workshops for physically handicapped persons.

The Ministry of Health operates twenty hospitals with 4331 beds, maintains fourteen district health offices, and employs about 450 doctors and 1750 nurses. Its medical services include maintenance of hospitals, mother and child care, sanitation, epidemiological services, an anti-malarial service, prevention and treatment of tuberculosis, mental hygiene, public health laboratories, and nursing and pharmaceutical services. It also carries on a program of health education. Six percent of the ordinary budget is spent on health services. Israel maintains the highest health standards of any country in the Middle East.

## Religion

Palestine has ever been a land of religion. Its mood has been that of piety, its literature that of the Bible. Its leaders have been the patriarchs, priests, prophets, the Messiah, the apostles, the Maccabees and the Crusaders; its foremost buildings, the tabernacle, the temple, the synagogue, the mosque, and the Christian church. These were ever and always pointing toward the one true, omnipotent, and all-wise God who requires righteous obedience of His children. In ancient times the Hebrews were the world's most devout worshippers, and they considered it their highest privilege to obey God.

Throughout all their wanderings the Jews have been symbolic of the hunger of man's spirit for God. On returning to their fatherland they have, for the most part, carried an acute awareness of being descended from Abraham, Moses, Amos, Micah, Isaiah, Jeremiah, and Ezekiel, and of being "the people of the Book." A minority have professed a sort of ideological atheism, or have endeavored to think of God as a philosophic concept to be figured in thought, and themselves as speculators whose daily work was their religion. But the majority of Jews have possessed a profound faith in forces far beyond the power of deterministic philosophy to interpret. They believe that in fulfillment of the prophetic vision, God has returned them to their land and that they are now fulfilling prophetic predictions spoken from these very hills more than two thousand years ago.

In rebuilding the country, the Israeli leaders have considered the restoration of Zion as a call of duty, a spiritual opportunity, a lasting obligation. They have, therefore, given the spiritual its rightful supremacy over the material. And in so doing their first thoughts have been for Judaism as practiced by the Jews. Yet they have realized that there were faiths other than their own. Therefore they enacted the following legal directives:[12]

> THE STATE OF ISRAEL . . . will be based on freedom, justice and peace as envisaged by the prophets of Israel; it will ensure concrete equality of social and political rights to all its inhabitants irrespective of religion, conscience, language, education and culture; it will safeguard the Holy Places of all religions . . . .
>
> The Sabbath and the Jewish festivals, namely the two days of New Year, the Day of Atonement, the first day of the Feast of Tabernacles and the Eighth day of Solemn Assembly, the first and seventh days of Passover and the Feast of Pentecost, shall be the prescribed days of rest in the State of Israel.
>
> Non-Jews shall have the right to observe their own sabbath and festivals as rest days.
>
> An employee's weekly rest shall be not less than thirty-six consecutive hours in the week.

> The weekly rest shall include—
> (1) In the case of a Jew, the Sabbath day.
> (2) In the case of a person other than a Jew, the Sabbath day or Sunday or Friday, whichever is ordinarily observed by him as his weekly day of rest.

Within the Ministry of Religious Affairs of the Israeli government there are four departments:

1. The Religious Council Departments supports and looks after the welfare of all Jewish religions, namely, the Ashkenazim, the Sephardim, the Karaites, and the Mizrachi.
2. The Department of Moslem and Druze Religious life in their respective communities. Arab clergymen from the neighboring Arab countries are granted the privilege of crossing the border and taking up residence in Israel.
3. The Department of Christian Communities fosters the interests of all Christian groups. These include the Greek Catholics, Greek Orthodox, Roman Catholics, Armenian, Gregorian, Maronites, Anglicans, Copts, Syrian Jacobites, Ethiopians, Assyrians, Church of Scotland, Baptist, and various other Protestant churches. There are over 160 places of worship for Christians in addition to about 50 religious schools and a score of charitable institutions and hospices. A Hebrew Christian settlement, consisting mainly of Jews converted to the Protestant Christian faith, has been established at Petach Tikvah, near Tel Aviv. Six other Hebrew Christian groups hope to set up similar settlements in the near future.
4. Other Religious Communities, which include Bahais, Ahmadiya, Carcassians, and Samaritans.

The way in which the Ministry of Religious Affairs functions is to exercise oversight of all Holy Places, encourage Sabbath observance, control Kosher foods, assist in the organization of pilgrimages, arrange for religious services, establish religious courts, and support religious education; also to repair and construct synagogues, churches, temples, shrines, and tombs; to purchase religious paraphernalia and equipment, support clergymen, allocate monies for charities, broadcast special services, and publish the *Christian News from Israel* and a bulletin giving news of the Moslem communities. They give all religious communities the right to their own courts of law and to exercise jurisdiction in matters of marriage and divorce.

Religion is one of the most obvious and most real forces in Israel. Jews frequent the synagogues, monks, nuns, and priests recite chants and responses from behind cloistered walls, the swart Muezzin calls "the faithful" to prayer, and godly men and women pass their lives in single-minded devotion. Among the Israeli there are lively Messianic expectations somewhat akin to Christian expectations of the second coming of Christ. "These Messianic hopes" says David Ben-Gurion, "have undergone repeated changes in form, but their essence has not changed, and will not change. They are closely coupled with the message of the redemption of Israel and the world."[13]

Israeli leaders feel that the upbuilding of their national life in Palestine is the "one great urgent and historically inescapable task of Jewry," but that there is no substitute for the religion that confronted Moses in the burning bush, filled Isaiah with prophetic zeal, and inspired the Psalmist to sing — religion which speaks of God, enjoins the worship of God and obedience to His commands, and urges the quest for God. This religion, many believe, will eventually culminate in the fulfillment of Isaiah's vision:

> And it shall come to pass in the last days, that the mountain of the Lord's house shall be established in the top of the mountains, and shall be exalted above the hills; and all nations shall flow into it.
>
> And many people shall go and say, Come ye, and let us go up to the mountain of the Lord, to the house of the God of Jacob; and he will teach us of his ways, and we will walk in his paths: for out of zion shall go forth the law, and the word of the Lord from Jerusalem."[14]

## CHAPTER XLII

# ISRAEL AND THE MIDDLE EAST CRISIS

THE JEWISH effort to rebuild Palestine has behind it a strong moral motive, and is backed by the force of a mighty religion. The overwhelming majority of Jews returning to Palestine earnestly endeavor to pick up the frayed threads of human life and weave them into a worthy pattern for their own future as well as for the welfare of those whom they will influence.

A considerable segment firmly or faintly cherish Messianic hopes for the world to eventually turn its spiritual foot-steps toward Jerusalem in sincere worship of the one true God of the universe. Others expect climactic success to come by material progress and by military might. However these expectations may be, ugly situations have been forming during the past few decades which have snarled up affairs throughout the Middle East and have repeatedly threatened to engulf the world in the final conflict of the ages.

As a land-bridge for three continents, Palestine and the Middle East have for 3000 years been considered of the utmost strategic military importance. Assyrian, Babylonian, and Persian rulers regarded it as important in their day. Alexander the Great, the Greeks, the Romans, the Saracens, the Arabs, the Crusaders, and the Turks all seized the Middle East in turn and made it the bulwark of their empires.[1] Knowing the importance of holding the Middle East, Napoleon endeavored to take it, but never completed the job. Previous to World War I, the Germans completed the "Berlin to Baghdad Railway," constructed executive buildings in Jerusalem, and laid extensive plans for the Middle East as a center for their own anticipated world empire. But General Allenby drove them out and took over the Middle East to make it the backbone of the British Empire. During World War II the German army under General Rommel was driving hard to take over Egypt, Palestine, and the Middle East when General Montgomery turned them back at El Alamein.

Only when united under a strong central government has the Middle East long enjoyed even a fair measure of security. Always, through the centuries, when one strong government yielded control or was forced out, there was created a general atmosphere of crisis into which another came in and took over. Although many in the family of nations had their turn, Russia had never been one of them. Yet, since the time of Peter the Great she had longed more than was generally known to control the Middle East. She would thereby gain a warm-water port for world trade, and use dominion here as a stepping-stone to still more distant areas. This desire was especially quickened in 1917 when the Communists took over Russia.

As usurpers and heirs of the old Czarist Empire, dark, shadowy, atheistic Communists donned the garb of Utopian idealism, and, untrammeled by any moral restraints, they went forth from Moscow throughout all the nations of the earth crying "Peace, Peace." In previous secret conclaves, decisions had been made, long-range plans formulated, and oaths sworn to in blood. Under the guise of democracy, and by fair promises and infiltration, by propaganda and subversion, by spying and lying, by abuse and character assassination, and by preaching peace and practicing revolution, they would, so they thought, march irrevocably toward their goal until they had attained world domination and forced all men to their way of life. No power could turn them back, not even death itself!

By the end of World War II — which they stealthily encouraged — the Communists had gained as satellites many smaller nations of Eastern Europe. Soon afterwards they took over China and other parts of the Far East, then gave themselves over to the centuries-old dream of occupying the Middle East and using it as a key to the conquest of the world. Following the war, they lingered in Azerbaijan, hoping to turn Iran into a Communist camp and to gain access to a warm-water port on the Persian Gulf. Allied pressure, through the United Nations, forced them out.[2]

Realizing that Great Britain blocked their way more directly than any other political power, the leaders of the Soviet Union secretly plotted the ruin of the enormous British Empire. In the main they would make it an East-West war in which they would urge native peoples to fight against "western colonialism" as represented in the British, the French, and the Dutch empires, but they would focus attention on destroying the British in piece-meal fashion. Or, at least, they would render them ineffective as a world power. In India, in Africa, and in the Middle East the Communists spread their propaganda, inveighed against "capitalistic imperialism," fostered nationalistic aspirations, and offered aid and comfort for the smaller nations who could be influenced against the British.

In the three-way conflict between the Arabs, the Jews, and the British, the Communists first worked to get the British out of Palestine. Then they placed their emissaries in both remaining camps, but definitely sided with the Arabs against the Jews. The Arabs were more numerous, they were hospitable, individualistic, highly emotional, and ready to take revenge because of resentment over any real or imaginary wrong done them.[3] And, too, the majority of Arabs were Mohammedans, and the Mohammendan world with some 350,000,000 adherents would prove invaluable to Communism in proportion to their ability to gain their good will. Even in the conflict between the East and West, or between the darker races against the white races, the Arabs were considered more useful to Communists than were the Jews.

The Arab-Jewish war, like most other wars, was woven, in its very fabric, with many dark and sombre threads. In its conduct the sharp edge of conflict had created so many ugly aspects and left so many deep antagonisms that only an armistice could be signed with Israel's neighbors. A treaty symbolizing peace was impossible with none of them. Especially so since Communist agents licked every Arab sore, magnified greatly every wrong — real or imagined — and stirred the war-brew more briskly still by always advising against any possible settlement.

Fear, born of war, augmented by a few atrocities, and coupled with appeals from their own misguided leaders, caused some 800,000 Arabs to forsake their homes and their lands and flee across Arab borders to become war-refugees. When the war was over, the terms of the armistice did not take them into account. Their Arab brethren did not want them, and the Jews would not permit them to return. Left friendless, homeless, and without compensation or proper accomodation, they became wards of the United Nations, and for the following eight years eked out a miserable existence in tattered tents and crude hovels erected just beyond the borders of Israel. Harried by the pitiless elements of cold and heat, beset by malnutrition, and plagued by the perennial longing to cross the border and return home, there festered in them a hatred for the Jews that grew more bitter with the years. And that bitterness entered into the hearts of ten or more millions of Arabs in nearby lands.

Seizing the opportunity to exploit Arab misfortunes and legitimate grievances, the Communist agents not only played upon Arab misery and stimulated irritation and hatred, but also actively hammered at the doors of seven Arab nations, offering them sympathy as well as economic and military aid. Communism was maneuvering for a firm foothold in the Middle East with its vast oil resources, its wealth of Dead Sea chemicals, its important Suez Canal, and its strategic position for air, land, and sea bases.

In waiting for the opportune time and the correct avenue of approach, they hoped for a sufficient measure of unity among the Arabs so that they might destroy Israel in war, but despite all encouraging, the Arabs seemed extremely difficult too unite. Once they had been united under the Prophet Mohammed, but after a short generation his followers had become divided over Ali, a cousin of Mohammed and the husband of the prophet's daughter, Fatima. The majority of the Mohammedans of Iraq, Iran, and India supported Ali's claim to the caliphate and became known as *Shiahs* or *"Shiites,"* while those of Arabia, Syria, Palestine, and Egypt opposed Ali's claim, elected their own caliph, and became known as *Sunnas,* or *"Sunnites."* Since then these two great Mohammedan families have developed further cleavages which hopelessly divide them, despite all well-meaning efforts to unite them. The Arabs have the common bonds of language, dignity and pride which hold them together. Moreover, politically they all believe in Arab nationalism, although in the end this usually simmers down to the nationalism of their own particular country.[4]

Developing an awareness of the Soviet Union's obvious aim to penetrate the Middle East countries, Iraq joined Turkey and Iran in the *Baghdad Pact* — a defensive alliance binding them in cooperative action in resisting any aggression directed against either of them by Russia in her program of expansion in the Middle East. Later this pact was signed by Pakistan and Great Britain. The majority of the population of these Middle East countries who signed the pact were of the "Shiite" persuasion, and in each case no one country was to interfere in the internal affairs of the other.

The United States endeavored to get other Arab countries to join the Baghdad Pact, but failed, largely because the majority were of the "Sunnite" persuasion, because of Communist influence, and because of the ambitions of Colonel Gemal Abdel Nasser of Egypt. As an officer in the Egyptian army, he was wounded and suffered humiliating defeat while fighting the Palestine war in the Gaza Strip during 1948-49. Feeling that the Egyptian government had brought on the debacle by its weakness, he secretly organized his forces, dethroned King Farouk, and assumed control of the army of Egypt in 1952. In 1954 he took over the government, and with the aid of his young officer friends he was made Chancellor and dictator of Egypt. Imbued with deep dreams of Egyptian greatness, he soon secured foreign diplomatic aid — principally that of the United States and Russia — and maneuvered the British into agreeing to evacuate the Suez Canal zone — their long-held bastion.

Having freed Egypt of "foreign occupation," Nasser's two immediate goals were to further confirm the fact that he was master in his own house by rebuilding and "Egyptianizing" the economic and social life of Egypt, and to emerge as a powerful leader who sincerely desired to "emancipate" the Arab world. His crowning effort for the material welfare of his own country, as he conceived it, would be to build a huge high dam at Aswan which would provide nearly two million additional irrigated acres to provide for Egypt's rapidly growing population. The high dam would be one of the world's largest, and competent engineers estimated that it would cost nearly a billion dollars. In his great need, Nasser appealed to the United States for $64,000,000 dollars to begin the work. The United States agreed to help him.

But Nasser dealt with a divided heart. In his flirtations with Russia, he had become infatuated by her sweet promise of economic aid. Then, too, she would see that his military needs were met.

Deep in Colonel Nasser's heart there rankled a bitter hatred for the Jews of Palestine. Moreover, he knew well enough that virtually all the Arab world shared in varying degrees a hatred for Israel, and the desire to see her destroyed. Feeling this to be his one grand opportunity of gaining sufficient might to destroy Israel and to become the hero and acknowledged leader of the Arab world, Nasser committed fifty per cent of Egypt's cotton crop for five years ahead to pay for some $200,000,000 worth of Soviet-supplied jet planes, tanks, guns, ammunition, and other war material. On September 27, 1955, Nasser, the Egyptian dictator, announced his deal to purchase arms from the Soviet bloc.[5] His intent to use these arms in a war with Israel was no guarded secret.

Once Communist weapons began moving into Egypt, Colonel Nasser extended the wave lengths of his radio broadcasting station so that his "Voice of the Arabs" program reached from Morocca to Iran and from Cyprus to Portugese East Africa. On four wave lengths he and his associates boldly represented Egypt as the center of modern Islam and the arch-foe of "Western imperialism and colonialism." He stimulated an interest in complete freedom of Arab countries from Morocco to Baghdad, championed the cause of the patriots of Algeria against the French, the Mau Mau in Africa against the British, and, with a fox-like cunning, influenced and encouraged Jordan in expelling Glubb Pasha, British Lieutenant General who had so effectively trained the Arab Legion and so faithfully served the Royal family of Jordan since 1930. And, above all, Nasser placed special emphasis on the defeat and destruction of Israel as the first and most important step in the process of clearing Arab countries of "foreign occupation."

Constantly affirming, despite armistice agreements, that Egypt remained in a state of war with Israel, Nasser reorganized and increased the *fedayeen* (commando army) and established centers for their training in Cairo, in Sinai, and in the Gaza Strip. Once trained, they were provided with rifles, machine guns, explosives, and hand grenades, then taken near Israel, where, in groups of from three to twelve men they crossed the border by night and penetrated as deeply as possible into Israel territory. They raided Jewish settlements, destroyed property, mined roads, ambushed buses, and demolished homes in which Jewish families were peacefully asleep.

At the village agricultural school of Shafrir near Ramle, the children were attending evening prayers when suddenly the lights went out and a hail of automatic rifle fire poured into the crowded assembly through the open door and windows, and the unsuspecting children were mowed down without mercy. The terrorists fled into the gathering darkness.

As students of the Old Testament, the Israeli forces struck back, exacting not merely "an eye for an eye and a tooth for a tooth," but endeavored in their reprisal raids to take the lives of five Arabs for the life of every Israeli killed. This only made matters worse by causing each side to regard the other as murderous invaders, and brought on many months of terrorist activities.

Border conflicts reached such a frightful state that United Nations Secretary-General Dag Hammarskjold journeyed to Egypt and Israel and not only obtained acceptance of the U.N. cease-fire, but induced Egypt and Israel on September 27, 1955 to sign an agreement to withdraw from the demarkation lines and each to respect the rights of the other. Yet, it was only a matter of days until the *fedayeen* were creeping back across Israeli borders. By late October the old terrorist activities were again in full swing.

Seeing Egypt's deep absorption in anti-Western propaganda, and that she was going so heavily in debt for Soviet arms that she would be unable to finance a fair share of the Aswan Dam project, the United States, on July 19, 1956, withdrew its offer of a loan to help finance the project.[6] Angered by this refusal, Nasser nationalized the Suez Canal Company on July 26, and took over operation of the Canal, although the internationally owned company held a concession for its operation until 1968. Nasser advised that he would use the profits from the Canal to build the Aswan Dam.

Britain and France protested against Nasser's seizure of the Canal company, and eighteen nations signed a proposal for international control of the Canal. Nasser countered by rejecting their proposal, and warned that Egypt would "defend the Canal to the last drop of blood."

Seizing her opportunity to stimulate trouble between the Middle East and the Western Nations, Soviet Russia came into open view and announced its approval of Nasser's nationalization of the Canal.

Having been pushed farther and farther out of the Middle East — out of Palestine, out of the Sudan, out of Iran, out of Iraq, out of Jordan, out of the Canal zone — and being deeply wounded by the series of fateful losses, and a dictator's usurpation of the waterway which to them was their very "life line," Britain called Nasser's bluff by dispatching a troop-laden aircraft carrier to the Mediterranean, called up reservists, and airlifted troop reinforcements to the island of Cyprus, the last foothold for the British army in the Middle East. France, who held large interest in the Suez Canal, joined Britain in warning Egypt that they were ready to use force if necessary to protect their rights in the Canal. Egyptian street rioters responded, in Communistic style, by marching through the streets of Port Said and along the quay where, in their angered determination to free their country of foreign influences, they destroyed the very monument of De Lesseps, the French engineer who built the Canal.

Then on October 24, 1956, an agreement was signed in Amman, placing the military forces of Jordan under the Egyptian High Command in the same way as the Syrian forces had previously been placed under Egyptian control. Immediately there was a resumption of fedayeen activities on a greatly extended scale. Thousands of well-trained fedayeen, formed into small suicide squads, penetrated Israel night after night, and left in their wake such destruction and death that life in Israel became almost intolerable.

When the Soviet bloc had made a half-billion-dollar build-up of arms in Egypt and Syria, and had sent large numbers of technicians to teach and direct the Arabs in the use of these planes, tanks, bombs, and explosives, the Egyptian High Command grew bold. Day by day and night by night, the "Voice of the Arabs" indicated Egypt's near readiness to launch the war that would destroy Israel. In a radio broadcast to all the Arab world, the Commander-in-Chief of the Egyptian army, General Abdul Hakim Amr, said:

> Now that the hour is approaching, I and the members of the Revolutionary Council will be in the front lines of battle. In this battle our enemies will be convinced of their weakness, and the victory will be yours and that of all the Arab states.

a little later General Amr said:

> The Israel danger no longer exists. Egypt has enough strength to wipe Israel off the map.[7]

Seeing there was little prospect for help from the United Nations, and feeling her peril was so acute that she might not reasonably wait longer, Israel alerted her military and civilian forces from Dan to Beersheba, and hastily girded for the final show-down. The Reservists — who included every able-bodied man between the ages of 18-49 — were called up. Over the week-end they swelled Israel's army to 250,000 in number.

On Sunday, October 28, 1956, Israel announced partial mobilization. On that day military vehicles were readied and untold numbers of civilian cars and trucks were smeared with mud and left in Jerusalem's parking lots with keys in the ignitions. As night stole along famous valleys and crept in to envelop the Holy City, prayers went up from thousands of lips while eager Israeli officers and troops crowded into hundreds of cars, trucks, jeeps, vans, tanks, and power wagons. Accompanied by armored half-tracks and artillery tow-trucks to form a mighty military cavalcade, they moved toward Beersheba. Here other similar cavalcades from other Israeli cities joined them, and the various columns — in keeping with orders issued by General Moshe Dayan — rolled on and, according to plan, took up positions near the Egyptian border from near El Auja to Elath.

At five o'clock in the afternoon of Monday, October 29, just forty minutes before dusk, Jewish task forces, at various take-off points in Israel, went into action against Egypt. In order to seal off the Egyptian land approaches, a fair-sized formation of Dakota transport planes had left Israel earlier and at 5:00 P.M. disgorged Israeli paratroopers one hundred and fifty miles within Egyptian territory near a cross-roads east of strategic Mitla Pass. A half hour later their weapons, jeeps, and supplies were dropped. After collecting them, the entire force proceeded through the gathering darkness to the foothills of Jebel Giddi, and dug in near the entrance of the winding gorge of Mitla Pass, through which runs the road from Port Suez.[8]

Meantime, also at 5:00 P.M., an Israeli armored column, after a difficult approach through the Southern Negev, crossed the Egyptian border and attacked the Egyptian battalion garrisoning Kuntilla. After fighting two and a half hours, and losing one hundred men, the Egyptians fled. At the same time another Israeli armored column from Elath captured the border post of Ras el Naqb and moved on westward, while the force that had already taken Kuntilla pushed on through the night and after a stiff fight captured El Themed at four in the morning.

The force from Kuntilla was then joined by the force from Ras el Nagb, and at dawn the combined Israeli force moved westward along the Pilgrim's Road. During the morning they were strafed by enemy jet planes. Yet by the middle of the afternoon they attacked and within forty-five minutes overwhelmed Nakhl, a fedayeen base and vital road junction. Here they captured Soviet-made armored cars, which they immediately pressed into service, and by that evening they were moving with speed and ferocity toward Mitla Pass, and the paratroopers. Arriving at Mitla Pass at ten that evening they found that their arrival had been none too soon, for already the Egyptian "Suez Brigade," composed of long columns of trucks, armored troop-carriers, mortars, and artillery, had moved up from Port Suez to the western entrance of Mitla Pass. The paratroopers had radioed for air support, and Israeli jets had attacked and inflicted loss on the columns on the other side of the mountains, but had not kept the Egyptians from taking up positions and attacking the paratroopers.

At dawn, on Wednesday the 31st, the Israelis were attacked by four Vampire jets, three of which were shot down. At noon the paratroopers and the armored cavalry set out to clear the enemy from Mitla Pass. When the long line of Israeli armored columns were deep inside the Pass they were hit by a rain of rifle and machine-gun bullets and strafed by Egyptian British-made Meteor jets. A gasoline tank-truck and an ammunition carrier blew up and blocked the pass, whereupon the intrepid Israeli soldiers jumped from their armored trucks and half-tracks, and on foot charged up the steep slopes with sub-machine guns, hand grenades, and bayonets, and settled the issue then and there. Nevertheless, it took them the rest of the day to entirely clear the Pass. That night they moved on through the Pass, and at dawn emerged on the Suez Plains with the Canal in sight.

The paratroopers, together with the armored column, turned back through the pass, and, leaving it in the hands of a reserve Israeli infantry, they turned south on an old Bedouin caravan track. Making their way amid mountain passes and along boulder-strewn water courses, they finally came down out of the mountains onto the shores of the Gulf of Suez some twenty miles south of the entrance to the Suez Canal. Turning left on the New Red Sea Road, the Israelis took the oil town of Ras Sudr, filled their tanks with gasoline, and pushed on to Tor, which, they found, when they arrived on Saturday, had been captured by another paratroop force that had been dropped there on the previous day.

Simultaneously, on Monday, October 29, at 5:00 P. M., a two-pronged Israeli armoured and infantry force rolled across the frontier below El Auja, and struck Quseima with its Egyptian force of one artillery and two infantry battalions, a fedayeen unit, engineers, and various other supporting units. Israel and Egypt were locked in battle all night. At dawn, air support came for Israel and the Egyptians yielded Quseima and the survivors retreated to Abu Aweigila, a strongly defended depot and supply base. By mid-afternoon the Israeli forces arrived and began the attack on Abu Aweigila. Being confronted with one of the strongest artillery concentrations of the war, the Israeli forces had tough going — so tough that it took them until nearly noon on Wednesday to take the place, although they used some of their best artillery, tank and air power.

That same afternoon the Israelis engaged in a furious but successful five-hour battle at a nearby stronghold known as the Egyptian Dam.

During the night they rested and regrouped. Early the next morning they were on the old Turkish Road marching westward toward Bir Rod Salem where, on Friday afternoon, with strong air support, they engaged and defeated a powerful force which Nasser had sent out from Ismalia. As the dawn's thin light turned the desert into a new creation, Israeli forces entered Bir Rod Salem and took over the big new air base stocked with Russian jet fuel. From there they sighted Ismalia and the Canal.

On Wednesday, October 31, at 8:00 P.M., an infantry and armored task force made up of hand-picked Israeli regulars crossed the border and attacked Rafah, with its crack Egyptian outfit supported by armored and artillery battalions. The Jewish ground forces exercised their best skill and daring, and their air support rocketed, bombed, and strafed the enemy. Yet, it took thirteen hours of hard fighting before Israel's armored battalions swept the field. They then turned and raced west toward El Arish, Egyptian army headquarters in Sinai, thirty-two miles away. Here the going was easier, for panic had been spread in El Arish by Egyptian officers fleeing there from Rafah with tales of the destruction wrought by huge Jewish forces armed with hundreds of heavy tanks and secret weapons. Hearing this, the officers at the garrison at El Arish deployed their troops in prepared defensive positions and then decamped westward "to fetch reinforcements." The abandoned troops fled or surrendered as soon as they saw the first clouds of dust raised by the oncoming Israeli armor on the horizon. From here the Israeli marched westward toward Egypt where they intercepted and virtually destroyed another crack armored brigade — the third army which Nasser had sent out to stop them.

Another Israeli infantry and armored task force attacked Gaza early Friday morning, and by noon the city had surrendered. They then went on to Khan Yunis, the headquarters of the Gaza army group, where the fiercest artillery duel of the war was fought. Israel broke through Khan Yunis' last defenses early Saturday morning, and the Gaza Strip was in Jewish hands.

The final phase of the Sinai campaign was carried out by Israel's intrepid Ninth Infantry Brigade, a reserve force which crossed into Egypt near Elath on October 30. Proceeding down the rough mountainous terrain of the western shores of the Gulf of Akaba, the Brigade captured Dahab, Naqb, Ras Nasrai, and Sharm el-Sheikh, where for six years Egyptian gun emplacements had prevented the passage of Israeli ships to and from the Israeli port of Elath.

Within one week the fast-moving, hard-hitting Israeli forces had overrun and cleared the entire Sinai Penninsula, destroyed or dispersed about one-quarter to one-third of the Egyptian army, and captured vast stores of supplies and Russian-built equipment. They had taken about 5600 prisoners, and had killed from 2000 to 3000 men at a cost of 171 dead, 600 wounded and 4 prisoners. It was so unusual a military campaign that many styled it "one of the most remarkable operations in world history."[9]

Israel's drive on Egypt elicited startling reaction throughout the world. Egypt was surprised, shocked, and bewildered. She had envisioned herself making the attack on Israel, and now, instead, Israel was attacking her, and with a rapid ferocity against which she seemed unable even to brace herself. Other national leaders were not only surprised but at once became exceedingly apprehensive lest other members of the "one world" order should be speedily drawn into the fray, and this should prove the beginning of the long-dreaded final conflict.

No one had to wait long to ascertain what would happen, for the week of the Sinai campaign was one of the world's busiest and most distressing up to that time. On October 30, the second day of Israel's Sinai campaign, Britain and France — already poised on the Island of Cyprus — announced that their troops would move into the Canal Zone to protect the Canal and so separate the belligerents. Israel and Egypt were given twelve-hour ultimatums to halt the fighting. Egypt rejected the demand, and on the following day British planes took off from Cyprus and began bombing military bases in Egypt, destroying much of the arms and munitions of war that Nasser had bought on credit from the Soviet bloc.

On November 2, the United Nations General Assembly, by a vote of sixty-four to five, adopted a resolution demanding an immediate cease-fire. But on Saturday, the 3rd, Britain and France continued to bomb strategic points in Egypt. On Sunday the U.N. set up an international "police force" of troops from small neutral nations to maintain peace in the Suez area. On Monday morning, November 5, after three days of inexplicable hesitation and disastrous delay, British and French paratroopers landed in the Suez Canal zone, took Port Said and soon drove southward one-third the distance of the Canal. Egypt sank ships and barges all along the Canal, in order to cut off Europe's oil supply and to make the Canal useless to the invaders. Syrian army detachments blew up the three main pumping stations on the Iraq pipeline, thereby cutting the remaining oil flow to European countries. That same day, in Moscow, Bulganin warned Britain, France, Israel, and the world that the Soviet Union was "fully determined to crush the aggressors and restore peace . . . through the use of force." Immediately President Eisenhower replied that "The United Nations, which would include the United States, would oppose Soviet volunteers."

Being under exceeding strong pressure from world opinion, and especially from the United States, Britain and France, on November 6, announced that they would obey the U.N. cease-fire order. Egypt and Israel indicated they would observe it. That day Russia announced that thousands of "volunteers" were applying to fight the "aggressors" in Israel. On November 8, Britain, France, and Israel agreed to pull their troops out of Suez as soon as the U.N. forces could take over effectively.

On Saturday, November 10, Russia renewed its threat to permit Soviet "volunteers" to fight in Egypt. That same day British officials reported that they had uncovered evidence to prove that the amount of Soviet arms supplied Egypt was sufficiently great not only to supply the Egyptians but also to enable Russia to quickly form an army in Egypt. The U.N. hastened to form its police force and to get it into the Canal zone ahead of the Communist "volunteers."

On November 14 it was reported that Egypt had asked for aid from Russia, and from Russia came the word that 50,000 "volunteers" had applied in the Soviet Union, 250,000 in Red China, and 65,000 in Indonesia. Russia grew bold with her threats, and warned Britain and France that they could be subjected to "rocket-bomb techniques." Thereupon General Alfred M. Gruenther, Supreme Allied Commander in Europe, told Russia she would be destroyed if she started a new war. Said he: "Retaliation will take place as day follows night, and the Soviet Union will be destroyed."[10] Nevertheless, Soviet jet aircraft began to arrive in Syria in larger numbers. President Eisenhower again warned that the U.S. would oppose entry of any new forces into the Middle Eeast. And to implement his words, the U.S. Sixth Fleet, consisting of 50 warships, 265 planes, and 25,000 men, slipped quietly into the Mediterranean. On the following day the first troops of the U.N. international "police force" arrived in the Suez Canal zone, and Egypt announced it no longer wanted any Soviet or Chinese "volunteers."

By Christmas the U.N. forces had control of the Suez Canal zone, and the British and French forces had completed their unconditional withdrawal. Israel withdrew until she held only "two strong points of resistance" — the Gaza Strip and the Gulf of Akaba. The Gaza Strip, captured by the Egyptians in 1948, had for years been used by the Egyptians as a center for their over-the-border commando raids against Israel's southern settlements. Premier David Ben-Gurion said they could not give it up until a pledge would be given that it would no more be used as a base of operation against Israel.[12]

The waters of the northern arm of the Red Sea, now known as the Gulf of Akaba, had for six years been closed to Israel shipping by Egyptian guns mounted at Sharm el Sheikh, opposite Tiran Island. Israeli arms had opened it to shipping, and had steadfastly refused to return it to the Egyptians without a pledge that it would henceforth be a free waterway for passage of Israeli ships.

Six times the U.N. ordered Israel to withdraw from the Gulf of Akaba and the Gaza Strip. Intent on getting the Jews out of Egypt and Gaza without losing the good will it had been endeavoring to build up among the Arabs, the United States took the initiative and endeavored to convince Israeli leaders that the U.S. understood their demands for guarantees in Gaza and Akaba, but was bound by its declaration that "an aggressor must not be rewarded." Israel retorted with the ancient adage that "victors *earn* soils." "Egypt," she said, "held Gaza because she won it by conquest" in the 1947-48 campaign. She had not been asked to return it. Why then should Israel be asked to return it when she had won it by conquest, without at least some assurance of peaceful intent on Egypt's part? And, as for the Gulf of Akaba, Ben-Gurion said:

> Israel's ships voyaged through these waters over 3,000 years ago in the days of King Solomon . . . these straits of the Red Sea are important to us — perhaps more then the Mediterranean. We have closer cultural affinity with the West, but economically we are perhaps closer to the East. To us trade with Asia and Africa is vital. Elath, at the head of the gulf, is our doorway to the East, and nobody has the right to blockade it.[13]

Then, on February 11, John Foster Dulles handed Israel's Ambassador Abba Eban a note assuring him that as soon as Israel pulled out of Egypt the U. S. would (1) itself proclaim the right of innocent passage in the Gulf of Akaba, and (2) support U.N. action to ensure that the Gaza Strip would not again be used as a base for guerrilla raids on Israel. While Ben-Gurion yet demurred, the Asian-Arab bloc introduced a U.N. resolution calling for sanctions against Israel. Some leaders favored the sanction, but more were reticent about voting sanctions against Israel when Russia, India, and Egypt had repeatedly refused to obey U.N. orders, without the imposition of sanctions.

After a long conversation with John Foster Dulles, Eban informed Ben-Gurion that Washington favored the idea of international administration for Gaza. Soon afterwards Prime Minister Ben-Gurion went before his cabinet in Jerusalem and announced his decision to evacuate Gaza and the Gulf of Akaba area. To the question, "What guarantees have we got?" Ben-Gurion explained developments in New York and Washington, and then added, "They have shown their understanding of our problems, and we must show understanding too." After two prolonged sessions a majority of the Jerusalem cabinet agreed with their Prime Minister, and soon Golda Meir appeared before packed galleries in the U.N. Assembly and announced Israel's decision: "Full and prompt withdrawal from the Sharm el Sheikh area and the Gaza Strip, in compliance with the resolution of February 2." Israel's action, she explained was based on three "assumptions": (1) that freedom of navigation would prevail in the Gulf of Akaba; (2) that the Gaza Strip would be administered by the UNEF "until there is a peace settlement . . . or definite agreement on the future of the Gaza Strip"; and (3) that Israel reserved the right under Article 51, the self-defense guarantee of the U.N. Charter, to send its ships through the gulf "by armed force" if there should be interference, and to "defend its rights" in the Gaza Strip if raids should start again.[14]

When Henry Cabot Lodge, of the U. S. delegation, endorsed Israel's decision, he limited the U. S. commitment to upholding Hammerskjold's view that the future of the Gaza Strip should be worked out "within the framework of the armistice agreement of 1949." Feeling that under such terms the Egyptians could conceivably return to Gaza almost as soon as Israel pulled out, the Prime Minister ordered Army Chief Moshe Dayan to postpone his scheduled conference with UNEF Commander Burns, pending future explanation of Lodge's U.N. statement.

Then on Sunday, March 3, when for weeks the world had talked as if Israel's withdrawal was the sole problem in the Middle East, President Eisenhower wrote a historic letter to Prime Minister David Ben-Gurion urging the "utmost speed" in the withdrawal of Israeli forces, and promised to work for conditions "more stable, more tranquil and more conducive to the general welfare than those which existed heretofore." Then the President concluded his letter with these reassuring words: "Israel will have no cause to regret its decision to withdraw."[15]

Feeling that this personal and moral commitment was more valid than any treaty between nations, because it was "the word not only of the President of the United States, but of an honorable man, a friend, and a general of armies," Prime Minister Ben-Gurion ordered General

Dayan to meet General Burns Monday morning and arrange for the withdrawal of the Israeli army from the Gaza Strip and the Gulf of Akaba area.

On Tuesday evening, March 5, an hour after sundown, a battalion of Danish and Norwegian troops, riding in jeeps and trucks bearing the blue and white flag of the United Nations, crossed into the Gaza Strip from Egypt and struck north toward the Biblical city of Gaza. The Israeli army's tanks and half-tracks fired shots intermittently as they pulled back. Shortly after 9:00 P.M., the U.N. column halted in the glare of the headlights in the central square of Gaza, and Danish Lieutenant Colonel Carl Engholm of the United Nations Emergency Force stepped from his jeep and said, "Everything is going well." "I wish you luck," replied Major General Moshe Dayan, and the Gaza Strip had come under U.N. control.

Two days later, at Sharm el Sheikh, three hundred miles to the south, an Israeli chaplain said prayers, Egyptian gun emplacements commanding the Strait of Tiran were blown up, the Star of David flag was lowered, a U.N. company of two hundred Finns took over the garrison, and Israeli soldiers sailed away for Elath and home.[16]

For 130 days Israeli troops had occupied Egyptian territory, days during which world leaders had been under unprecedented tension. For that matter, all men everywhere had been deeply concerned as the world's military might marched perilously on the very borderland of Armageddon, and none knew what a day might bring forth. Now that Israel was out of Egypt the world could again breathe more easily. The United States could enter the Middle East with its Eisenhower Doctrine of military and economic aid for those nations who desired to resist Communist aggression, and Israel could return to her great obsession — the rebuilding of Palestine. And the one place that received immediate attention was the new port city of Elath on the Gulf of Akaba.

Elath's location is strategic, its potential as a major harbor is "generous," and its planners are enthusiastic. A new harbor and new industrial developments along its seven-mile shoreline are already under way, and six hundred new homes, schools, hotels, and a hospital are being built. Port facilities for handling crude oil, and an eight-inch pipeline carrying oil 135 miles across the Negev to Beersheba, have been completed. In Israel and in certain capitals there is talk of large oil pipelines from Elath to an outlet on the Mediterranean which could provide "a supplement or even a substitute for the Suez Canal."[17]

Then, one day, Israel's "white-maned" David Ben-Gurion, Prime Minister, philosopher, founding father, and Israel's modern prophet, advised Curtis G. Pepper, special *Newsweek* correspondent, that he would prefer to sit down with leaders of the Arab world and work out a settlement that would end the unremitting eye-for-an-eye, and tooth-for-a-tooth Middle-Eastern struggle. But he saw little chance for that happening so long as Nasser was "irrevocably dedicated to the destruction of Israel."[18]

However, with firm reliance on the nations which morally pledged Israel's security, coupled with the Eisenhower Doctrine, he was confident affairs would somehow be straightened out so that Israel would be free from terror in the Gaza border and have peaceful passage through both the Suez Canal and the Strait of Tiran into the Gulf of Akaba. Then, donning his prophetic mantle, Prime Minister Ben-Gurion said:

> Come here in five to ten years and you will find that Israel, like America, has gone to its Westward heritage and founded its own San Francisco. [Ben-Gurion's "West" is the Negev Desert — Israel's southern triangle, whose apex rests on the Gulf of Akaba at the port of Elath.] Come and you will see that we will have railroads, highways lined with settlements, and a great pipeline filled with oil — an inland Suez across what is now the desert. And at Elath you will find a deep seaport with ships from all nations of the world — maybe, even our own.[19]

Rising from his chair, the seventy-year-old statesman-prophet reverently took down from a shelf the Old Testament, and opening it to Isaiah, he read from chapter 35:

> "The wilderness and the solitary place shall be glad for them; and the desert shall rejoice, and blossom as the rose . . . . And the parched ground shall become a pool, and the thirsty land springs of water . . . . And an highway shall be there, and a way . . . the unclean shall not pass over it . . . . No lion shall be there, nor any ravenous beast shall go up thereon, it shall not be found there . . . .

With reverence befitting a commentator of the Book of Books, the Bible-reading Prime Minister and colonizer added, "He meant a railroad as well as a highway, but he didn't say it because the people would not have understood or believed him. But it will come with time — it is the will of God."[20]

*Indexes*

## REFERENCE NOTES

### CHAPTER ONE

1. See Dr. Wooley's description of Ur in Harmsworth's *Universal History of the World,* Part 5, pp. 528-531.
2. Genesis 12:1-3.
3. Old Testament scholars of the critical school founded by Wellhausen once carelessly assumed that the patriarchal narratives were unreliable as historical documents. But the extraordinary accuracy of these narratives has been attested by rapidly accumulating materials discovered in archaeological and topographical researches. Even Prof. Bohl of Leyden, one of the foremost scholars among the Wellhausen group, now says, "Just as the Homeric Age stands at the beginning of Greek history, so does the Age of the Patriarchs in Israelite. Through the mist of ages we greet the figure of Abraham, whom Christians, Jews, and Mohammedans reverence as 'a friend of God' and as the 'father of all who believe'." (See Albright, *Archaeology and the Bible,* p. 130.)
4. Genesis 12:7.
5. Genesis 21:10.
6. Genesis 21:12-13.
7. Genesis 21:21 and Genesis 25:18.
8. Genesis 22:20-24 and Genesis 24:1-9.
9. Genesis 24:11.
10. Genesis 25:5.
11. Genesis 25:23.
12. Genesis 25:25-26.
13. Genesis 25-27.
14. Genesis 28:22.
15. Genesis 30:37-42 and Genesis 31:3.
16. Genesis 33:4. See also Geo. Adam Smith's *Historical Geography of the Holy Land,* p. 611.
17. Genesis 35:10-12.

### CHAPTER TWO

1. Genesis 36:6-9.
2. *Encyclopaedia Biblica,* Vol. IV, p. 5162; George Adam Smith, *loc. cit.,* p. 572.
3. The word *Seir* means "wooded region." (See Dr. Albright's note on this subject in the *Journal of the Palestine Oriental Society,* vol. XV, p. 188.)
4. Sayce, *Early Israel and the Surrounding Nations,* p. 113.
5. Luke, Harry C. and Garstang, J., *Handbook of Palestine and Syria,* p. 273.
6. Genesis 32:3.
7. Sayce, *op. cit.,* p. 115.
8. Genesis 28:9.
9. Genesis 19:31-38.
10. Genesis 25:18.
11. Genesis 25:15.
12. Sayce, *op. cit.,* p. 119 and I Kings 4:30.
13. Lamentations 4:21.
14. Isaiah 21:17.
15. Jeremiah 49:28-29.
16. Genesis 37:28.
17. Exodus 18:12-23.
18. Numbers 10:29-32.
19. Genesis 14:7.
20. This claim is in agreement with Biblical account. Genesis 10:21-30 and I Chronicles 1:17-23.
21. Barton, *Archaeology and the Bible,* p. 479.
22. I Kings 9:18, 26; I Kings 22:48.
23. Clark, *The Arabs and the Turks,* p. 29.
24. *Ibid.,* p. 30.

### CHAPTER THREE

1. Genesis 37:27-36.
2. Genesis 41:39-42.
3. Genesis 45:19-28.
4. Adams, *Biblical Backgrounds,* pp. 109-11.

5. Genesis 49:33.
6. Petrie, *A Vision of the Ages*, pp. 10-13.
7. Exodus 1:22.
8. The accumulated results of topographical and archaeological researches in Egypt, Transjordania and Palestine have convinced modern scholarship that Moses was not only a dynamic personality of his day, but a journalist, a leader, and a lawgiver, of the first magnitude. (See Kyle, *Moses and the Monuments*, pp. 86-90.)
9. Exodus 2:16.
10. Exodus 15:1.
11. Exodus 15:21.

**CHAPTER FOUR**

1. Exodus 20:2-17.
2. Exodus 24:7.
3. During the last century men arose to inform the religious world that the art of writing was unknown in Moses' day; but researches in Bible lands prove conclusively that there were *many* systems of writing known and used in Palestine in the days of Moses and Joshua. Writing had long been practiced, and the peoples of all the Near Eastern countries were well versed in the art of writing upon soft moist clay and engraving inscriptions upon stone. (See Dr. Albright's statement in *American Schools of Oriental Research Bulletins* Nos. 55 and 60; also Sayce's in *The Higher Criticism and the Verdict of the Monuments*, p. 313.)
4. Exodus 32:19.
5. The record tells us that the Israelites' principal diet was "manna" which they gathered "every morning" (except on the sabbath). One says: "Manna is the name given to the honey-like substance which was exuded from the tamarisk trees so common in that district. The little drops begin to form early in the morning, and attain the size of peas before the sun's rays cause them to melt away" (Kennedy, J. M., *The Religions and Philosophies of the East*, pp. 194-95). Such an explanation is extremely misleading. There is a species of tamarisk that exudes a meager portion of sticky gum, but this has no practical food value. It is medicinal rather than nutritive, and does not meet the description of the Biblical food.
6. Numbers 13:30.
7. Numbers 20:14-21. During the spring of 1934 Dr. Nelson Glueck, then Treasurer and now Director of the American School of Oriental Research, Jerusalem, led an expedition into Edom and located the ruined forts on all four sides of the country. Dr. Glueck assigned these forts to the fourteenth century B. C., which would be a bit late for the "early date" for the Exodus, but would go well with the "late date." If the earlier dating for the Exodus proves correct, then we could well reason that these forts were built as protection soon after Israel made the conquest of Canaan. (See *Illustrated London News*, July 7, 1934, also various reports in the 1934 *Bulletins of the American School of Oriental Research*.)
8. Numbers 21:11.
9. Numbers 28:8-10; 24:10-22. Various ancient altars are to be found in this section of Moab today.
10. There is no unanimity regarding the dating of Israel's entry into Canaan. Ussher would have them leave Egypt in 1491 B. C. and cross the Jordan during the year 1451 B. C. Some say they left Egypt in the year 1446 B. C. Prof. Garstang and Sir Charles Marston, the most recent excavators at Jericho, think Joshua must have destroyed Jericho about 1400 B. C. This they base upon a detailed examination of the stratifications relating to the outer wall. Dr. Albright says: "We would date this event preferably between 1360 and 1320 —but in the fourteenth century, in any case." Others would have them enter Canaan at a later date. Archaeological material

bearing on this question is as yet *incomplete.* An excavation at Hazor and further work at Jericho, Beth-el, and Ai will aid materially in assigning an exact date. (See *Palestine Exploration Fund Quarterly,* 1932, pp. 149-150. Also Marston, *New Bible Evidence,* pp. 151-159; Albright's "Archaeology and the Date of the Hebrew Conquest of Palestine" in *American Schools of Oriental Research Bulletin* No. 58, pp. 10-18; see also *Bulletin* No. 60, p. 13.)

11. The Biblical account of the fall of Jericho has been amply verified by the recent excavations carried on first by the Germans then by Dr. Sellin, and later by Dr. Garstang, and Sir Charles Marston. These excavations disclosed five strata, representing five successive settlements. The earliest began about 2500 B. C. Beginning of the second dates from about 2000 B. C.; the third from about 1800 B. C.; the fourth began about 1600 B. C.; and the last rebuilding was by Hiel about 900 B. C. The city which began about 1600 B. C. was destroyed by a fierce fire, which occurred at a time when the harvest had been gathered and the grain bins were full. The fire also left reddened masses of brick, cracked stones, charred timbers and ashes. Houses alongside the wall were found burned to the ground, their roofs fallen upon the domestic pottery within.

    The city of Joshua's day was surrounded by two parallel walls, the outer six feet, and the inner twelve feet thick. The entire eastern wall had entirely disappeared. Investigations along the west side show continuous signs of destruction and conflagration. The outer wall suffered most, its remains falling down the slope. The inner wall is preserved only where it abuts upon the citadel or tower to a height of eighteen feet; elsewhere, it and the remains of buildings upon it was found largely to have fallen. (See Prof. Garstang's article in *Palestine Exploration Fund Quarterly,* 1932, pp. 149-152; see also Barton, *Archaeology and the Bible,* pp. 142 and 170.)

12. The obscure ruins just east of Bethel commonly known as *et-Tell,* have long been identified as Ai. Mme Judith Krause-Marquet's excavations at this site indicate that the site was unoccupied from the Early Bronze Age to Early Iron I (*i.e.,* from 2000 to 1000 B. C.) The Kyle Memorial Excavation at Bethel, conducted by Drs. Albright and Kelso, show that Bethel was thoroughly burned about the time the Hebrews made the conquest of Palestine. This has led some to believe that "Bethel" should be substituted for "Ai" in the text of Joshua 7:2-8. Or, perhaps another site will prove to be Ai.
13. Deuteronomy 27:12, 13.
14. Joshua 8:30-35; 27:11-26.
15. Joshua 10:13.
16. Joshua 24:1-27; see also *Journal of the Palestine Oriental Society,* IX, p. 7.

## CHAPTER FIVE

1. Judges 2:7-23.
2. Judges 3:8-11.
3. Judges 3:12-31.
4. See Judges 12:31. The author regrets that he is unable to give the writer of these descriptive lines.
5. Judges 4:4-5.
6. Judges 4:6.
7. Smith, *Historical Geography of the Holy Land,* p. 393.
8. Judges 4:21.
9. Judges 5.
10. Judges 6:6-8.
11. Judges 6:28.
12. Stewart, *The Land of Israel,* p. 127.
13. Smith, *op. cit.,* p. 397.
14. Judges 7:12.
15. Judges 7:13, and Smith, *op. cit.,* p. 398.
16. Judges 7:20.
17. Judges 8:10.
18. Judges 8:23.

19. Judges 9:8-15.
20. Judges 11:31.
21. Lord Byron.
22. Smith, *op. cit.*, p. 217.
23. *Ibid.*, p. 216.
24. Judges 13:24-25.
25. Sangster, *The Women of the Bible*, p. 119.
26. *Ibid*, p. 119.
27. Judges 14:18.
28. Smith, *op. cit.*, p. 217.
29. Sangster, *op. cit.*, p. 121.
30. *Ibid.*, p. 122.
31. Judges 16:21.
32. Smith, *op. cit.*, p. 217.

## CHAPTER SIX

1. I Samuel 3:11.
2. I Samuel 7:13-17.
3. I Samuel 10:23-25. In 1933 Dr. Albright found King Saul's citadel at ancient Gibeah of Saul. It was rather large with a tower at each of the four corners. See *American School of Oriental Research Bulletin* No. 52, pp. 7, 8.
4. I Samuel 17:4-11.
5. I Samuel 17:17-20.
6. I Samuel 17:28-31.
7. I Samuel 17:44-52, See also Leary, *From the Pyramids to Paul*, p. 247.
8. I Samuel 26:19-25.
9. I Samuel 28:4-6.
10. Lord Byron.
11. I Samuel 31:1-6.
12. II Samuel 1:17-27.
13. Sachar, *A History of the Jews*, p. 35.
14. Lord, *Beacon Lights of History*, Vol. I, p. 214.
15. *Ibid.*, p. 238.
16. II Samuel 11:2, 3.
17. II Samuel 11:6-27.
18. II Samuel 12:1-31.
19. II Samuel 13:1-38.
20. II Samuel 15:1-6.
21. II Samuel 18:1-33.
22. Lord, *op. cit.*, p. 239.
23. Some have insisted that *forty* thousand horses were too many, but the number is conservative in view of the fact that soon after this, Shishak I, King of Egypt, invaded Judah with an army having *sixty* thousand cavalry and twelve hundred chariots. Furthermore, the recent excavations at Megiddo (one of the chariot cities) have disclosed the stables used by Solomon to accommodate many of these horses.

## CHAPTER SEVEN

1. I Kings 10:16-27.
2. Etham is supposed by many to have been located some seven miles south of Jerusalem on the Hebron road. There are at this present time three pools commonly known as "Solomon's Pools." The upper pool is 380 feet long, 236 feet wide at the eastern end and 229 at the western, and 25 feet deep. One hundred and sixty feet from this is the middle pool, 423 feet long, 250 feet broad at the eastern end and 160 at the western, and 30 feet deep. Two hundred and forty-eight feet from the middle pool is the lower pool, 582 feet long, 207 feet wide at the eastern end and 148 at the western, and 50 feet deep. They are partly hewn out of the solid rock, and partly built of masonry. All are lined with cement; all have flights of steps from top to bottom; and all three are connected by conduits, and with Jerusalem by an aqueduct. The topography of the nearby land is such as would have easily lent itself to just such a pleasure resort as Solomon would have desired.
3. Jones, *The Empires of the Bible*, pp. 185-186.
4. I Kings 11:9-10.
5. I Kings 11:31, 34, 35, 38.
6. Authorities disagree on the exact date of Solomon's death.
7. Shechem is located forty miles north of Jerusalem. It is in the center of Palestine—midway on the highroad from Dan to Beersheba, and poised high on the watershed between the Jordan river and the Mediterranean sea.

Here Abraham built his first altar to Jehovah, here Jacob reared an altar and digged a well on his return from Padan Aram; here Joseph was buried, here the blessings and cursings of the law were pronounced, here Joshua delivered his valedictory address; here Saul's, David's and Solomon's kingships had been ratified.

8. I Kings 12:14.

## CHAPTER EIGHT

1. A few years ago an archaeological expedition, under the direction of Dr. Sellin, discovered the site of ancient Shechem, (or perhaps, the *tower* of Shechem), at Balata, a mound one mile east of Nablus. The excavation revealed four "occupational" levels; that is, four stages of its history: (I) Canaanite 2000 to 1400 B. C. with bronze weapons, small figures of the goddess Astoreth; and proofs of Babylonian, Egyptian and Hittite influence similar to that afterwards found at Beth-shan. (II) Early Israelite 1400-900 B. C. broken about 1100 by Abimelech's destruction, but the walls were rebuilt. (Judges 9:30). (III) Late Israelite 800-700 B. C. with local altars for worship. (IV) Samaritan-Hellenistic with pottery inscribed with Aramaic letters of about the fifth and sixth centuries. (See *Palestine Exploration Fund Quarterly*, 1926, p. 206; 1927, p. 54; 1929, p. 59; See also G. Adam Smith, *op. cit.*, pp. 332, 333.)
2. Archaeological evidence indicates that Jeroboam not only used Penuel as a principal outpost, but that he fled there and used the place as his capital during the invasion of Shishak. This was at the same time that Shishak captured Rehoboam's territory.
3. I Kings 12:27. A beautiful jasper seal, known as "The Megiddo Seal," was found in the excavation at Megiddo, inscribed,

   *Belonging to Shema,*
   *officer of Jeroboam.*

   It is not yet made plain if the Jeroboam referred to is Jeroboam I who first ruled Israel after the division, or the wealthy Jeroboam II, in whose reign Amos prophesied about 755 B. C. But the evidence favors the latter. The seal is valued at $10,000. (See Albright's *Archaeology of Palestine and the Bible,* p. 30.)
4. I Kings 12:28; II Kings 17:16.
5. Hosea 2:13.
6. Hosea 13:2. Bowing down to a false god seemed to carry with it the practice of kissing the god or statue, as indicated in God's word to Elijah, "Yet I have left me seven thousand in Israel, all the knees of which have not bowed unto Baal, and every mouth which hath not *kissed him.*" I Kings 19:18
7. When Israel worshipped the golden calf at the foot of Mt. Sinai the record states that after the sacrifice was made "the people sat down to eat and to drink, and rose up to play" (Exodus 32:6) and their "playing" even degenerated into dancing, licentiousness and nudity (Exodus 32:9, 25.) There is reason to believe that they went farther into wrong at Bethel and Dan.
8. Under the direction of such men as Drs. Reisner, Fisher and Crowfoot, archaeological campaigns have been carried on at the mound of ancient Samaria. These excavations revealed no remains of a city before Omri's day, but laid bare the foundations of Omri's and Ahab's palaces, the ivory-ceiled palaces of Amos' day, and the senate and forum constructed by Herod the Great. (See *Palestine Exploration Fund Quarterly*, July, 1931.)
9. See Barton, *op. cit.*, p. 421, and Smith, *op. cit.*, p. 507, and II Kings 3:4-5.
10. Robinson, *Palestine in General History,* p. 33.
11. I Kings 16:33.
12. Joshua 6:26.
13. I Kings 16:34.
14. I Kings 20:34-43.
15. I Kings 21:1-14.
16. I Kings 21:19-23.
17. The Moabite Stone is a memorial pillar of black basalt three

and one-half by two feet wide, erected by Mesha, King of Moab, informing the world about the events of his reign. The inscription consists of thirty-four lines, and recounts how Mesha wrested back the cities of Medeba, Nebo and Jahaz, which Omri and his son Ahab had formerly taken from Moab. This stele was erected and dedicated by Mesha to his god Kemosh about 850 B. C. and was discovered in 1868 at Dibon, Transjordan, by Rev. F. A. Klien. It is now in the Louvre in Paris.

18. II Kings 9:30-37.
19. Harold M. Wiener, *Journal Palestine Oriental Society*, Vol. 8, p. 182; Robinson, *op. cit.*, p. 33.
20. *Ibid.*, p. 33.
21. *Ibid.*, p. 34.
22. Compare *Ibid.*, p. 35 and Sachar, *A History of the Jews*, p. 54.
23. The site of the ancient village of Tekoa is located twelve miles south of the city of Jerusalem. It is perched high up on the crest of a hill within the edge of the wilderness of Judea. The scenery is inspiring, but the place is so exposed as to receive the wind's worst blasts and the sun's hottest rays. The environment common to this section of Palestine had much to do with shaping the character of the inspired herdsman.
24. Remains of these ivory-ceiled houses have been uncovered at Samaria in the recent excavations conducted by Dr. Crowfoot of the British School of Archaeology. (See *Palestine Exploration Fund Quarterly*, 1931, pp. 139-142; 1932, pp. 63-70; 132-137; 1933, pp. 7-26. Also Albright, *Archaeology of Palestine and the Bible*, p. 225.)
25. Amos 2:8 and Exodus 22:26.
26. Quoted from Goldsmith's "Deserted Village."
27. Amos 1:2.
28. Amos Chapters 2-5.
29. Exodus 22:26.
30. Leviticus 19:35-36.
31. Amos 8:5.
32. Amos 7:12, 13.
33. Amos 7:14, 15.
34. The usual estimate given for one thousand Hebrew talents is about $1,750,000.00.
35. Hosea 1:5.
36. Hosea 2:14.
37. Hosea 4:17.
38. Hosea 6:4.
39. Hosea 7:8-11.
40. Hosea 11:1-4.
41. Hosea 13:9.
42. Hosea 14:1, 2, 4, 5, 7, 8.
43. Hosea 11:8.
44. Hosea 12:1 and II Kings 17:4.
45. II Kings 17:1-6.
46. This cylinder was discovered by Mr. Layard in the year 1890, and is now in the British Museum. This translation from Barton, *op. cit.*, p. 465. Sargon was King of Assyria from 722 to 705 B. C. His first residence was at Ashur, his second at Calah, his third at Nineveh, and his fourth in the great palace at Khorsbad, ten miles north of Nineveh. Sennacherib, his son, was his successor on the throne of Assyria.

## CHAPTER NINE

1. Jeremiah 41:5.
2. II Kings 17:24. Also see Josephus, *Antiquities of the Jews*, IX, 14.
3. Adams, *Biblical Backgrounds*, p. 284.
4. II Kings 17:25-39, and Josephus, *op. cit.*, IX. 14:3. Ezra 4:9-10.
5. II Kings 23:19 and II Chronicles 34:6.
6. Ezra 4:1-7.
7. Josephus, *op. cit.*, IX. 14:3 and XI. 8:6.
8. Ezra 4:2 and Josephus, *op. cit.*, XI. 4:3, 9 and XII. 5:5.
9. John 4:20.
10. Josephus, *op. cit.*, XII. 1:1.
11. *Ibid.*, XIII. 11:1-4.
12. Sachar, *A History of the Jews*, p. 105.
13. John 4:9, John 8:48, also Josephus, *op. cit.*, XX. 6:1.
14. Luke 17:16.

15. Luke 10:30-37.
16. Josephus, *op. cit.*, XVIII. 4:1-3.
17. Josephus, *Wars of the Jews*, III. 6:32.
18. Khadder, *Palestine Annual*, 1925, p. 38.
19. *Ibid.*, p. 39.

## CHAPTER TEN

1. These defense cities were Bethlehem, Tekoa, Adullam, Ziph, Etom, Bethzur, Hebron, Shoco, Gath, Mareshah, Adoraim, Lachish, Azeka, Zorah, and Aijalon.
2. II Chronicles 11:13-14.
3. II Chronicles 12:1.
4. II Chronicles 12:9-11, I Kings 14:25-28. There is an inscription at Karnak in which Shishak (Sheshonk) enumerates the cities he took and spoiled. (See Breasted, *A History of the Ancient Egyptians*, p. 362.)
5. II Chronicles 21:16-20.
6. II Chronicles 22:11.
7. II Chronicles 23:11.
8. II Kings 11:18, 20.
9. II Chronicles 24:17-22.
10. II Chronicles 24:25.
11. Knott, *Students' History of the Hebrews*, p. 231.
12. Isaiah 3:16-24.
13. II Kings 18:4; II Chronicles 31:1.
14. II Kings 18:14, Sachar, *op. cit.*, p. 56.
15. II Kings 19:21-23, 32-33.
16. The Assyrian account of this campaign informs us that Hezekiah, the Jew, was shut up "like a caged bird" in Jerusalem, but indicates retreat without decisive victory. (See Luckenbill's, *The Annals of Sennacherib*, p. 70.) Herodotus tells a story of field mice who gnawed at the military equipment of the Assyrians and rendered it useless, others hint at a fearful bubonic plague, but the Biblical account attributes it to the might of Jehovah manifest in answer to prayer.

    We are told that some years ago three travelers in England looked with interest on a stranger who entered their compartment just as the train was leaving one of the stations. A bag and sword-case indicated that he was a military man. Said one of them: "I am glad you have joined us, for we have been warmly discussing the comparative merits of Napoleon and Wellington. We should like your opinion as a military man as to which of these was the greater general strategically. We are of the opinion that Wellington was the greater."

    With considerable skill and graciousness, the military man brought forth convincing proof that strategically Napoleon held the first place. "Ah! then, who won Waterloo?" was the rejoinder.

    Reverently the man of arms replied, *"God won Waterloo!"*
17. Sachar, *A History of the Jews*, p. 71.
18. *Ibid.*, p. 71.
19. *Ibid.*, p. 72. See also II Kings 23:1-25.
20. II Kings 23:3-20.
21. Deuteronomy 6:4-5.
22. II Kings 23:29.
23. Jeremiah 5:1.
24. Jeremiah 5:4.
25. Sachar *op. cit.*, p. 74.
26. Jeremiah 36:23.
27. Sachar, *op. cit.*, p. 75; Lachish (Tell Duweir) stands on one of the foothills in the Shephela of Judea which rises gradually from the coastal plain. In ancient times it commanded the road that led from Gaza eastward to Hebron. Here Sennacherib received the deputation from King Hezekiah in Jerusalem. In 1859 Sir Henry Layard discovered, in the palace of Sennacherib at Nineveh, a relief which portrayed the siege of Lachish. This relief, which is now in the British Museum, shows the spearmen with their crested helmets, the Assyrian slingers and bowmen storming the city. The Jewish chiefs, with their curled hair, are shown humiliated before the king.

In March of 1935 Mr. J. L. Starkey discovered eighteen four-inch square pottery letters written with ink in pure Biblical Hebrew just like that previously found in the Siloam tunnel, and certainly like that used by Baruch, the private secretary of Jeremiah (Jeremiah 36:18), and like the letter delivered to Hezekiah after the departure of Sennacherib.

This find convinces many that our Scriptures were not always transmitted orally, but at least much of them in writing. Dr. Albright says it is hard to exaggerate their importance. (See *The Fortnightly Review*, September, 1935; also Miller's, *Footsteps in Palestine*, pp. 147-149.)

28. Jeremiah 28:10.
29. Sachar, *op. cit.*, p. 60.
30. Jeremiah 37:16-21.
31. Jeremiah 38:4-28.
32. Jeremiah 39:4-7.
33. Jeremiah 39:8-10.
34. Jeremiah 40:4.
35. Adams, *Biblical Backgrounds*, p. 256.
36. Lamentations 1:1; 12:2-15.

## CHAPTER ELEVEN

1. Adams, *Biblical Backgrounds*, p. 280.
2. Psalms 137:1-2.
3. Lord Byron.
4. Psalms 137:4-6.
5. II Kings 25:27-30.
6. Rohold, *Babylon and Its Jews*, p. 11.
7. Sachar, *A History of the Jews*, p. 79.
8. Ezekiel 1:3.
9. Sachar, *op. cit.*, p. 80; see also Ezekiel 36:25-38.

## CHAPTER TWELVE

1. Ezra 1:2-4.
2. Ezra 1:7.
3. Psalms 126:1-3.
4. Josephus, *Antiquities of the Jews*, XI. 1:4, and Ezra 2:64.
5. Josephus, *op. cit.*, XI. 1:3.
6. *Ibid.*, XI. 1:3. Josephus says that the number of the sacred vessels restored were as follows: 50 chargers of gold, and 500 of silver; 40 thericlean cups of gold, and 500 of silver; 50 basens of gold, and 500 of silver; 30 vessels of gold for pouring the drink offerings, and 300 of silver; 30 vials of gold, and 2400 of silver; with 1000 other large vessels. Also see Ezra 1:11.
7. Latimer, *Judea from Cyrus to Titus*, p. 29; see also Ezra 3:3-5.
8. Ezra 3:7.
9. Ezra 4:2.
10. Ezra 4:5.
11. Ezra 4:21.
12. Ezra 4:23.
13. Josephus, *op. cit.*, XI. 3:1.
14. Ezra 6:8.
15. Sachar, *A History of the Jews*, p. 86.
16. Ezra 9:3.
17. Latimer, *op. cit.*, p. 46; Dr. J. L. Kelso of Pittsburgh-Zenia Theological Seminary does not think that the temple was burned, or else it would have been mentioned in the Bible.
18. Nehemiah 1:3.
19. Nehemiah 2:3.
20. Nehemiah 2:10.
21. Nehemiah 2:13-18.
22. Sachar, *A History of the Jews*, *op. cit.*, p. 87.
23. *Ibid.*, p. 87.
24. Nehemiah 4:2.
25. Albright, *Archaeology of Palestine and the Bible*, p. 171.
26. Nehemiah 4:3.
27. Smith, *Historical Geography of the Holy Land*, p. 248.
28. Nehemiah 6:3.
29. Nehemiah 5:8.
30. Nehemiah 5:11-19.
31. Nehemiah 8:8.
32. Nehemiah 8:16.
33. Nehemiah 12:27-43.
34. Nehemiah 13:15-22.
35. Nehemiah 13:23-31.

**CHAPTER THIRTEEN**

1. Mathews, *The Riddle of Nearer Asia,* p. 60-61.
2. *Ibid.,* p. 62.
3. Hunkin, *Palestine in General History,* p. 61.
4. "Greece" was the name given by the Romans to the conquered land of Hellas, because they first came in contact with the tribe of *Graeci,* but the classical Greeks referred to themselves as "Hellenes," and to their culture as "Hellenism."
5. Mathews, *op. cit.,* p. 62.
6. Adams, *Biblical Backgrounds,* p. 301; Schurer, *A History of the Jewish People,* Vol. I. p. 195.
7. Hunkin, *op. cit.,* p. 62.
8. The "Sanhedrin" was for a long while known as the Council, and our first mention of it under the title of Sanhedrin is to be found in Josephus, *Antiquities,* XIV. 9:3.
9. *Ibid.,* XII. 3:3.
10. This was Ptolemy V, who was then but a boy twelve years of age.
11. Adams, *op. cit.,* p. 303; Schurer, *loc. cit.,* p. 196.
12. *Ibid.,* p. 302.
13. Kittell, *Great Men and Movements in Israel,* p. 433; Bentwich, *Hellenism,* p. 86.
14. *Ibid.,* p. 57.
15. This is the essence of Matthew Arnold's words regarding the two peoples, as quoted by Bentwich in his *Hellenism,* p. 88.
16. Exodus 20:26.
17. Sachar, *A History of the Jews,* p. 100.
18. Hunkin, *op. cit.,* p. 69.
19. Bentwich, *op. cit.,* p. 198.
20. Schurer, *op. cit.,* p. 198.
21. Sachar, *op. cit.,* p. 101.
22. Kittell, *op. cit.,* p. 433.
23. I Maccabees 1:11-14; Josephus, *op. cit.,* XII. 5:1; Schurer, *op. cit.,* p. 202.
24. II Maccabees 4:7-10.
25. I Maccabees 1:14-15; Schurer, *op. cit.,* p. 203.
26. I Maccabees 1:15.
27. II Maccabees 4:46-47.
28. II Maccabees 4:50.
29. I Maccabees 1:22-24; Schurer, *op. cit.,* p. 205.
30. I Maccabees 1:51.
31. II Maccabees 5:24.
32. Schurer, *op. cit.,* pp. 206-208.
33. I Maccabees 1:38.
34. Kittell, *op. cit.,* p. 438.
35. II Maccabees 6:10.
36. II Maccabees 6:18-31.

**CHAPTER FOURTEEN**

1. I Maccabees 2:7-14.
2. *Ibid.,* 2:19, 20.
3. *Ibid.,* 2:27.
4. Sachar, *A History of the Jews,* p. 103.
5. Moses, *Yahvism,* p. 247.
6. I Maccabees 2:64-68.
7. The name "Maccabeus" was a surname for Judas, and whatever it may have meant, it was later applied to the entire family —perhaps for the reason that Judas Maccabeus was the leading spirit of the movement for so long a time.
8. I Maccabees 3:18-22.
9. I Maccabees 3:27; 4:25.
10. Sellers, *The Citadel of Beth-zur,* p. 10; Schurer, *op. cit.,* p. 216.
11. I Maccabees 4:42-46; Gregg, *Between the Testaments,* p. 170.
12. The anniversary of this event continues to be celebrated in every Jewish home as the Festival of Rededication or, as they call it, "Hanukkah." The use of many lights at this feast has caused it sometimes to be called the "*Feast of Lights.*" Compare: I Maccabees 4:36-59; II Maccabees 10:1-8; Josephus, *Antiquities,* XII. 7:7; and John 10:22.
13. Schurer, *A History of the Jewish People,* Vol. I., p. 219.
14. Riggs, *A History of the Jewish People,* p. 41.
15. *Ibid.,* p. 43.
16. Schurer, *op. cit.,* p. 227.
17. I Maccabees 8:39-50; Schurer, *op. cit.,* p. 229.

18. Hunkin, *Palestine in General History*, p. 72.
19. Josephus, *op. cit.*, XII. 11:2. The Battle of Eleasa, in which Judas perished, was fought near Beth-Horon. See also I Maccabees 9:5-6.
20. Riggs, *op. cit.*, p. 57.
21. I Maccabees 13:12-30.
22. Riggs, *op. cit.*, p. 71.
23. The American School of Oriental Research of Jerusalem, in collaboration with the Presbyterian Theological Seminary of Chicago, recently excavated Beth-zur with Prof. O. R. Sellers as director and Dr. W. F. Albright as archaeological advisor. Strata belonging to the Middle Bronze, Early Iron I (period of the Judges), Early Iron II (Period of Monarchy), and to the Persian-Hellenistic ages were examined over a considerable area of the site. Most remarkable were the remains of the Maccabean age, including a great fortress which had been built and destroyed three times during the time of Judas, Jonathan and Simon. No fewer than 126 coins of Antiochus Epiphanes, "the redoubtable opponent of Judas" were discovered. (See Albright's *Archaeology of Palestine and the Bible*, p. 227, and Sellers, *op. cit.*, pp. 9-13; 69-71.)
24. I Maccabees 14:41.
25. I Maccabees 14:8-15.

## CHAPTER FIFTEEN

1. Hunkin, *op. cit.*, p. 74.
2. Josephus, *Antiquities*, XIII. 10:-2-3.
3. Hunkin, *Palestine in General History*, p. 74.
4. Josephus, *op. cit.*, XIII. 11:1-3, also Riggs, *A History of the Jewish People*, p. 118.
5. Riggs, *op. cit.*, p. 118.
6. *Ibid.*, p. 124.
7. Josephus, *op. cit.*, XIII. 14:2.
8. Latimer, *Judea from Cyrus to Titus*, p. 195.
9. Sachar, *A History of the Jews*, p. 107.
10. Josephus, *op. cit.*, XIV, 3:2.

## CHAPTER SIXTEEN

1. Herod became governor of Galilee about forty-five years before the birth of Jesus. It is generally believed that Joseph of Nazareth was but a baby boy, and that Mary, the mother of Jesus, had not yet been born.
2. Squires, W. H. T., *Peregrine Papers*, p. 101.
3. *Ibid.*, p. 103.
4. The object in disfiguring Hyrcanus seems to have been to disqualify him for the office of high priest; for the Jewish law decreed that no one should hold the office of high priest who was not physically whole.
5. Masada was a strong fortress built upon a rocky promontory which, like a miniature Gibraltar, towers above the western shores of the Dead Sea. Later it was to be used as the last stronghold of the Jews. Today its ladder-like approach is so difficult that few ever succeed in reaching its summit.
6. Sachar, *A History of the Jews*, p. 113.
7. Herod had divorced Doris, his former wife in order to make his appeal to Mariamne, the Jewess of royal birth, who was considered the most beautiful woman in all Judea.
8. Squires, *op. cit.*, p. 106.
9. Josephus, *Wars of the Jews*, I. 18:3.
10. Squires, *op. cit.*, p. 110.
11. *Ibid.*, p. 110.
12. Squires, *op. cit.*, p. 112.
13. *Ibid.*, p. 113.
14. Josephus, *Antiquities*, XV. 7:2-6.
15. Squires, *op. cit.*, p. 114.
16. Lord Byron.
17. Josephus, *op. cit.*, XV. 11:2.
18. The guides of today show these as "Solomon's stables"; and perhaps they were often used as stables, especially in the days when the Crusaders occupied Jerusalem.
19. John 2:20.
20. Josephus, *Wars*, V. 5:6.
21. We fear that modern men who attempt to cheapen the temple

structure only reflect their lack of knowledge respecting the subject.

22. Josephus, *Antiquities,* XVI. 4:-1-4.
23. The younger of the brothers left a daughter named Herodias. She married her own half-uncle, Herod Philip, but later became infatuated with Herod Antipas, his brother, and married him. John the Baptist condemned Herod for marrying his brother's wife. She resented the interference, and through Salome, her dancing daughter, brought about the murder of the fearless prophet.
24. Josephus, *Wars,* I. 22:5.
25. The "Parsees" of Western India are descendants of the ancient Persians, and claim that from among their number the "wise men" journeyed to Jerusalem at the appearing of the unusual star nineteen centuries ago.

### CHAPTER SEVENTEEN

1. Hodges, *The Early Church,* p. 1.
2. Tacitus, *Annals,* III, p. 48.
3. Luke 3:1. This fifteenth year is usually reckoned as being about 27 A. D.
4. The "locusts" of Palestine are very similar to the grasshoppers of America. The poorer people of Arabia frequently broil or boil and eat them. Few people of Palestine eat the locust at this present time.
5. Grandmaison, *Jesus Christ,* Vol. II, pp. 3, 4.
6. Hodges, *loc. cit.,* p. 1.
7. Matthew 3:11.
8. Grandmaison, *loc. cit.,* Vol. II p. 6.
9. John 1:29.
10. Matthew 3:15.
11. Milton, *Paradise Regained,* IV. 2, p. 437.
12. John 1:39.
13. Sharp, *Christ and His Times,* pp. 74-76.
14. Sachar, *A History of the Jews,* p. 128; Sharp, *loc. cit.,* p. 82.
15. Mark 16:20.
16. When beginning a journey to Rome, Herod Antipas visited the home of his brother Philip and while there became fascinated with Herodias, his brother's wife. Yielding to the fascination he proposed marriage to which Herodias gave assent. It was arranged that Herodias should secure a divorce from Philip, and that on Herod's return from Rome he should divorce his wife, the daughter of Aretas of Arabia, and should be married to Herodias. With this promise he proceeded on his journey to Rome. On his return his wife (the Arabian princess), who had meanwhile obtained information about the proposed procedure, asked that she be permitted to go to the palace fortress at Machaerus, near the hot mineral Springs east of the Dead Sea, where Herod the Great had often bathed. Antipas granted her request. But she had scarcely arrived at Machaerus when by the aid of her servants she fled to her father in Arabia and informed him of the unjust intentions of her husband. Aretas resented such a gross injustice toward his daughter, and from that time became an enemy of Herod Antipas, his former son-in-law. (Compare Schurer's *History of the Jews,* Vol. II, part I, p. 22, 23; Josephus, *Antiquities,* XVIII, 5:1; Renan, *Life of Jesus,* p. 157.)
17. Schurer, *op. cit.,* Vol. II. pt. I. p. 26.
18. Matthew 14:3-12. Mark 6:17-28; Luke 3:19, 20; Schurer, *op. cit.,* Vol. I, pt. two, p. 28; Papini, *The Story of Christ,* p. 55.
19. Matthew 4:17: Mark 1:15.
20. Matthew 14:2.
21. Luke 13:31-33; Schurer, *op. cit.,* p. 29, 30.
22. Woodrum, "The Campus Camera," Dec. 10, 1936.
23. Boaz, *The Great Question,* Rice Institute Pamphlet, Vol. XX, No. 4, p. 362.
24. To Victor Hugo goes the credit for having first given utterance to this thought.

25. Glover, *Influence of Christ in the Ancient World*, p. 112. Boaz, *loc. cit.*, pp. 360, 362.
26. Clark, *Christ and the Young People*, p. 17; Grandmaison, *loc. cit.*, p. 185.
27. Jones, *The Christ of Every Road*, pp. 62, 63, 68.
28. Glover, *op. cit.*, p. 87.
29. Morrison, *Christ in Shakespeare*, p. 50.
30. Glover, *op. cit.*, p. 114; Matthew 7:29; John 7:46; Luke 12:13-21.
31. Glover, *op. cit.*, pp. 10, 34.
32. *Ibid.*, p. 36.
33. Lamont, *Christ and the World of Thought*, p. 153.
34. Isaiah 61:1-3; Deuteronomy 18: 15-19; Jeremiah 23:5, 6; Micah 5:2.
35. Sachar, *op. cit.*, p. 129.
36. John 1:11, 12.
37. See a sermon by Rev. Dr. A. Guttmacher, Rabbi of a Baltimore Hebrew Congregation; reported in the *Baltimore Sunday Herald*, June 12, 1898.
38. *Christian Century*, Vol. 50, p. 1103.
39. Matthew 17:1-13; Mark 9:2-13.
40. John 11; 12:1.
41. Luke 19:1-10.
42. Clow, *The Secret of the Lord*, pp. 329, 330.
43. Luke 19:37-39.
44. Matthew 23:37; Luke 13:34.
45. Matthew 26:14-16; Mark 14:10, 11; Luke 22:1-6; John 13:18.
46. John Chapters 14-17.
47. Nevinson, *In the Dark Backwards*, p. 81.
48. See Morison's *A Lawyer Looks at the Crucifixion of Christ.*
49. Sachar, *op. cit.*, p. 132.
50. Some have been so *very* unkind as to speak of the Jewish people as "Christ killers," but a fair-minded person will not be guilty of such an accusation, for the Jewish people of today had nothing to do with the crucifixion of Jesus Christ. And even in that distant day the Jews *condemned* and *delivered* Him, while the Gentiles *scourged* and *crucified* Him. Both had part and both were in Christ's thought when He said, "Father, forgive them for they know not what they do."
51. Matthew 27:3-10.
52. Luke 23:6-11.
53. Broun, *loc. cit.*, p. 711.
54. John 18:38.
55. Broun, *loc. cit.*, p. 711.
56. *Ibid.*, p. 711.
57. Belloc, *The Battleground*, p. 219; From ancient times the law prescribed a washing of the hands when a person was innocent of the blood of another who had been slain, (Deuteronomy 21:1-9). Furthermore, the custom is to wash under *running* water to insure absolute cleansing. Therefore, it is almost certain that Pilate had water *poured* on his hands, rather than wash them *in* a bowl, as the average westerner supposes he washed.
58. Broun, *op. cit.*, p. 711; Pilate was unknown to historians before his arrival in Judea in the year 26 A.D. to take up the duties of procurator (Lieutenant-Governor). Within a short time he succeeded in gaining the bitter hatred of his subjects. However, all information concerning him comes from Jewish or Christian sources. But in 36 A.D. Lucius Vitellius sent him to Rome to answer charges against himself before Tiberius. The emperor died before Pilate arrived, but according to ancient tradition, Caligula sent him into exile in Gaul, where he committed suicide.
59. John 19:19-22.
60. Goodspeed, *Palestine, The Fifth Gospel.*
61. Boaz, *op. cit.*, p. 364.
62. Nevinson, *op. cit.*, p. 78.
63. Boaz, *op. cit.*, p. 357.


## CHAPTER EIGHTEEN


1. Eusebius, *Ecclesiastical History*, Vol. II, p. 7.
2. Through all these changes his brother, Herod Antipas (own son of Herod the Great) remained

tetrarch of Galilee, and it was to him that Pilate sent Jesus.

3. Acts 12:23.
4. Claudius afterward conferred Trachonitis and Abilene, to which a part of Galilee was added, upon young Agrippa before whom Paul afterward spoke at Caesarea.
5. Josephus, *Wars*, II. 18:10-11; 9:1.
6. The Christians fled to Pella, a city across the Jordan river, where their lives were preserved. This is supposed to have been the "flight from Jerusalem" of which Christ had prophesied. (Matthew 24:20-22.)
7. Latimer, *Judea from Cyrus to Titus*, p. 330.
8. Josephus, *Wars*, IV. 11:5.
9. Sachar, *History of the Jews*, p. 119.
10. Josephus, *op. cit.*, V. 11:2-4.
11. Sachar, *op. cit.*, p. 119.
12. Josephus, *op. cit.*, VI. 3:4.
13. Bishop Heber of Calcutta, India.
14. Graetz, *History of the Jews*, p. 307; Josephus, *op. cit.*, VI. 4:7; Knight, *The Arch of Titus*, p. 45-46.
15. Josephus, *op. cit.*, VI. 4-5.
16. Latimer, *op. cit.*, p. 358.

### CHAPTER NINETEEN

1. Leviticus 26:33.
2. Genesis 37:28.
3. Ruth 1:2.
4. I Samuel 22:4.
5. Adams, *Biblical Backgrounds*, p. 79.
6. Jeremiah 42:14 and 43:7.
7. Jeremiah 44:17.
8. Josephus, *Antiquities*, XII, 3:1.
9. *Ibid.*, XIII. 3; also Josephus, *Wars*, VII, 10.
10. The site of this temple is about twenty miles north of Cairo and is now known as Tel el-Yehudiyeh, or the "Tell of the Jewess." This mound was excavated by Dr. Petrie in 1905-1906. He found remains of the Jewish temple, which fully confirmed the statements of Josephus. He also found the remains of a Jewish settlement resembling the city of Jerusalem in its relation to the temple. He discovered a series of ovens for the roasting of Paschal lambs, and evidence that led him to believe that Jews came in large numbers from various places in Egypt to attend the annual Passover Feast. (See Petrie, *Hyksos and the Israelite Cities*, p. 191.)
11. *Jewish Encyclopedia*, Vol. IV. p. 560-561.
12. Barton, *Archaeology and the Bible*, p. 559.
13. *Ibid.*, p. 560.
14. Josephus, *Antiquities*, XII, 1:1; 2:1-3.
15. Tacitus, *Annals*, II, p. 85.
16. Josephus, *Antiquities*, XII, 3:6.
17. Requoted from Gregg, *Between the Testaments*, pp. 40-41.
18. Philo, *Works*, Vol. IV, p. 70.
19. Graetz, *History of the Jews*, p. 201.
20. James 1:1.
21. Raffaeli, *Journal of the Palestine Oriental Society*, Vol. III, No. 4, pp. 193-196.
22. *Ibid.* Here will be found a discussion of the other view in regard to the dating of the rebuilding of Jerusalem.
23. Numbers 24:17.
24. Giekie, *Holy Land and the Bible*, Vol. I, pp. 91-92; Vol. II, pp. 136-137.
25. Lord Byron.

### CHAPTER TWENTY

1. Smith, *Dictionary of Christian Antiquities*, Vol. I, p. 744.
2. It was claimed that a temple dedicated to Venus stood on this spot when Helena found it, but the claim has been left without adequate proof.
3. Smith, *op. cit.*, p. 744.
4. See Merrell, *Jerusalem*, p. 325.
5. Rappoport, *History of Palestine*, p. 262.
6. Compare Rappoport, *op. cit.*, p. 263.

7. Besant and Palmer, *Jerusalem*, p. 127.
8. Biggs, *Six Months in Jerusalem*, p. 215.
9. Rappoport, *op. cit.*, p. 257.
10. Besant and Palmer, *op. cit.*, p. 124.

**CHAPTER TWENTY-ONE**

1. Gibbon, *The Decline and Fall of the Roman Empire*, Vol. V. p. 401.
2. Clark, *Christ and the Young People*, p. 14.
3. Lodge, *History of the Nations*, p. 260.
4. The Persians mustered one hundred and twenty thousand soldiers and went against the invading Arabs, who had pitched their camp in the plain of Cadasia. The well-trained cavalry and archers of the Arabs depended largely on single combats, as they had done when fighting under Mohammed himself. On the fourth day a seasonable whirlwind drove a cloud of dust against the Persians; the Arabs taking advantage of the occasion, rushed in and began the slaughter. The clangor of arms reached to the tent of Rustum, the general of the Persian host, who was reclining in a cool and tranquil shade amid the baggage of his camp and the train of mules that was laden with gold and silver. On the sound of danger he started from his couch but was overtaken by a valiant Arab, who caught him by the foot and struck off his head, hoisted it on a lance, and instantly returned to the field of battle, carrying slaughter and dismay among the thickest ranks of the Persians.

   The standard of the Persian monarchy was overthrown and captured in the field. The battle of *Cadasia* was won and the Arabs advanced with victorious tread, for the morale of the Persians was destroyed by the belief that the last day of their religion and empire was at hand. And so it seemed, for the king with a part of his family fled from the country, while the Arabs took the capital by assault, shouting as they advanced: "This is the white palace of Chosroes; this is the promise of the Apostle of God." Thus did they conquer the Persian king and scatter his forces and take possession of his inheritance. (See Gibbon, *op. cit.*, pp. 405-7.)
5. *Ibid.*, Vol. V. p. 415.
6. *Ibid.*, Vol. V. p. 416.
7. *Ibid.*, Vol. V. p. 418-9
8. *Ibid.*, Vol. V. p. 422.
9. Lodge, *op. cit.*, Vol. I, p. 275, and Gibbon, *op. cit.*, p. 425.
10. *Ibid.*, p. 425.
11. *Ibid.*, p. 434.
12. Lodge, *op. cit.*, p. 282.
13. Gibbon, *op. cit.*, p. 436.
14. In those days (637 A.D.) mosques were usually built of wood and sun-dried bricks. Therefore, the building erected in Omar's day probably stood only about half a century, to be replaced about the year 690 A.D. by the present splendid structure — the Dome of the Rock — which is often called "The Mosque of Omar." See LeStrange, *Palestine Under the Moslems*, pp. 90-92.
15. Gibbon, *op. cit.*, p. 438.
16. *Ibid.*, p. 438.
17. Rappoport, *History of Palestine*, p. 252.
18. Lodge, *op. cit.*, p. 305.
19. See Newhall, *The Crusades*, p. 87.

**CHAPTER TWENTY-TWO**

1. Munro and Sontag, *The Middle Ages*, p. 243; Mombert, *A Short History of the Crusades*, p. 7.
2. The first striking example of Moslem finery filtering into Europe and influencing the Christians was in the days of Charlemagne (742-814), to whom Haraun al Rashid sent as presents: an elephant, a magnificent tent, costly silken garments, perfumes, balsam, two great brass candelabra, and a brass waterclock constructed with much mechanical

ingenuity. (See Munro and Sontag, *op. cit.*, p. 225.)
3. Newhall, *The Crusades*, pp. 27-28.
4. Archer and Kingsford, *The Crusades*, p. 21; Ridpath, *History of the World*, Vol. IV. p. 664.
5. Newhall, *op. cit.*, pp. 29-30.
6. Munro and Sontag, *op. cit.*, p. 243.
7. Cust, *Jerusalem, A Historical Sketch*, p. 162.
8. Much of the early life of Peter the Hermit is traditional. In fact, Dr. Munro and others question his having made a pilgrimage to Jerusalem, or having had much to do with the Crusades. Nevertheless, there is little in the traditional story of the Hermit that may not very well be true. His inferiority complex would have suggested just such a course, and he was in a proper position to have carried out the details. Often the first inspiration for great movements has come from some individual unencumbered by official duties. The story as it stands is both possible and probable.
9. Ridpath, *op. cit.*, p. 667.
10. The "Peace of God" and the "Truce of God" were movements inaugurated by the church to increase man's respect for the sacred things of the spiritual realm, and to increase the prestige and authority of the church.
11. Mombert, *op. cit.*, p. 26.
12. Newhall, *op. cit.*, p. 37; Munro and Sontag, *op. cit.*, p. 243. Ridpath, *op. cit.*, p. 668; Archer and Kingsford, *op. cit.*, pp. 28-31; Cox, *The Crusades*, pp. 29-31.

**CHAPTER TWENTY-THREE**

1. Archer and Kingsford, *The Crusades*, p. 35.
2. Ridpath, *History of the World*, Vol. IV. p. 670.
3. Archer and Kingsford, *op. cit.*, p. 37.
4. Ridpath, *op. cit.*, p. 670.
5. Archer and Kingsford, *op. cit.*, pp. 37-38.
6. Ridpath, *op. cit.*, p. 672.
7. Almost all records indicate that this rabble did in reality accept a *goat* and *goose* as the divinely appointed agents to lead them, but some have supposed they merely adopted banners on which, as symbols of the mysterious faith of Gnostics and Paulicians, the likeness of a goat and a goose were painted.
8. Mombert, *A Short History of the Crusades*, p. 42.
9. Ridpath, *op. cit.*, p. 672.
10. Archer and Kingsford, *op. cit.*, p. 42.
11. Robert of Normandy and William Rufus were sons of William the Conqueror.
12. Mombert, *op. cit.*, p. 46.
13. Ridpath, *op. cit.*, p. 675.
14. *Ibid.*, p. 677.
15. Mombert, *op. cit.*, p. 49.
16. Ridpath, *op. cit.*, p. 679.
17. Archer and Kingsford, *op. cit.*, p. 47.
18. Archer and Kingsford, *op. cit.*, p. 45.
19. This is the estimate as given by Baldwin's chaplain, which is usually regarded as an exaggeration. One hundred and fifty thousand is considered a fair estimate of both knights and foot-soldiers, but the exact number of the Crusaders is very uncertain. The chronicles of those days had a better basis for a proper estimate than ours of today.
20. Ridpath, *op. cit.*, p. 682.
21. Mombert, *op. cit.*, p. 52.
22. Archer and Kingsford, *op. cit.*, p. 55; Ridpath, *op. cit.*, p. 682.
23. Archer and Kingsford, *op. cit.*, p. 55.
24. Ridpath, *op. cit.*, p. 683; Archer and Kingsford, *op. cit.*, p. 57; Mombert, *op. cit.*, p. 55.
25. Ridpath, *op. cit.*, p. 683.
26. Mombert, *op. cit.*, p. 57.
27. Mombert, *op. cit.*, p. 57.
28. Ridpath, *op. cit.*, p. 685; Archer and Kingsford, *op. cit.*, p. 58.
29. Mombert, *op. cit.*, p. 58.
30. Archer and Kingsford, *op. cit.*, pp. 60-63.

31. Mombert, *op. cit.*, p. 60.
32. Archer and Kingsford, *op. cit.*, p. 67.
33. Ridpath, *op. cit.*, p. 687.
34. Archer and Kingsford, *op. cit.*, p. 69.
35. Ridpath, *op. cit.*, p. 689.
36. Archer and Kingsford, *op. cit.*, pp. 73-74.
37. Ridpath, *op. cit.*, p. 689.
38. Mombert, *op. cit.*, p. 65.
39. Ridpath, *op. cit.*, p. 690.
40. *Ibid.*, p. 690; Archer and Kingsford, *op. cit.*, pp. 75-76.

**CHAPTER TWENTY-FOUR**

1. Mombert, *A Short History of the Crusades*, p. 67; Ridpath, *op. cit.*, p. 691.
2. Archer and Kingsford, *The Crusades*, pp. 82-83; Mombert, *op. cit.*, p. 68.
3. *Ibid.*, pp. 69-70.
4. Archer and Kingsford, *op. cit.*, p. 85.
5. *Ibid.*, p. 88.
6. Ridpath, *History of the World*, Vol. IV. p. 693.
7. Archer and Kingsford, *op. cit.*, pp. 90-92; Mombert, *op. cit.*, p. 75.
8. Ridpath, *op. cit.*, p. 694.
9. Archer and Kingsford, *op. cit.*, p. 76.
10. Ridpath, *op. cit.*, p. 694.

**CHAPTER TWENTY-FIVE**

1. Archer and Kingsford, *The Crusades*, p. 93.
2. Ridpath, *History of the World*, Vol. IV. p. 695; Archer and Kingsford, *op. cit.*, p. 96.
3. *Ibid.*, p. 96.
4. Newhall, *The Crusades*, p. 46.
5. Ridpath, *op. cit.*, p. 696.
6. Archer and Kingsford, *op. cit.*, pp. 100-101.
7. Munro and Sontag, *The Middle Ages*, p. 250.
8. Ridpath, *op. cit.*, p. 699; Archer and Kingsford, *op. cit.*, p. 145.
9. Ridpath, *op. cit.*, pp. 701-705; Archer and Kingsford, *op. cit.*, pp. 170-177.
10. *Ibid.*, pp. 178-181.
11. Ridpath, *op. cit.*, p. 711.
12. Archer and Kingsford, *op. cit.*, p. 202.
13. *Ibid.*, p. 205; Ridpath, *op. cit.*, p. 712.
14. Clare, *Standard History of the World*, Vol. V. p, 2064.
15. Mombert, *A Short History of the Crusades*, p. 97.
16. *Ibid.*, p. 98; Archer and Kingsford, *op. cit.*, pp. 210-211.
17. Ridpath, *op. cit.*, p. 719.
18. *Ibid.*, p. 720; Archer and Kingsford, *op. cit.*, pp. 216-217; Mombert, *op. cit.*, p. 103.
19. *Ibid.*, pp. 104-106.
20. *Ibid.*, pp. 217-219; Ridpath, *op. cit.*, p. 720.
21. Archer and Kingsford, *op. cit.*, p. 220.
22. *Ibid.*, pp. 230-231.
23. Ridpath, *op. cit.*, p. 723.
24. Mombert, *op. cit.*, p. 114.
25. Ridpath, *op. cit.*, p. 725.
26. Munro and Sontag, *op. cit.*, p. 255.
27. Canton, *Dawn in Palestine*, p. 41.
28. Semakh was then known as *Ukhuwana.*
29. Stevenson, *The Crusades in the East*, p. 244.
30. Mombert, *op. cit.*, p. 124.
31. Stevenson, *op. cit.*, p. 231.
32. When one receives the hospitality of an Arab he is henceforth treated as a guest and accorded the protection of his host.
33. Archer and Kingsford, *op. cit.*, pp. 278-280.
34. Baker, *The Crusades*, p. 61.
35. Ridpath, *op. cit.*, p. 729.
36. Archer and Kingsford, *op cit.*, p. 312.
37. Mombert, *op. cit.*, p. 144.
38. *Ibid.*, p. 148.
39. Ridpath, *op. cit.*, p. 735.
40. Munro and Sontag, *op. cit.*, p. 301; Mombert, *op. cit.*, p. 157.
41. Ridpath, *op. cit.*, p. 735.

42. Archer and Kingsford, *op. cit.*, p. 337.
43. Mombert, *op. cit.*, p. 164.
44. Canton, *op. cit.*, p. 42.
45. Ridpath, *op. cit.*, p. 739.
46. Munro and Sontag, *op. cit.*, p. 302; Archer and Kingsford, *op. cit.*, p. 348.
47. Munro, *The Fourth Crusade*, p. 3.
48. Baker, *op. cit.*, p. 72.
49. Mombert, *op. cit.*, p. 203.

## CHAPTER TWENTY-SIX

1. Many writers of the thirteenth century gave accounts of the Children's Crusades, but none of them seem to have participated in the movements. Some of these writers feel free to "follow their own fancy" in explaining the movement, others are more reliable. Unconfirmed accounts make it all but impossible to know the exact truth. For a discussion of these accounts see Dr. Dana C. Munro's splendid article "The Children's Crusade" in the *American Historical Review*, Vol. XIX, pp. 516-524.
2. Munro, *op. cit.*, p. 518.
3. *Ibid.*, p. 518.
4. James, "The Children's Crusade," *Reader's Digest*, May, 1934, p. 68.
5. Some writers are of the opinion that the French children only marched about in their own country, and finally disbanded at the word of the king; others tell of their march to the sea, and their final destruction. (See Munro, *op. cit.*, p. 520; and Godfrey Lacker Lampson's account in *The Contemporary Review*, p. 192.)
6. Lampson, "A thirteenth Century Miracle," *The Contemporary Review*, Vol. CXXXVI, Aug. 1929, pp. 191-198.
7. Munro, *op. cit.*, pp. 519-520; Lampson, *op. cit.*, p. 193.
8. *Ibid.*, p. 194; Munro, *op. cit.*, p. 520.
9. *Ibid.*, p. 521.
10. *Ibid.*, p. 522.
11. *Ibid.*, p. 523.
12. *Ibid.*, p. 522.
13. Lampson, *op. cit.*, p. 197.
14. Baker, *The Crusades*, p. 75.
15. Munro, *op. cit.*, p. 524.

## CHAPTER TWENTY-SEVEN

1. Baker, *The Crusades*, p. 75.
2. Ridpath, *History of the World*, Vol. IV. p. 754.
3. *Ibid.*, p. 757.
4. *Ibid.*, p. 758.
5. *Ibid.*, p. 762.
6. *Ibid.*, p. 767.

## CHAPTER TWENTY-EIGHT

1. "Mameluke" in Arabic means a *slave.*
2. Rappoport, *History of Palestine*, p. 291; Muir, *The Mameluke Dynasty of Egypt*, pp. 60, 61.
3. DeHaas, *History of Palestine*, p. 303.
4. Rappoport, *op. cit.*, p. 292.

## CHAPTER TWENTY-NINE

1. Selim appointed a Turkish pasha over Egypt, but allowed the twenty-four Mameluke beys to govern the different provinces, to retain their position and a large portion of their power. The beys imported large numbers of slaves from the regions lying between the Black and Caspian Seas, and largely controlled the political state of Egypt for the following two hundred years.

   With twenty thousand infantry and several thousand cavalry these Mamelukes met Napoleon Bonaparte near the pyramids of Gizeh; but when three thousand of their number were left dead upon the field, the survivors fled in wild confusion to the nearby deserts. Their power, however, was never entirely broken until March 1, 1811, when Mohammed Ali summoned all the dignitaries of the realm to attend a celebration of unusual pomp and splendor at the royal palace.

The ceremonies were completed, and the Mameluke beys mounted their horses to leave the royal grounds, when to their great surprise they found the gates shut! "What does this mean?" For the first time a suspicion of dark treachery flashed across their minds. "We are prisoners in the citadel!" But their apprehensions had scarce time to ripen into fear, before a blaze like a lightning flash kindled about them and the sharp rattle of musketry, like a sudden thunder clap, broke in deafening peals upon the stillness of the night. From above them and around them, like the rattling hail, fell the leaden balls of death. Flight was in vain; valor availed nothing against an unseen and protected foe. Those who attempted to fly were picked off by the well-directed aim of sharp-shooting Albanian gunners. Of the four hundred and forty of their chief men who were gathered here on that fearful night but one escaped! He leaped his horse over a breach in the wall and down a fearful precipice, struck a heap of rubbish, and escaped into the desert.

2. Burckhardt, *Travels in Syria and the Holy Land*, p. 648.
3. Lane-Poole, *Turkey*, pp. 331, 332; Newett, *Canon Pietro Casola's Pilgrimage to Jerusalem*, pp. 227-233.
4. *Ibid.*, p. 11.
5. Hakluyt, *Early Voyages*, Vol. II, p. 270.
6. Eliachar, *A Jew of Palestine Before the Royal Commission*, p. 5.
7. Ali Bey, *Travels of Ali Bey*, p. 366.
8. *Ibid.*, p. 371; *Asia*, Vol. XIX, p. 163.
9. Bolton, *A New Survey of the Turkish Empire, History and Government*, chapter X, p. 176.
10. See Rappoport, *History of Palestine*, pp. 306-8.
11. *Palestine Annual*, 1925, p. 117.
12. *Ibid.*, p. 20.
13. Guedella, *Napoleon and Palestine*, p. 13.
14. *Ibid.*, pp. 45-47.
15. Rappoport, *op. cit.*, p. 311.
16. Beside the way leading to the gate of the palace, in the ancient oriental city, the ruler or his representative sat to hear cases. Thus in Constantinople the principle gate of the royal palace came to be called "the Sultan's gate." In the French language it was "the Sublime Porte." Within, the Sultan and his representatives decided cases of consequence that arose from time to time throughout the Turkish empire. Wherefore in time the people came to refer to the Turkish government at Constantinople as "the Porte."
17. Dr. Crawford, of the American University at Beirut, has informed the writer that his long residence in that country and his intimate acquaintance with Turkish problems of administration, has created a sympathy in his heart for the Turkish officials who, during the latter years of their occupation, were *handicapped* by throttling threats from other governments.

## CHAPTER THIRTY

1. Thomas E. Lawrence, said to be a descendant of Sir Robert Lawrence who fought as a Crusader under Richard Coeur de Lion, while an undergraduate at Oxford University became interested in the theme of the Crusades, choosing for the subject of his thesis, "The Influence of the Crusades on the Medieval Military Architecture of Europe." He donned the native dress of the Arabs and went on a two-year expedition to the Near East to study the castles and military history of the Crusades. The thesis not only gained him first-class honors in the final examination for his degree, but won Dr. Hogarth, the learned Orientalist, who influenced Magdalen College to give Lawrence a four-year senior traveling endowment.

While making use of this endowment he traveled with Dr. Hogarth and gathered information concerning the remains of the Hittites, studied Egyptian excavation under Sir Flinders Petrie, and was helping Dr. Leonard C. Wooley with the excavation at Carchemish when the World War began. The British war offices at Cairo needing some men who were intimately acquainted with the topography, the people and customs of the Near East, called for Lawrence as one man they could use in managing the native secret agents back and forth through the Turkish lines.

His phenomenal success in organizing and directing an Arab revolt of such huge proportions won for him the honor of being styled the foremost soldier among the allied forces of the World War and "The Uncrowned King of Arabia." Disgust with the Versailles peace conference led Lawrence to retire. He started writing his adventures but unfortunately lost the first manuscript. The second was published in 1926 under the title of "The Revolt in the Desert." Lowell Thomas later wrote of his experiences under the title, "With Lawrence in Arabia."

Wearied of being in the limelight, Lawrence resigned his rank, decorations and surname to enlist as a mechanic in the Royal Air Force under the name of T. E. Shaw. After two years in the tank corps and a number of years with the Royal Air Force, during which time he translated the "Odyssey," Lawrence resigned March 1, 1935. On the thirteenth of the following May he was fatally injured when he swerved his motorcycle to avoid hitting an automobile and collided with a butcher boy's bicycle. He died on the twentieth and on the following day was buried with simple rites in the little burial plot at the village of Moreton, England, in a grave unmarked by wreath or stone.

2. *Asia*, Vol. XIX, p. 1185.
3. *Ibid.*, pp. 828; 1002.
4. *Ibid.*, p. 1014.

## CHAPTER THIRTY-ONE

1. For many centuries Egypt had formed an integral part of the Turkish Empire, but for the past century had been "slipping from the grasp of the Turk." With the beginning of the nineteenth century Mohammed Ali rose to power in Egypt. Thereafter Turkey's rule was so nominal as to require only an annual money tribute paid to the Porte out of Egypt's revenues. In 1875 Disraeli—Britain's astute Jewish Prime Minister—by a brilliant stroke of diplomacy acquired the Suez Canal shares of the almost bankrupt Khedive, Ismail Pasha, thus linking Britain with her Overseas Empire. The extravagance of Egypt's officials precipitated a national crisis in 1882, resulting in a revolution which required the presence of British and French naval and military forces. After putting down the rebellion and restoring the government to the Khedive, it became necessary for the British forces to remain in the country to prevent further uprising. From that time onward Britain largely directed the government of Egypt. She became more intimately connected with affairs by participating in the Anglo-Egyptian military operations against the Soudan in 1885, under Gordon, and in 1898 under Kitchner. By the Anglo-French Entents Cordials she was assured that there would be no French interference in Egyptian affairs.

   The Khedive, Abbas Hilmi, was in Constantinople when the war broke out with Turkey. Since he was pro-Turk the British took advantage of the occasion and not only proclaimed Egypt an English protectorate but one day later deposed the absent Khedive and raised Hussein Kamel Pasha to the throne with the title of Sultan. The "Sultan" played second fiddle while Sir Milne Cheatham, the former *Charge d' Affaires*, functioned as High Commissioner until January 9, 1915, when Sir Henry M'Mahon took up the reins as the full-fledged High Commissioner. (For further details see MacMunn and Falls, *Military Operations in Egypt and Palestine,* Vol. I, pp. 7-18 and Major Lock's *With the British Army in the Holy Land,* pp. 1-3.)

2. Savage, *Allenby of Armageddon,* p. 185.
3. Lock, *op. cit.,* p. 2.
4. MacMunn, *op. cit.,* p. 19.
5. *Ibid.,* p. 20.
6. *Ibid.,* pp. 37-38.
7. *Ibid.,* pp. 38-39.
8. Lock, *op. cit.,* pp. 5-6, MacMunn, *op. cit.,* pp. 40-48.
9. In this connection it should be remembered that Russia's outlet to the Baltic and Atlantic had been blocked by the German fleet, aided by her mines. Thus Russia was obliged to receive her supplies of food, clothing and war materials from Japan and the United States by way of the long, expensive and dangerous land route across Siberia. The delay caused by this inconvenience not only rendered Russia inefficient, but even threatened to bring strained relations between her and the other Allies. Consequently the control of the Dardanelles by the Allies seemed a very important factor in the winning of the World War.
10. Lock, *op. cit.,* pp. 19-21. The pipes for this project were secured from the Standard Oil Company which had shipped them there with the expectation of drilling for oil.
11. Wavell, *The Palestine Campaigns,* pp. 43-45, MacMunn, *op. cit.,* pp. 160-166.
12. In his account in the *Encyclopedia Britannica* Wavell gives the Turkish total as eighteen thousand and the prisoners as four thousand. It is difficult to account for this discrepancy, unless it be that more authentic information reached him by the time he wrote for the *Encyclopedia.*
13. Wavell, *op. cit.,* p. 47.
14. Lock, *op. cit.,* p. 15.
15. *Encyclopedia Britannica,* 14th ed., Vol. 17, p. 138.
16. *Ibid.,* p. 138.
17. Lock, *op. cit.,* p. 18-19.
18. Practically all evidence would indicate that British officials had long planned the campaign into Palestine.
19. Wavell, *op. cit.,* pp. 77-79.
20. *Ibid.,* pp. 84-85, and Lock, *op. cit.,* p. 40.
21. When General Allenby had completed the reorganization of his forces, they consisted of: The 20th Corps, comprising the 10th (Irish), and 53rd (Welsh), the 60th (London) and the 74th (Dismounted Yeomanry) Divisions. The 21st Corps, comprising the 52nd (Scottish Lowland) the 54th (East Anglican) and the 75th (Wessex and Indian) Divisions. The Desert Mounted Corps, comprising the Australian Mounted Division, the Anzac Mounted Division; the Yeomanry Division. General Allenby had as his Chief-of-Staff Major-General L. J. Bols, B.B., D.S.C. In addition to the above troops there was on this front a composite brigade, consisting of French and Italians, familiarly known as the "Mixed Vermouth" Brigade. Other regiments were represented, such as Indian Imperial troops, and battalions of the British West India Regiment, while representative units of the Egyptian Army did duty upon the Lines of Communication. (Taken from Lock, *op. cit.,* p. 42.)
22. Wavell, *op. cit.,* pp. 123-24.
23. Allenby, "The Jerusalem Campaign" in *Current History,* Vol. VIII, p. 158.
24. *Ibid.,* p. 159 and Lock *op. cit.,* pp. 65-68.
25. Allenby, *op. cit.,* p. 71.
26. *Ibid.,* p. 160.
27. Lock, *op. cit.,* p. 71.
28. *Encyclopedia Britannica,* 14th ed., Vol. 17, p. 140.
29. The Canaanites, the Romans, and others had met their fate in these dangerous defiles.
30. Lock, *op. cit.,* pp. 74-75.
31. *Ibid.,* p. 78.

32. From time immemorial the word "gin" or "jinn" has been used in Palestine and Arabia to designate certain "evil spirits" to which the average native attributes excessive bodily power. (See Job 18:9; Isaiah 8:14; Psalms 140:5.)
33. *New York Times*, "Current History," April, 1918, p. 165.
34. Mayor Hussein Selim Husseieni was a relative of the High Sherif of Mecca, with whom Sir Henry M'Mahon had treated in regard to the Arab revolt against the Turks.
35. *New York Times*, "Current History," April, 1918, p. 165.
36. From the *Palestine Annual*, of 1926, p. 6.

**CHAPTER THIRTY-TWO**

1. Wavell, *The Palestine Campaigns*, p. 201.
2. Wilson, *With the Soldiers in Palestine and Syria*, pp. 66-67.
3. *Ibid.*, p. 67.
4. *Encyclopedia Britannica*, 14th ed., Vol. 17, p. 142.
5. *Ibid.*, p. 142.
6. Psalm 118:23-24, rev. ver.
7. *Encyclopedia Britannica*, 14th ed., Vol. 17, p. 137.
8. The poem is by Clinton Scollard, in *Asia*, Vol. XIX, p. 162.

**CHAPTER THIRTY-THREE**

1. Bentwich, *A Wanderer in the Promised Land*, p. 82.
2. Mr. C. R. Ashbee, Civic Adviser to the City of Jerusalem, (See also W. D. McCrackan's *The New Palestine*, pp. 274-302.)
3. Psalm 48:12.
4. Bentwich, *op. cit.*, p. 83.

**CHAPTER THIRTY-FOUR**

1. Psalm 137:4.
2. Thoraud, *The Chosen People*, p. 55.
3. *Ibid.*, p. 56.
4. Deuteronomy 4:30-31.
5. Deuteronomy 30:1-5.
6. Morning Prayer of Israel.
7. *Ibid.*
8. Prayers at conclusion of Passover Feast.
9. Judah Halevi, a noted Hebrew poet of the eleventh century.
10. Cohen, *The Zionist Movement*, p. 48.
11. Published in his official gazette, the *Monitor Universal*, and quoted by Israel Cohen on p. 48 of his *The Zionist Movement*.
12. Cohen, in *The Zionist Movement*, p. ......
13. *Ibid.*, p. 49.
14. Stein, *Zionism*, pp. 35, 36, 41.
15. *Ibid.*, pp. 36-37. Full text of appeal printed in N. Sokolow's *History of Zionism*, Vol. II, pp. 262-63.
16. *Ibid.*, p. 43.
17. *Ibid.*, p. 46.
18. Thoraud, *op. cit.*, p. 204, and Stein, *op. cit.*, p. 51.
19. *Eretz Israel*, p. 17.
20. Cohen, *op. cit.*, p. 49.
21. Thoraud, *op. cit.*, pp. 205-6.
22. *Eretz Israel*, p. 105.
23. Thoraud, *op. cit.*, p. 206.

**CHAPTER THIRTY-FIVE**

1. Holmes, *Palestine: Today and Tomorrow*, pp. 69-71.
2. Bentwich, *A Wanderer in the Promised Land*, p. 66.
3. As quoted in the *Palestine*, June 16, 1917.
4. *Ibid.*
5. *Ibid.*
6. *Ibid.*
7. Cohen, Israel, *The Zionist Movement*, pp. 112-113.
8. *War Memories of David Lloyd George*, Vol. I, pp. 348-50.
9. See Dunner's, *The Republic of Israel*, pp. 31, 32.
10. The author regrets having mislaid the source of this reference, but remembers it as coming from the account of the reception as narrated by Mr. Norman Bentwich.

### CHAPTER THIRTY-SIX

1. *The New Palestine*, Sept. 13, 1929. For much of the "on the scene" information of the disturbances at the Wailing Wall, the author is indebted to Dr. Wolfgang Von Weisl, noted German correspondent, and other writers who were in Jerusalem and wrote up the day by day events in *The New Palestine*. See also *The Western or Wailing Wall in Jerusalem*, by Secretary of the British Colonies, 1928.
2. Joseph Dunner, *The Republic of Israel*, pp. 47-48.
3. *Ibid.*, p. 49.
4. See Mr. Brilliant's "Underground in Palestine" in *Harper's*, March, 1947.
5. *Manchester Guardian*, Dec. 4, 1947; Dunner, *The Republic of Israel*, pp. 76-78.

### CHAPTER THIRTY-SEVEN

1. *Current History*, July, 1948.
2. *Palestine Year Book* and *Israel Annual*, Vol. 4, p. 68.
3. *Time*, January 31, 1949, p. 28.
4. State of Israel, *Government Year Book* (1953-54), p. 70.
5. *Palestine Year Book* and *Israel Annual*, Vol. 4, pp. 61-63.
6. *Ibid.*
7. From Dr. Weizman's oath of office as reported in the *United Palestine.*
8. William Foxwell Albright, *Land Reborn*, Jan-Feb. 1954 p. 3.
9. Isaiah 66:8.

### CHAPTER THIRTY-EIGHT

1. *Israel and the Middle East* (Special Issue), 1953, p. 156; Bilby, *The New Star in the Near East*, p. 31.
2. *Israel and the Middle East*, p. 156; Bilby, *op. cit.*, p. 33.
3. *Israel and the Middle East*, p. 166.
4. Shaw and Capa, *Report on Israel*, p. 6.
5. Bilby, *op. cit.*, p. 42.
6. *Israel and the Middle East*, p. 161.
7. Dunner, *The Republic of Israel*, p. 101.
8. Bilby, *op. cit.*, p. 46.
9. *Ibid.*, p. 47.
10. *Ibid.*, p. 50.
11. *Israel and the Middle East*, pp. 160, 165.
12. *Ibid.*, p. 165; and Bilby, *op. cit.*, p. 59.
13. Dunner, *op. cit.*, p. 177.
14. *Ibid.*, p. 70.

### CHAPTER THIRTY-NINE

1. Isaiah 43:5; 60:4, 6, 8, 9.
2. This act became known as "The Law of the Return."
3. *The Exodus from Yemen*, pp. 28, 29.
4. *Ibid.*, p. 33.
5. *Ibid.*, p. 41.
6. *Ibid.*, p. 42.
7. *Ibid.*, p. 43.
8. *Ibid.*, p. 43.
9. *Exodus from Iraq*, p. 3.
10. *Ibid.*, pp. 9, 10, 18, 19, 22.
11. *Ibid.*, pp. 25-27.
12. *Ibid.*, p. 30.

### CHAPTER FORTY

1. For the complete story of Eliezer Ben Yehouda see *Next Year in Jerusalem*, by Jerome and Jean Tharaud, pp. 132-172.
2. See *The Story of Modern Israel*, by Dorothy F. Zeligs, p. 113.
3. See *Christian Science Monitor*, May 17, 1950.
4. Isaiah 61:4.
5. For information on the various aspects of rebuilding Palestine in Israel, the author has received an abundance of literature from the Israel Office of Information in New York and direct from Jerusalem and Tel Aviv, but has been unable to secure information from the Jordan Govern-

ment regarding advancements made in that portion of Palestine.

6. Isaiah 55:13.

**CHAPTER FORTY-ONE**

1. See *Immigration* and *Absorption* (1954), published by Israel Office of Information.
2. *Agriculture* (Israel), p. 9.
3. *The Yarkon-Negev Project,* pp. 3-8.
4. State of Israel, *Facts and Figures,* 1954, p. 32.
5. *Natural Resources* (Israel), pp. 1-10.
6. The tonnage figures are taken from the *Literary Digest* report on the Dead Sea, and agree with other estimates.
7. *Economic Horizons,* pp. 3-11.
8. State of Israel, *Facts and Figures,* 1955, p. 54.
9. *Education* (Israel), 1954, pp. 2-10.
10. State of Israel, *Facts and Figures,* 1955, p. 56.
11. State of Israel, *Government Year Book,* 1953-54, pp. 48-50.
12. State of Israel, *Facts and Figures,* 1955, p. 23.
13. State of Israel, *Government Year Book,* 1953-54, p. 38.
14. Isaiah 2:2-3.

**CHAPTER FORTY-TWO**

1. See *U. S. News & World Report,* Nov. 23, 1956, p. 28.
2. *Ibid.*
3. "Glubb Pasha Analyzes the Arab Mind," *New York Times,* Nov. 18, 1956.
4. For a very splendid treatise of the Arab world, see Keith Wheeler's "Ferment of Nationalism in an Angry Arab World," *Life,* April 1, 1957.
5. *Newsweek,* December 3, 1956, p. 25.
6. *New York Times,* April 2, 1957.
7. This broadcast by General Amr was heard and recorded in Jerusalem as well as other areas of the Near East. See *Jewish Bulletin.*
8. The writer's account of the Sinai campaign is based largely on Mr. Lee Heiman's "Story of the Sinai Campaign" in *Commentary,* January, 1957.
9. *New York Times,* March 31, 1957, Section 7, p. 1.
10. *New York Times,* Nov. 18, 1956.
11. *U. S. News and World Report,* Nov. 23, 1956, p. 22.
12. The Gaza Strip had never been Egyptian soil since the time of Rameses the Great, 3500 years ago.
13. *Time,* March 11, 1957, pp. 23-24.
14. *Ibid.*, p. 25.
15. *Ibid.*, p. 27.
16. *New York Times,* March 10, 1957.
17. See Seth S. Kings, "Israel's Port of Hope—Elath," *New York Times,* March 31, 1957.
18. *Newsweek,* March 25, 1957.
19. *Ibid.*
20. *Ibid.*

## SUBJECT INDEX

## BIBLIOGRAPHY

Adams, J. McKee, *Biblical Backgrounds*, Broadman Press, Nashville, 1934.

Albright, William Foxwell, *The Archaeology of Palestine and the Bible*, Revell, New York, 1933.

Albright, William Foxwell, in *Land Reborn*, Jan.-Feb., 1954.

Ali Bey, *Travels of Ali Bey*, M. Carey, Philadelphia, 1807.

Allenby, General E. H. H., "Jerusalem Campaign," *Current History*, Vol. VIII, pp. 153-163.

*American Historical Review*, Volume XIX.

*American Schools of Oriental Research Bulletin*, Numbers 58, 60. Lewis C. Moon, 409 Prospect Street, New Haven, Conn.

Anonymous, "Acre," *The Palestine Annual*, 1925, pp. 109-121.

Anonymous, "The Delivery of Jerusalem," *Current History*, Vol. VIII, pp. 163-166.

Anonymous, "Gaza," *Living Age*, Vol. CCVIC, pp. 246-247.

Anonymous, "Turkey's Disaster In Palestine," *Current History*, Vol. IX, pp. 269-275.

Archer, T. A.; Kingsford, Charles L., *The Crusades*, G. P. Putnam's Sons, New York, 1906.

*Asia*, Vol. XIX.

Baker, Ernest, *The Crusades*, Oxford University Press, London, 1923.

*Baltimore Sunday Herald, The*, June 12, 1898.

Barton, George A., *Archaeology and the Bible*, American Sunday School Union, Philadelphia, 1933.

Bentwich, Norman, *Hellenism*, The Jewish Publication Society of America, Philadelphia, 1919.

Bentwich, Norman, *A Wanderer in the Promised Land.*

Besant, Walter and Palmer, E. H., *Jerusalem, the City of Herod and Saladin*, Scribner and Wilford, New York, 1889.

Biggs, *Six Months in Jerusalem*, Mawbrey, London, 1896.

Bilby, *The New Star in the Near East*, Doubleday & Co., Garden City, N. Y., 1950.

Bliss, *The Development of Palestine Exploration.*

Boaz, Hiram Abiff, *The Rice Institute Pamphlet*, Vol. XX, No. 4. The Rice Institute, Houston, Texas.

Bolton, Samuel, *A New Survey of the Turkish Empire, History and Government*, J. B. Bolton, London, 1664.

Breasted, James Henry, *A History of the Ancient Egyptians*, Scribner, New York, 1927.

Brilliant, "Underground in Palestine," *Harper's*, Mar. 1947.

Canton, William, *Dawn in Palestine*, Society For Promoting Christian Knowledge, London, 1918.

*Christian Century*, Vol. 50.

*Christian Science Monitor*, May 17, 1950.

Clare, Israel Smith, *Standard History of the World*, Vols. 3 and 5, Standard Historical Society, Cincinnati, 10 Vols. 1929.

Clark, *Christ and the Young People.*

Clark, Edson L., *The Arabs and the Turks*, Congregational Publishing Society, Boston, 1876.

Clow, W. M., *The Secret of the Lord*, Hodder and Stoughton, New York and London.

Cohen, *The Zionist Movement.*

*Commentary*, Jan. 1957.

Cox, Sir George W., *The Crusades*, Longmans, Green, London, 1891.

*Current History*, July, 1948.

De Haas, Jacob, *History of Palestine, Macmillan*, New York, 1934.

De Hass, Rudolph, *Galilee*, Syrian Orphanage Press, Jerusalem, 1933.

Dunner, *The Republic of Israel*, McGraw-Hill, New York, 1950.

Editorial, "A Classic Battleground," *The Nation*, Vol. CV, p. 683.

Eliachar, *A Jew of Palestine Before the Royal Commission.*

*Encyclopedia Biblica*, Vol. IV.

*Encyclopedia Britannica*, 14th Edition, Vol. 17.

*Eretz Israel.*

Eusebius, Pamphili, *Ecclesiastical History*, G. P. Putnam's Sons, New York, 1926.

*Exodus from Iraq.*

*Exodus from Yemen, The.*

Geikie, Cunningham, *The Holy Land and the Bible*, 2 Vols. James Pott, New York, 1888.

Gibbon, Edward, *History of the Decline and Fall of the Roman Empire*, 7 Vols., Oxford University Press, London and New York, 1925.

Glover, *Influence of Christ in the Ancient World.*

Glueck, Dr. Nelson, *Illustrated London News*, July 7, 1934.

Goodspeed, Frank L., *Palestine—"A Fifth Gospel,"* F. A. Bassette, Springfield, Mass., 1901.

Graetz, Professor H., *History of the Jews*, The Jewish Publishing Society of America, Philadelphia, 1893.

Grandmaison, *Jesus Christ*, 2 Vols.

Gregg, David, *Between the Testaments or Interbiblical History*, Funk and Wagnalls, New York, 1907.

Guedella, Philip, *Napoleon and Palestine*, Allen and Unwin, London, 1925.

Guttmacher, Dr. A., *Baltimore Sunday Herald*, June 12, 1898.

Hakluyt, Richard, *Early Voyages, Travels, and Discoveries*, 2 Vols., J. Mackinley and R. Priestly, London, 1810.

Heiman, L., "Story of the Sinai Campaign," *Commentary*, Jan. 1957.

Hodges, George, *The Early Church*, Houghton Mifflin, Boston, 1915.

Holmes, *Palestine: Today and Tomorrow.*

Hunkin, J. W., Robinson, Burkitt, *Palestine in General History*, Oxford University Press, London, 1929.

*Israel Annual*, Vol. 4.

*Israel and the Middle East*, Vol. V (Special Issue), Tel Aniv., 1953.

Israel Office of Information, 11 East 70th St., New York, 1954, *Absorption; Agriculture; Immigration; Natural Resources; The Yarkon Negev Project; Education; Economic Horizons* (in: *Israel* 1954).

James, Marquis, "The Children's Crusade," *The Reader's Digest*, May, 1934.

*Jewish Bulletin*, Kings, S.S., "Israel's Port of Hope — Elath, *New York Times*, Mar. 31, 1957.

*Jewish Encyclopedia*, Vol. IV.
Jones, E. Stanley, *The Christ of Every Road.*
Josephus, Flavius, *The Works of Josephus*, ed. by William Whiston, David McKay, Philadelphia.
*Journal of the Palestine Oriental Society*, Vols. III, VIII, IX, XV.

Kennedy, J. M., *The Religions and Philosophies of the East*, John Lane, New York, 1911.
Kittell, Rudolf, *Great Men and Momevents in Israel*, Macmillan, New York, 1929.
Kitto, John, *History of the Bible*, Henry Bill, Norwich, Conn., 1866.
Knight, *The Arch of Titus*, The Religious Tract Society, London, 1899.
Knott, Laura A., *Students' History of the Hebrews*, Abingdon, New York, 1922.
Krey, August C., *The First Crusade — Accounts of Eye-Witnesses and Participants*, Princeton University Press, 1921.
Kyle, M. G., *Moses and the Monuments*, Bibliotheca Sacra, Oberlin, Ohio, 1920.

Lamont, *Christ and the World of Thought.*
Lampson, Godfrey L., "A Thirteenth Century Miracle," *The Contemporary Review*, Vol. CXXXVI, August, 1929.
Lane-Poole, Stanley, *Turkey*, Fisher, Unwin, London, 1914.
La Strange, Guy, *Palestine Under the Moslems*, Houghton Mifflin, Boston and New York, 1890.
Latimer, Elizabeth W., *Judea from Cyrus to Titus*, A. C. McClurg, New York, 1899.
Leary, Lewis Gaston, *From the Pyramids to Paul*, Thomas Nelson and Sons, New York, 1935.
*Literary Digest.*
Lloyd George, David, *War Memories*, Vol. I.
Lock, Major H. C., *With the British Army in the Holy Land*, R. Scott, London, 1919.
Lodge, Henry Cabot, *History of the Nations*, J. D. Morris, Philadelphia, 1906-1908.
Lord, John, *Beacon Lights of History*, Fords, Howard, and Hulbert, New York, 1888.
Luckenbills, Daniel David, *The Annals of Sennacherib*, University of Chicago Press, 1924.
Luke, Henry C. and Garstang, J., *Handbook of Palestine and Syria*, American Colony, Jerusalem, 1925.

Macalister, Professor R. A. S., *A Century of Excavation in Palestine*, Revell, New York, 1925.
MacMunn, Sir George, and Falls, Captain Cyril, *Military Operations in Egypt and Palestine*, His Majesty's Stationery Office, London, 1928.
*Manchester Guardian*, Dec. 4, 1947.
Marston, Sir Charles, *New Bible Evidences*, Revell, New York, 1934.
Mathews, Basil, *The Riddle of Nearer Asia*, Doran, New York, 1919.
McCrackan, W. D., *The New Palestine.*
Merrell, Selah, *Ancient Jerusalem*, Revell, Chicago, 1908.
Miller, Madeline S., *Footprints in Palestine*, Revell, New York, 1936.
Milton John, *Paradise Regained*, Vol. IV.
Mombert, J. I., *A Short History of the Crusades*, News Printing, Paterson, N. J., 1894.
Morison, *A Lawyer Looks at the Crucifixion of Christ.*

Morrison, *Christ in Shakespeare.*

Moses, Adolph, *Yahvism*, The Council of Jewish Women, Louisville, Ky., 1903.

Muir, Sir William, *The Mameluke Dynasty of Egypt*, Smith, Edder, London, 1896.

Munro, Dana Carlton; Sontag, Raymond James, *The Middle Ages*, Century, New York, 1928.

Nevinson, Henry W., *In the Dark Backward*, Harcourt, Brace, New York, 1934.

Newett, *Canon Pietro Casola's Pilgrimage to Jerusalem.*

Newhall, Richard Ager, *The Crusades*, Holt, New York, 1927.

*Newsweek*, Nov. 26, 1956; Dec. 3, 1956; Mar. 25, 1957.

*New Palestine, The*, Sept. 13, 1929.

*New York Times*, Nov. 18, 1956; Mar. 10, 31, Apr. 2, 1957.

Nichols, Robert Hastings, *Growth of the Christian Church*, Westminster Press, Philadelphia, 1914.

*Palestine*, June 16, 1917.

*Palestine Annual*, 1925, Palestine Educational Co., Jerusalem.

*Palestine Exploration Fund Quarterly*, 1927, 1929, 1932, 1933, 1936.

*Palestine Year Book*, Vols. 1-6, Shulsinger Bros., New York.

Papini, *The Story of Christ.*

Parkes, James, *A History of Palestine from 135 A.D. to Modern Times*, Oxford, New York, 1949.

Petrie, Sir William Flinders, *A Vision of the Ages*, University College, Gower Street, London, 1930.

Petrie, Sir William Flinders, *Hyksos and Israelite Cities*, University College, Gower Street, London, 1930.

Rappoport, Angelo S., *History of Palestine*, Allen and Unwin, London, 1931.

Renan, Ernest, *Life of Jesus.*

Ridpath, John Clark, *History of the World*, Vol. IV., Riverside, Chicago, 1901.

Riggs, James Stevenson, *A History of the Jewish People*, Scribner, New York, 1903.

Rohold, S. B., *Babylon and Its Jews*, The Mount Carmel Bible School, Haifa, Palestine.

Sachar, Abram Leon, *A History of the Jews*, Knopf, New York, 1930.

Sangster, Mrs. Margaret E., *The Women of the Bible*, The Christian Herald, New York, 1911.

Savage, Raymond, *Allenby of Armegeddon*, Hodder and Stoughton, London, 1925.

Sayce, A. H., *Early Israel and the Surrounding Nations*, Service and Paton, London, 1899.

Sayce, A. H., *The Higher Criticism and the Verdict of the Monuments*, E. & J. B. Young, New York, 1894.

Schurer, Emil, *A History of the Jewish People*, 6 Vols.

Secretary of the British Colonies, *The Western or Wailing Wall in Jersusalem*, 1928.

Sellers, Ovid Rogers, *The Citadel of Beth-Zur*, Westminster, Philadelphia, 1933.

Sharp, Dallas Love, *Christ and His Times*, Abingdon, New York, 1933.

Shaw and Capa, *Report on Israel.*

Sokolow, N., *History of Zionism*, Vol. II.

Squires, W. H. T., *Peregrine Papers*, Private Publication, 1923.

State of Israel, *Government Year Book*, 1953-54.
*Facts and Figures.*
Stein, *Zionism.*
Stevenson, W. B., *The Crusaders in the East,* Cambridge University Press, 1907.
Stewart, Robert L., *The Land of Israel,* Revell, New York, 1899.

Tacitus, Cornelius, *The Annals of Tacitus,* J. Murray, London, 1904—1909.
Tharaud, J. and J., *Next Year in Jerusalem,* Boni and Liveright, New York, 1925.
Thomas, Lowell, *With Lawrence in Arabia,* Century, New York, 1924.
Thoraud, *The Chosen People.*
*Time,* Jan. 31, 1949; Mar. 11, 1957.

*United Palestine.*
*U. S. News & World Report,* Nov. 23, 1956.

Wavell, Colonel A. P., *The Palestine Campaigns,* Constable, London, 1928.
Wheeler, K., "Ferment of Nationalism in an Angry Arab World," *Life,* Apr. 1, 1957.
Wilson, John Plumpton, *With the Soldiers in Palestine,* Macmillan, New York, 1920.
Woodrum, Lon, "The Campus Camera," Dec. 10, 1936.
Wooley, Leonard C., "Ur of the Chaldees," *Universal History of the World,* Part 5, pp. 528-531, Amalgamated Press, London.

Yong, C. C., *The Works of Philo Judaeus,* Henry G. Bahn, London, 1855.

Zeligs, Dorothy F., *The Story of Modern Israel,* Block, New York, 1950.

# About the Author

G. FREDERICK OWEN has spent most of his life studying, teaching, and writing about the Middle-East area which is now the focal point of a world crisis. Dr. Owen received his B.A. degree from Northwestern Nazarene College, Nampa, Idaho, and his B.D. degree from Vanderbilt University, Nashville, Tennessee. He then earned his Ph.D. degree in education at George Washington University in Washington, D. C., making a survey of the education of Palestine for his doctoral dissertation. For some years he was professor of archaeology and Biblical literature at Eastern Nazarene College in Boston and for five years at Pasadena College, carrying on his research and writing at the same time.

As a member of the American Schools of Oriental Research and the Palestine Oriental Society, he has made three extended trips to the Middle East under the auspices of the first organization to carry on his fourfold research — the history, geography, archaeology, and customs of Bible lands. On each of his visits Dr. Owen, after about six months of research at the schools, engaged in excavations and traveled in the Middle-East area. He has also become a successful cartographer.

Dr. Owen now resides in Colorado Springs, Colorado, where he devotes his time to writing and lecturing.